J. Thomas Cook
Dept. of Philosophy
Vanderbilt University

MUIRHEAD LIBRARY OF PHILOSOPHY

An admirable statement of the aims of the Library of Philosophy was provided by the first editor, the late Professor J. H. Muirhead, in his description of the original programme printed in Erdmann's *History of Philosophy* under the date 1890. This was slightly modified in subsequent volumes to take the form of the following statement :

'The Muirhead Library of Philosophy was designed as a contribution to the History of Modern Philosophy under the heads : first of Different Schools of Thought – Sensationalist, Realist, Idealist, Intuitivist; secondly of different Subjects – Psychology, Ethics, Aesthetics, Political Philosophy, Theology. While much had been done in England in tracing the course of evolution in nature, history, economics, morals and religion, little had been done in tracing the development of thought on these subjects. Yet "the evolution of opinion is part of the whole evolution".

'By the co-operation of different writers in carrying out this plan it was hoped that a thoroughness and completeness of treatment, otherwise unattainable, might be secured. It was believed also that from writers mainly British and American fuller consideration of English Philosophy than it had hitherto received might be looked for. In the earlier series of books containing, among others, Bosanquet's *History of Aesthetic*, Pfleiderer's *Rational Theology since Kant*, Albee's *History of English Utilitarianism*, Bonar's *Philosophy and Political Economy*, Brett's *History of Psychology*, Ritchie's *Natural Rights*, these objects were to a large extent effected.

'In the meantime original work of a high order was being produced both in England and America by such writers as Bradley, Stout, Bertrand Russell, Baldwin, Urban, Montague, and others, and a new interest in foreign works, German, French and Italian, which had either become classical or were attracting public attention, had developed. The scope of the Library thus became extended into something more international, and it is entering on the fifth decade of its existence in the hope that it may contribute to that mutual understanding between countries which is so pressing a need of the present time.'

The need which Professor Muirhead stressed is no less pressing today, and few will deny that philosophy has much to do with enabling us to meet it, although no one, least of all Muirhead himself, would regard that as the sole, or even the main, object of philosophy. As Professor Muirhead continues to lend the distinction of his name to the Library of Philosophy it seemed not inappropriate to allow him to recall us to these aims in his own words. The emphasis on the history of thought also seemed to me very timely : and the number of important works promised for the Library in the very near future augur well for the continued fulfilment, in this and other ways, of the expectations of the original editor.

H. D. LEWIS

MUIRHEAD LIBRARY OF PHILOSOPHY

General Editor : H. D. Lewis

Professor of History and Philosophy of Religion at the University of London

The Absolute and the Atonement by Dom Illtyd Trethowan
Absolute Value by Dom Illtyd Trethowan
Action by Sir Malcolm Knox
The Analysis of Mind by Bertrand Russell
Ascent to the Absolute by J. N. Findlay
Belief by H. H. Price
Brett's History of Psychology edited by R. S. Peters
Broad's Critical Essays in Moral Philosophy edited by David R. Cheney
Clarity is Not Enough by H. D. Lewis
Coleridge as Philosopher by J. H. Muirhead
The Commonplace Book of G. E. Moore edited by C. Lewy
Contemporary American Philosophy edited by G. P. Adams and W. P. Montague
Contemporary British Philosophy first and second series edited by J. H. Muirhead
Contemporary British Philosophy third series edited by H. D. Lewis
Contemporary Indian Philosophy edited by Radhakrishnan and J. H. Muirhead 2nd edition
Contemporary Philosophy in Australia edited by Robert Brown and C. D. Rollins
The Discipline of the Cave by J. N. Findlay
Doctine and Argument in Indian Philosophy by Ninian Smart
The Elusive Mind by H. D. Lewis
Essays in Analysis by Alice Ambrose
Ethics by Nicolai Hartmann translated by Stanton Coit 3 vols
Ethics and Christianity by Keith Ward
The Foundation of Metaphysics in Science by Errol E. Harris
Freedom and History by H. D. Lewis
G. E. Moore: Essays in Retrospect edited by Alice Ambrose and Morris Lazerowitz
The Good Will: A Study in the Coherence Theory of Goodness by H. J. Paton
Hegel: A Re-examination by J. N. Findlay
Hegel's Science of Logic translated by W. H. Johnston and L. G. Struthers 2 vols
A History of Aesthetic by B. Bosanquet 2nd edition
A History of English Utilitarianism by E. Albee

Human Knowledge by Bertrand Russell

A Hundred Years of British Philosophy by Rudolph Metz translated by J. H. Harvey, T. E. Jessop, Henry Sturt

Hypothesis and Perception by Errol E. Harris

Ideas: A General Introduction to Pure Phenomenology by Edmund Husserl translated by W. R. Boyce Gibson

Identity and Reality by Emile Meyerson

Imagination by E. J. Furlong

In Contact with the Physical World by John Pennycuick

In Defence of Free Will by C. A. Campbell

Indian Philosophy by Radhakrishnan 2 vols revised 2nd edition

Introduction to Mathematical Philosophy by Bertrand Russell 2nd edition

Kant's First Critique by H. W. Cassirer

Kant's Metaphysic of Experience by H. J. Paton

Know Thyself by Bernadino Varisco translated by Guglielmo Salvadori

Language and Reality by Wilbur Marshall Urban

A Layman's Quest by Sir Malcolm Knox

Lectures on Philosophy by G. E. Moore edited by C. Lewy

Matter and Memory by Henri Bergson translated by N. M. Paul and W. S. Palmer

Meaning in the Arts by Louis Arnaud Reid

Memory by Brian Smith

Mental Images by Alastair Hannay

The Modern Predicament by H. J. Paton

Natural Rights by D. G. Ritchie 3rd edition

Nature, Mind and Modern Science by E. Harris

The Nature of Thought by Brand Blanshard

Non-Linguistic Philosophy by A. C. Ewing

On Selfhood and Godhood by C. A. Campbell

Our Experience of God by H. D. Lewis

Our Knowledge of Right and Wrong by Jonathan Harrison

Perception by Don Locke

The Person God Is by Peter A. Bertocci

The Phenomenology of Mind by G. W. F. Hegel translated by Sir James Baillie revised 2nd edition

Philosophy in America by Max Black

Philosophical Papers by G. E. Moore

Philosophy and Illusion by Morris Lazerowitz

Philosophy and Political Economy by James Bonar

Philosophy and Religion by Axel Hagerstrom

Philosophy of Space and Time by Michael Whiteman

Philosophy of Whitehead by W. Mays
The Platonic Tradition in Anglo-Saxon Philosophy by J. H. Muir-
    head
The Principal Upanisads by Radhakrishnan
The Problems of Perception by R. J. Hirst
Reason and Analysis by Brand Blanshard
Reason and Goodness by Brand Blanshard
Reason and Scepticism by Michael A. Slote
The Relevance of Whitehead, edited by I. Leclerc
The Science of Logic by G. W. F. Hegel
Some Main Problems of Philosophy by G. E. Moore
Studies in the Metaphysics of Bradley by Sushil Kumar Saxena
The Subject of Consciousness by C. O. Evans
The Theological Frontier of Ethics by W. G. Maclagan
Time and Free Will by Henri Bergson translated by F. G. Pogson
The Transcendence of the Cave by J. N. Findlay
Values and Intentions by J. N. Findlay
The Ways of Knowing: or the Methods of Philosophy by W. P.
    Montague

MUIRHEAD LIBRARY OF PHILOSOPHY

EDITED BY H. D. LEWIS

THE NATURE OF
PHYSICAL EXISTENCE

THE NATURE OF
PHYSICAL EXISTENCE

BY

IVOR LECLERC

Professor of Philosophy, Emory University, Atlanta, Georgia

LONDON: GEORGE ALLEN & UNWIN LTD
NEW YORK: HUMANITIES PRESS INC

Printed in Great Britain
in 11 point Baskerville type
by Clarke, Doble & Brendon Ltd
Plymouth

PREFACE

The central concern of this book is the understanding of the nature of the universe. Its field is thus that which until the eighteenth century had been known as *philosophia naturalis*, the philosophy of nature. The aim of the book is to elucidate and examine the fundamental concepts in terms of which the universe is understood. It could have been entitled an inquiry into the foundations of cosmology. I have, however, preferred the present title because as the inquiry proceeded I became increasingly convinced of the central importance of the concept of *physis*, nature, which the genius of Greek thought had discovered. This concept involves a basic reference to that which exists, that which is to be regarded as the existent in the full sense. But it also includes in its connotation that whereby the existent is *what* it is. Hence we speak of 'the nature of . . .'. The title therefore aptly reflects the primary issue of the inquiry, namely the problem of what is that which is to be taken as the natural, the physical existent. But the identification of the existent cannot be made in separation from the issue of how it is to be conceived, that is, the problem of what its nature is. The inquiry thus has to embrace the whole range of the fundamental problems of philosophy, especially metaphysical and epistemological.

This work started many years ago as an endeavour to gain an assessment of Whitehead's cosmology. It was not possible satisfactorily to do so, I found, short of a full-scale inquiry into the entire field. In the end I came to a position of my own which differs in many respects from that of Whitehead. My basic indebtedness to him is nevertheless evident. Other thinkers, more especially Aristotle and Leibniz, came to influence me perhaps quite as deeply. It is impossible to enumerate the many other writings which have been important to me in this work; they are not restricted to the ones receiving particular mention in the body of the book and in footnotes.

We are still at an early stage in the development of the new conception of nature, the necessity for which twentieth-century science has put quite beyond question. Indispensable in the future will be the formulation of alternative theories of nature as bases for alternative interpretations of scientific evidence. Through such interpretations the philosophical theories will be tested, and also the scientific evidence understood.

In this book, apart from some suggestions, I have refrained from interpretation in order to keep the philosophical issues as clear and unobscured as possible. Also, it is evident that there remains the further philosophical task of examining in detail the metaphysical, epistemological, theological, and other implications of the theory of nature which I have advanced in the last few chapters. That, however, must be the subject of another volume.

It remains for me here to acknowledge my indebtedness and deep gratitude to a number of friends and colleagues. I owe much to C. A. Campbell for his encouragement at the beginning stage of this inquiry, and to Charles W. Hendel for his constant readiness throughout, in successive summers at Lake Dunmore in Vermont, to read drafts, and for his valuable criticisms. To my colleagues Leroy E. Loemker and Gregor Sebba, to Hans Wagner of Bonn University, and to Walter Cerf of Brooklyn College, I am greatly indebted for their close reading of the final draft and for their suggestions and comments, which were most helpful in removing blemishes and improving the book in various ways; theirs is not the responsibility for the defects which remain. I am also indebted to my colleagues John P. Anton and William F. Edwards, the former for reading and commenting on the chapters on Aristotle, and the latter for his assistance with and verifying of many of the translations of quotations from Renaissance thinkers. I wish to express my gratitude to Rev. Edward C. Connelly for checking all quotations and references, and for a great deal of other assistance in the preparation of the typescript for the press. Finally I wish to acknowledge the financial assistance received from Emory University and a leave of absence which enabled me to spend a winter in Germany in research and writing.

I. L.

Emory University
September 1971

ACKNOWLEDGEMENTS

Permission has been gratefully received from the following for the citation of passages from works to which they hold the copyright:

Cambridge University Press:
  A. N. Whitehead: *Science and the Modern World* and *Process and Reality*
  E. S. Haldane and G. R. T. Ross translation of *The Philosophical Works of Descartes*

Dover Publications, Inc.:
  Isaac Newton: *Opticks*

Frommann-Holzboog:
  G. Bruno: *Opera Latine Conscripta*
  P. Gassendi: *Opera Omnia*

The Johns Hopkins Press:
  Alexandre Koyré: *From the Closed World to the Infinite Universe*

The Macmillan Company:
  A. N. Whitehead: *Science and the Modern World* and *Process and Reality*

Murnat Publications, Inc.:
  D. W. Singer: *Giordano Bruno, His Life and Thought*

Oxford University Press:
  The Clarendon Press: *The Oxford Translation of Aristotle* edited by W. D. Ross

Random House, Inc.:
  E. Gilson: *History of Christian Philosophy in the Middle Ages*

D. Reidel Publishing Company:
  G. W. Leibniz. Philosophical Papers and Letters translated by Leroy E. Loemker

University of California Press:
  Isaac Newton: *Mathematical Principles of Natural Philosophy*, the Andrew Motte translation revised by Florian Cajori

CONTENTS

PART III   THE MODERN CONCEPT OF NATURE

The dialectic of theories essential to investigation of the
fundamental issues and problems of philosophy of
nature: Aristotle; the sixteenth, seventeenth, and
eighteenth centuries; the present. Relation of science and
philosophy of nature. Present-day need to heal the breach
between science and philosophy in tradition of last two
centuries. The philosophy of nature again becoming
intrinsic to scientific enterprise. Consequent need for
revaluation of the nature of both science and philosophy.

I

INTRODUCTION

That the great developments in physical science which began towards the end of the nineteenth century have advanced us into a new era of thought is generally accepted. That this has involved a transformation of some fundamental concepts is also acknowledged. But the precise nature and extent of the changes in thought is still very much in dispute. An adequate comprehension is still very far from having been achieved.

One reason for this, and a most significant one, is the extent to which the fundamental scheme of concepts of the antecedent epoch still has its grip on present-day thought. Our situation is analogous to that which pertained at the beginning of the modern era when, for instance, the Aristotelian concept of substantial form continued as a basic presupposition well into the seventeenth century.

A manifestation of the hold of the scheme of the post-Newtonian epoch on the thought of the present is to be seen in regard to the concept of 'space' – one of the concepts most profoundly affected by the twentieth-century advances. By a long and complex process – which we shall subsequently investigate in some detail – extending from the sixteenth through into the eighteenth century, the concept of 'space' came to be developed as that of one of the fundamental factors in the constitution of the universe. It was the concept of an ultimate kind of existent, not reducible to any of the other fundamental factors, namely matter, time, and motion. Euclidean geometry, it came to be conceived, was the science of space, that is, the science which had space as its object.

By the nineteenth century this concept had become so completely accepted – with the entire cosmological scheme of which it was part – that the fact of its having been the product of an intricate and peculiar process of development was forgotten or not appreciated at all. It had, on the contrary, come to be assumed as an ultimate and generic concept, indispensable and

29

necessary to the understanding of the universe. All earlier thought was accordingly supposed to have possessed the concept, though usually in much less satisfactory forms. Because by that time the modern concept of 'space' had come to have the status of a tacit presupposition, with the seeming obviousness of the self-evident, nineteenth- and twentieth-century scholars have been interpreting the *chaos* of Hesiod and the early Greeks, the *chōra* of Plato's *Timaeus*, Aristotle's *topos*, the *kenon* of Democritus, the *vacuum* of Lucretius and the sixteenth-century thinkers, all as 'space' in the modern sense. This sense has so completely become a presupposition that it is extremely seldom appreciated that the very word *spatium*, or 'space', in pre-eighteenth-century thought had a significantly different connotation from that of the modern 'space' (or *der Raum*, *l'espace*, etc.).

Not only in general scholarship but in physical science too this presupposition continues its hold. Thus, although following Minkowski and Einstein, space has come to be held to be relative and not absolute, and has been brought into close relation with time in a 'four-dimensional continuum', the presupposition continues that it is itself some kind of ultimate existent. The question has to be faced, however, whether the twentieth-century physical theories do not entail the complete abandonment of that presupposition of some kind of ultimate existent which is 'space'. It is necessary to inquire whether this concept, instead of being the ultimate and generic notion which it is presupposed to be, is not in fact one which is special and peculiar to the cosmological scheme of the past couple of centuries, the scheme which is in this century in the process of supersession.

A similar continuation as tacit presuppositions of the antecedent scheme also applies with regard to the concepts of 'time' and 'motion'. There has come to be an appreciation in some degree of the special character of the concept of 'matter' in the theory of the last couple of centuries, but even this realization is still relatively partial, precisely because of the extent to which the presuppositions of the antecedent doctrine continue their effective sway over this concept too.

In this context it is particularly instructive to look at that earlier period of fundamental change. The thought of the early seventeenth century provides a singularly good exemplification not only of such concepts, belonging to a scheme in the process of supersession, being carried over as presuppositions, but also of the extent to which this carrying over is obstructive to advancement. From this point of view the philosophical endeavour of the seventeenth century can be seen as in one most important aspect a clarifying of fundamental concepts, determining their precise status and making clear their implications.

A very weighty factor enabling the achievement of that clarification was that the prevailing historical circumstances compelled the Aristotelian analyses to be the starting point of the new theories being developed. In the sixteenth and early seventeenth centuries medieval Aristotelianism was still dominant, indeed even enforced by the Church and universities, and opposition was not lightly tolerated. In consequence, it was not sufficient for the proponents of the new theories merely to put forward their views and positions; these had to be established in a grim struggle with the Aristotelian positions all along the line. A good knowledge of the Aristotelian texts was thus requisite, and out of this detailed, point-by-point confrontation of the new theories with the respective Aristotelian positions came a degree of understanding of what basically was at issue which could not otherwise have been possible. In this way it began to become clear to thinkers towards the end of the first quarter of the seventeenth century that, for example, 'matter' in the new theories which were then developing was in fact conceived fundamentally differently from what it was in the Aristotelian doctrine, and that this entailed a very different status for 'form'. Only when the special meaning of the concept of matter in the context of the Aristotelian doctrine came to be appreciated was it possible to be clear about what it meant in the new thought, and consequently that by this new conception the inherence of qualities in matter was excluded.

Evidently in this respect the historical situation in the twentieth century is very different from that in the sixteenth and early seventeenth centuries. The contemporary absence of an imposed orthodoxy is not the important factor in this difference, however. Rather, this factor is that, whereas in the antecedent period of fundamental change the scientific and philosophical concerns were closely associated, in the present century we are suffering the consequences of the separation of science and philosophy which followed upon the triumph of Newtonian physics in the eighteenth century. The result has been that, compared with the earlier period, there has so far been relatively scant philosophical preoccupation with and penetration into the developments which have occurred. The most serious deficiency is not the comparatively small number of interested philosophers so much as the lack of an adequate philosophical framework in terms of which to operate.

After Kant the 'philosophy of nature' virtually ceased being a field of philosophical concern and cultivation. The province of 'nature' had been handed over wholly to 'natural science'. This meant that the concept of 'nature' involved in the then current science was accepted without being subjected to philosophical scrutiny, the result being that in due course that concept became embedded in thought as a tacit presupposition – it is symptomatic that there gradually came about a loss of awareness that the term 'nature' had any particular significance at all, so that the adjective could be dropped, leaving only 'science'. As a presupposition, however, the eighteenth-century concept of nature has continued effective down to the present day, not only in scientific thinking but also in most philosophical attempts to interpret the scientific developments of the twentieth century – and these attempts consequently have been able to achieve little more than a somewhat more general formulation of the scientific theories. But there cannot be significant philosophical assessment without an exposure of presuppositions; for such an assessment involves being clear about wherein exactly fundamental differences from antecedent theories consist, and these differences are precisely what are obscured by tacit presuppositions.

By their very nature presuppositions are not easily detectable. One of the intrinsic difficulties is to know what to look for. In the present time this difficulty is vastly augmented by that feature of the twentieth-century situation indicated above. Because the fundamental concepts which are at issue have for so long ceased being objects of explicit philosophical concern and inquiry, the problem of how to enter upon and engage in this inquiry is singularly acute. This problem did not face the earlier period of change, because there was then a live tradition, proceeding from the Greeks, of concern with the relevant issues and problems. Our peculiar difficulty stems from the interruption of that tradition, for this has meant the loss of philosophical grasp and comprehension of what fundamentally is at issue, of the essential and ultimate problems. One significant manifestation of this loss is the contemporary lack of awareness of the carry-over of ideas as presuppositions. We are thus, in the present historical context, in a uniquely difficult position with regard to the inquiry into the fundamental concepts.

There is one way – perhaps it is the only one – to resolve this difficulty. This is by a reference back to the past. In the first instance, in order to achieve our aim of a proper comprehension of the contemporary developments, it is necessary to have an appropriate understanding of the immediately antecedent epoch. For to see the present in the perspective of that out of which it arose is the most effective means of gaining the contrast requisite for clear comprehension. But it is precisely here, in respect of the fundamental concepts, that we run up against our peculiar difficulty. For the carrying over of ideas as presuppositions obstructs that effort at distinction. It prevents our being able to discriminate clearly between what is truly generic and what is specific to the particular scheme.

To overcome this difficulty we need to go back further and study that antecedent epoch in its origins and development. This means that we need to concentrate particularly on the sixteenth and seventeenth centuries. The point of special relevance in this is not so much that this was the formative time in which modern science and philosophy arose, but rather that at that period the scientific and philosophical concerns were closely associated, and there was consequently a very considerable philosophical comprehension of the ultimate problems and issues. This period is thus of quite crucial significance for us in the present century.

To derive what we most need from the study of this period, particular attention is necessary to the earlier struggles with the revelant issues. It is in these struggles, in which the wrestling with the rejected Aristotelian positions was most explicit, that the fundamental problems and issues at stake came most clearly to the fore. Moreover, it was out of these earlier struggles that the new science and philosophy arose, and it was the issues and problems with which those struggles were concerned that determined the shape of the subsequent scientific and philosophical development. When we examine the thought of this earlier period it becomes evident that the central issues which exercised thinkers, those which were crucial in the emergence of the new science and

B

philosophy, were not centred on mechanics – the science to which
Kepler and Galileo made the epoch-making contributions. The
work of the latter in fact belonged to a later phase, which presupposed the developments with which I am now concerned.

A survey of the thinkers of the earlier period who were in the
forefront of the new development brings out that prominent
among them were medical men such as Paracelsus (1473–1541),
Fracastoro (1483–1553), Cardano (1501–1576), Scaliger (1484–
1558), William Gilbert (1540–1603), Daniel Sennert (1572–
1631), and Sebastian Basso.[1] This is indeed not surprising, for
already in the Middle Ages the province of 'nature' had come
to be the particular preserve of the medical men – so much so that
already the word *physicus* had come to have the meaning of
'medical practitioner', whence 'physician' in English. For it was
important to the treatment of illness that the composition of the
physical world be understood as well as the constitution of the
body. Only on the basis of such an understanding was it possible
to relate food and drugs to the problem of health. It is thus
readily appreciable that the theory of the elements and the theory
of chemical combination should take an eminent place among
their concerns. The theory of the elements was also prominent
in the thought of all the other thinkers of that period who contributed significantly to the rise of modern science and philosophy,
men such as Telesio (1508–1588), Patrizzi (1529–1597), Bruno
(1548–1600), Campanella (1568–1639), Lubin (1565–1631),
Francis Bacon (1561–1626), and David Gorlaeus (1592–1620).

For what was emerging in the thought of all these thinkers was
a conception of 'nature' radically different from that which had
prevailed since the time of the Greeks. And in the development
of this new conception the theory of the elements and the theory
of chemical combination played a singularly crucial part, as was
later most clearly brought out in the important book *Philosophia
naturalis* (1621) by Dr Sebastian Basso, the leading thinker among
the group of medical men and other intellectuals in Paris during
the second decade of the seventeenth century, whose vigorous
concern with the new anti-Aristotelian theories laid the basis for
the subsequent rapid advance by the Cartesians. There can be
little doubt about the influence of Basso's book on the con-

[1] The exact dates of Basso's life and death are not known. They are probably
roughly the same as those of Sennert.

temporary and later French thinkers such as Descartes, Gassendi, de Claves, Berigard, Magnenus, Mersenne, as well as others such as Jungius, Conring, Campanella, Sperling, and Leibniz beyond France.[2]

Fundamental to the new conception of nature was a new conception of matter. It was the outcome in the early seventeenth century of a gradual change, slowly beginning already in the late thirteenth century, from the concept of matter as the Aristotelian correlative of form to that of a self-subsistent actuality. It was in respect of this change in the concept of matter that the seventeenth-century concern with the theory of the elements and the theory of chemical combination played so decisive a rôle, for it was the scientific considerations which finally determined the acceptance of the new philosophical conception of matter which was so basically divergent from the Aristotelian.

In this new philosophical theory, matter was not only self-subsistent but was identified with the physical as such: the ultimate physical existent was 'material substance'. The subsequent philosophical thought of the seventeenth century was in its fundamental aspect the struggle with the implications of this new conception. Many of its most important and most radical implications were already clearly seen by Basso, for example, that matter as such is devoid of all qualitative form – which had consequently to be relegated to the mind of the perceiver. Another was that the Aristotelian plurality of kinds of motion was excluded; the only motion possible was change of place. The one respect in which Basso's insight was deficient was that he failed to see matter in a quantitative mathematical aspect. This was the great contribution of Galileo, who therewith founded the modern science of mechanics. But this science, far from settling a major philosophical issue, made it all the more acute – the issue namely of the relation of the physical and the mathematical.

For during the sixteenth century it was becoming increasingly clear to thinkers that the rejection of the Aristotelian conception of matter and of physical substance entailed the necessity of a reassessment of the nature and status of the mathematical. Many thinkers dealt with this issue, and Bruno's contribution was one of the most significant and influential. Consequently by the time

---

[2] cf. Kurd Lasswitz *Geschichte der Atomistik vom Mittelalter bis Newton* (Hamburg & Leipzig, 1890; Darmstadt, 1963), Vol. I, p. 467.

of the publication of Galileo's scientific results there was a considerable awareness of the question of the identification of the mathematical and the physical which seemed to be the implication of Galileo's work. Philosophical thought had therefore to turn attention to this issue as one of great urgency. The important philosophies of the seventeenth century, from Descartes and Gassendi through Leibniz and Newton and on to Kant in the eighteenth century, are to be seen as in a most fundamental aspect the attempt to resolve that issue of the relation of the physical and the mathematical.

During the sixteenth century it had also been clear that this whole issue was intimately bound up with a large number of related problems which Aristotle had raised and regarding which his solutions had been largely determinative of subsequent thought. There was the problem of divisibility and indivisibility, rendered acute by the recurring interest of sixteenth-century thinkers in the atomistic theory. There was the problem of continuity and discontinuity, also involved in the atomistic theory. There was the problem of infinity and finitude.

The reason why the thinkers of the sixteenth and seventeenth centuries were convinced that they were able to find a solution to these issues different from that of Aristotle was that by their time a vital new factor had entered the scene. This was a conception of infinity fundamentally different from that which had been maintained by Aristotle and all thinkers down into the fifteenth century. It is this change in the concept of infinity which constitutes the ultimate foundation upon which the entire edifice of modern science and philosophy has been raised. It is this which lies at the basis of that profound change in man's entire conception of the universe which is so fundamental to the modern era, distinguishing it from all previous ages, the change which Alexandre Koyré has so aptly epitomized in the title of his important book, *From the Closed World to the Infinite Universe*.[3]

Koyré was certainly correct in seeing that the beginning of that enormous change in man's thought has to be traced back to Nicolaus of Cusa in the first half of the fifteenth century, and therefore that a grasp of the philosophy of Nicolaus Cusanus is essential to the comprehension of the subsequent developments. But I do not think that even Koyré appreciated sufficiently the

[3] The Johns Hopkins Press, 1957.

extent to which Cusanus' concept of infinity was radically new. This concept, which the modern era has inherited from Cusanus, has come so much to be accepted as an ultimate presupposition that it is easy to read back the modern connotation of the term into earlier thought. It seems to me of the first importance for the understanding of modern thought to realize that until the fourteenth century the word 'infinite' (or 'infinity') had a profoundly different connotation from that which it came to have in the seventeenth century and subsequently. Moreover, an appreciation of this difference might turn out to be of the greatest significance to the developing thought in this century in science and philosophy.

We shall accordingly commence our inquiry, not as Koyré did his with Nicolaus Cusanus, but with an investigation of the meaning of the concept of infinity in antecedent thought, and of the vital changes which occurred in the late Scholastic period in respect of the concept of infinity which Cusanus was able to take over and construct into a whole new philosophy of the infinite.

The inquiry which is being here undertaken is not a history of thought. To a considerable extent it proceeds historically, but of necessity it has to be selective. It will emphasize some features and strands, and especially those which are less familiar, or which are not so well recognized in most treatments. In particular I shall stress those respects in which the thought or systems of the different thinkers are an endeavour to resolve the fundamental issues with which I shall be dealing, or are a carrying through – as a logical consequence of – the adoption of certain basic positions. Sometimes the thinkers in question will be seen to be themselves aware of such a logical carrying through. In other cases the sheer logic of the situation impels a thinker to certain conclusions without his being adequately aware of the basis upon which he is proceeding. In this inquiry the different thinkers will not be treated as so many lone individuals, each producing his own separate scheme or system, but as a number of persons struggling with the same fundamental problems and issues, each exploring a different possibility as an answer. That is to say, this inquiry will emphasize the dialectic of thought in order to obtain a clarification of certain basic issues, with the intention in the end of bringing this clarification to bear on the situation in which we are involved in this century.

PART I

The Concept of the Infinite

2

THE PROBLEM OF THE INFINITE:
THE ARISTOTELIAN ANALYSIS

For our inquiry into the development of the modern concept of
infinity it is necessary to start with Aristotle. He made the first
systematic analysis of the concept, and this analysis was determinative of later thought down into the sixteenth century. It was
therefore Aristotle's analysis with which the sixteenth-century
thinkers were forced to come to terms in the development of
their alternative theories. This history of the concept of the
infinite does not commence with Aristotle. His analysis is the
outcome of the whole great Greek tradition of inquiry into nature
which goes back to the Ionians, and in particular to Thales of
Miletos and his followers. In his characteristic method of procedure Aristotle takes this antecedent thought systematically into
consideration. For our purposes, however, it will suffice to take
aspects of it into account only in so far as they are important
for the appreciation of Aristotle's analysis and his own doctrine
of the infinite which emerges from that analysis.

That the concept of the infinite is highly important, Aristotle
points out, is testified to by the rôle it has played in antecedent
thought. But that the concept involves fundamental difficulties
and problems is evident from the fact of the great divergence in
the understanding of it by different schools of thought. The
problem with which we are ultimately presented is to determine
concerning the infinite whether it is or not, that is, whether there
is such a thing as the infinite or not, and if there is, what it is.[1]
We are indeed landed in difficulties whether we assert the existence of the infinite or deny it.[2]

If we reject the infinite entirely, Aristotle insists, we will be
up against insuperable difficulties, at least in respect of time, the
divisibility of magnitudes, and the number series.[3] The problem

[1] *Physics*, 202b35.   [2] ibid., 203b31–2.
[3] ibid., 206a9–12.

of time is tremendously complex and will be left for later consideration. But in regard to the last two, it is clear that mathematics in some sense involves the infinite in respect of divisibility and the number series, so that the complete rejection of the concept of the infinite runs into contradiction with the science of mathematics.[4]

We are thus compelled to accept that there is something which is the infinite, and accordingly are faced with the basic problem of what it is, how it exists, that is, what kind of existent it is. Specifically, we have to inquire whether the infinite is as such an *ousia*, a substantial or self-subsistent or actual existent; or whether the infinite is rather an attribute or determinateness of some substantial or actual existent; or if the infinite exists in neither of these ways, whether there is some other way in which there is an infinite and infinitely many.[5]

These alternatives are as pertinent today as they were in Aristotle's time. He found one or other of the first two being maintained by his predecessors and contemporaries, and was convinced of their ultimate untenability. We shall see that thinkers in the modern period reverted to one or other of these two positions, but after a most important development had taken place which enabled them to hold that an answer to Aristotle's objections had been found.

Let us start with the first alternative, namely that the infinite is itself a self-subsistent existent. Since it is itself a substance and not an attribute of a substance it must *be* infinite – for in the case of a substance, 'to be infinite' and 'infinite' cannot be different.[6] But what does it mean to say that the infinite is infinite? Is it infinite in the sense in which divisibility, for example, could pertain to it? For, as we have noted, the infinite is in some respect at least closely related to magnitude and number. But if the infinite be divisible, this would entail that it would have to be a magnitude or a multitude.[7] But this it cannot be. For since by hypothesis the infinite is a substance and not an attribute, it is entailed that every part or division of itself (if we admit such) must necessarily be infinite, which is impossible. Thus the infinite must be without parts and indivisible. But in that case the infinite

Rejection of alternative #1

[4] ibid., and *De caelo*, 271b10–14.   [5] ibid., 203b32–4.
[6] ibid., 204a23.   [7] ibid., 204a10.

could not be a fully complete existent, for a physical existent must necessarily be a definite quantity or magnitude.[8] In this argument Aristotle is concerned to demonstrate that the infinite conceived as a self-subsistent existent, cannot be infinite in the sense in which divisibility pertains to it. Thus it could be 'infinite' only in some sense which has no relevance at all to the concept of 'what admits of being gone through'.[9] Whether or not such a sense of 'infinite' could be regarded as self-consistent at all, it plainly has no connection with the sense of 'infinity' maintained by the thinkers concerned with the inquiry into nature. In the latter context, 'infinity' or 'the infinite' has a very decided relevance to 'what admits of being gone through'. For this is necessarily involved in the conception of a physical existent as having *megethos*, magnitude, that is, as being essentially extended. This means that it is impossible consistently to maintain the conception of an infinite physical existent in the sense of 'infinite' as a self-subsistent entity. This first alternative as to the conception of the infinite must be dismissed as self-contradictory.

It should be noted that the rejection of the first alternative is also for Aristotle a rejection of the conception of the infinite as such as a principle, a source from which other factors are derived, as was maintained for example by the Pythagoreans. It was because of the essential untenability of this alternative that the Pythagoreans were landed in the inconsistency of nevertheless tacitly adopting the second alternative, for instance when they regarded their void, identified with the infinite, as divisible into parts. The Milesians, in Aristotle's analysis, definitely held to the second alternative. This is plain in the case of Anaximenes, whose principle and element was air, to which he ascribed infinity as an attribute. But this holds too for Anaximander, the thinker who first specifically introduced the term *to apeiron*, the infinite.

It is important not only in connection with the immediate discussion but also for a general understanding of Greek cosmology to appreciate that Aristotle was correct in his interpretation of Anaximander. To Anaximander it was not *to apeiron*, the infinite, in the sense of the first alternative, which was the principle or source (*archē*) and element from which everything in the world is derived. For it was a tacit presupposition of Ionian

8 ibid., 204a20–8.
9 cf. ibid., 204a3–7.

thought that what exists, a physical existent, is necessarily extensive, in other words, that it is *sōma*, 'body'. Thales had proclaimed
one kind of body, namely water, as the principle and element
from which the determinate characteristics of all other kinds of
body are derived. That is to say, he sought to explain the manifold
characters of the plurality of bodies constituting the universe in
terms of the determinate characteristics of water. But the difficulty
with this, as Anaximander saw, was that the determinate
characteristics of water are no less in need of explanation than
are the determinate characteristics of other bodies. This meant
that no determinate characters can be explained in terms of other
determinate characters. Therefore they must be explained as
derived from an existent which itself does not have determinate
characteristics, that is, an existent which is *apeiron*, indeterminate. And since any existent whatever is body or bodily – having
megethos, size, extendedness – it must be *apeiron* not only in the
sense of 'indeterminate' (not determinately or definitely this or
that), but also in the sense of 'interminate' (not bounded, not
limited).[10] On this interpretation, therefore, Aristotle is correct in
viewing Anaximander as maintaining the second alternative,
namely of the infinite as an attribute of a substantial existent.[11]

Now the second alternative rests basically on the conception of
the substantial existent as body, for body is that which has extension in every direction,[12] and the infinite, as we have noted, has
essential reference to 'what admits of being passed through', of
which extension is at least one instance. (Aristotle does not restrict
'what admits of being passed through' to extension, for that
applies equally to time and the number series.) In this second
alternative, therefore, the hypothesis is the conception of a body
which is infinitely extended in every direction.

There are two points of great importance in connection with
this hypothesis. The first is that it involves an ultimate presupposition of Greek thought, from the Milesians onward, namely that
all physical existence, whatever exists physically, that is, as constituting 'nature', is necessarily extensive and thus bodily. It is
essential for the proper understanding of Greek thought to avoid

[10] Here the twofold sense of *to apeiron* in Greek thought comes clear; we shall leave
this, however, for later consideration, since it does not affect the present argument.
[11] cf. *Physics*, 204b22–4.
[12] *Physics*, 204b20: σῶμα μὲν γάρ ἐστιν τὸ πάντῃ ἔχον διάστασιν

reading back – as is all too frequently done[13] – the post-seventeenth-century concept of 'matter' into Greek thought and conceive body as 'material'. The modern concept of 'matter' is a complex one, as we shall see, and involves factors in its connotation which are entirely foreign to Greek thought. The basic Greek conception – which, incidentally, was taken over by later thought and continued to be maintained down into the seventeenth century and beyond – was that whatever is a physical existent is extensive and thus bodily. It is this general conception of body which Aristotle presupposes here.

The second point to be noted in connection with the hypothesis under discussion is the complete generality of the hypothesis. For with the rejection of the first hypothesis, it is invalid to maintain that there is extended body in the universe *and* another substance which is 'the infinite', under the tacit presupposition that this infinite is 'infinite extension'. If there be infinite extension it can be only as an attribute; which is to say that there can only be infinite extension of something, that is, of a physical existent, which means of body.

This position is the logical outcome of the long struggle with the problems of physical existence from the Ionians through Parmenides into Aristotle's day. This point is of great import not only to Aristotle's argument here but also to subsequent, including modern, thought, so we must discuss it in a little more detail.

The effort of Anaximander to find the *archē*, principle, source, of the perceived multiplicity of characters in an indeterminate existent could not be regarded as acceptable, as Anaximenes saw, since the determinateness could not come from what is in itself without determinateness. The Pythagoreans, however, had seen the aspect of validity and truth in Anaximander's argument, which is that the principle of explanation, that is, that in terms of which explanation is being made and understanding sought, cannot itself be of the same order and kind as that which is being explained. It was this truth which led ultimately to Plato's theory of Ideas or Forms. Since the characters of things which stood in need of explanation were manifestly sensory ones, the requisite principle must be something of a different order. The Pythagorean

13 As typical of this I shall mention only one of the most recent books, *A History of Greek Philosophy* by W. C. K. Guthrie – cf. e.g. Vol. I, pp. 279ff. See following footnote.

proposal was that the *archē*, the principle, the source, of all sensory things is number. They identified number as the ultimate *physis* of things; that is, the ultimate physical existent is number. And since a physical existent is necessarily extensive, number is extensive, which is to say that it is body or bodily.[14]

[14] cf. Aristotle, *Met.*, 1080b16–21: 'And the Pythagoreans, also, believe in one kind of number – the mathematical; only they say it is not separate but sensible substances are formed out of it. For they construct the whole universe out of numbers – only not numbers consisting of abstract units; they suppose the units to have spatial magnitude. But how the first 1 was constructed so as to have magnitude, they seem unable to say.' (Ross tr.)

I accept Aristotle's characterization as correct, in contrast to the view – shared by E. Zeller (*Die Philosophie der Griechen*, 1963, I.I., pp. 483ff.), F. M. Cornford (*Plato and Parmenides*, 1939, pp. 11ff.), G. S. Kirk and J. E. Raven (*The Presocratic Philosophers*, 1957, pp. 250ff.), and W. C. K. Guthrie (*A History of Greek Philosophy*, 1962, Vol. I, pp. 279ff.) – which would deny extension to the Pythagorean numbers. But the 'idealistic' conception of number which they attribute to the Pythagoreans is unacceptable; such a conception of number was not possible before Plato.

The Pythagoreans did indeed introduce the distinction between the sensible and the non-sensible. The numbers are non-sensible, and the sensible things are formed out of them, as Aristotle says in the above passage. These non-sensible numbers, however, have magnitude, which is to say that they are bodily.

The crux of the issue is the conception of 'body'. The recent thinkers have, contrary to Aristotle, identified body with the sensible (cf. e.g. Guthrie, op. cit., Vol. II, p. 111), and consequently have difficulty not only with Aristotle's analysis, but also with the concept of the void, as I shall indicate.

Numbers are non-sensible, but they have the essential features of body, namely, extensiveness, boundedness or limitedness, and fullness. Aristotle insists frequently, as in the above passage, that the Pythagoreans do not conceive numbers 'abstractly'; numbers are extensive, bounded, full existents.

A second epoch-making distinction was introduced by the Pythagoreans, namely that between the 'full' and the 'void'. Since the full is body, the void is accordingly non-body.

Guthrie is correct in saying that 'the only form of existence so far conceivable is bodily substance' (op. cit., Vol. I, p. 280), but from this he has concluded that 'hence it [the void] is thought of as a particularly tenuous form of matter' (ibid.), which means that void is a kind of body. I maintain that this conclusion is erroneous; the void for the Pythagoreans, as later for Leucippus and Democritus, was not body, but the very contrary of body. If the void were some kind of body it could not fulfil the function for which it was introduced – see below. It is because he has this interpretation of the void that Guthrie, in common with so many recent interpreters, has missed the fundamental significance of the position of Parmenides. For Parmenides, as for the Pythagoreans, 'the only form of existence conceivable is bodily substance'. But what he clearly recognized is that the void, as not bodily substance, is not-being. Thus, as opposed to recent interpreters like Guthrie, F. M. Cornford (op. cit.), Kirk and Raven (op. cit.), and G. E. L. Owen ('Eleatic Questions', *Classical Quarterly*, 1960, pp. 84–101), it seems to me that the view of Burnet, which they are united in rejecting, is more nearly correct. On this point Zeller is with Burnet in explicitly holding that the subject of *estin* is the 'full' (cf. op. cit., I. I., pp. 687ff., and *Outlines of the History of Greek Philosophy*, tr. Alleyne & Abbott, New York, 1890, p. 61, tr. Palmer, London, 1931, p. 49).

With this theory the Pythagoreans were validly able to deal with the Anaximandrian difficulty. But this theory involved profound difficulties of its own. The first basic problem is that if number be extensive body, how is plurality to be accounted for? For there is nothing in extensiveness as such whereby one extended body is to be separated off and thus distinct from another. Indeed, extendedness as such in no way requires or implies limits, boundaries, distinctions, at all. The Pythagoreans were here up against the fundamental character of extendedness, namely its necessary continuity. They were involved here in the general issue of continuity and discontinuity or discreteness. In the Ionian – and generally Greek – conception, that which is, in other words, what exists physically, is something necessarily extended. And bounds, limits, also necessarily belong to an extended something, that is, body – for what is not extended could not be bounded. Now since boundedness is not entailed in extension, which as such is continuous, the problem is how to explain boundedness. What is there in the extended something which would require its being bounded? It was also a feature of the Ionian, and generally Greek, conception of the physical that it is not only necessarily extended but also that it is necessarily *plērēs*, 'full' – if it were not there would simply be 'nothing there'. But the recognition of this does not help the problem at issue. For discreteness and bounds are no less entailed in *plērēs*, full, than in extendedness; so one 'full' would just join up with another 'full' to constitute ultimately one single plenum. Since discontinuity cannot derive from the essentially continuous, discontinuity, discreteness, and therewith plurality, can only come from a quite different *archē*, principle, source.

The proposal of the Pythagoreans in solution to this problem of the principle of discontinuity was momentous; its consequences have reverberated down the centuries into our own time. Since the Pythagoreans could not find the principle, the source, of discontinuity in the physical as such – conceived as an extensive full – they introduced the concept of the very contrary of the physical as the principle of discontinuity. Since what is, the physical, is *plērēs*, full, and what is the very contrary of 'full' is 'empty', 'void', the Pythagoreans postulated *to kenon*, the void, as the *archē*, the principle, source, of discontinuity and thus of plurality.[15] The reason why any one body is bounded, limited, and discrete is that its full extensiveness is separated from the full extensiveness of other bodies by a void between them. To be a discrete entity is to have a *peras*, limit, bound; thereby it is distinctively that entity which it is, in distinction from every other extended entity. Its limit implies its distinct numerical difference and separateness from every other extended entity, and it could not be thus distinct and separate unless it were separated off from the rest. It could not be 'separated off' by any other 'full', for that would not provide the necessary separation; it could only be 'separated off' by the very contrary of 'full', namely 'empty', *to kenon*. Now since *to kenon*, the void, is in every respect the contrary of the physical *plērēs*, full, it must accordingly be without *peras*, limit; that is, it must be *apeiron*, limitless. Thus that which is itself without limitedness is the *archē*, the principle, source, of limitedness – a vindication of the truth which Anaximander had divined.

But this Pythagorean theory involves a fundamental difficulty, as Parmenides – who had earlier been a Pythagorean – was the first clearly to see. It was this difficulty which led him to his distinctive philosophical position. It was this difficulty involved in the Pythagorean doctrine of the physical, and not a merely abstract logical problem,[16] with which Parmenides was dealing in the first part of his great poem.

From Thales, thinkers had been concerned to understand *physis*, nature, the physical existent. It is this which is by its own nature, which has its own nature, or what is in itself – as opposed to deriving it from something beyond. As Aristotle later put it, *physis*, nature, is that which has the *archē*, principle, source, of its *kinēsis* (process of change and development and thus being) in itself.[17] For Parmenides, the Pythagorean theory brought out, by its contrast between the full physical existent and the void, an ultimate presupposition of thought in regard to *physis*, the

---

[15] cf. Aristotle, *Physics*, 213b22–7: 'The Pythagoreans, too, held that void exists and that it enters the heaven itself, which as it were inhales it, from the infinite air. Further it is the void which distinguishes the natures of things, as if it were like what separates and distinguishes the terms of a series. This holds primarily in the numbers, for the void distinguishes their nature.' (tr. Hardie and Gaye).

[16] As is the favoured supposition of many; cf. e.g. Kirk and Raven, op. cit., pp. 269–70.

[17] cf. *Met.*, 1015a13–16. This will be discussed below, in Ch. 7, in some detail.

physical. It is this which is; what is, i.e. that which is, is *physis*. But when the Pythagoreans introduced to *kenon*, the void, this meant that they were introducing 'what is not'. Now the fundamental difficulty is, how can there *be* 'what is not'? That is, how can 'not-being' *be*? In other words, how can 'non-existence' *exist*? Indeed, how is it possible at all to think, to conceive, 'non-being', 'non-existence'? Parmenides concluded : it is impossible for 'non-being' to *be,* and it is impossible to think it.[18] The entire supposition involves an inherent contradiction.

The outcome for Parmenides was that the Pythagorean doctrine of the void is basically false and must be rejected utterly. Only 'what is' (in other words physical) can be, and only it can be thought. But the rejection of the void, of 'what is-not', means that the supposition of a principle of discontinuity, discreteness, plurality, is also invalid. What is, or, that which is, is one, and it cannot be other than one. It is *plērēs*, full, extended equally in all directions to be a well-rounded bulk (*ongkos*).[19] And since 'what is' is necessarily determinate, definite – as opposed to *apeiron*, indefinite, indeterminate – it must be a perfect, bounded sphere. And there can *be* nothing beyond it; for 'nothing' is 'non-being'. It is all there is, one, entire. And it must be eternal and unchanging, without beginning or end, without generation or destruction; for there can *be* nothing from which it could come, or from where it could come, or into which it could change or move. Only such could be *physis*, that which has the *archē*, principle, of its being in itself.

It is evident why Parmenides was such a challenge to subsequent Greek thought. He had brought to the fore the ultimate issue of *physis*, physical existence, as no one previously had done. The physical is what *is*. It is this which is extended, and only this which can be extended, for there cannot *be* an extended 'non-being' – 'non-being' is simply sheer nothingness, and 'nothing', 'non-being' cannot be extended – the very conception of an 'extended nothing' is a self-contradiction.

Aristotle accepted this portion of the Parmenidean argument as completely valid. Whatever is extended 'is'; it exists. And the sense of 'being' or 'existence' which is pertinent here is that of a self-subsistent, individual 'this' (*tode ti*) – to denote such an exis-

18 *Fragments*, 2, 3, 6 and 7.
19 *Fragment* 8, also for the rest of the paragraph.

tent the term *ousia* had come to be adopted by Aristotle's day.[20] This sense of 'being' or 'existence' is precisely that which had always been implied in the concept of *physis*. Thus it is to a physical existent, and only to a physical existent, that the concept of extension can validly pertain.

We can now appreciate Aristotle's position, enunciated at the beginning of this chapter, that an extended existent is body, and that the issue concerning the infinite as an attribute is whether it is possible at all that there can be an infinitely extended being.

The supposition of an infinitely extended being immediately runs into a general difficulty which is involved in the accepted Greek conception of the physical as body. If a body be defined as that which is bounded by a surface, it is evident that it is impossible for it to be infinite, for infinite here means without bounds, boundless. This is not a mere eristic objection based upon an arbitrary definition of 'body'. This definition is implied in the Greek conception of the physical as body – as was indeed very clear to Parmenides. For to be, to exist, is to be determinate, that is, definitely this or that – for an existent cannot be without any determinateness at all, *apeiron* – and an existent whose primary character is that of an 'extended full' is one whose extension or size, *megethos*, must be determinate, which is to say that it must have limits, bounds. So, Aristotle asserts, it is logically implied that an extended existent cannot be *apeiron*, infinite, interminate, without bounds.[21]

But Aristotle does not rest with this one general argument; the issue is too important and must be dealt with from other aspects, especially those more appropriate to physical theory.[22] It will be sufficient here to give only some of Aristotle's main points.

The universe conceived as an infinitely extended existent must be either compound or simple. Prima facie the more probable supposition is that it is compound.[23] The plurality of sensible bodies we encounter are readily recognizable as divisible and

---

[20] *Ousia* – the word is derived from the verb 'to be' – is that which is or exists in the full sense, as opposed to a derivative sense, e.g. that in which an attribute exists. An attribute (e.g. a colour) does not exist 'in itself'.

[21] cf. *Physics*, 204b5–8.

[22] *Physics*, 204b11.

[23] ibid., 204b11f.

composed of constituents.[24] Since this divisibility and composition cannot go on indefinitely, we come to certain ultimate constituents which are the elements out of which all other bodies are made up. These elements, it is to be noted, are also necessarily bodies; they are the elementary bodies. Thus the conception of an infinitely extended existent as compound means that this existent is a compound ultimately of certain elementary bodies. Since each of these elementary bodies cannot be infinitely extended, each must therefore be finite. Now the question is whether there be an infinite number of them. There cannot be a finite number of them, for a finite number of finitely extended existents cannot add up to constitute an infinitely extended whole. It would seem therefore that there must necessarily be an infinite number of finite elements. But can this validly be maintained? It is a plausible supposition, in fact maintained by many, such as the Democritean atomists – and indeed still very widely accepted today – but Aristotle rejects the supposition as invalid and false.[25]

Aristotle's argument here is of great importance, for the apprehension of his own position, as well as for the subsequent thought which was so profoundly influenced by him in this respect. Further, it is an argument which still needs to be taken into account. The plurality of elements or elementary constituents must each be a fully and definitely actually existing entity. But if each is actually and definitely existing, this means that there must be a definite number of them, that is, that they must be definitely numerable. The number may be vast (for instance, beyond the range of human numeration), but since each existent is definite and actual, their number must be definite, and this means in principle numerable. In other words, it is in principle possible to go through them. But that being the case, this implies that the number cannot be infinite, for the concept of the infinite is precisely that which in principle cannot be gone through to the end, since the infinite is that of which there is no end.[26]

This argument suffices to show that there cannot be an infinitely extended whole composed of a plurality of elements or constituents. Aristotle brings other arguments too,[27] but we can

[24] cf. *De caelo*, Bk I, Ch. 5, 271b2–25.
[25] cf. *De caelo*, Bk III, Ch. 4, 302b10 – 303b8.
[26] cf. *Physics*, 204a1–8.
[27] cf. *Physics*, Bk III, Ch. 5.

omit them here; this is the one which he regards as finally incontrovertible and which was subsequently accepted as such.

From this Aristotle draws the conclusion that if we accept the concept of a plurality of actually existing finite elements, then there must necessarily be a finite number of them. Accordingly the whole which they compose, the universe, must necessarily be finite.

The consideration of the other alternative, namely that the infinite physical whole is simple, that is, a single one not made up of constituents, also leads to the conclusion of its impossibility. Aristotle brings a number of arguments to demonstrate this,[28] but the general one given above[29] is conclusive, namely that an existent whose primary nature is that of extended body must necessarily be finite or determinate, for the primary character, extension, cannot be indeterminate, indefinite.

The foregoing will suffice for Aristotle's arguments against the conception of the All, the universe, as an infinitely extended body. The upshot of this is that the second main conception of the infinite, which is to regard it not as a self-subsistent existent but as an attribute of a self-subsistent existent, is also untenable.

What, then, is the alternative to these opposing theories? The alternative cannot be to deny the infinite entirely – we have seen that this would involve running completely counter to the science of mathematics. It is therefore necessary, Aristotle holds, to seek a quite different way to conceive the infinite.

[28] ibid.
[29] See p. 50.

3

ARISTOTLE'S DOCTRINE OF THE INFINITE

The fundamental problem concerning the infinite, as we saw in the preceding chapter, is to determine what it is, which is to say we need to find how it exists, what sort of being it is or has. We have seen that the infinite cannot be, that is, exist as, a self-subsistent being or existent; and also that the infinite cannot be or exist as an attribute of a self-subsistent existent. The question which now arises is whether this is exhaustive of the possibilities.

For an answer, Aristotle maintains, we must examine closely what is meant by 'to be'. Reflection on the antecedent discussion with particular attention to the meaning of 'to be' makes it clear that a simple, univocal meaning cannot be maintained. Thus in the first alternative the infinite has the 'to be' or being of a self-subsistent existent, and in the second alternative the infinite has a different, a derivative 'to be' or being, namely that of an attribute, which is to say that, but for the being of the self-subsistent entity, the attribute would not be at all. It is of the greatest importance to distinguish between these two ways or modes of 'being' or 'to be'.

But there is another equally important distinction in regard to 'being' which has to be observed if we are to avoid confusion and difficulty. This is the distinction between 'actual' being and 'potential' being. To speak of something being or existing does not necessarily imply that it exists 'actually'; we can equally validly speak of its existing 'potentially'.

Attention to this distinction, Aristotle maintains, will lead us to the solution of the problem of the infinite of which we are in search. All the theories exemplifying one or other of the two preceding alternatives respecting the infinite conceived the infinite as actual, that is, either as itself an actual self-subsistent existent or as an actual attribute of an actual self-subsistent existent. The upshot of Aristotle's examination of these two alternatives could

53

be expressed by saying that it is impossible for there to be an *actual* infinite: there can be no *ousia* or substance whose actuality, whose actual being, is infinity; and there can be no *ousia* or substance which is actually infinitely extended.

The alternative then would be to maintain that there is a 'potential' infinite.[1] But what could be meant by the conception of a 'potential infinite'? What could be meant by saying that the infinite is or exists 'potentially'? To clarify this, it is requisite to investigate the problem of what precisely 'the infinite' can properly and consistently be taken to pertain to. For example, if we say that a statue exists potentially, we mean that if a sculptor chips away appropriately at a block of marble then an actual statue will exist. But since an actual infinite or an actually infinitely extended body or substance is not possible, the phrase 'potential infinite' must have in some respect a different sense from that of a 'potential statue'. The statue as potential means that it is possible for there to be an actual statue; the infinite as possible cannot mean that it is possible for there to be an actual infinite.

Now we have noted before that in some sense the infinite does appropriately and legitimately pertain to multitude and number, that is in respect of division and addition of extensive magnitude and the number series. Some thinkers – and Aristotle agrees with them – would have the infinite pertain also to time and the generations of men.[2] We have noted too – and it is necessary specially to emphasize it again – that in some fundamental sense 'the infinite' connotes what admits of being gone through but without it being possible to reach an end.

Let us start with a consideration of the division of extensive magnitudes. Take any extensive magnitude and divide it in half, and divide one half again into half, and so on. This process of division into half can go on indefinitely without reaching an end, for however small a particular part we take, it will still be a part of an extensive magnitude and thus itself be an extensive magnitude, and accordingly divisible into half. In other words, extensive magnitude is infinitely divisible. This means that extensive magnitude 'admits of being gone through' by division without an end ever being reached or being possible to be reached.

This process of the infinite division of an extensive magnitude

[1] *Physics*, 206a17.   [2] cf. *Physics*, 206a25.

is the process of taking away a half, and then a half of the remaining half, and a half of that, and so on without end. There is also the converse process, of starting with a half, and then adding a half of that half to itself, and half of the latter, and so on. This process of addition of halves also can have no end; since we are concerned with extensive magnitude, there is always a smaller half to be added, without an end being possible to the process of addition. In other words, here we have an instance of infinite addition. Infinite division and infinite addition are here exact contraries.

Now we must note that in the foregoing it is not implied that there is an actually existing infinite division or addition; that is, the extensive magnitude is not *actually* divided into an *actual* infinite number of parts, but it is merely divisible, able to be divided, which is to say *potentially* divided into an infinite number of parts. Thus infinite division as 'potential' means that the process of division is able to go on indefinitely without it ever being possible to reach an end. The same meaning of potential holds for the converse process, namely of infinite addition as potential. Here 'potential' does not mean, as it does in regard to the statue, 'able to be actual', because in respect of this process of division, and its converse, addition, an actual infinite division, or addition, are by the very nature of the case impossible.

In this way, and only in this way, then, does the infinite exist, namely as potential, in the sense of potential exhibited in the division of extensive magnitudes.[3]

It is not the case, however, that this sense of potential is so different from that of a statue as potential that in the former sense the relation to the actual is absent. It must be recognized that potential (potentiality) is a correlative term; it is the correlative of actual (actuality), and essentially means 'able to be actual'. But since it is invalid and false to suppose that in the statement, 'the infinite is (or exists as) potential', it is implied that the infinite is able to be (exist as) actual, what then is the relation of 'potential' in this statement to 'actual'?

The respect in which the 'actual' validly pertains here is that which is exemplified when we say, 'it is day' or 'it is the games'.[4] A day is not actualized all at once; only a small portion of the whole day is actualized at a time. So when we refer to the whole

[3] *Physics*, 206b12–13.   [4] ibid., 206a22, 206b14.

day, the day is not actual; it is only successive portions of it which are properly actual. Likewise the Olympic games are not actualized as a whole, all at once; it is only particular individual games (or parts of them) which are being actualized. The same holds with regard to the infinite : the infinite as such is not actual; it is parts of 'that which is being gone through' which are actualized in the process of 'going through' – for example, in division or addition.

For it is crucial to appreciate that in the case of division and addition, as in the case of time and the generations of men, we are not dealing with instances of static entities which actually are, as a whole. Time is not something which actually exists as a whole; it is something of which there is successive actualization of a small portion. Only that portion, the present, is in the proper sense actual; only the present 'actually exists'. The past is the portion which has been actual and no longer is such, and the future is the portion which will be actual but is not yet actual. The same applies in the case of the generations of men. In all these cases we are not dealing with static entities but rather with some kind of process. In the case of division of an extensive magnitude we are not concerned with an extensive magnitude as one static actual thing which is actually divided into an infinity of parts; we are concerned with the *process of dividing*. This *process* is not actual as a whole all at once; in this, as in any process, only a portion is actualized at a time, namely that act of dividing that particular half. So the process of division *as a whole* is potential, while portions of that process are successively actual.

This, then, is what the infinite truly is, how it exists, what kind of existent it is. The infinite is not as such an actual entity or being; and the infinite is not an attribute of an actual being. The infinite does not exist as actual at all. It exists as potential, and the potentiality pertains not to a thing, a 'this' (*tode ti*), a substance, as an attribute, but it pertains to a process. The infinite as potential refers to a process of going through. The 'potentiality' of the infinite means that the process is able to be actualized, portion by portion. And the 'infinity' of this potentiality means that this process of successive actualization of portions can go on indefinitely without an end ever being able to be reached.

By seeing explicitly that the infinite or infinity pertains to a

process and not to an individual actuality as such, we can avoid
the error of implicitly taking it as applying as an attribute to an
actuality. Thus, for example, Aristotle maintains that 'infinite is
that, in respect to quantity, which is such that we can always
take a part outside what has already been taken'.[5] His statement
here is not that quantity is actually infinite in the sense of infinity
being an attribute of quantity. Infinity does not pertain to the
quantity as such, but to the *process* of being able always to take
a further portion beyond what has already been taken. This holds
whether the 'quantity' be an extensive magnitude or the number
series. The number series is not actually infinite; that is, there
is not an actual existent which is the number series having the
attribute of infinity. It is not merely that numbers do not exist
as themselves full actuals. When we speak of the number series
as infinite, this properly means that however far the process of
counting (or addition) has proceeded, it is always possible to go
beyond. It is the potential process of enumeration which is infinite
and not the actual numbers.

From the foregoing we can see another important implication
of the status of the infinite as potential. Since the infinite means
that it is always possible to go beyond, this entails that the infinite
is the contrary of a whole. For the concept of a whole is the
concept of what is complete, that is, the concept of that from
which nothing is absent or wanting – for example, a whole man
or a whole box.[6] Now the whole or wholeness pertains primarily
to actuality, to that which is actual, since it is only the actual
which can be whole in the full sense; for to say of something that
it is 'potentially whole' is to say that it 'is not whole but is capable
of being so', actually – but therewith it will have ceased 'being
potentially'.

Since *physis*, nature, the physical, is or exists actually, it must
be a whole, and since the infinite is the contrary of a whole, it
is evident that it is a contradiction to regard the All, the actually
existing universe, as infinite. Since the actual universe is an
extended magnitude it is an extended whole, and this means
that it must have limits – for the denial of this entails that it just
goes on without limit or end, which is to deny that it is a whole,

[5] *Physics*, 207a7–8: ἄπειρον μὲν οὖν ἐστιν οὗ κατὰ τὸ ποσὸν λαμβάνουσιν αἰεί
τι λαμβάνειν ἔστιν ἔξω. (My tr.).
[6] *Physics*, 207a9–10.

and this contradicts its being actual. The actual extended whole which is the physical universe is, by virtue of its actuality and thus wholeness, complete, beyond which is nothing – and particularly no extension, it itself being a whole of actual extension. To postulate an infinite extension beyond the limits of the universe is to commit the error of regarding the infinite as an actual attribute. The ontological status of the infinite is that of potentiality and not of actuality. Its potentiality pertains to a process and not to an actual entity as such.

There cannot be an actual infinitely extensive magnitude, but the concept of the infinite pertains particularly to an extensive magnitude in respect of the process of divisibility, as we have seen. It is in the same sense that the infinite pertains to quantity in general.

Analogously, time and motion (*kinēsis*) can validly be referred to as infinite. For they are not infinite in the sense of an actual attribute, but by reference to the process entailed in each. In respect of time there is the endless, that is, infinite, process of actualization of the present. The *kinēsis* of the physical universe is infinite in that physical existence is a perpetual process of coming into being, and *kinēsis* is precisely the process involved in coming into being. This perpetual process of coming into being of physical existence, Aristotle argues – for reasons which we shall have to examine later – is necessarily without beginning and end. It is therefore in this respect *apeiron*, infinite. But clearly to speak of the universe as in this respect infinite is not to mean by the term 'infinite' an actual attribute, for the infinite here pertains to the process of actualization, in which the actualization is not all at once but successive. Here the meaning of infinite is exactly that which was elucidated above: it means that however much actualization has taken place, the *process* of actualization is such that necessarily further actualization is always possible. Thus Aristotle defines *kinēsis* as the actualization of the potential in so far as it is potential.[7]

For the purposes of our inquiry this will suffice for the understanding of the essentials of Aristotle's analysis of the infinite and his own conception of the infinite which emerges from that analysis. This Aristotelian analysis gave to the concept a precision which was determinative for thought down to the modern time.

[7] This will be explained in detail in Ch. 7.

4

THE CHANGED CONCEPT OF THE
INFINITE IN MEDIEVAL THOUGHT

Within two centuries after Aristotle there began to occur changes in the intellectual climate which were to be of the greatest consequence for the concept of the infinite in subsequent history. For our purposes it will not be necessary to enter into the discussions of the infinite in Hellenistic thought; this produced nothing new, but continued the debate which had existed in classical times and before. The changes with which I shall be dealing were not directly related to the concept of the infinite but affected it only incidentally, at least at first.

These changes began occurring in the later Hellenistic period and came to a climax in the era which saw the birth of Christianity. We need not investigate the causes; it will suffice to indicate some salient features and not the outcome. For reasons connected with the disappearance of the Greek city-states and therewith the closely related world of Greek thought, values, art, and culture, there accurred a weakening of the hold of Greek ideals and modes of thought. One outcome of this was a profound loss of confidence of man in himself, one manifestation of which was the prevalence of a wide-ranging scepticism. In the classic Greek view and ideal, man was master of himself through his possession of reason, whereby he was able not only to command truth, but to effect the harmony through which goodness and beauty were achieved in life and art. In the period under review there had set in a loss of faith in the power of reason, indeed in the very laws of reason, and in the determinacy of harmonious form, in life and in art. The lack of confidence of men in themselves, in their capacity to command their own destiny, turned men to seeking a source of help in something beyond man, in the divine conceived as absolutely transcendent, not only of man but also of the entire universe of physical existence. That is to say, the breakdown of the Greek view and ideals led men to a transcendent religion for their salvation.

Now the feature of fundamental significance to our theme is that this conception of the divine is one contrary to that manifested in the classical Greek view of man and the All. In this Greek view the divine is integral to the All and included in it as an ultimate and necessary factor. In the view now coming into acceptance – which was influenced in this respect by oriental thought and religion – there is not only a distinction to be made between the universe as such and the divine, but there is also a clear separation to be recognized between them. The divine is wholly transcendent of the universe, and wholly other than the universe. Further, the universe is wholly dependent upon the divine.

The exaltation of the divine into a transcendent eminence, which had its impulse in a religious motive that had become widespread, and was implicit in the religious trends of the time, received its first clear theological and philosophical expression in the thought of the Alexandrian Jewish theologian, Philo, who was well acquainted with Greek philosophy. Greek thought in general had conceived the All as eternal. On the basis of the conception of the divine as completely transcendent and the universe as dependent, this Greek doctrine of the eternity of the All or of the universe had to be utterly rejected. God alone is eternal – and Philo was able to find some Biblical texts in support of this – and only God can be eternal. The world, accordingly, is essentially perishable and passing, and must be completely dependent upon God for its existence.

For the next millennium and a half this position, explicitly formulated by Philo, became the fundamental position which lay at the basis of all medieval thought. It was this position and its implications which characterized medieval thought and distinguished it from the thought of other epochs, before and after.

The Neoplatonists, Plotinus and his followers, were the first systematically to develop the implications of this position, and in doing so they advanced trends of thought which had already appeared earlier among the Hellenistic sceptics. The loss of confidence in reason had among them led to the characterization of the highest, the divine, as the unknowable. Their aesthetic thought, too, exhibited the same trend. The Greeks of classical times had found beauty and artistic excellence in the harmony of form, that is, in a perfect definiteness. In later Hellenistic thought this was replaced by a tendency to seek beauty in the sublime, in the incomprehensible. The fundamental departure from classical Greek thought constituted by these trends, which linked up with the theological insistence on the divine alone as eternal, is of the utmost significance to the changes in the concept of the infinite with which we are concerned, and must therefore be examined more fully.

It was fundamental in classical Greek philosophy, as we have already had occasion to note, that to be, to exist, is to be definite, that is, to be limited in this way rather than that. Aristotle had made quite explicit what was in fact pretty generally agreed in Greek thought, that unlimitedness, unboundedness, indefiniteness, implied the unformed, that which is without form, and, as Parmenides had insisted, can neither be nor be thought. *To apeiron*, the unformed, implied the unknowable, the incomprehensible, for there can be no knowing, no comprehending, of what has no form to be grasped.[1] To know an entity is to comprehend what distinguishes it, that is, to grasp that whereby that entity is distinct and separate (limited) from other entities.

Aristotle did not agree with Parmenides that *to apeiron* simply *is not* in every sense of 'to be'. It cannot exist as actual; but it is potential. Thus Aristotle's *hylē* (matter), for example, is *apeiros*, indefinite, without any form of its own (it is on the contrary that which is formed, that which takes form), and can thus have no actual existence; it has or is the mere potentiality of being; *hylē* strictly *is* only as informed by some or other definiteness.

In Greek thought the being, the existence, of the universe itself implies its full definiteness, and this implies its limitedness in extension, its boundedness, which as we have seen in the previous chapter, Aristotle had emphasized. God also cannot be infinite (*apeiros*), but on the contrary God is the complete and perfect definite. Once more Aristotle's doctrine is characteristic. God, for Aristotle, is first in complete reality,[2] the eternal *ousia* and actuality,[3] which is without *hylē*.[4] God as a being without *hylē*

[1] Aristotle had emphasized this point, too, in regard to the universe conceived as infinite, *apeiron*. cf. *Physics*, 187b7–13.

[2] *Met.*, 1071a36: τὸ πρῶτον ἐντελεχείᾳ.

[3] ibid., 1072a25: ἀΐδιον καὶ οὐσία καὶ ἐνέργεια οὖσα.

[4] ibid., 1074a35–6: τὸ δὲ τί ἦν εἶναι οὐκ ἔχει ὕλην τὸ πρῶτον· ἐντελέχεια γάρ.

means that God is a being without *dynamis*, potentiality, and thus that God is a being whose very *ousia*, being or beingness, is *energeia*, actuality,[5] which, since it is without potentiality, is the perfect definiteness.

With this background we can pass on to Plotinus. Plotinus explicitly accepted what was to become the fundamental medieval position of the complete transcendence of God, implying his complete otherness from the world or universe, and the complete dependence of the world on God. God is that from which everything derives, and therefore God must necessarily transcend all things, and God must necessarily be one. It was what is entailed in this transcendence on which Plotinus primarily focused. Accepting the Greek conception that to be is to be definite, which means that every being must have some form, and combining this with the conception of a transcendent God, Plotinus saw it to follow that all definiteness and form must derive from God. But since all form derives from the One or God, the One must necessarily be without form,[6] for if the One had form he would be merely one definite thing among other definite things, and so could not be the *archē*, principle, source, origin, of all definiteness. In this Plotinus was exemplifying that insight which had first been manifested by Anaximander and then by the Pythagoreans, and later by Plato when he went beyond Socrates and insisted that the form of the beautiful, for example, could not itself be a beautiful thing. But Plotinus carried this insight further. If that which is the principle or source of all definiteness or form be itself without form, it follows that it is not a being, an *ousia*, at all,[7] for an *ousia* is a 'this' and a 'this' is necessarily determinate, a definite thing (*hōrismenon*). But if the One be not one of the particular definite things, the One can only be said to be 'beyond' (*epekeina*) them.[8] This means that, since these things are 'beings' and 'being' (*ta onta kai to on*),[9] the One is therefore 'beyond being' (*epekeina ontos*).[10] Further, if the One be without

---

[5] ibid., 1071b20: δεῖ ἄρα εἶναι ἀρχὴν τοιαύτην ἧς ἡ οὐσία ἐνέργεια.

[6] *Enneads*, V, 5, 6: ἀνάγκη ἀνείδεον ἐκεῖνο εἶναι.

[7] *Enneads*, V,5, 6: ἀνείδεον δὲ ὂν οὐκ οὐσία. τόδε γάρ τι δεῖ τὴν οὐσίαν εἶναι· τοῦτο δὲ ὡρισμένον.

[8] ibid.: τὸ δὲ οὐκ ἔστι λαβεῖν ὡς τόδε. ἤδη γὰρ οὐκ ἀρχή, ἀλλ' ἐκεῖνο μόνον, ὃ τόδε εἴρηκας εἶναι. εἰ οὖν τὰ πάντα ἐν τῷ γενομένῳ, τί τῶν ἐν τούτῳ ἐκεῖνο ἐρεῖς; οὐδὲν δὲ τούτων ὂν μόνον ἂν λέγοιτο ἐπέκεινα τούτων.

[9] ibid.

[10] ibid.

form or definiteness, it follows that the One is necessarily beyond knowledge, for only that which is definite is capable of being known. Plotinus' doctrine, therefore, is that God or the One is 'beyond thought and knowledge and even what we can speak of as being'.[11]

There is a further profound departure from the characteristic position of Greek philosophy in this doctrine which accords a transcendent eminence to God. Since Greek thought had placed a fundamental emphasis on the definite (to be is to be definite), for the Greeks accordingly it was the definite which was the supreme : for example, Parmenides' One Being, Plato's pure Forms or Ideas, Aristotle's *ousiai*. Now for Plotinus the supreme is that which stands in complete contrast and opposition to the definite or finite. Here has fully taken place the complete inversion of the Greek identification of the supreme with the definite; in Plotinus the supreme is identified with the infinite, the indefinite.

This inversion, which was systematically formulated by Plotinus, was implicit in the Christian religion and theology which had accepted the transcendence of God as basic, and it became to some extent explicit in the thought of the early Christian theologians. The eternity of God stood in sharp contrast to the transitoriness and finitude of creation. Created life and being is of limited, finite duration. The eternity of the transcendent God, who is the creator, means that he does not come into being, nor does he have an end; he is thus the unlimited, the infinite. The concept of eternity thus became identified with that of infinity. Likewise did the concept of eternity become identified with the unknowable, the incomprehensible – an identification which was already implicit in Old Testament times, the Hebrew word for eternity, *olam*, having had the original meaning of the veiled, the hidden. With his grounding in Greek philosophy Philo had drawn the conclusion that the incomprehensibility of God meant that God is *apoios*, without quality or attribute, in this respect analogous to *hylē* as *apeiron*, indefinite.[12] Among the earliest of the Apologists, Justin Martyr spoke of God as unutterable (*arrēton*), incomprehensible (*akatalēpton*), unborn or ungenerated

---

[11] *Enneads*, V,4. 1: οὗ μὴ λόγος μηδὲ ἐπιστήμη, ὃ δὴ καὶ ἐπέκεινα λέγεται εἶναι οὐσίας.

[12] cf. E. Zeller, *Philosophie der Griechen*, III, II, II, 403.

(*agenētos*), and almighty (*pantokratōr*).[13] The world by contrast, Justin Martyr maintained, is limited in extent, and of limited duration – here repeating the doctrine of the Stoics, with whom he had earlier been associated, of an endless, infinite succession of worlds.

Evidently in the early centuries Christian theologians had already run into the problem of the infinite. Its impingement on them was complex and presented supreme difficulty, for their new basic position of a completely transcendent God, so contrary to that of Greek thought, necessitated a new conception of the infinite; and since the very framework of fundamental concepts in terms of which they were operating was of Greek philosophical origin, they were inevitably involved in confusion in respect of the concept of the infinite. The struggle was protracted for centuries; indeed it was not till toward the end of the medieval period that the new conception of the infinite fully emerged.

The conflict of the Greek conception of the infinite with that implied in the Christian doctrine of a transcendent God manifested itself first most sharply in the thought of the two thinkers who had earliest most extensively brought Greek philosophy into use in developing a Christian theology, namely Origen and Augustine. Origen, who like Plotinus had been a student of the Platonist Ammonias Saccas in Alexandria, maintained that since of that of which there is no limit there can be no conception, God accordingly could not conceive an unlimited number of creatures, and therefore God must have created the world as finite. However, the conception of God as eternal transcendent creator involved an important problem. If the world is necessarily finite, then it had a beginning. But what was the situation antecedent to that initial creation? It is inconsistent with the conception of an eternal creator that antecedently to the creation of the world he was simply idle. An eternal creator must always be creating, and since the world is necessarily finite, that is, with beginning and end, it follows that God creates a succession of finite worlds. Thus creation, that is, the act of creation and that which is created, is finite. It is to be noted that the conception of 'infinite' here is strictly consistent with the Greek conception, and in particular with that of Aristotle.

Another significant respect in which Origen ran up against the

[13] cf. A. Harnack, *History of Dogma* (New York, 1958), Vol. II, p. 205.

problem of the infinite was in regard to the power of God. God was being characterized as *pantokratōr*, almighty, and this was interpreted as limitless power. But unlimitedness, *to apeiron*, is indeterminateness, and of the indeterminate there can be no knowledge or comprehension. So in regard to power this would imply that God could have no comprehension of his own power. Further, God's power as indeterminate would mean no one thing in particular, that is, the power to do neither one thing nor another, and this implies not having or exercising power. It is worth having his own pungent statement of his argument and his conclusion : 'We must say that the power of God is finite, and not, under pretence of praising him, take away his limitation. For if the divine power be infinite, it must of necessity be unable to understand even itself, since that which is naturally illimitable is incapable of being comprehended. He made things therefore of such a size as to be able to apprehend and keep them under his power, and control them by his providence; so also he pre-pared matter of such size (that is, in such quantity) as he had power to ornament.'[14]

It is evident that Origen, though he was trying to formulate a theology of the new conception of a wholly transcendent God – as opposed to a Platonic *demiourgos* who formed a pre-existent stuff – still had his thought determined by the Greek conception of the infinite. One contribution of Origen, however, was of the utmost importance for the future of the conception of the infinite. Origen, proceeding from a basis in Platonism, was the first to introduce into Christian theology the explicit denial of God as corporeal, maintaining the conception of God on the contrary as a spiritual being. The significance of this for the concept of the infinite was that it could be detached from the concept of the corporeal, with which it had been essentially united in Greek thought, as we have seen. This step of detachment was taken by Augustine.

The doctrines of Origen were a main target in Augustine's polemics. Origen's argument that God could not have infinite knowledge because it is not possible to conceive what is infinite, was rejected by Augustine as being based upon thinking of God in human terms. Human minds can grasp only what is finite,

---

[14] Origen, *De principiis*, II, 9, 1. (tr. Etienne Gilson, *History of Christian Philosophy in the Middle Ages* (New York and London, 1955), p. 38.)

limited; but God's mind is immutable and is capable of grasping all infinity and enumerating all number without transition of thought.[15] Number is certainly infinite, and to suppose that God cannot grasp the totality of numbers is impious.[16]

In opposition to Origen, Augustine was here advancing a conception of the infinite very different from that of Greek thought. It involves conceiving the infinite as actual, but now the actual was not what it had been in Greek thought, namely the universe or some element or elements of the universe, but on the contrary of what completely transcends the universe. In this new intellectual position the universe is finite (more particularly extensively), in this respect confirming the Platonic-Aristotelian analysis and indeed carrying it further. Augustine accepted, too, the Platonic-Aristotelian correlation of time with the world process. Thus, if the world be finite, as created, so also is time; time was created with the world, and the doctrine of Origen of an unlimited series of successive worlds is accordingly false. In Augustine's doctrine the universe, as created, is in every respect finite, and the infinite pertains wholly and exclusively to the transcendent God.

Augustine rejected the doctrine of Plotinus that God transcends also being. Created being, it is true, is finite and definite, as Plotinus maintained, and God transcends this. But the creator of finite being *is* also; his is infinite being, the source of all finite being.

But how precisely is 'infinite being' to be understood? Certainly there can be no human comprehension of infinite being, not because 'infinite' means, as it did for the Greeks, the indefinite and thus what in essence is incapable of being grasped, but because the human intellect, as created, is finite and for this reason not able to comprehend what transcends it as the infinite. The infinite is the fully intelligible, but incomprehensible to finite human minds.

The only way of approach to some comprehension by finite minds of the infinite is a negative one: starting with the features of finitude – which are fully comprehensible – and saying that God is not that, God is not-finite. In other words, the infinite is to be understood only as what stands in complete contrast to

---

[15] *Civ. Dei* XII, 18: '*Mentem divinam omnino immutabilem cuiuslibet infinitatis capacem et innumera omnia sine cogitationis alternatione numerantem.*'

[16] ibid., XII, 18.

the finite, the not-finite. Thus it is that we can also validly speak of the being of God as the not-finite being.

This essentially negative way of approach to the infinite prevailed in Christian theology until high Scholastic times. Thomas Aquinas refined it by making a distinction between the privative infinite and the negative infinite. God is not privatively infinite, for in saying that God is infinite we are not denying characters and definiteness of God. On the contrary, we are asserting characters, goodness, for example, and knowledge; not however goodness and knowledge as we have it, namely finitely, but not-finitely.[17]

In the late thirteenth century another approach to the infinite was introduced first, as Etienne Gilson pointed out, by Henry of Ghent, an approach which was to be of the utmost import for the future. Gilson is correct in insisting that the significance of the development of the conception of infinity in Christian thought has had too little attention paid to it.[18] His concern is primarily theological, but his comment on Henry of Ghent is highly pertinent to our wider theme :

'let us note in the theology of Henry of Ghent the new meaning attributed to the divine "infinity". Like all his predecessors, Henry considers infinity a negative notion. It essentially points out the non-existence of any limits set to the divine being or to the divine perfection. But Henry has stressed the fact that, negative as it is in its mode of signifying, the notion of infinity points out a most positive perfection of the divine being. We are here witnessing a complete reversal of the Greek idea of infinity conceived as the condition of that which, being left unfinished, lacks the determinations required for its perfection. Henry conceives infinity as the positive power whereby the divine being transcends all possible limitations. The passage of his *Summa* II, art. 44, qu. 2, in which Henry extends this notion of infinity from God to creatures marks an important date in the history of the notion. The world, Henry says, is finite, but its finitude does not result in it from any perfection. On the contrary, "the word *infinite*, not only in God but in creatures as well, principally signifies that something is being posited, or affirmed"; and again, "in God as

---

[17] cf. Thomas Aquinas, *Summa Theologica*, I, Quest. 7.
[18] Gilson, op. cit., pp. 571–2.

well as in creatures, the word *infinite* really imports an affirmation, although it expresses it under the form of a negation or of a privation (of limits)". This positive interpretation of the notion of infinity will play a decisive part in the theology of Duns Scotus.'[19]

This change of meaning, begun by Henry of Ghent, was carried a good deal further by John Duns Scotus. The meaning of the word still derives by contrast with 'finite' : it is that which stands in contrast to the finite. But since created being is dependent upon God the perfect being, the finiteness or limitedness of created being is conceived as implying its relative imperfection – in this respect agreeing with Aquinas. By contrast with this, the infinity of God is correlated to the perfection of God, and the term 'infinite' thus for Scotus comes to connote perfection or the supreme degree beyond which there is no other. So when Scotus speaks of the 'infinite being' of God this is not the merely negative assertion that God's being is not finite; it is the positive assertion of the supreme and ultimate perfection of being. So also the infinite goodness and the infinite wisdom of God mean God's complete perfection in goodness and wisdom, beyond all degrees. Further, for Duns Scotus, because God is infinite being he is necessary being. Created being is contingent, dependent, so by contrast with God, finiteness implies the contrary of necessity, namely contingency.

Here with Scotus a complete inversion of the antecedent procedure or way of approach to the infinite has taken place : instead of, as was previously done, starting from the concept of the 'finite' to arrive at an understanding of God as 'not-finite', Duns Scotus starts from an understanding of God as perfect (=infinite) to arrive by contrast with this at the status of the 'finite'. Finiteness, definiteness, accordingly connotes limitedness in the sense of derogation from perfection, deficiency. This is the complete opposite of the Greek view, according to which perfection could only be attained by definiteness.

Thus it was with Duns Scotus that the reversal of the Greek position, a reversal which began explicitly with Plotinus more than a thousand years previously, was completely effected. According to the fundamental Greek position there can be no

[19] ibid., pp. 448–9.

being without definiteness; that is, being is necessarily finite. Now with Duns Scotus the finiteness of being involves an essential contingency, that is dependence upon infinite being. This means that, in the ultimate and primary sense, being is necessarily infinite.

With Duns Scotus therefore became explicit a new conception of being and a new conception of infinity. But the full potentialities of the new conception are not realized by a single thinker or a single school. A vastly important new development became possible through the adoption of this positive conception of infinity by a Christian Neoplatonism. This was the work of a thinker of great philosophical power, Nicolaus of Cusa, in the first half of the fifteenth century.

5

THE NEW PHILOSOPHY OF THE
INFINITE OF NICOLAUS CUSANUS

To Cusanus must be accorded a special place in the history of the concept of the infinite, because it was his development of the concept which made possible the transition from the 'closed world' of ancient and medieval thought to the 'infinite universe' of modern thought – to use Koyré's characterization of the contrast. We have seen that the former position was anything but the outcome of ignorant prejudice; it rested on very firm foundations. In the case of Greek thought the conception of the universe was grounded in a particular conception of being. The universe had to be finite, that is determinately bounded, for it to be definite, and the universe accordingly could not actually exist as an indefinite, indeterminate, unbounded entity. This fundamental philosophical position was carried over into medieval thought, with the highly important qualification that the necessary definiteness of being on which the Greeks had insisted applied truly only to created being. The finiteness of created being is the necessary implication of its contingency. Thus the consequence of the fundamental doctrine of medieval thought, namely the complete transcendence of God and the complete dependence of the world on God, was to strengthen considerably the conception of the world as finite in extent.

Evidently a quite extraordinary development was required for this conception to be departed from, indeed for the conception of an 'infinite universe' to be rendered seriously possible at all. A mere denial of the medieval doctrine of the essential contingency of the world, for example, would not have achieved this possibility, for this denial would have left intact the Aristotelian analysis of the concept of the infinite and therewith also Aristotle's conclusion. It was a new conception of the infinite which was here indispensable, one altogether different from that of the

Greeks. And this was possible only upon the basis of a very different conception of being.

Fundamental changes in thought do not occur as radical breaks, but as developments from antecedent positions. The new conception of the infinite came not as the outcome of a repudiation, but on the contrary with a full acceptance of the basic position of medieval thought, of the complete transcendence of God, and of the changes in the Greek conception of the infinite which this necessitated. These, as we have seen, had been, in the first instance, to remove the concept of the infinite from an essential reference to the universe, that is, to the physical or natural, which it had had for the Greeks, and instead to make it pertain essentially to the transcendent divine. The second fundamental change effected by medieval thought was to have attained to a positive conception of the infinite as opposed to a negative conception as the 'not-finite'. The course of advance to the modern position was through a continuation of the medieval development by Nicolaus of Cusa.

Cusanus was essentially a medieval thinker, fully accepting the basic position of medieval thought, that of the transcendence of God and the dependence and otherness of the world. Indeed Cusanus saw in the late thirteenth-century development of a positive conception of the infinite the possibility of realizing the theocentricity of traditional Christian thought more thoroughly and consistently than ever before. What was required was to go in the direction of a Neoplatonism rather than in that of the Aristotelianism of the dominant tradition of Scholastic thought. Duns Scotus, in the latter tradition, had centred his metaphysics on the concept of being, and had developed a positive conception of infinite being. Cusanus agreed that the concept of being is fundamental, but, he maintained, equally so is the concept of unity – it had indeed long been realized that the concepts of being and unity are convertible. So, Cusanus insisted, God is not only infinite being but also infinite unity. Following the Neoplatonic emphasis on unity, Cusanus saw the momentous implications of the new positive conception of the infinite when applied to the concept of unity.

To elicit these implications the first necessity was to concentrate on the positive conception of the infinite. To express this positive conception of the infinite as complete perfection, beyond all degrees, Cusanus used the term 'maximum': 'I call maximum that than which nothing can be greater.'[1] It was very considerably by his employment of the concept of the maximum that Cusanus was able to attain a further and most significant development of the conception of the infinite. For this development consisted in establishing a precise, positive connotation to the concept of the infinite which made it the key and central concept in the entire process of understanding.

In previous Christian philosophy the concept of the infinite had played a relatively subordinate part in understanding. The human mind, since it is finite, can properly comprehend only the finite. Its proper objects are finite things, and at its highest, finite being qua being. The human mind is not able to attain an understanding of the divine except negatively, that is, as the not-finite. Now, with the development of a positive conception of the infinite, Cusanus saw that the antecedent procedure of understanding, of starting with the finite and going from that to the not-finite, could be reversed. With a positive conception of the infinite it is possible to start with the infinite as the highest, and proceed from that to achieve an understanding of the finite. The antecedent procedure was one which Christian thought had taken over from Greek philosophy, but it was rendered invalid, Cusanus maintained, by the new conception of being, namely the primacy of infinite being. Accordingly Cusanus proclaimed the necessity of the reversal of the entire procedure of understanding and put it into effect in his important book, *De docta ignorantia*. His doctrine is that, contrary to antecedent thought, we cannot attain to a sound and true understanding of the finite except in terms of the infinite, for the finite is not self-contained and self-subsistent but is utterly dependent upon God, the infinite. Thus what usually is taken to be knowledge – that is, what is attained by concentrating on the finite – is not really knowledge at all; it is ignorance, learned ignorance. True knowledge is in the first instance and primarily knowledge of God, the infinite, and from this knowledge we can attain to a real knowledge of the world, the finite.

This reversal of the antecedent procedure of understanding which Cusanus introduced came gradually and increasingly into

---

[1] Nicolaus Cusanus, *De docta ignorantia* I, 2. All translations from this book are my own.

acceptance, and by the seventeenth century it was not only the explicit doctrine of the leading thinkers such as Descartes, Spinoza, and Leibniz, but had become very widely adopted and was a major factor in the development of the modern concept of space, as we shall see. The following passage from Descartes' *Principles of Philosophy*[2] brings out clearly how fully Cusanus' doctrine had come into effect:

'Being thus aware that God alone is the true cause of all that is or can be, we shall doubtless follow the best method of philosophising, if, from the knowledge which we possess of his nature, we pass to an explanation of the things which he has created, and if we try from the notions which exist naturally in our minds to deduce it, for in this way we shall obtain a perfect science, that is, a knowledge of the effects through their causes. But in order that we may undertake this task with most security from error, we must recollect that God, the creator of all things, is infinite and that we are altogether finite.'

Cusanus insisted that it is possible for the finite intellect to attain to a true knowledge of God, for the finite intellect can achieve a positive insight into the infinite. The way to do this is to concentrate on the concept of the maximum. The maximum is that than which nothing can be greater, and this means that the maximum, as the greatest, is beyond all degrees, all more or less. The implication of this is quite crucial and leads Cusanus to his new doctrine. The maximum as 'beyond all degrees, all more or less', is not to be conceived negatively, as that which is without degrees – this is the old negative theology which Cusanus is repudiating – for how then could it be the maximum of anything? The maximum must be positively conceived as 'beyond' degrees.

The maximum can be a meaningful concept only if it means the maximum of everything. Now 'everything' must mean all the diverse manifold of what actually is and what is possible, in all its differences, kinds, and degrees. But diversity of kinds implies opposites and contraries, which are thus mutually exclusive, so how can there be a 'maximum' of them? There can be only if the maximum contains them in a transcendent integration.

2 Part I, 24; Haldane and Ross tr. p. 229.

An evident instance of such a 'containing' is that in which the genus dog, for example, 'contains' all the variety of individual dogs, with their different sizes, colours, shapes, sexes, etc. Further, the genus transcends the individuals. The maximum, understood in this way, is the *coincidentia oppositorum*, the coincidence or coming together of all opposites and diversities.

It is in this conception of the maximum as *coincidentia oppositorum* that Cusanus finds the positive meaning of the infinite. The infinite is an absolute unity which is the integration of all opposites and diversities. Basically we have here a rendering of the Neoplatonic conception of the One in a new interpretation. The One is the ultimate source and origin of everything. Therefore the One must in some respect contain the divergent plurality. It cannot contain the diversity as its mere sum, since then it could not be the source, the origin – to be the source of diversity it must itself transcend the diversity. Since the One cannot in itself be actually diverse, that diversity must coincide in the One in a unique unity.

This crucial notion of coincidence, Cusanus maintains, can be readily grasped from a mathematical exemplification. Indeed in mathematics we have a singularly good way to the positive understanding of the concept of infinity. All mathematical figures are finite, but we are readily able to conceive them as infinite. For example, every straight line is finite, but we can easily conceive an infinite straight line, namely one which proceeds interminably in both directions. Now consider a triangle. It is a plane figure bounded by three straight lines, forming three angles, the sizes of which add up to two right angles or 180°. What happens if we extend the length of one of the sides indefinitely? Clearly the angle opposite it becomes ever greater and the other two angles ever smaller. As this side approaches infinite length the opposite angle approaches 180°, and when that side is infinite in length, the opposite angle will be fully 180°, which implies that the other two sides will have collapsed into the infinitely extended one. This means that the infinite triangle coincides with the infinite straight line. A similar coincidence occurs in the case of an infinite circle. A circle is a plane figure constituted by a line all the points of which are equidistant from a central point, this line therefore being a continuous curve. The diameter of a circle is a straight line, necessarily shorter than the circumference. Now the longer the diameter the less will be the curvature of the circumference. If the diameter be extended infinitely the curvature of the circumference will disappear entirely, and this means that the infinite circle will coincide with the infinite straight line. In both cases we have an exemplification of the concept of *coincidentia oppositorum* : at infinity the contraries, the straight line, circle, and triangle, all come together and coincide – more precisely, the circle and triangle and other geometrical figures all coincide with the straight line.

This coincidence at infinity of the triangle and circle with the straight line does not mean that the triangle and circle simply disappear in every respect. On the contrary, they must in some respect remain, for otherwise there would not be a 'coincidence'. They remain *complicans*, 'enfolded', in the infinite straight line, and because of this *complicatio* there can be an *explicatio*, 'unfolding', of them – just as the conclusions of an argument are 'explicated' because they are 'contained', *complicans*, in the premises.

Now we are able to see the full positive conception of the infinite as developed by Cusanus. To be infinite is to contain *complicans*, in other words to have 'enfolded' in it that which is capable of being 'unfolded', *explicans*. With this conception we are able to grasp the way in which the absolute infinite, which is God, is the absolute *coincidentia oppositorum*. God as infinite means absolute being having all diversity *complicans*, and thereby being the absolute unity of all. This is Cusanus' new conception of being – which is completely divergent from that of the Greeks. For Cusanus being is primarily infinite, not finite, and to be infinite being is to have everything, every possibility, *complicans*.

With this positive conception of infinity as *coincidentia oppositorum* it is then possible to proceed to an understanding of the world. Fundamental to the understanding of the world is the fact of the dependence of the world, and this means ultimately its derivation from God. Since God is the infinite source of all, the infinite unity which is the infinite *complicatio* of all things, the world must derive from God by an *explicatio*, an unfolding, of that unity. The world, therefore, is *explicatio Dei*, the unfolding of God.

This conception of the world as *explicatio Dei* is the momentous conclusion to which Cusanus was led by his new conception of infinity. It is momentous for what it implied and for what in fact followed from it in subsequent history.

The implications can be readily seen by considering Cusanus' doctrine in the context of the issue with which thinkers had struggled from early on in the medieval period, namely the fundamental problem inherent in the basic position of medieval thought of the absolute transcendent otherness of God and the dependence of the world. For if God be the source and origin of the world, then the being of the world derives from God, and the problem which becomes acute is the ultimate problem of 'being'. Plotinus, as we have seen, continued to maintain the Greek conception of being and accordingly held that being is not to be ascribed to God; God as the source of being is beyond being. The Christian tradition, in this respect becoming fully explicit with Augustine, rejected this doctrine and insisted on the primacy of being, which means that God is being, the supreme being, being as such – for which a favourite Scriptural authority was the passage in *Exodus* 3, 14, where Yahweh answers Moses : 'Thus shalt thou say to the children of Israel : He who is, hath sent me unto you.' This Christian doctrine, however, involves the following basic problem with regard to being : is there one essential meaning of 'being', irrespective of whether we speak of the being of God or the being of creatures? If a univocal meaning be accepted, then the doctrine of the transcendent otherness of God is threatened, since if God's being be the same being as that of creatures, then God does not absolutely transcend creatures in being. On the other hand, if it be maintained that 'being' is equivocal, the word meaning something completely different in respect of God from what it does in respect of creatures, then the doctrine of the transcendent otherness of God is secured, but at the price of having God intrinsically beyond any creaturely relationship, including knowledge, as Scotus insisted, and thus of making the doctrine of the dependence of the world on God unintelligible : the statement that the being of the world derives from the being of God is vacuous, since the 'being' of God can have no meaning for creatures. Aquinas sought to solve this problem by his doctrine of the analogy of being, a doctrine which, however, many subsequent thinkers felt still essentially leaves the fundamental difficulty regarding being intact.

It is in respect of this that Cusanus took a new line. Instead of following the antecedent Neoplatonists in maintaining God as beyond being, Cusanus saw that, with the positive conception of the infinite, the orthodox Christian tradition of the primacy of being could be consistently accepted. God as infinite being means for Cusanus that God is the being which has all other being *complicans* in an absolute unity, and therefore that the world must derive by the *explicatio* of that unity which is God. Cusanus stated this doctrine as follows : 'Deus ergo est omnia complicans in hoc, quod omnia in eo; est omnia explicans in hoc, quod ipse in omnibus' : 'God therefore is all [things] enfolded, in this that all [things] are in him; he is all [things] unfolded, in that he is in all [things]).[3] The implication is evident that the being of the world is an *explicatio* of the being of God.

In this position Cusanus is not only in full accord with the basic medieval doctrine of the complete dependence of the world on God, but he renders that dependence more intelligible than it is in the orthodox doctrine of creation, for the very being of the world derives by *explicatio Dei*. However, this position of Cusanus entails an inconsistency with the other basic medieval doctrine, that of the complete transcendence and otherness of God. If the world be *explicatio Dei*, then God cannot be completely other than the world, that is, in an absolute sense transcending the world. It was on the ground of this inconsistency that the main Christian tradition had rejected the Neoplatonic doctrine of the coming into being of the world by emanation from God. Cusanus was now explicitly asserting the emanationist theory.

Cusanus himself strongly denies, however, that this theory, as he is maintaining it, involves inconsistency with the Christian doctrine of the transcendence of God, insisting that his conception of God is infinite unity clearly entails the transcendence of God – the infinite as *coincidentia oppositorum*, which is the source and origin of all, necessarily means that it is a One, a unity, which transcends the divergent and contrary many; that which is all things *complicans* must necessarily be transcendent if there is to be an *explicatio*.

Nevertheless, in a certain most important respect Cusanus' doctrine is inconsistent with the fundamental medieval doctrine

[3] *De doct. ig.*, Bk II, Ch. 3.

of the transcendent otherness of God. For that doctrine had maintained this transcendent otherness in a sense distinctively different from that now proclaimed by Cusanus. The sense in which the complete transcendent otherness of the divine had earlier been maintained is well exemplified both in the doctrine of Plotinus of the One as beyond all knowledge and being, and in the Christian negative conception of the infinite. This sense was departed from by Cusanus with his positive conception of the infinite; the sense in which his doctrine admits transcendence is a significantly different one from that which had formerly been maintained.

We have here indeed the crucial respect in which the doctrine of Nicolaus Cusanus constitutes a fundamental divergence from the basic position of medieval thought. It is by reason of this that the philosophy of the infinite of Cusanus effected the transition to the modern conception of the universe. Cusanus himself went a considerable way toward that modern conception through drawing the implications for the nature of the universe when it is conceived as *explicatio Dei*.

The fundamental implications become clear by attaining to a fuller comprehension of what is entailed in the conception of the world as *explicatio Dei*. How, for example, does that *explicatio* take place? This can be understood from a consideration of God as having the diverse plurality of the world *complicans*. We have already noted that this is to be conceived analogously to the way in which the genus dog, for example, contains the diverse plurality of species of dogs and of individual dogs. Alternatively stated, this genus-species-individual relationship means that the genus manifests itself in the species and the species manifests itself in the individual. To make this point more precise Cusanus adopted the Neoplatonic conception of *contractio* : the genus manifests itself, that is, exists, in the species because the genus, which is wide and includes a great diversity of species, is 'contracted to' that particular species; and further, the species likewise manifests itself, that is, exists, by 'contraction' to an individual.

Cusanus claims that 'when we correctly consider contraction, all things are clear'.[4] That is, it fully explains the conception of the world as *explicatio Dei*. The world or universe comes into being as the 'contraction' of God. God is the absolute infinite

---

[4] *De doct. ig.*, Bk II, Ch. 4: '*quando recte consideratur de contractione, omnia sunt clara*'.

unity which becomes contracted to the universe. The universe, as the very word indicates, is a one or unity, but it is a contracted unity, a contraction of the infinite absolute unity to a particular form. This contracted unity, the universe, is then further contracted to the many actual individual existents, which are thus each a contracted unity.

From this conception of the universe as the *contractio Dei* a number of most important implications for the nature of the universe follow. First, there is a general epistemological one of very considerable significance. If the universe be *explicatio Dei*, then it is evident that the depreciatory view of and attitude toward the universe or nature, which had been pervasive from earliest Christian times, is entirely false. Far from it being the case that an interest in nature, in the sensory, is to be deplored as distracting attention and effort from the only worthy object of contemplation, God, the very contrary must be maintained : through a study of the world we have one most important way of arriving at an understanding of God. For since the universe itself and the multitude of finite actual things are so many contractions of God, by studying the manifold characters of the world, we see in contracted forms what is infinite in God. By this doctrine Cusanus provided a positive philosophical justification for the interest in nature which had been steadily growing from the twelfth century onward, under a number of influences, prominent among which were that of St. Francis of Assisi, and that of the discovery by the West of Arabic philosophy and through this the philosophy of Aristotle, which had brought a certain attention to nature as an object of knowledge. More frequently and with renewed significance there had begun cropping up reference to the 'Book of Nature' in which the Creator had revealed himself no less than in the other Book, the Holy Scriptures. The effect of Cusanus was a strong impetus to this trend, in this respect directly influencing important sixteenth-century thinkers like Agrippa of Nettesheim, Paracelsus, Cardanus, Scaliger, who were medical men seeking to understand nature, but basic to whose work was the conviction that the world itself is a worthy object of inquiry since it is the manifestation of God. The conception of the real justification of the study of nature being that it contributes to a knowledge of God is fundamental to the rise of modern science and goes through into the seventeenth century and beyond. The following statement of this conception by Leibniz epitomizes the attitude of that time : 'The greatest usefulness of theoretical natural science, which deals with the causes and purposes of things, is for the perfection of the mind and the worship of God.'[5]

From the conception of the universe as *explicatio Dei* and *contractio Dei* Cusanus drew a number of conclusions as to the nature of the universe which were of the greatest import for the future. To appreciate not only his position but also the future developments, it should be noted that the term 'universe' was for Cusanus not a mere collective noun denoting the totality of the many individual existents, as the word had antecedently commonly been used, and as it was used subsequently – though merged with Cusanus' conclusions, with consequences of the utmost moment, as we shall see. The difference is that whereas in the usual usage the universe stands in relation to the plurality of individual things as their total, in the conception of Cusanus the relation of the universe to the many individual things is that of genus to individuals. The many individual things are, in the philosophy of Cusanus, contractions of God, not directly however but mediately; the individual things are contractions of the universe. It is the universe which is the immediate contraction of God, and the universe is thus for Cusanus an entity transcending the plurality of individual things, but having them *complicans*. However, just as a genus is not an actual individual existing completely separately from the many, but exists as contracted to the many actual individuals, so, Cusanus maintains, 'there is no universe unless contractedly in things, and everything actually existing contracts the universe'.[6]

With this clarification of the ontological status of the universe we can more readily appreciate the implications for the nature of the universe which Cusanus found to be contained in his conception of the universe as *explicatio Dei*. God is the infinite unity,

⁵ G. W. Leibniz, *Elementa physicae*, tr. by L. E. Loemker under the title *On the Elements of Natural Science* and published in *Gottfried Wilhelm Leibniz: Philosophical Papers and Letters*, Translated and Edited by L. E. Loemker, 2nd ed. (Dordrecht-Holland, 1969), p. 280. All English translations of Leibniz's writings, unless otherwise stated, will be those from this edition, and will be referred to under the abbreviation of 'Loemker'.

⁶ *De doct. ig.*, Bk II, Ch. 5: '*Non est autem universum nisi contracte in rebus, et omnis res actu existens contrahit universa.*'

as we have seen, and the universe is a contracted unity, that is, an immediate contraction of God's unity. Since God's unity is infinite, what are we to infer about the unity of the universe? It would be incongruent with the nature of God as infinite to suppose the primary manifestation of the divine infinity to be a finite, bounded entity. Since God is absolute infinite unity, the primary manifestation must be a contracted infinite unity. But what is a 'contracted infinite unity'? Cusanus held that the solution to this problem is to be found in the character of the universe as extensive; it is in this that he saw the primary manifestation of the infinity of God. That is, God's absolute infinity is contracted to an interminate, unbounded extension. The fundamental character of the universe, therefore, that in which God has most fundamentally manifested his infinity in a contracted form, is an interminate, endless, extensiveness.

This is the basis upon which Cusanus rejected the Greek and medieval conception of the universe as finite, bounded. It should be noted, however, that Cusanus did not maintain that therefore the universe is infinite. For infinity strictly can pertain to God only. The universe, Cusanus held, is not infinite but a 'contracted infinite', that to which infinity is contracted, and this is extension without bounds or limits. So while God is *infinitum*, infinite, the universe is *interminatum*, unbounded, endless. Descartes, in the seventeenth century, was careful to maintain this distinction.[7]

Cusanus saw in this conception of the status of extension another implication for the fundamental nature of the universe which has had equally momentous consequences for subsequent thought. It had been recognized since Greek times that mathematics, and geometry especially, has the feature of extensiveness as its particular object. On the basis of his conception of the universe as *explicatio Dei* Cusanus now saw the justification for the Pythagorean doctrine, which had been continued by Plato, of mathematics as fundamental to the nature of the universe. The universe, in its fundamental and essential nature, is a mathematical structure. 'Admirabili itaque ordine elementa constituta sunt per Deum, qui omnia in numero, pondere et mensura creavit' : 'thus in admirable order the elements are arranged by God, who created all things according to number, weight and

[7] cf. for instance, Descartes, *Principles of Philosophy*, Pt I, 26 & 27.

measure'[8] – Cusanus using here the oft-quoted phrase from *Ecclesiasticus* 11, 21.[9]

In this conception of God's absolute infinity being contracted to an unbounded geometrical extensiveness, Cusanus presented the philosophical foundation for the conception of the universe as a mathematical structure, the conception which has been basic in the development of modern science, through Newton and beyond. It was this Cusanian conception of the nature of the universe which Galileo proclaimed two centuries later as foundational to knowledge when he wrote:[10] 'Philosophy is written in this great book which continually stands before our eyes (I mean the universe), but we do not understand it if we do not first learn the language, and know the characters, in which it is written. It is written in the mathematical language, and the characters are triangles, circles, and other geometrical figures, without which it is humanly impossible to understand a word of it; without which one wanders about vainly through an obscure labyrinth.' At that period in the history of thought the conception of the universe as a mathematical structure would hardly have been acceptable without a grounding ultimately in God, and this requirement continued right through the seventeenth century, and played a most important role, as we shall see, in the development of the modern concept of space.

When a fundamental conception such as this of the nature of the universe is adopted, its implications are usually not so evident at first, but the advance of thought is nevertheless determined by them, and their explicit realization is usually the work of genius. It says a great deal for the philosophical perspicacity and power of Cusanus' mind that he elaborated some implications many generations before they began to dawn on others.

One such implication, that which was later involved in the work of Copernicus, was that the new conception made in principle untenable the entire medieval view of the place of man at the centre of the world – and therewith also the medieval view of the relation of man to God. Nearly two centuries before this realization dawned on the Church and produced one of the

---

[8] *De doct. ig.*, Bk II, Ch. 13.

[9] '*Pondere, mensura, numero Deus omnia facit*'

[10] Galileo Galilei, '*Il Saggiatore*', in *Le Opere di Galileo Galilei* (Firenze, 1964–6), Vol. VI, p. 232, (my tr.).

greatest crises in its history, Cusanus saw very clearly that the long dominant doctrine of the earth as the fixed centre of the universe was without a basis if his conception of the universe as a contracted infinite be maintained. Since the universe is boundless it can have no circumference, and without that the concept of a centre is strictly without objective meaning. In other words, there can be no real centre; the centre can be but apparent. In a world with all things in motion, any point of reference will be at rest relatively to all others. The earth accordingly, Cusanus maintained, is really in motion, but because it constitutes our point of view it appears to be stationary, and the celestial bodies appear to be in motion round it. Likewise, in an unbounded universe without a centre, there can be no fixed and immovable poles; relativity is universal. The fundamental problems involved in this began to emerge in the seventeenth century, and they are still a prominent feature of twentieth-century thought.

Further, the earth having been deprived of its unique status in the universe, the basis is removed for regarding the earth as composed of any different stuff from that of the planets and other heavenly bodies, or of being any more noble and perfect. Cusanus explicitly maintained, on the contrary, the essential homogeneity of the universe throughout its range. This conception was to be a necessary presupposition of the scientific investigation of the universe.

The centuries after Cusanus witnessed the gradual acceptance of the fundamentally new philosophical position which Cusanus had introduced, and the struggles with the problems and difficulties which it involved.

6

THE CONCEPTION OF THE
UNIVERSE AS INFINITE

On the basis of his new philosophical theory of the infinite, Cusanus had been led to conclusions about the nature of the universe which were far ahead of his time. It was to be another century and a half before Cusanus' doctrines were enthusiastically accepted and propagated by Giordano Bruno. Meanwhile the geocentric conception and the conception of the universe as finite came into question as part of the increasing general criticism of Aristotelianism. The theories of other ancient thinkers were resuscitated and contributed to the growing ferment – Empedocles and Anaxagoras, Democritus and Lucretius, Seneca and Cicero, Asklepiades and Galen, and the mathematicians Aristarchos, Archimedes, Euclid, and Heron of Alexandria. The sixteenth-century thinkers became ever more alive to the complexity of the issues involved, indeed the entire range which Aristotle had so penetratingly examined, and which were now thrown into renewed and fervent controversy. Only some of these will be considered in this chapter; others will be the topic of the next two Parts.

As himself part of the Neoplatonic revival of the fifteenth century, Cusanus was steadily influential. His doctrine of the universe as *explicatio Dei* was sympathetically received by an appreciable number of thinkers, more particularly in the sixteenth century when there first occurred on a marked scale a turning to the Book of Nature. It is a significant fact that modern science and modern philosophy did not start with a repudiation of the theocentricity of the medieval tradition; in a fundamental aspect modern thought was the outcome, after the disintegration of the Scholastic synthesis, of a renewed endeavour to understand God and his relation to the world. This motivation is evident in all sixteenth-century thinkers who were immersed in the inquiry into nature, whether explicitly influenced by Cusanus or not. Cusanus clearly had an effect on his countrymen, such as Agrippa of Nettesheim, Paracelsus, and Scaliger; he was also, however, well known elsewhere, especially in Italy, Cardano, for example, holding him in highest esteem and explicitly accepting the Cusanian ground for the inquiry into nature. This general attitude, which was evidenced also by other prominent Italian researchers such as Fracastoro, Telesio, and Patrizzi, was glowingly expressed by Bruno. The following passage in his *De immenso et innumerabilibus* is characteristic: 'it behoves him to turn the keenness of his eyes and the intentions of his internal sense to the surrounding heaven and worlds; there is presented to him a picture, a book, and a mirror, where he can look at and read and contemplate the trace, law, and likeness of the supreme good in a certain disposition, structure, and image . . .'[1].

My purpose here is not to trace the historical influence of Cusanus; my concern is to elucidate the ideas which were fundamental to the development of the modern conception of the universe. In this Cusanus is accorded special attention not only as originator but more particularly because of the singular clarity of his grasp of some of the basic ideas and the logical rigour with which he developed them. When these have been comprehended in Cusanus they become much more readily recognizable in subsequent thinkers, where they appear either in more complex or involved forms, or are obscured by other concepts. Thus, too, we are able more easily to see the changes undergone by the relevant ideas in later thinkers, and to assess the validity of their combination in different schemes.

Our primary topic in this chapter is the change in the conception of the infinite which took place in the couple of centuries after Cusanus. In the doctrine of Cusanus the concept of infinity pertains in a strict sense to God alone. Only God can be truly infinite as the absolute *coincidentia oppositorum*. The universe as a contraction of the infinite has all the plurality of actual individuals *complicans*; but although this means that the universe is a coincidence of the manifold diversity of actuality, this is very far from being a coincidence of all possibility. The universe is a restricted *coincidentia oppositorum*; the term infinity implies

---

[1] Giordano Bruno, *Opera Latine Conscripta*, 3 vols in 8 parts, ed. by F. Fiorentino, F. Tocco, H. Vitelli, V. Imbriani, C. M. Tallarigo (Naples and Florence, 1879–91; Stuttgart, 1962), Vol. I, Pt I, p. 203 (tr. of Bruno mine unless otherwise indicated).

an absolute *coincidentia oppositorum*. The universe, Cusanus quite explicitly maintained, is neither infinite nor finite;[2] the universe is *interminatum*. This feature of boundlessness is a particular contraction of infinity, and only error can be the consequence of forgetting or ignoring the distinction. It was precisely the minimization or loss of this distinction which was involved in the development during the next couple of centuries.

Cusanus had, as we have seen, placed the primary emphasis on God as infinite. The procedure of knowledge is from the infinite to the finite. In this later period, however, Cusanus himself, acceding to the logic of his doctrine of the world as *explicatio Dei*, came to attach increasing weight to the investigation of the world, of nature, as a way to know God. This shift of emphasis became characteristic in the sixteenth century, and is of special significance in the thought of Bruno, who had wholeheartedly embraced the philosophy of Cusanus, adopting all its fundamental doctrines.

Bruno fully accepted Cusanus' conception of the universe as *explicatio Dei* and *contractio Dei*, and thus of God alone as the absolute unity of all possibility. As he put it in *De la causa* :

'Every potency and act, therefore, which in the principle are enfolded (*complicato*), united, and one, are in other things unfolded (*esplicato*), dispersed, and manifold. The universe, which is the great simulacrum, the great image and only-begotten nature, is still all that it can be, through the same species and principal members, and a containing of all matter, to which nothing is added, and from which nothing is lacking, it is of all and one form; but it is yet not all that it can be through the same differences, modes, properties, and individuals; however it is nothing other than a shadow of the first act and first potency; and yet in it potency and act are not absolutely the same thing because no one of its parts is all that it can be.'[3]

Characteristic of his time, Bruno put the emphasis on the universe; it is through knowing the universe that we come to know God. But in contrast to his contemporaries who were investigating the manifold actualities, Bruno concentrated on the

2 cf. *De doct. ig.*, Bk II, Ch. 1.
3 *De la causa, Principio e uno*, in *Opere Italiane*, I (Bari, 1907), pp. 212–13.

universe. In doing so Bruno strictly adhered to Cusanus' conception of the universe as an entity transcending the actual individuals. It is the universe so conceived which was for Bruno the *explicatio*, the manifestation of God.

However, this shift in emphasis by Bruno to the universe involved a difference between Bruno and Cusanus which is of the greatest significance. Cusanus still adhered fully to the theocentricity of the medieval tradition of thought, and was not aware of the extent to which his doctrine of the universe as *explicatio Dei* implied a divergence from the conception of the complete transcendent otherness of God. But by the sixteenth century the sheer logic of this doctrine of Cusanus began to assert itself : God is not absolutely transcendent of the world but exists in and through the universe. Here the original meaning of the verb 'to exist', *exsisto*, comes to the fore : 'to step out or forth, emerge, appear; to be visible, manifest'.[4] God manifests himself in the universe, which is to say that God exists in that manifestation. That manifestation does not exhaust all that God is, but the crucial point is that the universe is God manifesting himself. Here the former clear distinction between the otherness of God and the universe has broken down. That this is what they were committed to by the conception of the universe as *explicatio Dei* was not always clearly realized by thinkers who accepted the doctrine, but the implications of ideas become effective in thought despite the lack of conscious realization. It was mostly in this implicit way that the changed conception of the relation of God and the world came into force in the sixteenth century, particularly among thinkers who were investigating nature as a way to knowing God.

Bruno was the sixteenth-century thinker who explicitly and most fully accepted and carried through this new conception of the relation of God and the universe, in this respect as in so many others characterizing the advancing thought of his time. In this conception the fundamental position of medieval thought has been completely abandoned, and this constitutes Bruno's crucial divergence from Cusanus. For on the basis of this conception of the relation of God and the universe Bruno was able to accept the doctrines of Cusanus and give them a significantly different interpretation. Thus, since God exists as manifesting himself in

4 *A Latin Dictionary*, Lewis and Short.

the universe, the sharp Cusanian distinction between the nature
of God and the nature of the universe tends to be lost. The nature
of God is that which is manifest in the universe. In particular
it is the infinity of God which is manifest in the extension of
the universe, so that the universe is validly to be conceived as
infinite. Thus it is that what Cusanus had ascribed to God in
distinction from the universe, Bruno is able to ascribe to the
universe itself :

'The universe is, therefore, one, infinite, immobile. One, I say, is
the absolute possibility, one the act, one the form or soul, one the
matter or body, one the thing, one the being, one the maximum
and optimum; which is not capable of being comprehended; and
yet is without end and interminable, and to that extent infinite
and interminate, and consequently immobile. It does not move
itself locally, because it has nothing outside itself to which it might
be transported, it being understood that it is all. It does not
generate itself since there is no other being which it could desire
or look for, it being understood that it has all the being. It is not
corruptible, since there is no other thing into which it could
change itself, it being understood that it is everything. It cannot
diminish or increase, it being understood that it is infinite, thus
being that to which nothing can be added, and that from which
nothing can be subtracted, for the reason that the universe does
not have proportional parts. It is not alterable into any other disposition, because it does not have anything external through
which it could suffer and through which it could be affected. In
addition, through comprehending all contraries in its being in
unity and fitness, through being able to have no inclination to
another and new being, or to this or that mode of being, it cannot
be subjected to mutation according to any quality, nor could
it have a contrary or different thing which could alter it because
it is every concordant thing. It is not matter because it is not
figured, nor figurable; it is not terminated, nor terminable; it
is not form, because it does not inform or figure anything else,
it being understood that it is all, maximum, one, universal. It
is not measurable, nor does it measure. It does not include itself
because it is not greater than itself. It is not included because it is
not less than itself. It is not equal to itself because it is not other
and other, but one and the same. Being the same and one, it

does not have this being and that being; and because it has not this being and another being, it does not have this part and another part; and because it does not have this part and another part, it is not composite. It is a term of a sort which is not a term; it is a form in such a way that it is not a form; it is matter in such a way that it is not matter; it is soul in such a way that it is not soul; because it is all indifferently, and yet it is one, the universe is one.'[5]

In summary, for Bruno it is the universe which is the unity of all, the universe which is *coincidentia oppositorum* and which has all actual things and all possibility *complicans*. The universe is all this not in distinction from God, but as God in manifestation:

'Here then we see how it is not impossible but necessary that the optimum, the maximum, the incomprehensible, is all, is throughout all, is in all, because as simple and indivisible it can be all, be through all, be in all. And thus it was not said in vain that Jove fills all things, inhabits all parts of the universe, is the centre of that which has all being, one in all, and through whom one is all. Who, being all things, and comprehending all things in itself, brings it about that everything is in everything.'[6]

This position of Bruno's involves two points of particular import for the concept of infinity. The first is that whereas for Cusanus the concept of infinity could pertain strictly only to God, Bruno had made it, by his development of Cusanus' doctrine of the universe as *explicatio Dei*, pertain equally to the universe. The second point is that thereby Bruno had achieved the conception of the universe as an *actual* infinite. This was Bruno's momentous development of the concept of the infinite. The fundamental significance of this lies not in the fact of this concept having come into increasing acceptance in the seventeenth century; it is rather that Bruno had achieved a conception of an actual infinite which could circumvent the Aristotelian argument that an actual infinite is inherently impossible.

Through the entire medieval period down to and including

---

[5] Opening to the 5th Dialogue, *De la causa*, op. cit., pp. 239–40.
[6] ibid., p. 242.

Cusanus, thinkers were able to avoid Aristotle's arguments against the possibility of an actual infinite by ascribing infinity exclusively to God – the 'actual' with which Aristotle had been concerned was exclusively the universe as the physical existent. Bruno's development brought him up against the Aristotelian objections, and he had to take issue with them. It will suffice to give the gist of Bruno's counter-argumentation, which he elaborated in considerable detail.

In general Bruno's contention was that Aristotle had not grasped the essential nature of an actual infinite. Indeed to have been able to do so had not been possible till Cusanus and his doctrine of the infinite as *coincidentia oppositorum*. It is only when this as the true nature of the infinite had come to be understood that Aristotle was able to be rebutted.

An implication of Cusanus' conception of the infinite, as he had himself shown, is that the universe as *interminatum*, unbounded, can have no centre and no circumference. But a great many of Aristotle's arguments, such as those seeking to prove the impossibility of motion in an infinite whole,[7] involve and are based upon the conception of centre, circumference, radii, etc., and since there are no such in an infinite whole, Aristotle's arguments can be dismissed as completely lacking in validity.

Equally invalid, Bruno insisted, are Aristotle's arguments against the conception of an infinity of parts in an infinite whole. Here again it is Cusanus who had made possible the answer. For Cusanus had shown, with his doctrine that everything is everything, that the universe is a macrocosm and all the contracted actual individuals are microcosms of that macrocosm. Thus each individual (i.e. part), which is itself a fully definite, finite being, as a contraction of the whole is a microcosm. But since the whole or macrocosm is infinite, it follows that the individuals, which in their own particular modes are finite, are, as microcosms, infinite. Thus Cusanus' macrocosm-microcosm doctrine establishes, contrary to Aristotle, that the parts of an infinite whole not only can be, but necessarily must be at once finite and infinite.

Aristotle's argument that finites, because of their definite finitude, must be of a definite number, is not valid because at infinity number and numerability no longer apply: 'we are not forced

---

[7] cf. *Physics*, Bk III, Ch. 5, and *De caelo, passim*.

to define number, we who say that there is an infinite number of worlds; "there" there is neither an equal distinction nor an unequal, because the differentiae are those of number and not of the innumerable.'[8]

To thinkers like Kepler who did not accept the Cusanian conception of the infinite, the Aristotelian arguments against the possibility of an actual infinite were incontrovertible. Kepler vigorously countered the kind of reasoning of Bruno with the essentially Aristotelian argumentation of the *reductio ad absurdum* kind:

'How can we find in infinity a centrum which, in infinity, is everywhere? For every point taken in the infinity is equally, that is, infinitely, separated from the extremities which are infinitely distant. From which it would result that the same [place] would be the centre and would not be [the centre], and many other contradictory things, which most correctly will be avoided by the one who, as he found the sky of the fixed stars limited from inside, also limits it on the outside.'[9]

Bruno would have replied to this (Kepler's book was published six years after Bruno's death) that it is precisely by virtue of the universe being infinite that the implications, which Kepler thought to be contradictory, are not contradictory. But this implied a very different conception of infinity from that maintained by Aristotle and Kepler. On the basis of the latter, the suppositions that the universe can be actually infinitely extended and that there can be an infinite number of celestial bodies spread through an infinitely extended universe are completely untenable, as Kepler forcefully argued:

'though it cannot be denied that there can be many stars which, either because of their minuteness or because of their very great distance, are not seen, nevertheless you cannot because of them assert an infinite space. For if they are, individually, of a finite

---

[8] *De immen. et innum.* in *Op. lat.*, Vol. I, Pt II, p. 274.

[9] *De stella nova in pede Serpentarii*, Cap. XXI, p. 691, *Opera omnia*, Vol. II (Frankoforti & Erlangae, 1859). For this and the following quotation I have used the excellent translation of Alexandre Koyré in his *From the Closed World to the Infinite Universe*, p. 70.

size, they must, all of them, be of a finite number. Otherwise, if they were of an infinite number, then, be they as small as you like, provided they are not infinitely so, they would be able to constitute one infinite [star] and thus there would be a body, of three dimensions, and nevertheless infinite, which implies a contradiction. For we call infinite what lacks limit and end, and therefore also dimension. Thus all number of things is actually finite for the very reason that it is a number; consequently a finite number of finite bodies does not imply an infinite space, as if engendered by the multiplication of a multitude of finite spaces.'[10]

In taking this stand Kepler is commonly regarded as having been, despite the brilliance of his scientific thought, still too much under the sway of notions which the modern enlightenment was revealing to be so much pathetic ignorance. This view of the situation is too superficial, however; in adhering to this position Kepler was on much stronger ground than is usually admitted, and it is not surprising that Galileo was in so much doubt about this question – his apparent vacillation was genuine uncertainty and not, as is so often supposed, a fear of authorities. It is important for a correct understanding of the situation to appreciate that unless Cusanus' conception of the infinite were accepted, as it was by Bruno, but apparently not fully by Galileo, and definitely not by Kepler, then Aristotle's arguments were difficult indeed to counter. And further, what is of particular relevance here is that it was fundamentally the Cusanus-Bruno conception of infinity and not that of Aristotle which came into effect in the great seventeenth-century schemes – in Descartes, Leibniz and Spinoza, in Henry More and in Newton the concept of the universe as infinite was grounded ultimately in the infinity of God, as we shall see in due course – whence the importance of Bruno's thought at this stage.

The Aristotelian analysis, however, played a profound rôle for several generations, from the late sixteenth century onward, and not merely as the ruling adversary of the newly advancing conception of the universe as infinite. For this conception had perforce brought into renewed consideration and re-examination the

[10] *Epitome astronomiae Copernicanae,* lib. I, pars II, p. 136 in *Opera Omnia,* Vol. VI (Frankoforti & Erlangae, 1866); tr. Koyré, op. cit., pp. 85–6.

entire set of issues which Aristotle had so fully investigated. Bruno as well as other thinkers had to face up to these issues and re-think them, and he, no less than others, owed his grasp of what was fundamentally at issue and of the relevant problems very largely to a study of Aristotle. Here I shall restrict myself to one of these issues as crucial to the conception of the universe as infinite; other issues will be the topics of succeeding chapters. In respect of this issue I shall concentrate particularly upon Bruno as the thinker who most vigorously and penetratingly came to grips with it.

Aristotle had maintained as implicit in the conception of the universe as finite 'that neither are there now, nor have there ever been, nor can there ever be formed more heavens than one, but this heaven of ours is one and unique and complete',[11] from which 'it is therefore evident that there is also no place or void or time outside the heaven. For in every place body can be present; and void is said to be that in which the presence of body, though not actual, is possible.'[12] Since the universe is absolutely inclusive of all that is, there can in no sense *be* anything beyond; beyond the universe is sheer nothing, and nothing can no more constitute a place than it can constitute a container. Any supposition of a place beyond is thus strictly meaningless.

Bruno saw that the crucial contention in this argument was that the concept of a 'beyond' makes no sense, that it is meaningless. He insisted, on the contrary, that it is rather the concept of a boundary to the universe which is the meaningless notion : 'If thou wouldst excuse thyself by asserting that where naught is, and nothing existeth, there can be no question of position in space nor of beyond or outside, yet I shall in no wise be satisfied. For these are mere words and excuses, which cannot form part of our thought. For it is wholly impossible that in any sense or fantasy (even though there may be various senses and various fantasies), it is I say impossible that I can with any true meaning assert that there existeth such a surface, boundary or limit, beyond which is neither body, nor empty space, even though God be there.'[13] He brought forward the old argument of Archytas :

[11] Aristotle, *De caelo*, 279a9–11 (tr. J. L. Stocks).

[12] ibid., 279a12–14 (tr. J. L. Stocks).

[13] Bruno, *De l'infinito universo e mondi, Opere Italiane*, (Bari, 1907), Vol. I, p. 282; tr. by D. W. Singer in *Giordano Bruno, his Life and Work* (New York, 1950), p. 252.

what if a man were to get to the outermost sphere of heaven and stretched out his hand 'beyond'? The essential point Bruno is concerned to make is that the concept of 'beyond' is meaningful.

"Thus let this surface be what it will, I must always put the question, what is beyond? If the reply is NOTHING, then I call that the VOID or emptiness. And such a Void or Emptiness hath no measure and no outer limit, though it hath an inner; and this is harder to imagine than is an infinite or immense universe. For if we insist on a finite universe we cannot escape the void. And let us now see whether there can be such a space in which is naught. In this infinite space is placed our universe (whether by chance, by necessity or by providence I do not now consider)."[14]

Bruno has here turned the tables on the Aristotelian position: 'if we insist on a finite universe, we cannot escape the void', that is, the concept of 'nothingness beyond'. But on the Aristotelian position such a concept is self-contradictory, since 'nothing' cannot be extended – let alone infinitely so. Therefore, Bruno's conclusion is, since the concept of 'beyond', *ad infinitum*, has necessarily to be admitted as valid, and since the beyond cannot be 'nothing' – that, he fully agrees with Aristotle, involves a contradiction – there must accordingly necessarily be 'something' beyond, that is, some existent. That is to say, there must necessarily be an infinitely extended existent.

The question now arises as to what that existent is. Bruno was in agreement with Aristotle that it cannot be an infinitely extended body. His principal reason against this, however, is different from that of Aristotle. Bruno, like many of his contemporaries in the new developments, was impressed by the argument, contrary to Aristotle, that a physical, bodily plenum would render motion impossible. Motion necessitates that there be void extents, that is, extents free of body, into which bodies are able to move.

This, however, raises the big problem of what precisely is meant by 'void'. This problem, which had become the subject of considerable controversy at that time, was dealt with by Bruno

[14] *Op. Ital.*, pp. 283–4; Singer, p. 254.

with very much greater consistency than many of his contemporaries were able to attain. In the first place, the void could not mean sheer empty nothingness, as many such as William Gilbert, held – Gilbert had maintained not only that there is a void between and beyond the heavenly bodies, but also that because of this the issue between finite and infinite was settled, since a void can be neither finite nor infinite. Bruno, with the majority of thinkers, accepted the validity of Aristotle's argument that an extended nothing is a contradiction in terms; only an existent can be extended, so the supposition of the void as sheer nothingness has to be rejected as false. This does not mean, however, that there is no valid concept of a void possible. The void means, Bruno agreed with Aristotle, a place where no body is but where a body might be.[15]

'We do not posit a void space as something in which there is nothing in act, but a space certainly in which now one and now another body is necessarily contained, and which is first generated to be filled with air. For it is to us an infinite being, and there nothing is, in which something is not. Hence we define a void, space or limit, as something in which there are bodies; but not at all as something in which there is nothing. Since however we say that void is a place without body, we separate it not really but in reason from bodies . . . [16] It is called plenum inasmuch as it has mass and can receive mass; it is called void inasmuch as it is understood without mass; it is called place inasmuch as it contains mass.'[17]

It is not in Bruno only at this time that there is an important connection between the concepts of the infinite and that of the void – this connection will concern us further later in regard to other implications, especially those concerning the concepts of place and continuity. What is here most relevant is that Bruno was presenting with remarkable clarity and consistency the fundamental logic of the development which was characteristic of the sixteenth and seventeenth centuries, up to and including Newton. And this is that the concept of the void, since it cannot mean

---

[15] cf. Aristotle, *Physics*, 213a28, 213b32–4, 214a17.

[16] Bruno, *Acrotismus seu rationes articulorum physicorum* in *Opera latine conscripta*, Vol. I, Pt I, pp. 130–1.

[17] ibid., p. 133.

mere extended nothingness, implies that an existent other than body has to be admitted.

This existent, Bruno maintained, is the universe itself, in distinction from the contractions which are the plurality of bodies. It is this conception of the universe – which is essentially that of Cusanus – that enabled Bruno to meet the objections which could legitimately be brought against the concept of the void as maintained in many theories of the time, especially those of the atomists. It is Bruno's fundamental position here which was accepted by Descartes and by Henry More, from whom this conception was taken over as basic in the philosophy of Newton.

One feature of this existent, the universe, must be mentioned here as fundamental to Bruno's doctrine and as one which is, in a slightly different form, equally fundamental in Descartes and Newton. This too is a Cusanian doctrine, namely that the universe in its ultimate nature is mathematical. Cusanus' doctrine had been that God manifests his infinity in the geometrical extensiveness of the universe. Bruno's version of this is that the universe, 'through being actually all that which it can be, has all measurements, has all species of figures and dimensions, and because it has them all, it has none; because it is necessary that that which is so many different things be not any one of those particular things. It is fitting to that which is all to exclude every particular being';[18] that is to say, the universe as the infinitely extended existent is not of a particular geometrical form or size, but it is that which has all particular geometrical sizes, shapes, and dimensions *complicans*; it is not itself a dimensional structure, but is that from which all dimensionality derives.

Here we are brought to the ultimate issue of the relation of the physical to the mathematical which was to play so fundamental a rôle in the thought of the seventeenth century, and more particularly in the systems of Descartes, Gassendi, Galileo, Newton, and Leibniz. Bruno brought this issue very much to the fore, making it clear that one of the profoundest philosophical problems any scheme has to face is that of the relation of the mathematical to the physical. The great schemes of the seventeenth century are in one basic aspect so many attempts at different solutions to this problem.

That there is an intimate connection between the infinite and

[18] Bruno, *De la causa*, in *Op. Ital.*, p. 228.

the mathematical is evident from our analysis in this Part. In Aristotle's doctrine it is to the mathematical that the infinite essentially and properly pertains and not to the physically actual. In Bruno the infinite comes to pertain to the actual universe. But does this imply an identification of the mathematical and the physical? Many subsequent thinkers were to come to hold this position. In order to examine this fundamental issue of the relation of the mathematical to the physical it is manifestly necessary to get clear on what is meant by the 'physical', 'nature'. We have here a problem of very considerable complexity.

PART II
The Concept of the Physical

7

THE GREEK CONCEPTION OF
THE PHYSICAL

In the last two hundred years the conception of the universe as infinite has come so much to be taken for granted that what this concept entails, the issues and problems which it involves, have tended to retreat into the background and to be largely lost sight of. Something analogous has happened to the concept of the physical. The very words, the 'physical', the 'natural', 'nature', have undergone a dissipation and have considerably lost their former significance. Yet the fundamental concept of the physical continues even in our time to play a basic role in thought despite the scant awareness of this fact. The most effective way to make this concept and its rôle explicit is to go back, not to the sixteenth and seventeenth centuries, when certainly it was very much alive, but to see it in its origin and development, and this means that we must start our inquiry with the Greek conception of the physical. For it was Greek thought which had first arrived at the concept and recognized it as fundamental. With Aristotle was achieved the most penetrating analysis of what the concept entailed.

The concept goes back to the beginnings of Greek philosophy among the Ionians whose treatises, according to Plato, Aristotle, and the doxographers, were *peri physeōs*, 'concerning nature'. That the Presocratic thinkers in fact entitled their treatises *peri physeōs* is questionable, but not that this phrase accurately indicated the subject-matter. Their concern was with *physis*, to discover the *physis* of things. What did this word *physis* mean?[1]

[1] It seems to me that the earlier controversies over the meaning of this term arising from the divergent interpretations of thinkers such as Burnet (*Early Greek Philosophy*, 4th ed. 1930, Introduction, Sect. 7), F. J. E. Woodbridge (*Phil. Rev.* X, 1901, pp. 359–74), W. A. Heidel (*Archiv für Gesch. der Phil.*, 1906, pp. 333–79, and *Proc. Amer. Academy*, 1910, 77–133), A. O. Lovejoy (*Phil. Rev.*, XVIII, 1909, pp. 369–83), can be regarded as resolved in a more balanced conception. My interpretation is in the main in agreement with that of Guthrie, op. cit., Vol. I, pp. 82–3. Cf. also J. W. Beardslee, *The Use of* ΦΥΣΙΣ *in Fifth Century Greek Literature*, Chicago, 1918.

We get some way towards the answer if we pursue the question why that word was chosen to denote that with which they were basically concerned. The word *physis* is derived from the verb φύ , 'to bring forth, produce, put forth; to beget, engender; to grow, wax, spring up or forth'.[2] In its primary and general sense the word *physis* accordingly means 'origin', or as Aristotle more fully put it, 'the genesis of growing things'.[3] And when we seek to explicate this concept of 'origin', or of 'genesis' as Aristotle phrases it, it is clear that *physis* connotes, again in Aristotle's words, 'that immanent part of a growing thing, from which its growth first proceeds'.[4] Live things, growing things, quite evidently have something inherent or immanent from which they spring or originate (for example, the seed) and which determines their subsequent growth to be of a certain kind or character whereby they are that particular thing and not another. That is to say, there must be some fundamental *archē*, principle, source, the 'that from which', and as that according to which there is a process of growth, by virtue of which that thing is uniquely itself.[5] From this accordingly comes the main derivative sense of *physis* (which is most frequent in literature[6] as opposed to the more technical sense in philosophy). In this sense *physis* means character, the qualities of a person or thing whereby they are uniquely that person or thing; the innate or original character – often opposed to what is acquired – which is that which a person or thing most truly is.

To come now to the particular philosophical meaning which specially concerns us here, the Presocratics were endeavouring to find the *archē*, the principle, source, of all things, that is to say, that which is immanent in all and whereby things are what they are, that immanent something which ultimately accounts for 'the all' having the character which it does have. This could be put by saying that what they were seeking is the ultimate *physis* of things, for this is precisely what *physis* means, in the second sense

---

[2] Liddell & Scott, *Lexicon.*

[3] *Met.* 1014b16: φύσις λέγεται ἕνα μὲν τρόπον ἡ τῶν φυομένων γένεσις. (Ross tr.).

[4] *Met.* 1014b17–18: ἕνα δὲ ἐξ οὗ φύεται πρώτου τὸ φυόμενον ἐνυπάρχοντος. (Ross tr.).

[5] cf. *Met.* 1014b18–20: ἔτι ὅθεν ἡ κίνησις ἡ πρώτη ἐν ἑκάστῳ τῶν φύσει ὄντων ἐν αὐτῷ ᾗ αὐτὸ ὑπάρχει.

[6] cf. Lovejoy, op. cit., pp. 376ff., and Beardslee, op. cit., esp. Chs 2 and 6.

above, namely that immanent something whereby what is is as it is. That the Presocratic thinkers should have found the word *physis* singularly fitting is thus readily understandable.

The Milesians had a fundamental hypothesis about that *physis* : since what is is extended, bodily, that *physis* must be an extended something : for example, for Thales it was water, for Anaximenes it was air, for Anaximander it was an indeterminate extended something. The particular hypothesis, however, is not the important point here; rather it is that in seeking the *physis* of things they were seeking that ultimate something in things by virtue of which they *are*, and are what they are. The inquiry into the *physis* of things is thus the inquiry into the 'being' of things, what in later terminology was called the 'existence' and 'essence' of things. This is the fundamental meaning which still persists when we speak of the 'nature of' something. For when later the Latins wanted a word to render the Greek *physis* they derived *natura* from the verb *nascor*, the Latin equivalent of the Greek φύομαι. It is in this connection with 'birth', 'origin', 'coming into being', that for the Greeks the fundamental philosophical sense of *physis* is to be understood. Thus for them the inquiry into *physis* was the inquiry into the source and origin and thus into the ultimate being of things. And this is why the phrase *peri physeōs* in reference to the Presocratics in one respect meant simply philosophy or the philosophical inquiry. Aristotle also accepted and insisted on this fundamental connection of *physis* with being, beingness, *ousia*, as we shall see.

But while one can in a general way refer to the 'nature of' anything whatever, the Greek philosophical concern was with *physis* in its basic sense, which is to say that their inquiry was into the *physis* of, the nature of, that which has a *physis*, a nature, intrinsically – as opposed to having it derivatively, as for example does an artefact – and which can accordingly be distinguished as *kata physin*, 'according to nature', 'natural'. In this fundamental sense therefore that is 'natural' which has its *physis*, its nature, in itself intrinsically, by virtue of itself. The connection with 'being' is again evident, and Aristotle pointed out that accordingly *physis*, nature, 'means the *ousia*, the beingness, of natural things'.[7]

---

[7] *Met.* 1014b35–6: ἔτι δ' ἄλλον τρόπον λέγεται ἡ φύσις ἡ τῶν φύσει ὄντων οὐσία. (My tr.).

Further, the word *physis*, nature, is used collectively to denote those things which are natural, which have a nature intrinsically. But, it should be noted, in earlier Greek philosophical thought, as indeed also in Plato and Aristotle, in this collective meaning *physis* was not used in a personified sense – as when in English Nature is spoken of and spelt with a capital. Although this use is to be found, especially in poetry and literature, this personified use is to be distinguished from the more precise philosophical sense in which it refers to the 'nature of' things in general or to the ultimate nature of things, from which is derived the sense in which things collectively as exhibiting that nature are referred to as *physis*, nature, the physical.

The word 'physical' has come now to have a much more restricted connotation than that in which I have just used it. In Greek thought, too, the word *physis* had a more specific in addition to the generic sense so far discussed. The Presocratics on the whole, and not only the Milesians, as we have seen, conceived what is as extended. This applied also to *psychē*, soul, which thinkers identified usually with the finest extended entities, those which are furthest removed from the gross bodily : by Leucippus and Democritus with the spherical atoms of fire, by the Pythagoreans with air, by Heraclitus with 'warm exhalation', this being an instance of the widespread belief in the connection between *psychē* and *pneuma*, breath. This Presocratic conception of what is means, as Aristotle pointed out, that for them 'what is is all that which is perceptible and contained in the so-called heavens'.[8] Accordingly *physis* for them is in itself corporeal and having extension, *megethos*.[9] In other words, it is the bodily extended which for the Presocratics is *physis*, nature, the natural, the physical, and it was this restriction of *physis*, the natural, the physical, to the extended bodily which Plato, Aristotle, and later thinkers particularly had in mind in referring to these Presocratics as the *physikoi* or *physiologoi*.

This connotation of the physical as the bodily came to play a most important role throughout the history of thought. Among the Presocratics themselves the conception was implicit. The explicit recognition of *physis*, the physical, as having this specific

---

[8] *Met.* 990a4–5: ὅτι τό γε ὂν τοῦτ' ἐστὶν ὅσον αἰσθητόν ἐστι καὶ περιείληφεν ὁ καλούμενος οὐρανός. (My tr.).

[9] cf. *Met.* 988b23: καὶ ταύτην σωματικὴν καὶ μέγεθος ἔχουσαν.

connotation for the Presocratics came only with Plato and Aristotle, for it was not until there had arisen the conception of an existent or existents as non-bodily that there was gained the contrast necessary for making the Presocratic connotation explicit; without the conception of non-bodily being, there was no particular significance in conceiving existence as 'bodily' – so long as 'to be' meant 'to be bodily', the latter phrase was a pointless tautology. The conception of being, of what is, as non-corporeal was the great achievement of Plato. In the *Phaedo* is the first clear enunciation of the conception that there are two kinds of existing things, one which is extended and known by the senses and one which is non-extended and known by the mind.[10]

Plato did not, however, identify only the former kind as *physis*, the natural, the physical. On the contrary, because the latter kind of being was regarded by him as more fundamental, as being, existing, in a more ultimate sense – since all the characters of the sensible kind were derivative from the non-sensible kind – it was the non-sensible kind of being which was for him more truly *physis*. Accordingly, fully accepting the basic meaning of *physis* as that immanent something whereby things are and are what they are, Plato was concerned to controvert the Presocratic restriction of *physis* to the sensible extended bodily;[11] it is by virtue of the Ideas, the Forms, that things are and are what they are, and therefore for Plato the *physis* of things is to be identified with the Ideas.

Aristotle rejected the Platonic bifurcation of what is into two quite different kinds. But the work of Plato had put it beyond dispute that there is more to what is than the merely sensible bodily extended. This meant for Aristotle that the entire issue of *physis* had to be opened up again, gone into anew in a fundamental analysis. It was necessary to inquire once more and afresh into the problem of what is that immanent something whereby things are and are what they are.

There can be no doubt that the existents which we encounter in perception are extended: ourselves and beings like us, the animals; also plants and all inanimate things; the earth and what we perceive above and beyond the earth. Thus it could be said

---

[10] *Phaedo*, 79A.
[11] cf. *Phaedo* 96A–100B, *Apology*, 26D, *Laws*, 893C, 967, *Sophist* 265C–266E, *Philebus*, 28–30, *Timaeus*, 46C–E.

that it belongs to their *physis*, their nature, to be extended. But does this imply that the *physis*, the very nature of these things is to be found in their extendedness? That is, is it by virtue of their extendedness that they are, that they exist? Extendedness is certainly one fundamental character, and thus *physis* in this derivative sense of the word. But is their *archē*, the principle and source of their being, to be found in extendedness; is extendedness that whereby they are? Is extendedness their *ousia*, their very beingness?

In the first place, Aristotle contended, when we carefully consider their theories, even the Presocratic *physiologoi* did not in fact hold this; they did implicitly realize that there is more to being than extendedness. For extendedness is not the only general character or feature of these existents. Another is – and it is this which Plato had fastened on as a general character distinguishing this sensible kind of existent from the other kind which he was concerned to maintain, the Ideas or Forms – that these sensible existents are in constant change, of a variety of kinds: there is *genesis*, generation or coming-into-being, and *phthora*, perishing or going out of existence; there is change of character or qualities; there is change in size and shape; there is *phora*, translation or change of place.[12]

Of these kinds of change, the first, *genesis*, is the primary one, for the other kinds can all be conceived as involved in this one: things which come into being – animals are a paradigm instance – involve, in the very process of their generation, change of the qualitative kind, and of the quantitative kind, and change of place; that is, they cannot be in a process of generation without exhibiting the other three kinds of change. The fundamental connection of *physis* with this general character of change rather than with that of extendedness is thus manifest, for *physis* in its primary sense, as we have seen, means 'the genesis of growing things'.

Accordingly, in seeking the *physis* of, the nature of, these things, we are seeking that in them whereby they come into being, that by virtue of which there is a process of generation and change. And a *physei* (natural) being is one which has the *archē* (principle, source) of this *kinēsis* (change) in itself. The *physis* which we are seeking is that which is the very *ousia* (beingness,

[12] cf. Aristotle, *Met.*, Bk I, Chs 3–5, and *Physics*, Bk II, Chs 2, 3, and 7.

essence) of these natural beings. Aristotle summarized his conclusion in a famous sentence: 'From what has been said, then, it is plain that *physis* (nature) in the primary and strict sense is the *ousia* (beingness, essence) of things which have in themselves, as such, an *archē* (principle, source) of *kinēsis* (change, movement).'[13]

Thus for Aristotle, unlike for the Presocratics, *physis*, the natural, the physical, does not connote 'the extensive bodily'; for him the fundamental connotation relates rather to the process of change, to *kinēsis*. More particularly, *physis* refers to that in a being which is the very principle or source of this process of change: 'nature [*physis*] in this sense is the source [*archē*] of the process of change [*kinēsis*] of natural beings [*physei ontōn*], which is somehow inherent in them, either potentially [*dynamei*] or in complete attainment [*entelecheia*].'[14] And from this, in a general derivative meaning, *physis*, the physical, denotes that, whatever it is, which involves a process of change [*kinēsis*] in its essential being.

The concept of *kinēsis* is clearly quite fundamental according to Aristotle's analysis of the physical, and it is therefore necessary to pay some special attention to it. This is the more important for us since it is in respect of this concept that in the early seventeenth century the great divergence from Aristotle took place which is at the basis of the modern conception of the physical.

The term *kinēsis* is usually rendered into English by the words 'motion' or 'movement'. Because of the special connotation which these words have acquired in the modern period – which we shall have to investigate in due course – their use in the translation of Aristotle is apt to be misleading. In the foregoing two paragraphs I have used the phrase 'process of change' as a more apt rendering of Aristotle's meaning.[15] It is not completely satisfactory, however, and the only way to get at Aristotle's meaning is to study especially those passages in which he has explicitly explained the word. The main relevant text is Book III of the

---

13 *Met.* 1015a13–15: ἐκ δὴ τῶν εἰρημένων ἡ πρώτη φύσις καὶ κυρίως λεγομένη ἐστὶν ἡ οὐσία ἡ τῶν ἐχόντων ἀρχὴν κινήσεως ἐν αὑτοῖς ᾗ αὑτά· (Based on the Ross tr.).

14 ibid., 1015a17–19. (My tr.).

15 cf. John P. Anton, *Aristotle's Theory of Contrariety* (London, 1957), p. 10, for a similar interpretation..

Physics, especially chapter 1, and the parallel passages in the *Metaphysics*, Book XI, chapter 9.

Aristotle starts Book III of the *Physics* with the statement: 'Since nature [*physis*] is the principle [*archē*] of *kinēsis* and change [*metabolē*], and our inquiry is concerning nature [*peri physeōs*], we must understand what *kinēsis* is; for if we do not know this, necessarily we shall not know what nature [*physis*] is.'[16] There is a consensus among commentators that here, and in this chapter as a whole, Aristotle uses the terms *kinēsis* and *metabolē* (change) synonymously. While in a certain respect this is true, yet the latter word, like our English word 'change', has a very general meaning, and this is not the case with *kinēsis*, the meaning of which is much more particular and special. This special meaning emerges in the course of Aristotle's analysis.

First we must recognize that change – *kinēsis* or *metabolē* – is not itself some kind of self-subsistent existent: 'there is no such thing as *kinēsis* over and above the things.'[17] It is always 'something' which changes, and 'change' is not itself something. That is, change is always 'with reference to' something, and this something can be fourfold. As Aristotle puts it, 'that which changes changes always with reference to an *ousia* [a self-subsistent individual], or to quantity, or to quality, or to place'.[18]

Next, we must recognize that the subject of change *(ousia)* with which we are concerned here is a natural being, that is, one to which change *(kinēsis)* belongs in its very beingness or essence. This means that the being of a natural being is the very contrary of the being which Plato had conceived for his Forms, which eternally are what they are, fully actual and not subject to any change or alteration or transition into anything different from what they are; that is, their being is totally exempt from any change of any kind. A natural being, Aristotle holds, involves change in its very beingness; it is essentially in transition. This is manifest if we attend to the primary meaning of *physis* as 'the genesis of growing things'. Genesis primarily pertains to natural beings, and this means that beings in their generation

16 200b12–15: 'Ἐπεὶ δ' ἡ φύσις μέν ἐστιν ἀρχὴ κινήσεως καὶ μεταβολῆς, ἡ δὲ μέθοδος ἡμῖν περὶ φύσεώς ἐστι, δεῖ μὴ λανθάνειν τί ἐστι κίνησις· ἀναγκαῖον γὰρ ἀγνοουμένης αὐτῆς ἀγνοεῖσθαι καὶ τὴν φύσιν. (My tr.).

17 200b32–3: οὐκ ἔστι δὲ κίνησις παρὰ τὰ πράγματα. (My tr.).

18 200b33–4: μεταβάλλει γὰρ ἀεὶ τὸ μεταβάλλον ἢ κατ' οὐσίαν ἢ κατὰ ποσὸν ἢ κατὰ ποιὸν ἢ κατὰ τόπον (My tr.).

involve a transition from a certain origin or beginning to a final
culmination. This transition or passage is the very contrary of
instantaneousness; it is a process in which there is the gradual
continuous transition to the achievement of an end-state. This
is the fundamental change involved in natural beings; this is
their *kinēsis*.

But the analysis of *kinēsis* must be carried much further. Since
kinēsis is a transition to the achievement of an end-state, this
implies that there is a beginning or origin of the process of transition. Further, it is evident that there is a significant difference
between the two, the origin and the end, which we could put
as follows. From the standpoint of the end-state and in contrast
to it, the origin was potential *(dynamis)*; for in order for that
end-state to have been actually attained, at the beginning or
origin of the process it must have been able to be, that is, it must
have been capable of attainment. And the end-state means that
this potentiality, *dynamis*, has then become actual, *energeia*,
which is to say fully achieved, *entelecheia* – 'having its end in
itself'.

Now this distinction between potentiality *(dynamis)* and
actuality *(energeia)* or, what is in this respect synonymous with
it, the full achievement, the having-its-end-in-itself *(entelecheia)*,
is of the greatest importance for the accurate understanding of
kinēsis. *Kinēsis* is a process of transition towards the achievement
of that end, and when that end has been attained or actualized,
it as an actuality transcends the process of transition towards it.
The process, the *kinēsis*, therefore, pertains primarily to the
dynamis, the potentiality for that end, and not to the end in its
actuality, *energeia*. This is evident also if we attend to the meaning of *dynamis*, potentiality: it entails potency, that is, power
to attain that end, and potency or power exercised or in effect
involves a process of transition. It is this process of transition
involved in potentiality which Aristotle denotes by the term
kinēsis. As he put it in a brief definition: 'the achievement
[*entelecheia*] of that which exists potentially [*hē tou dynamei
ontos*], in so far as it is potential [*hē toiouton*], is *kinēsis*'.[19]

The English phrase 'process of transition', while having a
certain usefulness in elucidating Aristotle's conception of *kinēsis*,

[19] *Physics*, 201a10–11: ἡ τοῦ δυνάμει ὄντος ἐντελέχεια, ᾗ τοιοῦτον, κίνησίς ἐστιν.
(My tr.).

is not satisfactory as a translation of the word *kinēsis*. It is highly desirable to have a single English word, but there is none without the disadvantage of some distracting differences in connotation. There is much to be said in favour of the word 'process', which has been used in an excellent recent translation of and commentary on Aristotle's *Physics*,[20] but 'process' has the limitation of being deficient in the grammatical flexibility of ready verbal and adjectival forms. From this point of view the word traditionally used, namely 'motion', has a decided advantage. For another reason, too, it will be advisable at this stage to recover the earlier connotation of the word 'motion' – the English word comes from the Latin *motus* which is the precise equivalent of the Greek *kinēsis*: this reason is that the recovery of the earlier traditional connotation is important for an adequate appreciation of the change in the concept of motion which began to come into currency in the early seventeenth century.

In the Aristotelian analysis motion, *kinēsis*, is the process of achievement of an end. That is to say, motion is not change merely, but change with reference to an end, and, moreover, with reference to the *achievement* of the end; motion, *kinēsis*, is indeed the very *process of achievement*, the achieving, whereby there is a 'having of the end in itself', which is the natural being existing fully in itself. However, because this process, the motion, pertains primarily to the potentiality and not to the final actuality as such, it must not be supposed that there is first motion, a process, and then, lo and behold, a natural being exists; for that would entail that motion, the process, is something existing by itself apart from a subject, a mover – which, as we have seen, Aristotle rejects as untenable – and it would also contradict the fundamental conception of a natural (*physei*) being as one which involves motion (*kinēsis*) in its very *ousia* (beingness). Potentiality and actuality cannot be separated as the foregoing supposition implies. Rather must they be seen as constituting an integral whole in a polar relationship. The concept of *dynamis*, potentiality, implies a potency to move or change, that is, a power as the spring or impetus of motion; and the concept implies also that which is capable of being actualized by the motion. But since motion is the motion of something, an *ousia*, that which is capable of being actualized, namely the

20 Hans Wagner, *Aristoteles: Physikvorlesung* (Berlin, 1967).

ousia, must itself be involved as the subject of the motion. This
means that it must in some respect be actual – the *ousia* as the
subject of motion cannot be merely potential, for a potential
subject is not a subject, and mere potentiality in any case would
be only the capacity to move without the process of moving
taking place.[21] This means that in so far as there is *kinēsis*, motion
there is a full being in-act, and the motion is the process of attaining, of actualizing, the potentiality. Therefore *kinēsis*, motion,
is the *process of attaining* in contrast with *what* is attained. This
is what Aristotle has stated in a slightly fuller (and somewhat
more difficult) definition of *kinēsis* than that which was quoted
above: 'Motion [*kinēsis*] takes place when the full achievement
itself exists, and neither earlier nor later. The achievement of
the potentially existent, when it is a fully achieved being in act,
not qua itself, but qua movable, is motion [*kinēsis*].'[22]

It is not necessary for our purposes to pursue the analysis of
kinēsis, motion, into the much greater detail into which Aristotle
enters. This is sufficient for the elucidation of Aristotle's conception of *physis*, nature, the physical, as that which has the
principle of motion in itself, that to which *kinēsis*, motion, belongs as to its essence or beingness (*ousia*).

In this Aristotelian analysis, *physis*, nature, the physical, involves motion, not as a mere flux, as mere change, and especially not as some change which just happens. To understand the
change which is manifest in the universe we must see it as
grounded in the very being (*ousia*) of natural or physical existents. The fundamental change is the *kinēsis*, motion, which is
the process of transition involved in the actualization of existents.
Thus it is basic and essential in Aristotle's conception of the
physical that every physical existent is in a constant process of
actualization. Its very being, its very existing, is to be found in
the process of actualization. That is, a physical being does not
exist as simply actual, but as in-actualization – as is clear from
the many passages in Aristotle in which the noun *energeia* retains
the force of the verb, *energeō*, to be in action or activitiy – its
meaning is better captured by 'in-actualization' than by the more
abstract 'actuality'.

21 cf. *Physics*, 201b28–31.
22 *Met.* 1065b21–3: ἡ δὴ τοῦ δυνάμει ὄντος, ὅταν ἐντελεχείᾳ ὂν ἐνεργῇ, οὐχ ᾗ
αὐτὸ ἀλλ' ᾗ κινητόν, κίνησίς ἐστιν. (My tr.). cf. *Physics*, 201a27–9.

When we examine the *kinēsis*, motion, which is the process of actualization of a natural or physical being, we find that it is analysable as constituted by three forms of change : qualitative change, quantitative change, and change of place. That is to say, the transition constituting actualization is analysable into one or other, or more likely, all three together, of these three forms of change. Some natural beings of the higher kind – the heavenly bodies are an instance – do not involve *genesis*, coming-into-being, and also are not subject to qualitative or quantitative change; their process of actualization is confined to the third, change of place, that is, translation or locomotion. But the motion of most physical beings, and especially when they are generated beings, consists in change of all three forms. It needs to be emphasized that for Aristotle *kinēsis*, motion, is not equated with translation or locomotion, change of place; locomotion (*phora*) is a form of motion, one among others. This is of the greatest importance for understanding correctly the concept of locomotion in Aristotle.

At the beginning of Book III of the *Physics*, as we have noted, Aristotle stated that it is necessary to understand *kinēsis*, motion, if we are to understand *physis*, nature, the physical. Although the theory of motion which we have elaborated, and consequently the conception of *physis*, nature, can be regarded as peculiarly Aristotelian, yet in a basic respect this Aristotelian conception characterizes, and makes completely explicit, the fundamental Greek conception of *physis*. For the conception of *physis*, nature, as that which has the *archē*, principle, of its *kinēsis*, motion, in itself, as well as the conception of this *kinēsis* as the process involved in actualization, is also that of the Presocratics in a basic respect. For while *physis*, the physical, is for them the sensible bodily extended, for almost all of them – Parmenides is the notable exception – the bodily extended essentially involves *kinēsis* in its being, that is, a *kinēsis* which is essentially related to their beingness, their *ousia*. This Greek conception of physical existence has often been characterized as 'organic' which, as far as it goes, is correct. This being so, it is seriously inaccurate to characterize the Presocratic conception of the physical, as has so frequently been done, as 'material' – especially when the word 'material' is understood in its modern sense. For this word, 'material', has a particular complex connotation, the outcome of a long and involved development, which makes it distinctly inapposite in the present context. It is important to avoid the fallacy of reading back a modern conception into ancient thought. When Aristotle said that the *physiologoi* identified *physis* with *hylē*, 'matter', he understood this term in a very different sense from that which it has come to have in the modern period.

The Greek conception of nature, of the physical, was in its essentials carried over into subsequent thought, through the Hellenistic into the medieval, not merely in a general way and as a tacit presupposition, but also quite explicitly so, especially by medieval theorists. For in the Hellenistic period it was the medical men who were most actively interested in nature, in the problem of physical existence; and it was through them that the inquiry was perpetuated and taken over by the medieval Arab medical men, through whom it came to the West at the beginning of the Scholastic period. It will not be necessary for our purposes, however, to trace the history of the concept of the physical through these thinkers. For the changes which were most significant for the new sixteenth and seventeenth-century conception of the nature of physical existence, were changes which gradually began taking place in the concept of 'matter' in medieval thought, changes which were in some respects parallel to those in the medieval conception of the infinite, and like the latter the outcome of the doctrine of the transcendance of God and the dependent existence of the world. To understand these changes in the concept of matter it is necessary to start with an examination of the Aristotelian concept.

8

THE CONCEPT OF MATTER:
(i) ARISTOTELIAN *HYLĒ*

In the preceding analysis of the Greek conception of *physis*, nature, the physical, the concept of matter was purposely omitted. In the first place the Presocratics did not have a concept of matter; as an explicit philosophical category this concept was introduced by Aristotle. And even for the treatment of Aristotle's analysis of *physis* this concept could be left aside, not because it is unimportant, but because it was desirable to maintain the emphasis on what is fundamental in Aristotle's analysis of *physis*, namely *kinēsis*, motion. That the concept of matter is important, however, in the Aristotelian conception of *physis*, nature, is amply evidenced in the following passage : 'Now natural comings to be [generation, *genesis*] are the comings to be of those things which come to be by nature; and that out of which they come to be [*to ex hou gignetai*] is what we call matter [*hylē*]; and that by which they come to be is something which exists naturally; and the something which they come to be is a man or a plant or one of the things of this kind, which we say are substances [*ousiai*] if anything is – all things produced [*gignomena*] either by nature [*physis*] or by art [*technē*] have matter [*hylē*]; for each of them is capable [*dynaton*] both of being and of not being, and this capacity is the matter [*hylē*] in each – and, in general, both that from which [*ex hou*] they are produced is nature, and the type according to which [*kath' ho*] they are produced is nature (for that which is produced, for instance, a plant or an animal, has a nature [*echei physin*]), and so is that by which they are produced – the so-called "formal" [*eidos*] nature, which is specifically the same (though this is in another individual); for man begets man.'[1]

Here in this passage the essential connotation, which we saw in the previous chapter, between *physis*, nature, and *genesis*,

[1] *Met.*, 1032a15–25. (Ross tr.).

generation or coming into being, is evident. What is added in this passage is the designation of that out of which there is generation (*to ex hou gignetai*) as *hylē*, matter, and the further designation of *hylē* as the capacity (*dynaton*) to be. This latter designation clearly ties up with our preceding analysis in which the coming to be or generation of a natural being was seen essentially to involve a transition from potentiality (*dynamis*) – which implies the capacity (*dynaton*) to be – to being actually (*energeia*), that is, in full attainment (*entelecheia*). In this passage Aristotle explicitly connects potentiality with that out of which there is generation; there must be 'something out of which' that has the capacity or potentiality to be. Further, our previous analysis had made clear that the transition from potentiality to actuality necessarily involves something undergoing that transition – if it were not it would be a case of one thing going out of existence and another coming into existence, and the kind of change is not that which is *kinēsis*.[2] In the above passage the something undergoing transition, that which underlies (*hypokeimenon*) change, is connected with the 'that out of which'. How does Aristotle conceive the 'that out of which' which he denotes by the word *hylē*?

In this use of the word *hylē* Aristotle was not employing an antecedent technical term; this technical term was one of his own coinage. He did not introduce the term merely to have a single word for the phrase 'that out of which'; the Aristotelian concept of *hylē* is very much more complex. Its elucidation has to be gradual.

The Greek word *hylē* literally means 'a forest, wood, woodland', the Latin word for which is *silva*. Derivatively it also means 'wood cut down', 'timber', as does the English word 'wood', and in a further derivation it means this timber used in the construction of something.

It was this last meaning which Aristotle took for his purposes, generalizing it quite beyond any specific connection with the literal meanings. The generalization was effected by the procedure of analogy – literally, according to due *logos*, ratio, that is, proportion or proportional relationship : as the timber out of which an artefact is made stands to the finished product, so in general stands any 'that out of which' to the respective completed thing. That is to say, Aristotle in this way established or

2 cf. *Physics*, Bk V, Ch. 1, etc.

created a new generalized meaning for the word *hylē* which had nothing to do with timber as such except that timber used in construction is one convenient instance of the general relationship which he wished to bring out.

Aristotle's basic concern was the fundamental instance of this relationship, that namely between the underlying subject of the transition which is the process of actualization and the actualized being, the *ousia*. This underlying something is the *hylē,* in the new completely generalized sense. As Aristotle put it : 'The knowledge [*epistēmē*] of this underlying nature [*hypokeimenē physis*] is by analogy. For as the bronze is to the statue, the wood [*xylon*] to the bed, or the *hylē* and the shapeless before receiving shape to the thing which has shape, so is this [underlying nature] itself to *ousia*, i.e. the 'this' [*tode ti*], the being [*to on*]'.[3]

It is to be noted that not only has the technical term, *hylē,* been arrived at through proceeding by analogy, but the concept for which this technical term was introduced is itself an analogical concept. That is to say, *hylē* does not denote any one specific and definite thing, some sort of stuff for example, which can be identified as an ultimate constituent in every physical existent. Rather, the concept of *hylē* is a relative one; the *hylē* is always relative to the particular actual thing. Artefacts provide a ready illustration : in respect of this particular statue the *hylē* is bronze, but of that one it is marble. Likewise also of a natural being : the *hylē* of a horse is different from that of a tree; and even if the horse be a Trojan horse, its *hylē* will be different from that of a tree, for the *hylē* of the tree involves the capacity to become a tree and not a horse (even a Trojan one) – it is the actual grown tree which then becomes the *hylē* for the Trojan horse.

Now this means that because the concept of *hylē* is a relative, analogical concept, accurate or true knowledge, scientific knowledge (*epistēmē*) of *hylē*, as Aristotle said at the beginning of the last quotation, has to be gained by an analogical procedure, and not by a procedure such as that by which a chemist, for example, might set about discovering the particular constituents of which something is made up. The *hylē* is relative – there is no absolute something which is *hylē* – and thus the concept has to be under-

---

[3] *Physics,* 191a8–12 (my tr.) : ἡ δὲ ὑποκειμένη φύσις ἐπιστητὴ κατ' ἀναλογίαν. ὡς γὰρ πρὸς ἀνδριάντα χαλκὸς ἢ πρὸς κλίνην ξύλον ἢ πρὸς τῶν ἄλλων τι τῶν ἐχόντων μορφὴν [ἡ ὕλη καὶ] τὸ ἄμορφον ἔχει πρὶν λαβεῖν τὴν μορφήν, οὕτως αὕτη πρὸς οὐσίαν ἔχει καὶ τὸ τόδε τι καὶ τὸ ὄν.

stood relatively : with reference to this particular thing the *hylē* in question will be that out of which *this* thing comes to be; it is that which has the capacity to, and does, receive the particular form whereby the actuality which then comes into being is a 'this' – that is, a particular being, this and no other, with this character whereby it exists as this being. In other words, *hylē* has to be thought of, not as an entity by itself, on its own, but in relation to form (*eidos*) : as that which is formed, the recipient of form, in contrast to the form which it receives. As Aristotle put it : '*hylē* is relative (*pros ti*); to each form (*eidos*) there is a special *hylē*.'[4]

Since the concept of *hylē* is the concept of that which receives form, as opposed to the form received, in the completely general and primary sense of the concept, *hylē* must be in itself wholly devoid of form and thus of any particular individuality. As Aristotle stated this : 'By *hylē* I mean that which in itself is neither a particular thing nor of a certain quantity nor assigned to any other of the categories by which being is determined.'[5] The concept of *hylē* in this primary sense is to be distinguished from *hylē* in a secondary sense, that which is the *hylē* in particular instances – for example the bronze which is the *hylē* of this statue of the charioteer. The form of the charioteer is the form of the statue, but the bronze as the *hylē* which receives that form itself has a form, whereby it is bronze and not gold or iron. This means that the bronze, which is the *hylē* of the statue, itself has a *hylē*. If that *hylē* in turn be designatable as this kind as opposed to that, it too will be an instance of secondary *hylē*. The progression is, however, not *ad infinitum* : ultimately one comes to primary *hylē*, that devoid of determinateness of any kind. Since it is thus devoid of definiteness, it is evident that primary *hylē* cannot be any kind of stuff, not even an *Urstoff*. If primary *hylē* be conceived as a stuff this would entail a departure from, a negation of, Aristotle's fundamental position in respect of *hylē* as a relative, analogical concept.

It is this relative conception of *hylē* which enabled Aristotle to distinguish between a 'perceptible' (*aisthēton*) *hylē* and an 'intellectual' (*noēton*) *hylē* as the *hylē* respectively of perceptible

4 *Physics*, 194b9–10. (My tr.).
5 *Met.*, 1029a20–1. (Ross tr.). I have substituted *hylē* for 'matter' in this and subsequent quotations.

entities and intelligible entities (for example, a bronze circle and a mathematical circle): 'Some *hylē* is perceptible and some intelligible, perceptible *hylē* being for instance bronze and wood and all *hylē* that is changeable, and intelligible *hylē* being that which is present in perceptible things not qua perceptible, that is, the objects of mathematics.'[6] This distinction between perceptible and intelligible *hylē* is not possible with a stuff conception of *hylē*.

Another important implication of Aristotle's relative conception of *hylē* is that '*hylē* is unknowable in itself'.[7] This follows because it is only possible to know what is definite, determinate, and since *hylē* is *per se* lacking all determinateness (which comes entirely from form), *hylē* cannot be an object of knowledge -- except in the way we have seen, namely the way or procedure of analogy.

The concept of *hylē* makes possible a further elucidation of the concept of *physis*, nature, the physical. This is most readily approached through Aristotle's analysis and criticism of the Presocratic conception of *physis* in terms of this conception of *hylē*. In their search for the *physis* of things, Aristotle says, the earliest philosophers believed this to be constituted by 'that out of which all things that are consist, the first out of which they are generated, and that into which upon destruction they are ultimately resolved, of which the very being persists though changed in its modifications'.[8] Thus they were plainly identifying the nature (*physis*) and being (*ousia*) of natural existents with that which Aristotle had distinguished as *hylē*.[9]

But since *physis*, nature, is that which has the *archē*, principle or source, of its *kinēsis*, motion, in itself, the question must be raised as to whether *hylē*, the 'that out of which' and the substrate of change, can itself be regarded as 'that from which comes the beginning [source] of the movement [*kinēsis*]'.[10] There is a distinction to be made, Aristotle insists, in the concept of that

---

[6] *Met.*, 1036a9–12. (Ross tr.).

[7] ibid., 1036a8–9.

[8] *Met.* 983b6–10: τῶν δὴ πρώτων φιλοσοφησάντων οἱ πλεῖστοι τὰς ἐν ὕλης εἴδει μόνας ᾠήθησαν ἀρχὰς εἶναι πάντων· ἐξ οὗ γὰρ ἔστιν ἅπαντα τὰ ὄντα καὶ ἐξ οὗ γίγνεται πρώτου καὶ εἰς ὃ φθείρεται τελευταῖον, τῆς μὲν οὐσίας ὑπομενούσης τοῖς δὲ πάθεσι μεταβαλλούσης (My tr.).

[9] cf. *Physics*, 193a9–11, 28–30.

[10] *Met.* 984a27: ὅθεν ἡ ἀρχὴ τῆς κινήσεως (Ross tr.).

from which a process of *kinēsis* starts, between the 'that out of which there is generation' (*to ex hou gignetai*) as that which underlies (*hypokeimenon*) the process, and the 'that from which as a source' (*hothen hē archē*), which is to say that which is the spring, the impetus, of change, the motive principle, that which is responsible for getting it going. These two are not the same; we have two different concepts. And we can have one without the other : 'For at least [in certain cases] the substratum itself does not make itself change; for instance, neither the wood nor the bronze causes the change of either of them, nor does the wood manufacture a bed and the bronze a statue, but something else is the cause of the change.'[11] All the more important, then, to observe this distinction in natural beings, in physical existents, those which have the source of their *kinēsis*, motion, in themselves.

The early philosophers, the *physiologoi*, had not observed this distinction. In their conception of *physis* they had put all the emphasis on *hylē* as the *hypokeimenon*, substrate, of change, and identified the underlying *hylē* as the *physis* of things, the nature of things. It is not *hylē*, however, which is basic in the concept of *physis*. Rather this is, as we have seen, 'the that from which the primary motion in a natural being initiates in each being, in virtue of itself'.[12] Thus in seeking an underlying *hylē* the earlier thinkers had missed what is truly basic in *physis*, namely *kinēsis*, motion, and they had consequently not seen that for the ultimate *physis* of things it is necessary to look for the source, the spring or impetus of motion.

Since Aristotle does not find this source, this spring or impetus of *kinēsis*, and accordingly the ultimate *physis*, nature, of things in *hylē*, where then does he find it? Correctly to see Aristotle's position in respect of this it is necessary to bear in mind carefully his insistence that *hylē* is a relative concept. It is precisely this that the Presocratics, who had implicitly employed the concept of *hylē*, had failed to appreciate and consequently conceived of a substrate which is *per se* a full and complete *ousia*, being. Therein lay their basic error; *hylē* cannot *per se* be *ousia*, for there is no *hylē* which *per se* is a self-subsistent existent. *Hylē* is relative to form, *eidos*.

11 *Met.*, 984a22–5. (Ross tr.).
12 ibid., 1014b18–20: ἔτι ὅθεν ἡ κίνησις ἡ πρώτη ἐν ἑκάστῳ τῶν φύσει ὄντων ἐν αὐτῷ ᾗ αὐτὸ ὑπάρχει (My tr.).

With this appreciated we can move to the proper conception of *physis*, nature. Although *hylē* certainly is involved, and most importantly so, it is form, *eidos*, which is crucial 'Hence as regards the things that are or come to be [*gignetai*] by nature, though that *from which* [*ex hou*] they naturally come to be or are is already present, we say they have not their nature yet, unless they have their form [*eidos*] or shape [*morphē*].'[13] That is to say, both *hylē* and *eidos* are essential to that which exists by nature.[14] And because *hylē* is involved, it is correct to refer to *hylē* as *physis*, nature, but only in conjunction with form, *eidos*, for strictly a natural being has a nature (*physin echein*) only when it has 'the *eidos* [form] or *ousia* [being] which is the end [*telos*] of the process of becoming or generation [*genesis*]'.[15] The point is that in Aristotle's philosophy it is *eidos* (form) rather than *hylē* (matter) which is the *ousia*, the very beingness, of natural beings – this is the overall outcome of his long and complicated analysis in Book VII of the *Metaphysics*. We can now more fully appreciate Aristotle's conception of *physis*, nature, when he says (in a passage quoted in the previous chapter): 'From what has been said, then, it is plain that nature [*physis*] in the primary and strict sense is the *ousia* of things which have in themselves, as such, a source of *kinēsis*.'[16]

The *ousia* of things is to be identified with *eidos*, form, rather than with *hylē*, matter, and it is accordingly in *eidos* and not in *hylē* that is to be found the source, the spring, the impetus, of *kinēsis*. This is what Aristotle said in the passage quoted at the beginning of this chapter: the formal nature (*he kata to eidos physis*) is that *by which* (*hyph' hou*) things are produced.[17]

This Aristotelian conception of form as the spring of action came to play a profound role in subsequent, and especially medieval, thought. This conception was brought into issue by Bruno in a way which deeply affected the sixteenth and seventeenth-century developments of the concept of matter. Bruno maintained the spring of action to be in matter rather than in form. But before this could be maintained, highly significant changes had to take place in the concept of matter. These were in

13 *Met.*, 1015a3–5. (Ross tr.).
14 cf. *Met.*, 1015a6.
15 ibid., 1015a9–10. (My tr.).
16 ibid., 1015a13–15. (Ross tr. with modifications.)
17 *Met.*, 1032a24–5.

part the outcome of the shift in fundamental philosophical position effected by the medieval doctrine of the transcendence of
God, but in part they were the product, too, of difficulties which
subsequent thinkers found in Aristotle's concept of matter.

One of these concerned that connection which we saw earlier
in this chapter which Aristotle made between *hylē* and *dynamis*,
potentiality. In the passage quoted, Aristotle had said that 'the
capacity of each thing to be or not to be [*dynaton gar kai einai
kai mē einae hekaston autōn*]' is the *hylē* of each.[18] The problem
is that if *hylē* be in itself wholly devoid of determinateness, how
does it have a 'capacity to be'? In the first place, to be is to be
definite, determinate, and definiteness, determinateness, is from
form, so that strictly the *capacity* to be would seem more appropriately assignable to form. It could be said that since *hylē* is
that which is formed, that which receives form, this implies that
hylē has the capacity to be formed or to receive form, and that
therefore this is the strict sense in which *hylē* is 'capacity'. But
this raises the further problem that there is an implication of
'potency', 'power', in the concept of capacity – it is unquestion-
ably there in the Greek word *dynamis* (as in the Latin *potentia*)
to which *dynaton* is related. Capacity means 'able to', having the
power to, and how can there be the ability to, the power to, without a 'drive', 'impetus', 'spring of activity', which puts it into
effect? And was it not in form rather than in matter (*hylē*) that
Aristotle had found the 'spring of activity', the source (*archē*)
of *kinēsis*, the motive principle? These and related problems
played a determinative part in the subsequent changes in the
concept of matter.

18 ibid., 1032a21–3. (My tr.).

9

THE CONCEPT OF MATTER:
(ii) MEDIEVAL *MATERIA*

The concept of *hylē* was taken over from Aristotle by the Hellenistic schools and through them it entered medieval thought. Latin thinkers had to find a suitable word to render the Greek *hylē*. The strict Latin equivalent of *hylē* in its ordinary meaning of forest, woodland, is *silva*, but this Latin word had the disadvantage of not having a relatively much-used derivative sense, as had the Greek *hylē*, of timber used in the construction of things. (Indeed also in Greek the word in this sense was not the common one, the usual word being *xylon*, so that in referring to a wooden article, that is, one made out of wood, the adjective from *xylon* was used and not that from *hylē*.) The Latin thinkers accordingly sought another word to render Aristotle's *hylē*, and in doing so proceeded from the technical sense of Aristotle's term rather than from the literal meaning of the word. This sense they understood as that out of which a thing is made, itself remaining as the substratum, undergoing a change of shape or form. Thus they chose the word *materia*, which derives from the root *ma-*, 'to make' (having this root in common with *mater*, mother, this being also the root of the Greek μάτηρ, μήτηρ, mother), meaning that which is used by a maker, that out of which he makes things.

The word *materia* was certainly suitable for rendering the Aristotelian concept of 'that out of which', the enduring substrate. It had the effect, however, because of its general ordinary usage in the sense in which we speak of the 'material' used in the production of things, of strengthening any tendency toward conceiving 'that out of which' as a 'stuff'. This tendency was kept in check by the continuation of the strict Aristotelian philosophical concept as analogical and relative, but the tendency nevertheless began quite early to assert itself. Throughout medieval thought, however, and down into the sixteenth century the philosophical concept of *materia* retained the essential Aristotelian sense of the correlative of form, that which receives form, in itself therefore devoid of definiteness. *Prima materia* can accordingly *per se* neither be, exist, as an independent, self-subsistent existent, nor can it *per se* be known.

This concept of *materia* accorded well with the fundamental medieval doctrine of the transcendence of God and the complete dependence of the world. Basically this dependence of the world was in respect of its being, which it derived from God by creation. Now the verb *creo* literally means to make, in the sense of a workman making an artefact, and this thus implied something out of which, a *materia*, the artefact is made. The relevance of Plato's doctrine in the *Timaeus* was manifest, of God as a *demiourgos*, a workman, an artificer, fashioning the world by using the eternally existing forms and the equally eternally existing 'receptacle', that is, that whose essential nature was to be recipient of form – Aristotle had explicitly and consistently interpreted Plato's 'receptacle' as *hylē*.[1] Plato's doctrine, however, was inconsistent with the medieval conception of the complete transcendent eminence of God which, following Philo, the tradition had insisted, implied that God alone could be eternal. There could accordingly be no pre-existing *materia* out of which God created, made, the world; God's creation had necessarily to be *ex nihilo*. This was indeed completely consistent with the philosophical concept of *materia*, for *prima materia* is not something which could at all exist self-subsistently, to be used in making. Of the earlier medieval thinkers it was Augustine who most clearly saw and expressed this. The coming into being of the world necessarily involved form, since to be is to be definite, and for there to be a definite something necessitated a recipient of form. But it was not necessary that the recipient, *materia*, pre-exist the incoming of form. God's act of creation was the bringing into being of form with matter.

Augustine's conception of matter, which derived from Neo-platonism, strongly influenced subsequent thought. Plotinus had accepted Aristotle's conception of *hylē* as in itself without definiteness; it is thus *apeiron*, the indefinite. This he interpreted as meaning that *hylē*, the indefinite, is at the opposite pole to being, the definite, which is form; *hylē* is not-being. Augustine

[1] cf. e.g. Aristotle, *Physics*, 209b11–12.

accepted this Neoplatonic position. The form, which is the principle, source, of the being of the world, is that constituted by the Platonic Ideas, which Plotinus had regarded as having emanated from the One, and which Augustine now located in the divine intelligence as the exemplars or archetypes of the forms of actual created things whereby they are or have being. It is the forms in things which are the active principle, the potency or power, the spring of activity, the efficient or motive principle in things. Form must be the active source since an active source cannot be ascribed to what as such is at the opposite pole to being, that is, not-being. Matter in itself is pure passivity, the contrary of activity. In the Augustinian conception, therefore, potency is not accorded to matter but to form, which is implanted by God in matter as *rationes seminales* (the *logoi spermatikoi* of Neoplatonism and Stoicism).

Thus while Neoplatonism continued the Aristotelian conception of matter as the correlative of form, the Neoplatonist polarization of form and matter as being and not-being constituted a great divergence from the Aristotelian doctrine. This enabled Neoplatonism to resolve the problem which arose for Aristotle in his connecting *hylē*, matter, and *dynamis*, potentiality; they resolved it by rejecting that connection. For in the Neoplatonic position only forms can be regarded as active sources, and thus potentiality must be grounded entirely in form.

The Neoplatonic interpretation of the concept of matter continued largely unchallenged in medieval thought until the Scholastic period. But the rediscovery of Aristotle by Western thinkers did not result in a full recovery of the Aristotelian conception of matter. One factor hindering this was that the Neoplatonic conception had become to such an extent a tacit presupposition of thought that it was difficult to conceive matter differently. And not much help in this respect was forthcoming from the Arab philosophers from whom the West had regained a knowledge of Aristotle. For an inheritance of Neoplatonism had strongly coloured the Aristotelianism of the Arab thinkers.

Characteristic of the Neoplatonic influence on the Arab interpretation of Aristotle, and more particularly in respect of the concept of matter, was the thought of Ibn Sina, known as Avicenna to the West. Avicenna, as a medical man, was especially interested in the inquiry into nature – indeed it was he who

effectively initiated the return to this inquiry which culminated
in the sixteenth-century developments.

Following Aristotle, Avicenna accepted matter and form as
the two fundamental, correlative principles of natural beings.
Matter is not only the recipient of form but, as Aristotle had
maintained, that whereby natural things have a capacity to be
and not to be, that whereby there is generation and corruption –
for form in itself is not susceptible of generation; form in itself
cannot undergo change, but something, a substratum, under-
goes a change through a supersession of forms. Now since matter
in itself is without any definiteness, it cannot exist even as some
inchoate extended stuff, an *Urstoff*; there is requisite a completely general form whereby matter is an extensive existent at
all, that is, whereby matter can be bodily. This is the form of corporeity (*forma corporeitatis*). Matter, Avicenna held, is never
without the form of corporeity, and it also always has a variety
of other forms, specific forms (*formae speciales*) and accidental
forms. The Neoplatonic influence in this is clear : matter in itself
is not; it exists at all only through form, the general form of
corporeity and the other forms. So strictly all capacity, even to
be a corporeal substrate, comes from form. The formal is manifestly the superior and dominant principle; the material principle or cause is much the subordinate one.

Form as the superior principle comes out, too, in Avicenna's
interpretation of nature. Aristotle had admitted *hylē* as in some
respect *physis*, as we have seen. On Avicenna's interpretation,
however, this is not so. The nature of a thing is, as Aristotle maintained, 'the that from which the primary motion in a natural being
initiates in each being, in virtue of itself',[2] and this, Avicenna
affirmed, could only be form. Thus, in the doctrine of Avicenna, nature is conceived dominantly in terms of form. There
is nature, or natural being, by virtue of form. Each natural
being has a nature, constituted by the form which is its motive
principle, its spring of action. All internal sources of motion or
activity, all internal 'energies', are natures. Thus in animated
beings souls are natures. But in general, all natures are forms.
Also, forms as determining the definiteness of natural beings, that
which they are, are their 'essences'. It is clear that in this philosophy, due to the Neoplatonic influence, forms are accorded a

[2] *Met.*, 1014b18–20; cf. above, Ch. 8, p. 119.

far more independent, and almost self-sufficient, status than they are in the philosophy of Aristotle, in which the concepts of form (*eidos*) and matter (*hylē*) are much more definitely correlatives. Aristotle did not think of *eidos* as something apart from *hylē*, or of *hylē* as something apart from *eidos*; his essential way of thinking was to conceive them in conjunction, in relation to each other, as one required by the other. Neoplatonism, with is conception of matter as a *prope nihil*,[3] introduced a great change in the way of thinking of matter and form : since matter is *prope nihil*, form is elevated to a kind of independence which it did not have for Aristotle. In this respect, therefore, the effect of Avicenna was to affirm the conception of matter inherited from Augustine.

An influence which significantly countered this conception came from the system of the Spanish Jewish thinker, Salomon Ibn Gabirol (Latinized as Avicebron, or Avicembron, or Avecebrol), a slightly later contemporary of Avicenna, whose book, *Fons vitae*, made a considerable impact on Christian thinkers. Gabirol decisively accepted the Aristotelian principles of matter and form. All beings other than God are composed of matter and form – thus distinguishing God fundamentally from all other beings. Although Gabirol's doctrine was appreciably under Neoplatonic influence in that he conceived all beings as being what they are in virtue of forms, it is in distinctive contrast to Neoplatonism in the emphasis it placed on matter. For Gabirol matter is not a *prope nihil*; on the contrary, for him matter is the fundamental principle, that which is the source or spring of activity. This reversal of matter and form in respect of the ultimate principle of being, that is, the potency, the that from which springs the activity of being, was to come to be of the greatest consequence for the future.

Gabirol conceived of a universal primary matter, which in itself is without form. Since matter, however, cannot exist without form, the universal primary matter with a correlative universal form composes a universal entity (*essentia*). This, however, does not in itself exist in actuality, but in potency; it exists in act by the various forms it takes. By virtue of forms the universal primary matter differentiates into universal spiritual matter and universal corporeal matter, respectively the matter of spiritual

---

[3] I am using this phrase here because of its significance in the sixteenth century; see below, p. 131.

and corporeal beings. The forms determining matter as spiritual are the intelligible forms, and those determining corporeal matter are the sensible ones. In both cases there are levels of generality of forms in the relation of genus to species. Thus, for example, the most general form by virtue of which there is corporeal matter is the form of 'corporeity', which is actualized in particular bodies by specific forms which determine the bodies as mineral, vegetable, animal, and by the forms of quantity, surfaces, lines, figures, and colours, to an ever-increasing differentiation into singular individuality.

For our purposes it is not necessary to enter further into the details of the system of Gabirol. Its significance lies in the influence of this concept of matter on later thought, particularaly on the thirteenth-century Franciscans. In this conception matter is no longer ontologically subordinate. The historic importance of this is that it was a basic step in the development of the conception of the independence of matter. In the late thirteenth century Richard of Middleton conceived matter as having a minimum of actuality since God can create matter without form.[4] Henry of Ghent and John Duns Scotus both insisted on an 'essence' of matter not attributable to or derivable from form, so matter could exist as such if God chose to create it so. Before them Roger Bacon too had conceived matter as having its own essence as matter whereby it is different from form.

Also contributory to the conception of matter as independent was the doctrine of Ibn Rochd (Averroës), a Spanish Arab who was perhaps the most influential authority on Aristotle during the Scholastic period and later. All sensible substance has matter and form, which means that it is in passage or change from potentiality to actuality, this change being motion. Through matter it is in potency to become; through form, which is act, it is. Averroës fully accepted the Aristotelian argument that it is impossible that motion should either have come into being or cease to be.[5] This implies the eternity of the world, which means the eternity of matter. Form likewise must be eternal. And since matter cannot exist without form, form cannot be brought into matter from without – as was maintained by Avicenna – but must be in matter as potentiality. This does not mean that forms

---

[4] cf. Gilson, op. cit., p. 348, for the connection of Richard and Gabirol.
[5] cf. Aristotle, *Met.*, 1071b6–10.

are latent, hidden, in matter, merely to be extracted or disengaged. Rather, since in the process of becoming there is the arising from matter what there was in potentiality with respect to the form actualized, it means that the forms are educed from potentiality to actuality, and therefore that forms are immanent in matter. They are immanent not as actual forms, but as intrinsic to the potentiality of matter. This conception therefore restores the ontological status to matter which it had in Aristotle and which was lost in the Neoplatonic interpretation.

The Averroistic doctrine of the eduction of forms through the mediation of higher forms as movers, in a hierarchy of movers, dominated by the intelligences moving the celestial spheres, and culminating in God as the first unmoved mover, enabled the conception of a system of the world functioning by its own inherent principles, the knowledge of which is to be gained by the examination of natural beings themselves. We shall here, however, stress only that aspect of the conception which contributed significantly to the eventual conception of matter as itself as self-subsistent existent. For if matter has forms intrinsic to it, matter cannot be unknowable as had formerly been maintained; matter itself can be an object of knowledge. This is not a conclusion at which Averroës himself could arrive, since he very definitely retained the Aristotelian relational conception of matter. But in so far as that is weakened, Averroës' conception of matter strengthened the tendency to elevate the ontological status of matter to the point of conceiving matter *per se* as the physical existent – the intermediate stage of which was the Renaissance conception of ensouled matter.

Thomism, too, in the end proved influential in the development of the conception of matter as independently existent, although it did so in a different way. Aquinas, unlike Aristotle and Averroës, did not make matter and form principles coordinate with potentiality and actuality. For him the latter were wider, holding in respect of all created being, whereas only sensible being had matter. Matter is that in each sensible being which particularizes and individualizes it. Although a thing is what it is by virtue of its substantial form, since matter is the principle of individuation, matter is more than the general concept of that which receives form. The individuation here is into separate bodies, so matter is essentially extensive stuff – corporeality, for Aquinas, is not due to a general form of corporeity, as in the doctrines of Avicenna and Gabirol. That is to say, in Thomism there is corporeality by virtue of matter as extensive stuff. In itself matter, this extensive stuff, is inert, deriving all potency and being from form. Matter is accordingly not something which could exist by itself. Although Thomism, because it continued to hold firmly to the Aristotelian conception of matter and form as correlatives, was far from according an independent existence to matter, nevertheless it contributed significantly to the tendency so to view matter by its conception of matter as extensive inert stuff. This conception came to be increasingly accepted as the fundamental connotation of the term matter, and therewith provided one of the bases for the new conception of matter which arose in the early seventeenth century.

Another aspect of Thomism which contributed to the later development was the sharp distinction it made between the act of being (*esse*) and form, as opposed to their tacit identification in Neoplatonism. For Aquinas, form is not being, but form receives its act of being (*esse*) from God, to become the source of agency in individual substances. It is not a far step to conceiving matter with its own act of being, received from God.

This was the step taken in the sixteenth century, a step which was indispensable to the achievement of the modern concept of matter in the seventeenth century.

10

THE CONCEPT OF MATTER:
(iii) RENAISSANCE CONCEPTION
OF ENSOULED MATTER

Sixteenth-century thought played a crucial role in the development of the modern conception of matter, that which arose in the seventeenth century and which became basic to the new physical science, from then through to the end of the nineteenth century. The Renaissance pushed through those tendencies in late medieval thought toward the conception of matter as having some independence of being, qua matter, to their extreme, which was the conception of matter *per se* as substance. The way to this was, however, complex and fraught with philosophical problems. Certainly this conception could not have been easily attained, involving as it did a radical departure from the conception of matter which had dominated thought for two thousand years, that of matter as the correlative of form.

One of the particular difficulties facing the conception of matter as substance was, in the sixteenth-century context, that on the inherited philosophical analysis, to be an independent existent, that is, substance, implied *actio*, activity or action, which entailed a source of activity, and this, in the medieval tradition, had been ascribed decisively to form. To conceive matter *per se* as substance clearly involved the problem of ascribing the source of activity to matter itself.

This considerable change from medieval thought was mediated by the re-emergence of Neoplatonism in the fifteenth and sixteenth centuries. We have already dealt with Cusanus in a different context as a crucial thinker in the new development of thought; in the present context he is of equal significance. For in respect of the issue with which we are here concerned it was the Neoplatonic emanationist theory which was of determinative consequence. Cusanus had developed this theory in terms of his doctrine of the world as *explicatio Dei*, of its coming into being by *contractio*. The infinite being of God is contracted to the universe;

in this contraction, form, which in God is infinite, is contracted to the *spiritus mundi*, the world soul. The world soul is indivi-dualized by further contractions to the souls of the individual existents. So in this doctrine all individual existents are ensouled.

At the beginning of the sixteenth century this doctrine was vigorously embraced by Agrippa of Nettesheim, who saw all nature as alive. The conception of a world soul and of all sub-stantial existents as ensouled became a prominent feature of Renaissance thought, exemplified in the leading thinkers, such as Paracelsus, Fracastoro, Cardano, Scaliger, Telesio, Patrizzi, Bruno, and Kepler.

This doctrine constituted a most important stage in the development of the conception of matter as an independent exis-tent or substance. It made it possible to elevate the ontological status of matter, that is, conceiving it as itself substance, with a solution to the problem of ascribing the source of activity to matter. This line of thought was manifested in Cardano, Telesio, and Patrizzi, but it was in Bruno that it was exemplified most fully. In this respect as in others Bruno characterized the thought of his time. By his singular penetration into what was at stake he achieved a clarity about and analysis of the issues beyond what was attained by others.

Bruno strongly attacked the Aristotelian theory of matter – or what he understood as Aristotle, which was in fact the Neo-platonic Aristotle of so much medieval thought. In the Aristote-lian theory, he argued, since matter is without any of the deter-minations of being, it is a *prope nihil*, and thus a 'pure potency, bare, without act, without power and perfection',[1] while form and act, as the contrary of matter, have to come into matter from without. The conception which Bruno opposed to this came from Nicolaus of Cusa, who accepted the Aristotelian conception of matter and form as correlatives, co-ordinate with potentiality and actuality. But where antecedent thought rigidly excluded matter and potentiality from God, Cusanus, by his doctrine of *coincidentia oppositorum*, included them in God. In God poten-tiality and actuality are one; that is, God is absolute potency as well as absolute act.[2] Further, Cusanus maintained, act 'is not

[1] Bruno, *De la causa, Op. Ital.*, I, p. 231. (My tr.)

[2] Cusanus, *De doct. ig.*, Bk II, Ch. 8: 'wherefore absolute possibility in God is God, and outside him there is in truth no possibility'; and Bk II, Ch. 9: 'it is not possible for there to be an absolute potency or absolute form or act which is not God'.

absolute except in potency; and potency is not absolute unless it is contracted by act'.[3] The contraction of God is the universe, and the contracted potency, qua potentiality, is the matter of the universe, while the contracted form or act is the soul of the universe – 'a universal form which has in itself enfolded all the forms'.[4] Cusanus was very well aware of the divergence of this doctrine from Aristotelianism; he regarded it as a necessary corrective to a basic weakness in the Aristotelian system, namely that it fails to carry the co-ordinate principles of matter and form, and potentiality and actuality, to full metaphysical generality as applying also to God. As a consequence he equally rejected the Neoplatonic conception of the status of matter.

This radically changed status of matter effected by the Cusanian doctrine is the fundamental position accepted by Bruno, who carried it even further in a momentous development, Bruno being influenced not only by Cusanus but also by Gabirol's conception of a universal primary matter, Averroës' doctrine of the eduction of forms from matter, and David of Dinant's identification of matter and intellect (*nous*) with God – a doctrine which had been influential on Cusanus too. Bruno thus embraced all the tendencies which we have noted in Scholastic thought to the enhancement of the status of matter and carried them through.

The potency and act, that is, matter and form, which in God are 'enfolded, unified, and one',[5] as unfolded (*explicans*) or contracted to the universe become two distinct principles, matter and form. The universe, that is, is composite, of a universal matter and a universal form (the world soul).[6] But Bruno's universal matter is no mere passive substrate awaiting the entry of

---

[3] ibid., Bk II, Ch. 8.

[4] ibid., Bk II, Ch. 9.

[5] Bruno, *De la causa*, *Op. Ital.*, p. 212; see above p. 86.

[6] cf. Introductory Epistle to *De la causa*, summarizing the argument of the Second Dialogue, Bruno states his doctrine of the world soul: 'that the first and principal natural form, the formal principle and efficient nature, is the soul of the universe; which is the principle of life, vegetation, and sense in all things which live, vegetate, and feel . . . [It] is a thing unworthy of a rational subject to be able to believe that the universe, and its principal bodies are inanimate, it being the case that from the parts and residuals of those the animals which we call most perfect derive . . . [Thus] there is no thing so lacking, corrupted, diminished, and deficient which, for that which has a formal principle, does not likewise have soul, even though it does not have the act of a subject that we call animal.' (*Op. Ital.*, p. 132.).

form from without. In itself certainly matter is without form, since form is the correlative principle, but, Bruno maintained, 'I say that [matter] is deprived of forms and without them, not as ice is without heat, and as the deep is deprived of light, but as the pregnant woman is without her progeny, which she sends forth and draws out of herself';[7] 'therefore it ought to be said then that matter contains the forms and includes them, than to think that it is empty of them and excludes them. That, therefore, which unfolds (*esplica*) what is enfolded (*implicato*) must be called a thing divine and a best parent, genetrix, and mother of natural things; indeed, nature entire in substance'.[8] The conceptions of Cusanus, Gabirol, Averroës, and David of Dinant here merge to constitute a new concept of matter in which, although matter and form are still correlatives, it is matter which is the dominant principle. It is in matter, not form, that all potency is to be found. It is matter which contains in itself, and is, the principle or source of activity or motion and thus of being. This is why Bruno was able to identify matter with nature. Thus in Bruno matter, ontologically, takes the place previously occupied by form. In the antecedent doctrines, under Neoplatonic influence, matter was a *prope nihil* and form was identified with being; so for them it was form which essentially was substance. Bruno completely reversed this status of matter: for him it was matter which essentially is substance.

This universal substantial matter is that which has everything in it *complicans*. Because that is so, universal matter in itself can be neither corporeal nor incorporeal, but it is contracted now to corporeal being and now to incorporeal or spiritual being. Thus this conception of matter is very different from the Thomistic conception of extended stuff. It can be said to be extended, but not in the sense of extension being an attribute or quality of a stuff; rather it is extendedness *per se*, ultimate mathematical extendedness, which has all particularities of extension, dimensions, shapes, etc., *complicans*. 'That matter, through being actually all that which it can be, has all measurements, has all species of figures and dimensions, and because it has them all, it has none; because it is necessary that that which is so many different things be not any one of those particular things. It is

[7] ibid., p. 231.
[8] ibid., p. 234.

fitting to that which is all to exclude every particular being.'[9]
This conception, derived from Cusanus, was to have a most fruit-
ful future in the seventeenth century, particularly in Descartes,
in Henry More, and in Newton.

In Bruno's conception, though matter is potency, both passive
and active, and therefore the very beingness of substance, form
is nevertheless necessary, and matter is not without form. Also,
Bruno exemplified the Renaissance identification of form as the
soul of things. We can now in retrospect see these two sixteenth-
century developments, so clearly exemplified in Bruno, of the
elevation of the ontological status of matter and of the conception
of all things as ensouled, as being the necessary steps to the
seventeenth-century development of the concept of matter as an
independent existent, and of soul as another, but separate existent. This seventeenth-century development, however, did not
spring simply from a pursuit of the problem of the conception
of matter as such; it came rather by a somewhat different route,
as the outcome of the pursuit of other problems which, however,
converged on the concept of matter. These problems, which particularly impinged on the medical men during the sixteenth and
early seventeenth centuries, centred on the theory of the elements
and the theory of chemical combination.

[9] ibid., p. 228.

THE CONCEPT OF MATTER:
(iv) EARLY SEVENTEENTH-CENTURY CONCEPTION OF ELEMENTARY BODIES

The line of thought into which we now have to inquire is not distinct from the foregoing; it is but another aspect of the complex development of the modern concept of nature. In the sixteenth century, medical men were prominent among those concerned with the investigation of nature. Their interest centred on an understanding of the human body in its relation to nature as a whole, not least in respect of the body ingesting various kinds of natural existents as nourishment and as medicaments. The body's assimilation of these entities implies that there is no fundamental difference in nature between them and the body. The problem was one of knowing the elements of which the body and the other entities are constituted, of how these elements are combined in the various instances. Most important, therefore, was the theory of the elements and the theory of chemical combination. The theory of the elements in particular played a basic role in the developments with which we are here concerned and we shall consider that first.

In this theory it was once again Aristotle's doctrine which was the point of departure, and it is accordingly necessary first to state Aristotle's argument. Since there undoubtedly is change (*metabolē*) of various kinds[1] in the bodies we encounter in perception – change of size and shape, alteration (*alloiōsis*) of a qualitative kind, locomotion (*phora*) and that change constituted by the coming-into-being (*genesis*) of things and their destruction or passing-away (*phthora*) – we have to conclude that these bodies are in some respect complex, composed of certain other bodies as their elements. 'An element [*stoicheion*], we take it, is a body into which other bodies may be analysed, present in them poten-

[1] cf. Aristotle, *De gen. et corr.*, Bk I, Chs 1–5.

tially or in actuality (which of these, is still disputable), and not itself divisible into bodies different in form. That, or something like it, is what all men in every case mean by element.'[2] The problem is to determine the kind, number, and nature of the elements, whether for example there is one kind of element or many kinds, of a limited number or of an unlimited number, and whether the elements as such are the sources of agency.[3]

The issue which we have here centres not only on the fact of change but on the fact that that change entails contrariety,[4] manifestly so for example when we consider change in the senses of alteration and of coming-into-being and passing-away, for qualitative change is change from one quality to a contrary quality, and coming-into-being and passing-away are change from one thing into a contrary thing. Now this change into contraries implies some substratum underlying the change; for it is not the case that we have here simply the existence of something with a particular character and then, in an absolute or unqualified sense, that thing ceasing to exist and another thing, again in an absolute or unqualified sense, coming to exist in its stead; rather there is something undergoing the change, something which is continuous throughout the process of change. And when we recognize the need for a substratum we must also acknowledge that contrariety constitutes a principle different from that of substratum. For contrariety cannot be reduced to or identified with the substratum; that is, the substratum cannot itself as such be two contraries, for then there could be no change from one into the other. Thus both a substratum and contraries are necessary as *archai*, principles, sources, of change.[5]

The question now is whether the elements are to be identified as the substratum of change. This was the position taken for example by Leucippus and Democritus. Their atoms were the elements of which complex bodies were constituted and they were the substratum of change, they themselves remaining constant throughout change. For in their doctrine the atoms were eternal, that is, not subject to generation and destruction, so that it was compounds to which coming-into-being and passing-away

2 Aristotle, *De caelo*, 302a16–18. (tr. J. L. Stocks.).
3 cf. *De gen. et corr.*, Bk I, Ch. 6.
4 cf. ibid., Bk I, Ch. 7, esp. 323b29ff.
5 cf. ibid., Bk II, Chs 1 and 2.

pertained – this meant that it was only compounds which
changed. But in that case how is this change, which involves
contrariety, to be accounted for? Coming-into-being can only be
constituted, on this theory, by an association of atoms. But the
bare grouping of unchanging atoms cannot give rise to or generate
a character in the group which is contrary to the character or
characters of the individual constituents severally.

It is clear from this, Aristotle maintained, that it is fallacious
not only to identify the elements with the substratum, but also
to conceive the elements as unchanging, that is, not coming into
being. Hence his conclusion : 'The elements of bodies must there-
for be subject to destruction and generation.'[6]

Since generation or coming-to-be in the primary sense pertains
to *ousiai*, substances, this means that the elements are substances.
Now substance, as we have seen,[7] involves *hylē*, and since *hylē*
is the capacity to be,[8] therefore '*hylē* in the chief and strict sense
is the substratum which is receptive of coming-to-be and passing-
away'.[9] Here then we have the true relation of the substratum
of change and the elements : the substratum is the *hylē*, matter,
involved in the elements, these being the substances. *Hylē* is not
itself a substance; it exists only as informed, as having form, and
the form here is the set of basic contraries requisite for change.
As Aristotle put it : 'our theory is that there is a *hylē* of perceptible
bodies, but it does not exist separately but always with contrariety; and it is from this [that is, from *hylē* and the contraries]
that the so-called elements come into being.'[10] In this way Aristotle's theory fulfils the requirement noted above of the substratum and the contraries as the principles, sources, of change.
That is, with *hylē* and certain basic contrary forms Aristotle is
able to account for change as involving contrariety; *hylē* is the
capacity to become or generate, and the contraries are *what* are
generated, that is, the character which comes into being.

But since in nature change is always going on and never ceases,
and since it is fundamentally the elements as substances which
change – and more particularly in the primary sense of change
which is generation, coming-into-being, and passing-away – the

6 *De caelo*, 305a13 (tr. Stocks).
7 In Ch. 8 above.
8 cf. *Met.*, 1032a21–3.
9 Aristotle, *De gen. et corr.*, 320a3–5. (My tr.)
10 ibid., 329a25–7. (My tr.)

elements must constantly be coming into being and passing away. That is to say change, especially in the primary sense, is not accounted for on the supposition that the elements come into being once and for all and then simply are; that supposition leaves us with the fundamental difficulty of the atomistic theory noted above. How then can we conceive the elements as in constant generation and passing away?

The generation of the elements must be either from something incorporeal or from something corporeal. It cannot be from something incorporeal, for every natural being is corporeal, so there does not exist anything incorporeal from which the elements could be generated. Matter and form certainly are as such not corporeal, but then they are not themselves self-subsistent existents out of which there could be generation. This leaves the alternative that the generation of the elements must be from something corporeal. Now it is impossible that the elements should be generated from some kind of body which is not an element, for that would involve a body distinct from the elements and prior to them,[11] and no such is possible. For any body must be either simple or compound; if it be compound it will itself be constituted of elements, and if it be simple it must itself by an element. The only alternative which remains, therefore, is that the elements are generated by changing into each other.[12]

Thus we have one most important and characteristic feature of Aristotle's theory of the elements, namely that the elements must necessarily be in constant change, that this change must necessarily be the inner process of change which is generation, and that this generation must necessarily be constituted by a change of the elements into each other.

The other characteristic feature of the Aristotelian doctrine which was of great importance in the sixteenth and early seventeenth-century debates and developments derives from the role of contraries in his conception. Aristotle maintained that the basic contraries are the two qualitative pairs, hot and cold, wet and dry. From these and the conception of four kinds of elements, fire, air, water, and earth, all the characteristics of compound bodies are explicable. These four essentially qualitative elements are bodies, simple bodies (*hapla sōmata*), but they are not found

---

[11] *De caelo*, 305a23–4.
[12] ibid., 305b28; cf. also ibid., 305a32–3.

existing by themselves, simple and unmixed, but as combined in various proportions in the compound bodies constituting the experienced physical existents.

Early in the sixteenth century Agrippa of Nettesheim, under Pythagorean, Platonic, and Cabbalistic influence, introduced some quantitative characteristics into the otherwise essentially qualitative Aristotelian elements – some elements being double, some threefold and some fourfold as mobile, as fine, or as sharp as others.[13] But the change in respect of the theory of the elements which had the most momentous consequences originated with Agrippa's contemporary, Paracelsus, and was spread through his influential medical school.

Paracelsus[14] rejected the Aristotelian four, fire, air, water, earth, as being truly elementary. The real elements, he maintained, are the three primary substances (*tres primae substantiae*), sulphur, mercury, and salt – which had long played a basic role in the theories of the alchemists. Typical of sixteenth-century thinkers, he conceived all things as ensouled. Each of the three elements had its own individual *Archeus* or spirit of life which constituted its individual character and also its active power (*virtus*). Since all ordinary bodies are composed of these elements, it is the *Archei* of the elements which ultimately constitute the powers (*virtutes*) whereby bodies of various kinds come into being through association and have the characters which they do and also behave as they do.

Of particular significance in this doctrine from our present point of view are the following. First, it instantiates the sixteenth-century development whereby the conception of ensouled matter came to oust the medieval conception of substantial forms. Bodies, which are identified with matter, have their own inner power of being and living, so that the sources of change are to be found in bodies themselves, in their own inner power and activity.

But the point of greatest importance is that Paracelsus' conception of the elements differs from that of Aristotle in one quite fundamental respect. The Aristotelian elements change into each other, but the elements of Paracelsus are conceived as generically different from each other, each being what it is, sulphur, mercury, and salt, and each essentially remaining that, unchanged. They

---

[13] cf. Lasswitz, op. cit., Vol. I, pp. 290–3.
[14] cf. ibid., pp. 298–306.

go into combination with each other, but in this each remains exactly what it is, exerting its efficacy through its own individual power (*virtus*). This theory in which the elements are in themselves changeless – and this includes their being completely devoid of any internal process of change or becoming – is the new conception which entered thought in the Renaissance period and gradually made its influence felt. It is to be expected that the Paracelsian doctrine, as part of the general anti-Aristotelian movement of thought, would also contribute to bringing the theories of the Presocratics and those of the Roman medical schools, into renewed significance as lending support to this anti-Aristotelian conception of changeless elements.

The grip of the Aristotelian theory of the elements remained strong, however; most sixteenth-century thinkers, like Cardano and Gilbert, and even some in the seventeenth century, like Campanella and van Helmont, continued to maintain the Aristotelian conception, with some modifications, such as reducing the number of the elements to three or to two – fire being the one most thinkers abandoned. Also most thinkers were still strongly under the influence of the concept of substantial form. But gradually the trend which we investigated in the previous chapter towards the conception of matter as itself substance, came to have an impact on the theory of the elements. The elements had always been considered substances, and now they were conceived as material substances – of course ensouled. Also, the elements were corporeal. Thus was effected an identification of the concepts of substance, matter, and body.

The first step towards this identification, which was crucial for the modern conception of nature, was however not explicitly taken till during the first quarter of the seventeenth century, and then it came as the outcome of a complex development. It was this development which finally accorded to matter the full status of an independent substance, while conclusively breaking the hold of the conception of substantial form. The result was the modern conception of matter.

The factor which basically brought this about was a renewed examination of the theory of chemical combination in the light of the growing influence of the two sixteenth-century developments which we have outlined, namely, (1) the sixteenth-century conception of matter – so seriously at variance with the Aristotelian – especially when combined with (2) the anti-Aristotelian trends in the theory of the elements. In regard to the theory of chemical combination it was the second of these, the growing strength of the conception, contrary to the Aristotelian, of the elements as themselves changeless, which was decisive. Contributing to the increasing acceptance of this conception were the anti-Aristotelian developments in the conception of matter as stuff, as well as the influences from the school of Paracelsus.

In the theory of chemical combination once again the starting point was the Aristotelian doctrine. Aristotle pointed out that there are two kinds of combination. One is that of a putting together (*synthesis*) of ingredients in a compound in which the ingredients remain separate and distinct, like grains of barley and wheat in a heap constituted of both.[15] That is to say, in this kind of compound there is a mere aggregate juxtaposition of the constituents. In the other kind of combination there is a blending (*krasis*) or mixing (*mixis*) of the constituents, with the result that the whole is homoeomerous, that is, having parts like one another and like the whole of which they are parts – 'just as any part of water is water, so also with what is blended'.[16] The former kind Aristotle usually referred to as a *synthesis*, and the latter as a *mixis*. It is important to distinguish between the two, Aristotle argued, for either there is genuine *mixis*, or *mixis* is but apparent, which is to say that there is a mixing only relatively to perception (*pros tēn aisthēsin*),[17] *mistio ad sensum* – which anyone with the keen eyesight of a Lynceus would see is but an instance of *synthesis*, aggregate juxtaposition.[18]

It is equally important to distinguish *mixis* from generation and destruction, for if one or more of the ingredients, when coming into a compound, were to cease to exist or be completely absorbed, *mixis* would not have occurred, but rather there would have taken place the generation of one substance and the destruction or passing away of one or more others.[19] In other words, there can be no genuine *mixis* unless the constituents of the compound in some respect continue to exist in the compound – for it is an empirical fact that 'the constituents of a mixture first come to-

15 *De gen. et corr.*, 328a2–4.
16 ibid., 328a11–12. (My tr.).
17 ibid., 328a14.
18 ibid., 328a15.
19 ibid., 327b1–7.

gether after having been separate, and can be separated again'.[20]

The problem which arises in this conception of *mixis* is how it is possible for the constituents to continue to exist in a *mixis* without this being a case of merely aggregate juxtaposition, *synthesis*, in which there is only a *mistio ad sensum*. Aristotle maintained that we have a solution to this problem in terms of his distinction between actual and potential existence. His formulation of the solution is important; since there is only this one statement of it in his writings, it became the key statement for interpretation by later thought. 'Since, however, some things *are-potentially* while others *are-actually*, the constituents combined in a compound can "be" in a sense and yet "not-be". The compound may *be-actually* other than the constituents from which it has resulted; nevertheless each of them may still *be-potentially* what it was before they were combined, and both of them may survive undestroyed.'[21]

The theory of chemical combination was brought into prominence again in the middle ages by Avicenna in his medical treatise *Canon medicinae* as well as in his physics treatise, *Sufficientia*, and his commentary on Aristotle's *De generatione et corruptione*. He took over Aristotle's analysis and his theory, which thereafter became the accepted doctrine down to the Renaissance. Aristotle's theory, however, involved an important difficulty, which became clear with the criticism by Averroës of Avicenna's interpretation of Aristotle's doctrine, and this set going a protracted controversy, continuing throughout the Scholastic period. It will be helpful to consider very briefly some main points in the controversy in order to bring out the difficulty in Aristotle's theory.

This difficulty consists in the problem of precisely how to conceive the 'potential-being' of the constituents in a chemical combination. Avicenna, interpreting this in terms of the conception of substantial form, maintained that the potential being meant that the substantial forms of the constituents remain undisturbed in the mixture, though their attributes affect each other

[20] ibid., 327b28–9. (My tr.).
[21] ibid., 327b23–7. (tr. by H. H. Joachim.) ἐπεὶ δ' ἐστὶ τὰ μὲν δυνάμει τὰ δ' ἐνεργείᾳ τῶν ὄντων, ἐνδέχεται τὰ μιχθέντα εἶναί πως καὶ μὴ εἶναι, ἐνεργείᾳ μὲν ἑτέρου ὄντος τοῦ γεγονότος ἐξ αὐτῶν, δυνάμει δ' ἔτι ἑκατέρου ἅπερ ἦσαν πρὶν μιχθῆναι, καὶ οὐκ ἀπολωλότα.

and undergo change. Averroës rejected this interpretation on the ground that if the substantial forms remain unchanged, this entails that the constituents exist 'actually' in the mixture, which means that it could not be a genuine mixture at all but only an aggregate juxtaposition – the Aristotelian *synthesis*. For our purposes it is not necessary to enter into a discussion of the alternative solutions by Averroës, Aquinas, Scotus, and others. The Scholastics submitted the theory of *mistio* to detailed and subtle analysis,[22] and it remained an important topic down into the Renaissance. However, as was clear from the controversies, no solution to the problem of potential existence was without serious objections.

A big change in the theory of chemical combination came in the first quarter of the seventeenth century as the outcome of the sixteenth-century developments in respect of (1) the theory of the elements whereby the elements came to be conceived as in themselves changeless, and (2) in the concept of matter. It was on the medical men, of whom Daniel Sennert and Sebastian Basso were the outstanding examples, that the implications for the theory of chemical combination of the conception of the elements as unchanging made their strongest impact. For these medical men this conception tied in well with the influence on medical thought of the ancient anti-Hippocratic medical school of the Methodists who had maintained an atomistic theory, as well as with Avicenna's interpretation of the theory of chemical combination – the influence of Avicenna having continued strong in medical thought down into the seventeenth century.

But the changes in the concept of matter were of equal significance for the theory of chemical combination, as was particularly clear to the Dutch thinker David van Goorle (Gorlaeus) and the French medical man Sebastian Basso. Of the thinkers of the first quarter of the seventeenth century, it was Basso who on the whole had the clearest appreciation of the developments taking place. His thought can be taken as particularly representative of the time, and his own contribution, moreover, was of considerable significance. Basso was a leading member of the circle of scientifically and philosophically interested thinkers in Paris who during the first quarter of the seventeenth century

[22] cf. Anneliese Maier, *An der Grenze von Scholastik und Naturwissenschaft*, (Essen, 1943), pp. 7–140, and Lasswitz, op. cit., Vol. I, pp. 239–54.

vigorously discussed among themselves the anti-Aristotelian theories then still under strict ban by the University of Paris and the Church. These discussions, and the developments of thought which resulted from them, were crucial for the next generation of thinkers – Descartes and Gassendi may be mentioned as two outstanding figures – for it was upon that foundation that these later thinkers carried the new conception to maturity.

Basso saw very clearly that a new conception of matter, fundamentally different from the traditional Aristotelian one, was emerging, and that the theory of chemical combination was especially significant for this conception. Indeed he saw this theory as a test case of the anti-Aristotelian theory of matter, and accordingly devoted the first two Books of his volume *Philosophia naturalis*[23] to 'De Materia et Mixto'.

In a running polemic against the Aristotelian doctrine of matter, Basso advanced a conception of matter in which matter *per se* was substance, that is, a self-subsistent existent, the instances of this being the elementary constituents of all compounds. These elementary substances – which under the influence of ancient thought he referred to as 'atoms' – he conceived as created by God as unchanging and unchangeable, all of them remaining exactly what they are, whether they exist separately or in combination.[24] A number of thinkers had come to essentially the same conception of material substance about the year 1620 – Gorlaeus,[25] Sennert,[26] and Francis Bacon[27] may be specially men-

---

[23] *Philosophia naturalis adversus Aristotelem Libri XII. In quibus abstrusa veterum physiologia restauratur, et Aristotelis errores solidis rationibus refelluntur* (Geneva, 1621), pp. 1–129.

[24] cf. Bk I, Int. I, Art. 6: p. 14 *'Cum agimus de atomis, censemus eas a Deo creatas, quod fuit praemonendum.'* ibid., Bk I, Int. I, Art. 5, p. 13: *'Sed esto, hos Veteres circa illa prima rerum principia discrepasse, certum tamen est, illos in eo convenisse, quod & verissimum esse demonstrabimus, & ad mutationum naturalium causam rationemque inveniendam sufficit. Quod scilicet agnoverint omnes ex minimis, diversissimisque particulis res construi, quae ut ab invicem seiunctae naturas haberent dissimiles, eandem naturae differentiam coniunctae retinerent, quocumque tandem nomine res illas voces.'* Bk I, Int. II, Art. 3, p. 26: *'Materiamque talem nos cum Veteribus asserere, quae constet ex partibus diversissimis. Ita ut in parte ossis, vel carnis quam minimam reris, sit particularum diversi generis conjunctio, quae in illa compositione propriam naturam retineant.'*

[25] *Exercitationes Philosophicae quibus universa fere discutitur Philosophia Theoretica. Et plurima ac praecipua Peripateticorum dogmata evertuntur. Post mortem auctoris editae cum gemino indice* (Lugd.-Batavorum, 1620).

[26] *Epitome scientiae naturalis* (Wittenberg, 1618); *De Chymicorum cum Aristotelicis et Galenicis consensu ac dissensu* (Wittenberg, 1619).

[27] *Novum Organum Scientiarum* (London, 1620).

tioned. Basic to this conception was the conviction that all natural bodies evident to our senses are compounds, that they are not themselves unitary, homogeneous substances, and that they must therefore be constituted by certain elementary bodies, which must accordingly be the true substances. Because the theory of atomism, as was evident from the Aristotelian criticism of it, presented difficulties (these will be discussed subsequently), it was sufficient to regard the elements as the smallest constituent bodies of compound bodies – Sennert accordingly chose the term *corpuscula* rather than atoms for the elementary bodies. The important point is that these 'corpuscles' or 'atoms' are bodies, that they are the true substances, that these substances are conceived as matter only – the characteristic instances being stuffs such as sulphur, mercury, and salt – and that these material substances are in themselves changeless.

Basso saw the theory of chemical combination as of quite unique importance in this context, for it could settle the issue between the Aristotelian doctrine of matter and the new conception. Sennert, independently of Basso, had come to the same opinion, and they were in this respect the leaders of a general trend. Both these thinkers insisted that the fact that the constituents of a chemical compound could by appropriate processes be separated from each other amply proved that the constituents remain actually existent in the combination or *mixtum*. Both, and Basso especially, brought forward a wealth of empirical evidence which, they argued, was explicable only on the supposition of the unchanged existence of the constituents in chemical combination. And further, clearly under the influence of the anti-Aristotelian conception of the elements as changeless in themselves, they insisted that the constituents remaining actually existent in chemical combination implied that a chemical combination could not be an instance of an Aristotelian *mixis*. For, as Basso said, since some cases in which the compound had all the appearance of a completely homogeneous entity proved on close examination to be domonstrably instances of aggregate juxtaposition, there was no justification to regard any compound as a *mixis* on the ground of apparent homogeneity. On the contrary, the alternative theory of all combination being what Aristotle had termed *synthesis*, that is, an aggregate juxtaposition of the constituents, and that the *mistio* is a *mistio ad sensum* only, is fully adequate to account for all the evidence.[28]

Thus, considerably through the influence of the theories of the elements and of chemical combination, there emerged a new conception of matter as completely self-subsistent substance, in which the true substances were identified as the elementary bodies constituent of all compound bodies.

The logical implications of this new conception immediately began to assert themselves, though restricted and retarded by the implicit carrying over of presuppositions from the rejected conceptions. Basso, for example, continued to hold to a conception of elementary bodies as extremely diverse in size and shape, and as having the basic qualitative characters of hot and cold. Gorlaeus held a similar view. And the conception of substantial form had a fairly firm grip on Sennert.

A fundamental implication of the new conception, clearly seen by Basso, is that since all perceptible bodies are aggregate compounds of changeless elements, the differences between these bodies can only be constituted by different groupings of these elements. From this it follows that the fundamental change whereby there is change in bodies is change of place or locomotion. Since the elements are in themselves changeless, coming-into-being and passing-away can pertain only to compound bodies, and coming-into-being can only be constituted by the occurrence of a new grouping of the elements through their locomotion and, correspondingly, passing-away can only be due to the constituents of the group ceasing to be together, again through their locomotion. Here we have the basic position of the mechanistic conception of nature as it came to be developed during the rest of the century.

A further implication of this new conception is that qualitative change, too, and not only generation, is accountable for in terms of locomotion. Basso did not draw this implication fully, for as noted he continued to regard the qualities of hot and cold as inherent in the elements. It was Galileo, in his *Il Saggiatore* (1623), who first fully appreciated this implication; heat in the thing called hot is nothing but the motion of particles. The sensible quality of heat, like all other sensible qualities, exists purely

[28] cf. Basso, op. cit., Bk I, Int. IV, Arts. 2 and 3, pp. 37–42.

in the sensibility of the experiencer.[29] Thus what, after Locke, came to be known as the doctrine of primary and secondary qualities, is grounded in this new conception of matter, and was from the start of the conception realized to be an implication of that conception; it is not surprising that it came into rapid and widespread acceptance.

This new theory of matter not only entailed the reduction of all the kinds of change which Aristotle had maintained to be distinct – the coming-into-being (*genesis*) of things and their passing-away (*phthora*), alteration (*alloiōsis*) of a qualitative kind, and of a quantitative kind – to one, namely locomotion (the Aristotelian *phora*), but it also gave a quite fundamental status to this kind of change in another respect. Aristotle had maintained[30] that *physis*, the natural, the physical, is that which has the source of *kinēsis* in itself, and that this *kinēsis* is basically the process of the attainment of actuality, involving the transition from potentiality to actuality. Now on the new conception of material substance, as Gorlaeus most clearly saw and forcefully stated, the Aristotelian conception of substance as involving a transition from potentiality to actuality is completely invalid. Since the elementary bodies which are the substances are in themselves entirely changeless, they are as such fully actual, and they accordingly cannot involve any Aristotelian process of attaining actuality. The Aristotelian distinction between potentiality and actuality has thus to be completely rejected. This means that there is no *kinēsis* as Aristotle had maintained it except in the sense of locomotion (*phora*). In other words, in the new doctrine all motion (*kinēsis*) is locomotion (*phora*), and therewith the term 'motion' came to acquire the restricted connotation which it has since had.

And therewith, too, the modern conception of nature, of the physical, was born. Taking over from Aristotle that the natural, the physical, is that which has the principle of its motion in itself, since the only motion possible in the new theory is locomotion, this meant that the concept of nature, of the physical, is the concept of the ultimate constituents of compounds, as in themselves changeless substances, undergoing change of place. This is what is meant by the mechanical conception of nature,

29 cf. *Le Opere di Galileo Galilei* (Firenze, 1964–6), Vol. VI, pp. 347–8.
30 See Ch. 7 above.

which is that nature is completely understandable in terms of changeless substances and their locomotion.

In this conception of nature, of the physical, the science of nature, physics, becomes the study of the laws of motion of these corpuscular substances – in other words, physics becomes mechanics. This new physics rapidly became immensely successful. The new conception of nature involved great philosophical problems, however, and in a basic respect the philosophical endeavour from the end of the first quarter of the seventeenth century up to and including Kant consisted in a protracted struggle with the problems and difficulties involved in this new conception.[31]

[31] The thought of the first quarter of the seventeenth century and its significance for the rise of modern philosophy has been much neglected. Lasswitz's analyses of the relevant thinkers (op. cit.) remains the most extensive and valuable. cf. also A. G. van Melsen, *From Atomos to Atom*, (1952).

PART III

The Modern Concept of Nature

12

MATTER, MOTION, AND THE
CONCEPT OF PLACE

Foundational in the modern theory of nature is the concept of
matter as an independent actual existent or substance, in itself
devoid of any internal process of change or becoming, and capable only of change of place, that is, of locomotion. Nature is
basically to be understood in terms of this matter and its locomotion. Because of the tremendous divergence of this new conception of nature from that which had antecedently prevailed,
it necessitated a complete re-thinking of the entire range of philosophical issues involved in the concept of nature, the issues which
had been so penetratingly analysed in Aristotle's *Physics*. This
re-thinking was a basic concern of the philosophical endeavour
of the seventeenth century. The consequent new analysis and
the problems it involved will be the topic of this Part.

The new concept of matter involved a new concept of motion,
of activity, and of the ontological status of form and the soul.
The new doctrine was also immediately plunged into the problems of the continuum, that is, of divisibility and indivisibility, of
continuity and discreteness, and of finitude and infinity. For in
this doctrine the macroscopic bodies evident in perception were
composite of elementary bodies, and according to Aristotle's
analysis of the continuum, atomism had to be rejected as an
untenable concept. In addition, matter and the problem of the
continuum also was soon seen to involve the very difficult issue
of the relation of the physical and the mathematical, the resolution of which led finally to the development of the modern concept of space, a concept which in the eighteenth century was
recognized as equally fundamental to the modern concept of
nature as was that of matter. This range of problems and others
to which they led will be examined in succeeding chapters. In
this one we shall commence with the examination of motion.

Aristotle had brought out that the factor which is fundamental in the natural, the physical existent, is that of *kinēsis*. The new doctrine maintained this Aristotelian insight, but its subjected the complex Aristotelian concept of *kinēsis*, *motus*, motion, to a considerable simplification : whereas for Aristotle *kinēsis*, motion, was a generic concept of which qualitative change, quantitative change, and change of place were the species, in the new doctrine motion is conceived as solely locomotion or change of place, to which all the other kinds of change are finally reducible. In this chapter we shall be concerned with the concept of locomotion and what its analysis involved, namely an examination of the concepts of place and the void. The present chapter will be devoted largely to the former concept; the inquiry into the latter will carry over into the next chapter.

Since locomotion is change of place, it is evident that the concept of place is basically involved in the concept of motion. Aristotle, in his discussion of locomotion (*phora*), had subjected the concept of place to a detailed analysis. The Platonic revival of the Renaissance and its attendant anti-Aristotelianism had in the sixteenth century brought Aristotle's analysis of the concept of place into renewed and critical scrutiny even before it became urgent because of the new concept of matter. Seventeenth-century thought was thus the heir to a long tradition of vigorous debate on this topic. The full import of the concept of place in the modern doctrine of nature is apt to be obscured when the examination of modern philosophical thought is commenced, as is all too frequently the case, with the seventeenth century, for seventeenth-century theories are essentially the outcome and conclusion of that antecedent debate; this being the case, and since the background out of which they arose was so generally familiar, it was not necessary to the seventeenth-century thinkers to rehearse the whole debate. Here, however, we must survey the essentials of it.

Since the sixteenth-century examination of these problems had started from the Aristotelian analysis, it is necessary to consider the latter first. Aristotle had pointed out that, with regard to locomotion (*phora*), the crucial concept is that of *topos*, place, since locomotion is that kind of motion which is constituted by a change from one place to another; and indeed place would not have been recognized at all but for the occurrence of locomotion.[1]

[1] *Physics*, 211a13–14

It is the crucial concept even for those who, like the atomists, maintain the existence of *to kenon*, the void, on the ground that it is the essential condition of locomotion since, if there be not a void for a body to fill, the body will not be able to move, Aristotle's point being that in this sense 'the void is place deprived of body'.[2] Thus the problem which has particularly to be considered is what *topos*, place, is; in other words, what exactly are we concerned with when we speak of place, and how precisely is it to be defined?

It is clear, when we consider the usage of the term *topos*, place, that it is closely connected not only with locomotion but also with body. First, we recognize place by the fact of bodies changing positions with each other.[3] A second connection is that when a body is occupying a place the magnitude of the place must be the same as that of the body;[4] it is evident that the magnitude of the place cannot be smaller than that of the body, but it also cannot be larger since, if it were, another body could be included in that dimensional area or room, in which case the place would not be strictly that of the first body.[5]

But because there is this dimensional coincidence between place and body, it does not follow that place and body are therefore to be identified. Place is not something corporeal,[6] nor can it be any kind of part or element of the body.[7] On the contrary, place must be separate and distinct from body, since it can be left behind by body in locomotion.[8] Further, we speak of a body being *in* a place, so place must be what in some respect *contains* the body.[9]

With these clarifications made, what then is place to be taken to be? What is its ontological status? It is something dimensional, and yet it is not either itself corporeal or to be identified with the body it contains. Also it cannot be incorporeal, for nothing incorporeal can make up an actual dimensional extent.[10] In general, place cannot be an actual existent, an *ousia*. But might it not be form, *eidos*? For the shape (*morphē*) of the body and of place would seem to be the same, since 'the extremities of what contains and of what is contained are coincident'.[11] But

[2] ibid., 208b26–7: τὸ γὰρ κενὸν τόπος ἂν εἴη ἐστερημένος σώματος. (My tr.).
[3] ibid., 208b1.　　　　[4] ibid., 211a2.　　　　[5] ibid., 209a5–12.
[6] ibid., 209a5–7.　　　[7] ibid., 209a14–17; 211a1.
[8] ibid., 208b7; 211a3.　　　　[9] ibid., 209b1–4; 210b35–211a1.
[10] ibid., 209a15–16.　　　　[11] ibid., 211b12. (tr. Hardie and Gaye).

place cannot be form, since form is necessarily the form of an actual existent (*ousia*), and this means of body; and because place is not an *ousia* it is thus not able to have a form.[12] For a like reason, place cannot be identified with *hylē* either.[13]

Another possibility is that the interval (*diastēma*), extent or extension, between the extremities is what place is. But this too must be rejected, since an extension cannot exist by itself, not being an actual existent. An extension could exist only as the extension of an actual existent. Since the only actual existent here is body, this means that the extension must be the extension of the body. Thus extension is not separate from the body in question as it would have to be if extension were place.[14]

There remains only one further possibility, Aristotle argued, and this is that the extremities of place, which are coincident with but not identical with those of the contained body, are those constituted by the interior limiting surface of a containing body.[15] This entirely fulfils all the requirements for the concept of place, namely that it be dimensional, that it be coincident with the extremities of the contained body, and that it yet can not be itself an actual existent. Hence Aristotle's conclusion : 'the innermost motionless limit of the container, that is place'.[16]

This is the classic Aristotelian definition of place which subsequent thinkers either accepted – as did most of the medievals – or disputed and sought to overthrow – as did many of the sixteenth-century thinkers. For most of these thinkers the primary reason for the rejection of the Aristotelian conception of place was that it involved that the existence of *to kenon*, *vacuum*, the void, was impossible, and they were coming to the conclusion that the void was required as the necessary condition of locomotion and also of condensation and rarefaction. The concept of the void was thus held to require renewed analysis, to which we must now turn.

[12] ibid., 211b10–13.   [13] ibid., 211b30–212a2.
[14] ibid., 211b14–29.   [15] ibid., 212a2–7.
[16] ibid., 212a20–1: ὥστε τὸ τοῦ περιέχοντος πέρας ἀκίνητον πρῶτον, τοῦτ' ἔστιν ὁ τόπος. (My tr.).

13

PLACE, THE VOID, AND SPACE

The argument that the void is necessary as a condition of locomotion was one which had been prominent in Greek thought,
and Aristotle had subjected it to careful analysis, showing the
intimate connection between the concepts of *to kenon*, the void,
and *topos*, place. This connection became crucial in the sixteenth-
century reconsideration of the philosophical implications of the
concept of locomotion or change of place.

The supporters of the concept of the void, Aristotle said, held
that the void is the cause or condition of locomotion as being
that in which movement occurs.[1] Now the first problem is, what
precisely is meant by this concept of the void? By it, according
to Aristotle, its protagonists essentially meant 'that in which there
is no "this" or *ousia* which is bodily'.[2] This implied that the void
was conceived as a separately existing extent which can be
occupied by body. This meant that in this conception the void
is a sort of place deprived of body.[3] Thus the concept of place
is intrinsic to the concept of the void.

But, as we have seen in the previous chapter, the concept of
place cannot be that of a separate existent, and if void be place
deprived of body it would entail that void be some kind of
separate existent which is extensive. Since place as a separate
existent is not possible, the conception of void as a separate existent must be rejected.[4] Aristotle's argument here does not rest
on an identification of void and place. It is that void is conceived
as an independently existent dimensional extent, and this was
one of the possibilities as to the nature of place which Aristotle
had investigated and found to be untenable, as we have seen.
That is to say, Aristotle's argument was not that an independently
existent dimensional extent was untenable conceived as place, but

---

[1] *Physics*, 214a23–5. [2] ibid., 214a13. (My tr.).
[3] ibid., 214b17–18; 208b26–7; cf. p. 153 above.
[4] ibid., 214b24–8.

that the concept of an independently existent extent as such is untenable, for the reason that an extensional interval or extent is not something which is capable of existing simply by itself; for in order to do so it would have to be some kind of individual being, *ousia*, and mere dimensional extent *per se* plainly cannot be an *ousia*. Thus Aristotle's argument basically is that it is an independently existing extent, that is, a dimensional extent existing as itself an actual being, which is impossible; and therewith a void, conceived as such an independently existing extent without body in it, must be rejected. Aristotle's conclusion was that the universe must thus necessarily be a bodily plenum.

With this Aristotelian argument as the background, it was clear to the sixteenth-century thinkers that it was the concept of place which was in need of reconsideration. For, since they wanted to maintain a conception of 'void place', a place without body in it, into which a body could move, it would be impossible to do so as long as the Aristotelian definition of place was accepted. For since on that definition place is constituted by the interior limiting surface of a containing body, this implies that there necessarily must be a contained body in that place – there cannot be 'no body' at all in that place because 'no body' or 'nothing' would here mean that place be an extent of non-existence, that is, a non-existent extent. So if the concept of the void, the concept of an extent without body in it, were to be admitted at all, a different definition or conception of place would have to be found.

One of the main attacks of the sixteenth-century thinkers on Aristotle's definition and conception of place was that it tied the concept of place so completely to that of body that place was not able to be anything in itself. But, they insisted, if place be that 'in which' bodies are, that is to say, if place be that which contains bodies – an implication of the concept which Aristotle had recognized[5] – then the Aristotelian definition is unsatisfactory because what it really comes to is that it is not place which contains body, but body which contains body, since in this doctrine place is but the name for the interior surface of a containing body. So if *place* is to be the container of bodies, and moreover if it be something into which bodies move, then place must be not only logically but also ontologically distinct from bodies.

The earliest attempt to find a solution to this problem was that

5 See above, p. 153.

of Julius Caesar Scaliger. He did so by arguing for the existence of the void on the ground that it is necessary as the condition of movement, directing his attack not only against Aristotle but also against his younger contemporary Hieronymus Cardanus, who had accepted the Aristotelian conception in his book *De subtilitate*. Scaliger maintained : 'In nature it is necessary that there be a void. For if there be not one, either there is no motion, or body comes over into body.'[6] The reason why this had not been clearly seen is that, since antiquity, an erroneous conception of the void had prevailed. 'For they maintain a void without body';[7] that is to say, the void had been conceived as an extent empty of body. The conception which Scaliger put forward instead of this was that of an extent with body in it, that is the conception of the extent *in which* the body is : 'But we proclaim, that [is] a void in which a body is.'[8] The implication of this is that 'void and place are the same and do not differ except in name. For unless there be a void, there will be no place. Therefore void is an extent (*spatium*) in which there is body. For its nature is of such a kind that if a body yields to another, a void comes into being and is filled. Therefore void is the principle of motion.'[9] With this new conception of void and its identification with place, Scaliger achieved the separation of place from body. With regard to the definition of place, he held, the error of the Aristotelian doctrine was in its putting the entire emphasis on the interior bounding *surface* of the containing body, identifying that with place, and completely ignoring the extent or space *within* those bounds. Instead of this, Scaliger maintained, place is to be identified with that interior space or extent : 'Thus place is not the encompassing surface of the exterior body; but it is what is contained within this surface.'[10] Not the limiting boundary is place, but the entire room or extent within that boundary. But this space or extent, which is place, has to be distinguished from

---

[6] J. C. Scaliger, *Exetericarum exercitationum liber ad Hieronymum Cardanum*, 1557. Exercit., V. 2 : '*In Natura vacuum dari necesse est. Nempe si non daretur, aut non esset motus, aut subiret corpus in corpus.*'

[7] ibid., '*Illi enim ponebant vacuum sine corpore.*'

[8] ibid., '*At nos illud profitemur vacuum, in quo corpus est.*'

[9] ibid., '*Idemque esse vacuum, & locum: neque differre, nisi nomine. Sane si non esset vacuum, non esset locus. Est enim vacuum spatium in quo est corpus. Cuius natura per se talis est, ut cedente corpore corpori, fiat vacuum, ut impleatur. Erit igitur vacuum principium motus.*'

[10] op. cit., exercit. V, 3 : '*Non est igitur locus, exterioris corporis ambiens superficies: sed id, quod intra eam superficiem continetur.*'

the dimensional extent of the body as such; it is that extent which contains the body. It was accordingly to achieve this distinction, of place as dimensional extent from body as extended, that Scaliger identified place with void, and redefined the concept of void for this purpose.

Telesio, too, similarly argued that the movement of body requires that the concept of place be not only distinguished from body but that it also be separated from it. He maintained that, rather than with the Aristotelians conceiving place as dependent upon body, place should instead be identified with the extent (*spatium*) which bodies occupy and which they leave behind in moving. Place must be regarded as a certain capacity to receive bodies,[11] and it must be without any agency of its own.[12] When a body moves, place stays constant:

'Thus place can become the receptor of any entities whatsoever, and, when the entities existing in it recede or are expelled, [place] itself never recedes, nor is expelled, but remains perpetually the same, and promptly receives all the succeeding entities, constantly becoming just as great as the quantity of the entities located in it, perpetually, that is, equal to the things which are located in it, but never identical with any of them, and entirely different from all of them.'[13]

Telesio did not regard it as necessary, in order to distinguish place as the extent in which body is from the body as such, to identify this place with void, as Scaliger did. Thus he could retain the concept of void in its original meaning of extent without body in it. And since place is distinct from body it must therefore be possible, he held, for there to be places without body in them. This means that, contrary to Aristotle, an empty extent, *vacuum spatium*, is possible.[14]

These two thinkers will suffice here to illustrate not only the

---

[11] Bernadino Telesio, *De rerum natura*, 1586, lib. I, cap. 25: '*aptitudo modo quaedam sit ad corpora suscipienda*'.

[12] ibid.

[13] ibid., '*Itaque locus entium quorumvis receptor fieri queat, et in existentibus entibus recedentibus expulsisve nihil ipse recedat expellaturve, sed idem perpetuo remaneat, et succedentia entia promptissime suscipiat omnia, tantusque assidue ipse sit, quanta quae in ipso locantur sunt entia.*'

[14] ibid.

character of the sixteenth-century debate, but that it resulted in a change in the concept of place, removing the Aristotelian emphasis upon the exterior bounding surface of the body and putting the emphasis instead on the whole interior extent, maintaining that place must be identified with the extent (*spatium*) within those bounds. By the early seventeenth century this had become characteristic of the conception of place. Thus by that time and in this way was achieved what was of the greatest importance for the subsequent development, namely the separation, not only logically but also ontologically, of the concept of place from body.

In respect of this whole issue of motion, place, and the void, it was once again Bruno who specially characterized his time and advanced thought by his penetrating analyses. Bruno agreed with the argument that extents or intervals vacant of body are necessary to enable movement of bodies to occur. But Bruno was more clearly aware than other thinkers of the time of the manifold implications of this concept of extents vacant of bodies. Thus he saw that the separation of these extents from bodies involved the problem of the ontological status of these extents. This problem was indeed implicit in calling these extents *vacuum*, void, for the Aristotelian analysis of void could not be simply ignored. Aristotle had been entirely correct in insisting on the contradiction in the concept of void if what was meant was a completely empty extent, that is, strictly an extent of nothing, for an extent of 'nothing' is a non-existent extent, since 'nothing' cannot be extended. Therefore not only was the problem of the definition of place urgent, but even more, and more fundamentally so, was the problem of the ontological status of these extents vacant of body.

The Aristotelian argument had made it sufficiently plain that an extent just as such could not exist. Accordingly if there are to be extents vacant of body, then these extents must be extents of something, and the something must be non-bodily. Moreover, it was essential that this non-corporeal existent be itself intrinsically extensive if there were to be any extensiveness at all. Bruno maintained that in his philosophy there is such a necessary extensive existent.

Following Cusanus, Bruno had conceived the universe as *explicatio Dei*, God's absolute infinity being contracted to the infinite extension of the universe. Now Bruno, as we have seen,[15] had regarded matter as the fundamental principle, as opposed to the Neoplatonic doctrine of form as fundamental. This meant that the infinite extension is the extension of the universal matter of the universe. But this universal matter in Bruno's doctrine, as we have also previously brought out, is not corporeal – and neither is it spirit as such, but that which has body and spirit *complicans*. Bodies are constituted by contractions of this universal matter. But the concept of this universal matter involves no necessary implication that it must be everywhere contracted to body, in which case the universe would be one bodily plenum as it was for Aristotle. On the contrary, since bodies require to move, there are places where the universal matter is not contracted to body, and it is these places which constitute the vacant extents. Thus, far from its being the case that these extents are extents of nothing, of non-existence, they are extents of the fundamental existent, the universe itself. So in Bruno's doctrine the infinite universal matter, by its essential extensiveness, constitutes the ultimate places of things, that is the places in which bodies are, and the vacant places into which bodies can move. Thus Bruno's theory secures the separation of place from body and provides it an ontological status.

Because the word *vacuum*, void, had the undesirable connotations which we have noted, Bruno preferred on the whole not to use it. Instead he spoke of the universal matter, in respect of these extents vacant of body, variously as *aether*, *aer*, and *spiritus* (that is, the world soul). And when he was referring to this extent purely as such, and not in respect of its content (in which case it would be called *aether*, etc.), he used the Latin word for extent or interval, namely *spatium*.

Here we have a new use of the word *spatium*, space, in a technical sense, and this sense was the beginning of what was eventually to develop into the modern concept of space. Bruno's conception here, however, is importantly different from the modern concept of space, and to read Bruno with the modern connotation of the term in mind is seriously to misunderstand him. The full modern conception was not achieved for another century, and the sixteenth-century analyses we are here considering contributed most important ingredients to its development.

[15] See above, pp. 132f.

Properly to appreciate the emergence of the modern sense, it is important to be clear about the meaning of the word *spatium* in the usage of the time – which was indeed not different from that of the Roman and medieval. The word *spatium* derives from the root *spa-*, to draw (from the Greek σπάω, to draw, draw out), cognate with *span-*, to stretch (cf. German *spannen*). In its original use *spatium* meant 'a certain stretch, extent, or area of ground, an expanse',[16] and it was frequently employed in specific reference to such a stretch or expanse used for running races. It is thus closely related to the Doric Greek σπάδιον, (στάδιον in Attic Greek), a race-course, a stadium. In classical Latin the general meaning of *spatium* was that of 'a stretch or extent or interval', and we find this as the earliest use of 'space' in English in the fourteenth century. From this, in Latin, came a number of derivative meanings, of which the following are some of the most prominent. Thus, *spatium* was used *de loco, in quo ambulatur*, that is, it meant 'a place, an expanse, in which to walk'; and from this it came to refer also to 'a walk', and the action of 'walking' – in this way was derived also the German *spazieren*. Another derivative meaning is *de intervallo loci*, 'the interval between places', hence 'distance' – *spatium* in this meaning of distance is the equivalent of the Greek διάστημα. And in a more generalized derivation, 'magnitude, size, bulk, bigness'. One of the most frequent uses of *spatium* was in respect of time, *intervallum et longitudinem temporis*, 'an interval and stretch of time' – as we have had it in English since the fifteenth century, 'a space of time'. Another derivative use of *spatium* was that of 'an enclosed area or extent or interval', for instance in a dwelling, this being equivalent to the English word 'room'.[17]

16 cf. *The Universal Latin Lexicon* of Facciolatus and Forcellinus, New Edition by James Bailey, London, 1878. (*Totius Latinitatis Lexicon* Consilio et cura Jacobi Facciolati opera et studio Aegidii Forcellini).

17 The word 'room' derives from the Germanic *rum*, which is cognate with the Latin *rus*, open country. These have in common with *spatium* the basically similar connotation of 'stretch, expanse, extent, interval'. Whence the German equivalent of *spatium*, space, has come to be *der Raum*. The English 'room' (as also the German *der Raum* in one of its senses) means 'an enclosed area or extent or interval' in a dwelling. While this is perhaps the most common meaning of the word, it also has a more generalized meaning in which it is synonymous with 'space' as 'extent, interval, expanse', e.g. in the phrases 'to make room for', 'there is plenty of room for another. . .'. The word 'space' in which it is equivalent to 'room' in this generalized sense is that which is now most prominently current in connection with the recent development of interplanetary rocketry – this is not 'space' in the sense in which we are concerned with the concept in this book.

The general meaning of *spatium* at the beginning of the modern era was still that of 'extent, stretch, interval', and when this is borne in mind together with Bruno's conception of the extent vacant of body as filled with the universal matter, his new use of *spatium* becomes clear : 'Space therefore is a certain continuous physical quantity consisting in a triple dimension, in which the magnitude of bodies is captured, by nature before all bodies, and subsisting without all bodies, indifferently receiving all things, without conditions of action and passion, intermixed, impenetrable, not formable, not locatable, exteriorily embracing all bodies, and incomprehensibly within, containing all bodies.'[18] This conception, very close to that of Telesio, is of a three-dimensional extent, in its nature distinct from body, and which is the place in which body is or which is capable of receiving body. With regard to the ontological status of that extent or space, Bruno identified it with universal matter, in this respect going well beyond Telesio, who had not made a systematic attempt at the establishment of its ontological status.

Leaving aside for the moment this issue of ontological status, the point I wish to bring out is that a number of sixteenth-century thinkers had come to maintain that such a three-dimensional extent, distinct from body, is necessary as the place in which body is or might be. That is to say, they maintained that place is to be identified, not as by Aristotle with the exterior bounding surface of body, but with the extended area or room within those bounds. Because the emphasis came so strongly to be on this internal room or extent, distinct from body, it is not surprising that a convenient word to indicate it should be desirable, and that the word *spatium*, space, should gradually acquire this technical usage, with the connotation of extent or room in which body is or might be as the place of body. It is to be noted that this new connotation of the word is quite neutral as to the ontological status of that space, that is, as to the problem concerning what it is an extent of – this issue came very much to the fore during the seventeenth century. But during that whole period, and until the controversy over that issue had achieved

18 Bruno, *De immenso*, I, 8; *Op. lat. con.*, I, i, p. 231: '*Est ergo spatium, quantitas quaedam continua physica triplici dimensione constans, in qua corporum magnitudo capiatur, natura ante omnia corpora, et citra omnia corpora consistens, indifferenter omnia recipiens, citra actionis passionisque conditiones, immiscibile, impenetrabile, non formabile, illocabile, extra et omnia corpora comprehendens, et incomprehensibiliter intus omnia continens.*'

an accepted outcome, the new special connotation of the word *spatium*, space, remained simply that of extent or room in which body is or might be, and throughout the century we frequently find the phrase *spatium vel locus internus*, space or internal place, as for example in Descartes.[19]

Although Bruno's analyses were influential, his doctrine of the ontological status of this extent distinct from body which is the place of body received little adherence, and far into the seventeenth century the controversy raged over the concept of the void, the renewal of atomism at the end of the first quarter of the seventeenth century serving to intensify interest in the issue. On the whole the Aristotelian argument, the validity of which Bruno had accepted, against the possibility of a void tended to prevail. Thus Jean Bodin maintained that the corpuscular atoms must be densely packed constituting a plenum, since a void was impossible.[20] William Gilbert maintained this position, too, though he admitted a void between the heavenly bodies and beyond them.[21] Francis Bacon, in different writings, held conflicting views as to the tenability of atomism, in some accepting it, in others rejecting it as impossible, and accordingly took different positions in regard to the possibility of the void. He brought to the fore the distinction, which had been made by Heron of Alexandria (*c.* 100 B.C.), between a void of large extent (a massed or heaped void, *vacuum coercervatum*) and a void of small extent (an intermixed void, *vacuum commixtum*) constituting pores in and between bodies. Bacon rejected the former, but wavered in regard to his acceptance of the latter.[22] The chemist J. B. van Helmont definitely accepted the existence of such pores of void as necessary for the explanation of condensation and rarefaction, but denied that they could be just nothing, maintaining them to be constituted by a kind of existent of a nature in between matter and spirit.[23]

Differences of view regarding the void prevailed also among

[19] cf. e.g. *Principles of Philosophy*, Pt II, Principles X–XII.
[20] J. Bodin, *Universae naturae theatrum*, (Hanoviae, 1605), pp. 147, 226.
[21] W. Gilbert, *De Mundo nostro sublunare Philosophia nova* (opus posthumum), (Amstelodami, 1651), pp. 65, 68.
[22] Compare, e.g. his position in *Cogitationes de natura rerum* with that in *Novum Organum*, II, 8, and II, 48.
[23] J. B. van Helmont, *Ortus medicinae id est Initia physicae inaudita*, (Amsterdam, 1648), §21.

those early seventeenth-century thinkers, Sennert, Gorlaeus, and Basso, who we had earlier seen to have become strong proponents of atomism. Sennert implicitly rejected the existence of the void since he conceived the atoms to be completely contiguous. With regard to the concept of place, Sennert followed Scaliger in identifying place with the room or space within the boundary of the body, explicitly rejecting the Aristotelian identification of it with the inner bounding surface of the container.

Gorlaeus, too, was directly influenced by Scaliger, not only rejecting the Aristotelian conception of place, but following Scaliger also in identifying place with void. Void, however, he held, is sheer nothingness and is therefore not to be found *actu* in the world, that is, without body in it, though there is a void beyond the world.[24] Basso accepted the argument that movement and the phenomena of rarefaction and condensation necessitated something like a void, but since a void *per se* is impossible, we have to admit the existence of a subtle, tenuous, corporeal-like aether, a *Spiritus* (the *anima mundi* of the Stoics).[25] Galileo also rejected the supposition of completely void spaces. Movement, he held, can be explained with a conception of infinitely small atoms – a conception which we shall examine later.

The outcome of thought on this topic had thus on the whole been an agreement about the need to separate the concept of place from the close tie with body which it had been accorded by the Aristotelian doctrine, and to identify place instead with the room or space within the bounds of body. But as to the question whether place can exist as a space void of body, there was no widespread agreement. The majority of thinkers rejected the possibility of void space. However, the entire issue is more complex even than has appeared so far; the problems of place and the void are involved too in another set of problems, namely those of the composition of the continuum. In the period under discussion these came particularly to the fore with the renewal of the theory of atomism.

[24] cf. D. Gorlaeus, *Exercitationes philosophicae* (1620), p. 214, and *Idea Physicae* (1651), pp. 29, 30.
[25] cf. S. Basso, *Philosophia naturalis*, Bk *De Natura et Anima Mundi*, Int. II and III, pp. 321–45. He ends Intentio II, Art. 5 with the conclusion: '*Ergo vacuum est necessarium, . . .*', and begins Int. III, Art. I, identifying it with the Stoic *anima mundi* (pp. 332–3).

14

THE THEORY OF ATOMISM AND THE PROBLEMS OF THE CONTINUUM

In a previous chapter[1] we examined the developments which had led to the firm conviction that the macroscopic bodies evident to our sensory perception are compounds and not homogeneous unitary substances, that they must accordingly be constituted ultimately by certain elementary bodies. These compounds are bodies, so their ultimate constituents must be bodies, and the latter must be elementary or elements since, as the ultimate constituent bodies, they cannot themselves be composed of other bodies. This meant strictly that the elementary bodies were not further divisible. That is to say, they must be atoms – in the strict meaning of the Greek *atomos*, that cannot be cut, indivisible.

This, however, raised a problem. A fundamental and necessary character of body is that it is extensive, and extensiveness implies divisibility. How then is it possible that there be indivisible extents, that is, atoms or atomic bodies? This is a problem which had arisen for the Greeks, especially with the doctrine of Leucippus and Democritus, and had been thoroughly examined by Aristotle, of whose analyses the thinkers of the sixteenth and seventeenth centuries were very much aware. That the problem is very complex had been made clear by Aristotle. In this chapter we shall be concerned with some aspects of the problem; others will be taken up later.

The Aristotelian doctrine with which the modern thinkers had to contend was that 'it is impossible for what is continuous to be composed of indivisibles, for example a line cannot be composed of points, the line being continuous and the point indivisible'.[2] The geometrical line or an extensive magnitude – such

[1] Chapter 11.
[2] *Physics*, 231a24–5 (my tr.): ἀδύνατον ἐξ ἀδιαιρέτων εἶναί τι συνεχές, οἶον γραμμὴν ἐκ στιγμῶν, εἴπερ ἡ γραμμὴ μὲν συνεχές, ἡ στιγμὴ δὲ ἀδιαίρετον.

as that of a body – has the basic feature of continuity. Now what is continuous implies having parts which are *ephexēs*, in order one after another, that is, in succession, and that 'the touching extremities of each are one, and, as the word [*syneches*, continuous] indicates, held together; there cannot be continuity if these extremities be two things'.[3] What is crucial here, as Aristotle pointed out,[4] is that for there to be continuity it is not sufficient that the extremities merely be together by contact, for in that case the extremities remain two; for there to be continuity the extremities must be together in such a way that they are one.

Next, it must be recognized that a continuous magnitude is divisible – for example, every line is divisible – and, moreover, that the parts into which it is divisible must themselves be continuous magnitudes. Since each of these parts, as itself a continuous magnitude, must itself be divisible, 'it is evident that every continuum is divisible into divisibles that are always divisible',[5] which is to say that the divisibility of a continuum is infinite.

It is not possible for a continuum to be divided into indivisibles, 'for of an indivisible there is no extremity which is other than some part'.[6] That is to say, for an entity to be truly indivisible it could not have parts, and this implies that it could have no extremity or limit, for the extremity and that of which it is the extremity must be distinct;[7] and if it have no extremity there is nothing at which it could be 'held together' with another.

The evident instance of an indivisible is a geometrical point. Since as indivisibles points have no extremities, there is nothing whereby they can be together as one and in succession, and thus able to be continuously 'held together'. Points either coincide wholly, or are apart. Accordingly it is impossible for points to constitute a continuum.[8] Thus a line cannot be composed of points. There are an indefinite number of points in a line, but the line is not composed of them.

What is basic in Aristotle's argument is that any continuous magnitude, such as a line, is qua continuous magnitude divisible,

[3] ibid., 227a11–13 (my tr.).   [4] ibid., 227a21–3.
[5] ibid., 231b15–16 (my tr.).
[6] ibid., 231a26–7 (my tr.): οὐ γάρ ἐστι τὸ μὲν ἔσχατον τὸ δ' ἄλλο τι μόριον τοῦ ἀδιαιρέτου.
[7] ibid., 231a28–9.   [8] cf. ibid., 231b1–5.

and the parts into which it is divided must themselves be continuous magnitudes. A point by definition is not a magnitude, so it cannot be a part of a continuous magnitude. The relation of point to magnitude is a different one from that of part to whole.

The science of geometry requires both concepts, that of continuous magnitudes, that is lines, and that of indivisibles, that is points. Moreover, it is necessary and fundamental in geometry that a continuous magnitude, a line, be indefinitely divisible. Therefore there can be no minimum magnitude beyond which it is in principle impossible further to divide. 'Admit, for instance, the existence of a minimum magnitude, and you will find that the minimum which you have introduced, small as it is, causes the greatest truths of mathematics to totter.'[9]

On the basis of the foregoing analysis Aristotle completely rejected the theory of atomism. This theory, he insisted, is inconsistent with geometry : 'a view which asserts atomic bodies must needs come into conflict with the mathematical sciences'.[10] But to consider his argument more fully : atoms are maintained to be indivisible bodies. Now, in the first place, if they truly be indivisibles, they cannot have extremities whereby they can be together as one to constitute a continuum, so that if the macroscopic bodies evident to our senses be continuous, they cannot be composed of atoms. In the second place, if these so-called atoms be truly indivisible, they could not have parts, and therefore they could not be extensive, and accordingly they could not be bodies. And thirdly, if they be bodies, they must necessarily be extensive, and as extensive they must be divisible, and what is more, infinitely divisible, so that they could not in any strict sense be atoms, that is, indivisible.

This was the argument which confronted those thinkers of the late sixteenth and seventeenth centuries who had become convinced, contrary to the Aristotelian doctrine, that macroscopic bodies are not homogeneous unitary substances but composites. This implied, as we have seen, that they had to be composed of smaller bodies as their constituents. The elements, that is to say, had to be bodies, and since they were elements, these constituent bodies could not themselves be composed of still smaller bodies. They had, accordingly, to be minimal bodies, themselves

9 *De caelo*, 271b11-2. (tr. H. H. Joachim.)
10 ibid., 303a20-1 (tr. Joachim).

indivisible. It was in this respect that these thinkers were faced with Aristotle's argument against the possibility of minimal bodies, the argument which throughout the Middle Ages had effectively countered any inclination to the acceptance of atomism.

Now in the period under consideration it was very largely medical men who were responsible for the resuscitation of atomism, and the factor which played an appreciable role in this was the influence on them of the doctrines of the ancient medical school, calling themselves the Methodists, who in opposition to the humourism of Hyppocratic medicine – whose doctrine was that the principal determinants in health were the bodily humours or liquid constituents – maintained that the body is a porous structure, the pores (*poroi*) being formed by the interstices between the *ongkoi*, corpuscles, which constituted the bodily whole, health depending upon the proper relation between the width of the pores and the corpuscles. This doctrine of the porous structure of the body was originated by the medical man Asklepiades of Bithynia, a contemporary of Cicero. The constituents of the body, he held, are themselves extensive bodies, and Asklepiades, taking account of the Aristotelian arguments, rejected the Democritean doctrine of their indivisibility, and called the constituents not *atomoi* but, following Heraklides Ponticus, simply *ongkoi*, bulks.[11]

The significance of this doctrine to the modern thinkers – besides the encouragement from the fact of an ancient school which had opposed Aristotle – was that for physiological theory it was not necessary to maintain the indivisibility of the bodily constituents, that for the purposes of physiological theory this whole question of the ultimate divisibility or indivisibility of the constituents could be ignored. At least it was not crucial in the acceptance of the doctrine of the body as composite. It was under this influence that there was introduced the word *corpuscula*, small bodies – as a rendering of the Greek *ongkoi* – for the elementary constituents of composite bodies.[12] This emphasized that it was basic in the modern doctrine that the constituents are bodies.

The philosophical issues, however, as we shall see, are not thus

11 cf. Lasswitz, op. cit., Vol. I, pp. 211–14, 229–32.
12 cf. Lasswitz, op. cit., Vol. I, p. 403.

to be evaded. Sennert in fact did not ignore them. More strictly following the implications of the conception of the macroscopic body as a composite, he came in his later work[13] to the firm view that the constituents are indivisible, calling them *atoma corpuscula* and *corpora indivisibilia*, and countered Aristotle's objections to atomism by maintaining that Aristotle had mistakenly ascribed the characteristics of the mathematical continuum to the actual physical existents. Mathematically a continuum certainly is divisible *ad infinitum*; but the divisibility of a physical body ends in certain minimal bodies, not themselves further divisible.

This argumentation of Sennert, shared by many, shows however an insufficient awareness of the implications of the separation it involves of the mathematical from the physical. The full awareness of these implications came only later in the seventeenth century. The inheritance from Cusanus, which was so crucial in the development of modern science, was that the universe is a mathematical structure, and this prima facie seemed to imply the identification of the mathematical and the physical. Before Descartes, Bruno was the thinker who most clearly appreciated this and faced up to its implications. It was accordingly necessary, Bruno saw, to take full account of the Aristotelian arguments.

One of the many respects in which Bruno was characteristic of his time was in his realization of the strength of the case for regarding the body evident to sensory perception as composite. The basis, however, upon which the concept of atoms must be accepted, Bruno insisted, is finally not physical but logical. That is, we must accept the atom not because we will arrive at it if we proceed to divide the body – we can never be certain anyway that our actual division has reached an indivisible – but because, if it be maintained that the body is composite, there must be minima as the necessary beginning of any composite. The concept of an atom therefore is that of an indivisible minimum, that is of a part which does not consist of parts, and if there be not such there would be nothing with which to begin composition, nothing to constitute a composite.

The earliest modern appearance of a full-scale atomism was that of Bruno, and it was a development from essentially philo-

13 In the 3rd ed. of his *Epitome scientiae naturalis*, 1633 (1st ed. 1618); cf. Lasswitz, op. cit., p. 438, fn. 6.

sophical considerations such as the foregoing, that is, from a consideration of the problems of the continuum, well before the problems of physical theory led thinkers like Sennert, Basso, Gorlaeus, and Galileo to the acceptance of atomism.

Bruno's theory of atomism, like his theory of the universe as infinite, is a direct derivative from the doctrine of Cusanus. The special significance of Bruno from our present point of view is not this historical one, however, but that he advanced the theory of atomism in a very clear awareness of the philosophical problems involved, in particular of the problems of the continuum – that is, of continuity and discontinuity, of divisibility and indivisibility – as well as of the problems of the relation of part to whole, and of the finite and the infinite. Moreover, in his examination of these problems Bruno took full and detailed issue with the Aristotelian analyses all along the line, thereby contributing considerably to the seventeenth-century developments.

In the doctrine of Cusanus the actual individual existents are contractions to individual plurality of the one universe. As such they are microcosms of the macrocosm, and each is accordingly an individual unity. The universe has the fundamental character of geometrical extensiveness – this is fundamental because it is this interminate extensiveness which is the primary manifestation of the infinity of God – and accordingly the individual contractions must each be extensive.

The bodies evident to sensible perception are obviously divisible, so, Bruno argued, they cannot be the ultimate units. Since bodies are composite they must be constituted by minimal bodies which are not themselves further divisible. These are the true microcosms, the true units. Bruno accordingly used the term *monas* for the ultimate unit, as well as the term *minimum*.[14]

These units or monads are the ultimate individual beings. In other words, they are, from the ontological or metaphysical point of view, the primary individual existents which constitute plurality. But they are equally the primary physical existents. And, what is more, Bruno maintained, since the fundamental character of the macroscopic one, the universe, is extensiveness, and these monads are the ultimate contractions to unity of that extensiveness, they must be indivisible units of extensiveness. So

---

[14] cf. Bruno, *De min.* I, Ch. 2: 'The minimum is the substance of all things. . . . Here is the monad, the atom. . . .' (tr. Singer, op. cit., p. 74.).

from the mathematical point of view they must be identified as geometrical points. Thus for Bruno the monad, which is the ultimate metaphysical existent, is also the physical unit, that is, the element or atom of which all physical composites are constituted, and it is the unit of geometrical extension, the point, as well as also of number.[15]

Bruno's doctrine thus quite explicitly involved the identification of the physical and the mathematical. Aristotle's analysis of the continuum, therefore, was all the more a challenge to Bruno. Particularly it was Aristotle's conception of the continuum as necessarily divisible without end which affected Bruno. This accordingly had to be rejected. Thus Bruno maintained: 'The source and basis of all error not only in physics but also in mathematics is the resolution of the continuum into infinity.'[16] But it was not sufficient merely to proclaim this; Aristotle's argument had to be met in detail.

Since for Bruno the physical units are atomic, that is, indivisible, and were identified with geometrical points, he had to refute the Aristotelian argument that an extensive magnitude cannot be constituted of indivisibles. Aristotle had maintained, as we have seen, that an indivisible, since it is without parts, cannot have a boundary, and therefore that there is nothing whereby it can be united to another. Accordingly, if two such indivisibles touch at all they must do so wholly, that is, they must coincide, and consequently cannot make up an extensive magnitude, how-

[15] Bruno, *De minimo*, in *Op. lat.* I, Pt 3, Ch. 2, Scholium, pp. 139–40: '*Minimum est substantia rerum, quatenus videlicet aliud a quantitatis genere significatur, corporearum vero magnitudinum prout est quantitatis principium. Est, inquam, materia seu elementum, efficiens, finis et totum, punctum in magnitudine unius et duarum dimensionum, atomus privative in corporibus quae sunt primae partes, atomus negative in iisce quae sunt tota in toto atque singulis, ut in voce, anima et huiusmodi genus, monas rationaliter in numeris, essentialiter in omnibus. Inde maximum nihil est aliud quam minimum. Tolle undique minimum, ubique nihil erit. Aufer undique monadem, nusquam erit numeros, nihil erit numerabile, nullus numerator. Hinc optimus, maximus, substantiarum substantia, et entitas, qua entia sunt, monadis nomine celebratur.*

Numerus est accidens monadis, et monas est essentia numeri; sic compositio accidit atomo, et atomus est essentia compositi. Principium numeri monas cum numero, sicut et principium magnitudinis atomus cum ipsa magnitudine, reductive vel principaliter sunt in genere quantitatis, et accidentia substantiae, quae sunt monas antecedens, vere et per se minimum principium magnitudinis, in quo non ex quo; et in hac omnia sunt unum, sicut in veritate atomi secundum speciem omnes atomi secundum numerum. Ad corpora ergo respicienti omnium substantia minimum corpus est seu atomus, ad lineam vero atque planum minimum quod est punctus.'

[16] ibid., I, Pt 3, Ch. 6. Schol., p. 153: '*Principium et fundamentum errorum onmium, tum in physica tum in mathesi, est resolutio continui in infinitum.*'

ever small. What Aristotle clearly had in mind here as the paradigm of the indivisible is the point as conceived in Greek geometry, namely as without any extension at all.

But Bruno's identification of the point with the physical atom implies that the geometrical point is extensive. So for Bruno the paradigm of the indivisible was the extensive atom. He accordingly countered Aristotle's argument by insisting that it fails to make a distinction between a *minimum* and a *terminus*, boundary. A minimum is that which has no parts, but which is itself an ultimate part of a composite. But its not having parts does not preclude its having a boundary (*terminus*), since a boundary is not a part but that which separates either two parts or two wholes. An indivisible body, a physical atom, is a minimum, and thus without parts, but as an extensive body it must have a boundary – certainly a boundary is not a part, for a body cannot be made up of boundaries as a whole is made up of parts. Having a boundary, therefore, a minimum can be in contact with other minima, and thereby they can constitute a continuum.

This position, however, involves grave difficulties. How exactly is a continuum constituted by the contact of such *minima*? For in the contact of two minima their *termini* must either coincide or be distinct. If they be coincident this would mean that these *termini* or boundaries would be one, and this would completely conform to Aristotle's conception of what is requisite to constitute a continuum.[17] However, in that case there could not be two strictly discrete entities as the atomistic theory presupposes.

On the other hand, if the *termini* be distinct, does not this imply that there is not strictly a continuum – at least not in the sense in which Aristotle had maintained it? In that case the concept of continuity would require redefinition, as being constituted by a contiguity in which there is no empty extent separating the *termini* in question. This is indeed the conception of the continuum entailed by the atomic theory. But the question is whether this conception is adequate. Aristotle had insisted that it is inconsistent with geometrical theory.[18] Bruno implicitly acknowledged this in recognizing that his doctrine, which identifies the geometrical point with the physical atom, requires a

[17] See above, p. 166.
[18] See above, pp. 166f.

pretty radical revision of geometrical theory, one which he himself sought to provide by developing a geometry upon an atomic basis.[19] His attempt, however, but helped to make clear in what insuperable difficulties such a conception was involved.

Besides the inherent difficulties of this conception of the continuum, there was the further one for Bruno, in that it constituted an incoherence with the conception of the continuum implied in his doctrine of the universal matter of the universe as continuously extensive and in itself undivided. The latter, it is to be noted, conformed to Aristotle's conception.

All these difficulties which Bruno's thought served to bring to light were ones involved in and which arose out of the identification of the physical and the mathematical. Does it follow from this that this identification is false, that it would have to be abandoned? Seventeenth-century thinkers did not come to this conclusion, for they saw that Bruno's conception of this identification was but one alternative. His proving unsatisfactory, other alternatives would have to be explored. The most important of these were the theories of Descartes and Galileo.

[19] cf. *De min.*, especially Bk 4.

15

THE CONTINUUM, THE PHYSICAL,
AND THE MATHEMATICAL

The conception of the universe which was gaining increasing acceptance in the seventeenth century as fundamental to the new science was that of the universe as a mathematical structure. Bruno had interpreted this, as we have seen, as involving the identification of the physical and the mathematical. This meant that for him the mathematical continuum is the physical continuum; there is no distinction *in re*, but only a distinction in thought.

That there are profound problems in the distinction of a physical and a mathematical continuum was clear to Aristotle. In some important respects a distinction had to be made – the science of mathematics is not simply identical with the science of physics, for example. But it raises the problem of the relation between the two, and this involves the very difficult issue of the ontological status of the mathematical. That is to say, the question has to be faced as to what status in being the mathematical has; what sort of being has it? What kind of existence do mathematical entities have? For Aristotle, as we have seen, the fundamental being or existence is that of the physical. What, then, is the relation of the mathematical to the physical?

This issue is brought much to the fore in the consideration of the problem of the continuum. A physical, a natural, body is a single integral whole, Aristotle maintained, and thus constitutes a continuous magnitude – it is not a kind of whole constituted by the mere juxtaposition of discrete parts, as would be the case, for example, with an artificial construct. In other words, a physical, a natural body is a continuous magnitude, and is not constituted of parts which are discrete and thereby themselves actual beings. An actual physical body has parts, to be sure, but these are not themselves actual physical bodies. For instance, the top half and the bottom half of a natural body are each parts of the whole actual body, but they are not, as parts of that whole, themselves discrete bodies. If they were to become discrete bodies, for instance, by the original body being cut in two, they would no longer be parts of that body since the original body would, as an actual, have ceased to exist.

Now an actual physical body, since it is a continuous magnitude, must be divisible; it is evidently possible to cut it into halves, quarters, and into further pieces of indefinitely small dimensions. But how is this feature of its divisibility to be analysed; what precisely does this divisibility involve? If the natural body were to be cut up, each of the consequent parts would have the status of an actual, that is, each would then necessarily be itself an actual body. But what is the status of those parts prior to the cutting up? It cannot be that of an actual. Aristotle maintained that it can only be that of a possible or potential. Therefore, when we are considering the divisibility of a continuum – as opposed to its actual division – we are dealing with potentiality and not actuality.

In Aristotle's analysis of the continuum the distinction between actuality (*energeia*) and potentiality (*dynamis*) thus plays a fundamental role. This distinction is equally fundamental for him in respect of the contrast of the physical and the mathematical. The physical continuum is actual, that is, it is the continuous magnitude of an actual physical body. Mathematically a continuous magnitude is divisible *ad infinitum*. There can be no actual division into an infinite number of parts for, as we have seen earlier,[1] actual parts must necessarily be discrete and definite, so there must necessarily be a definite, that is, finite number of them in any definite magnitude – which is to say that it is impossible for there to be an infinite number of actual parts constituting an actual finite magnitude. Accordingly, in Aristotle's doctrine, mathematical divisibility necessarily pertains to potentiality and not to actuality.

But what does this imply for the ontological status of the mathematical? Aristotle had explicitly rejected the Platonic doctrine that mathematical entities are themselves some kind of actual existents distinct and separate from the physical. Mathematicals, Aristotle agreed with Plato however, are forms, and form (*eidos*), in Aristotle's doctrine, can exist only as informing

[1] See above, pp. 50f, and Ch. 3 *passim*.

matter (*hylē*) in a natural *ousia*. Thus mathematical forms, as we know them intellectually, are abstractions from the physical – this 'abstraction' for Aristotle being an intellectual 'extraction' of the form from matter. For Aristotle, therefore, the mathematical, while not in itself an actual existent, is a form of the actual physical existent.

There is, accordingly, in Aristotle's doctrine a very close relation between the mathematical and the physical. The mathematical is however not identified with the physical, as is clear when we consider the continuum : the mathematical continuum is definitely to be distinguished from the physical continuum. The actual physical continuum is one and undivided; it is divisible, but not infinitely so, whereas the mathematical continuum is infinitely divisible. Aristotle has characterized the distinction between these continua as that between potentiality and actuality. But since for Aristotle the mathematical exists in the physical, as a form in and of the physical, what exactly does its status as potentiality mean? For example, in Aristotle's doctrine, is the actual extensiveness of a physical body quite distinct from geometrical forms informing its *hylē*? Here again, as in the theory of chemical combination, Aristotle's doctrine of potentiality poses considerable problems, the resolution of which later thought was much concerned to achieve. These attempts exposed the complexity of difficulties involved in the question of the status of potentiality; it was this question which was basically at issue in the long medieval controversy between the realists and nominalists. We can, however, omit consideration of these medieval debates and turn to the seventeenth-century struggles with the issue.

The Platonic revival of the Renaissance had particularly brought to the fore the Platonic emphasis on mathematics, and this had resulted in the conception of the universe as a mathematical structure, as we have seen. This seemed to involve the identification of the mathematical with the physical, and Bruno's was but one of the attempts to work out the implications of such an identification.

Galileo, aware of the difficulties into which Bruno had run in his endeavour to develop a geometry upon an atomistic basis, explored a different alternative in the conception of the identification of the mathematical and the physical. Like Bruno he was convinced of the truth of atomism, and though also like Bruno he was much alive to the significance of the Aristotelian arguments against atomism, he did not agree with Bruno that 'the source and basis of all error not only in physics but also in mathematics is the resolution of the continuum into infinity'.[2] As a mathematician it was clear to Galileo that Aristotle had been completely correct in insisting on the infinite divisibility of the continuum.

Further, Galileo also agreed with Aristotle that the concept of the void as an extent of nothing is untenable, since it involves a contradiction. Bruno's metaphysical solution to the problem was unacceptable to him, however. Bruno's universal matter was strictly 'meta' the physical, and Galileo was in agreement with the doctrine of the other seventeenth-century atomists in conceiving matter not only as an independent existent, that is, substance – which of course Bruno also accepted – but as the physical existent. This was to become the dominant doctrine down into the twentieth century.

The problems of the continuum in respect of the physical, and the problems respecting atomism, motion, and the void, Galileo held, are all resolved by a strict identification of the physical, conceived explicitly as matter, and corporeal, with the mathematical. In this doctrine the ultimate nature of matter, that is, the essential feature of matter whereby it is matter, is its mathematical character.

With this conception it is clear that the fundamental attribute of matter is its geometrical extension. Now since extension implies continuity, this means, in the first instance, that the parts of extended matter are continuous with each other, and therefore that there can be no gaps of non-matter or void between them. Secondly, since continuous extension implies infinite divisibility, there can be particles of any variety of sizes and shapes. Thirdly, and most important, by virtue of the infinite divisibility of the continuum, there can be no minimum extension beyond which divisibility is not possible. But Galileo did not agree with Aristotle that therefore atomism is an untenable hypothesis. On the contrary, he held, atomism is acceptable provided we admit atoms of infinite smallness, a conception to which we are indeed logically driven by the identification of the physical and the mathematical.

[2] See above, p. 171.

Moreover, this theory of infinitely small atoms is able to deal with the problems that come to the fore with the theory of atomism which, it was argued, necessitated the concept of the void. If it be accepted that the atoms can be of any variety of size and shape, inevitably there will be unfilled and unfillable interstices between them. This is even more evidently the case when the atoms are conceived, as for example by Bruno, as spherical in shape. But if atoms be of infinite smallness, it is possible for all interstices to be filled without remainder, and thereby the concept of the void is rendered unnecessary. Secondly, with the theory of infinitely small atoms, the argument that the void is necessary in order to account for locomotion loses its validity. For if the atoms be infinitely small, extended matter will be completely fluid, without a hindering rigidity, thus rendering any variety of movements possible.

This theory also provides a solution to the problems of the continuum as these arise for the atomistic theory. Ancient atomism had postulated the void as fundamentally necessary for the discreteness of the atoms and therefore as the principle of plurality. For unless there were non-corporeal extents to separate the bodies, the atoms, by their contiguity, would be continuous with each other and so would constitute the whole world one bodily plenum; that is, with nothing to separate them, all bodies would merge into one, and atoms would be impossible. Now many of the modern thinkers, as we have seen, accepting the validity of the arguments against the void, maintained that the atoms are completely contiguous,[3] ignoring the implications respecting the problems of the continuum which this conception involved. For if in their contiguity the boundaries of the atoms remained separate and did not coincide, there would be no physical continuum in the sense of a continuum required in mathematics. Accordingly this implies a distinction, and not an identification, of the physical and the mathematical. On the other hand, if the identity of the physical and mathematical be insisted on, atoms as discrete minimal extents will be impossible. If the mathematical be identified with the physical, there can be no escaping the infinite divisibility of the continuum, and the only possibility for atomism is to maintain infinitely small atoms.

Some important implications of Galileo's doctrine need to be

3 See above, pp. 163f.

carefully examined. First, his conception means that the divisibility of the continuum entails its actual division, *ad infinitum*. Thus Aristotle's conception of 'divisibility' as meaning 'potential division' as opposed to 'actual division' is thereby rejected; what is divisible is in actuality divided. Secondly, since the divisibility, and thus division, is necessarily *ad infinitum*, the actual divisions, the atoms, must be infinitely small. And when we explicitly bear in mind the identification of the mathematical and the physical it becomes evident that the infinitely small atoms must be identified with geometrical points. Hence, as Galileo recognized,[4] his atoms must be *atomi non quanti*. That is to say, the infinitely small atoms are atomic, that is, indivisible, by virtue of their having no extension at all.

But this conception runs into another set of difficulties respecting the continuum which Aristotle's analysis had brought out. Aristotle had argued, as we have seen,[5] that no finite extension can be made up of the juxtaposition of extensionless entities such as points. Galileo countered this by insisting that extensionless atoms or points can make up a finite extensive magnitude if there be an infinite number of them. Galileo's argument, however, involves a confusion of divisibility and composition. If each of the constituents of a finite extension be discrete and definite, then there must necessarily be a definite, that is, finite, number of them. In other words, no finite whole can be made up, composed, of an infinite number of constituents if the constituents be discrete and definite. On the other hand, a whole can be held to be infinitely divisible only because that divisibility does not imply any final discrete divisions. The crux of the issue is therefore whether infinite divisibility is consistently reconcilable with the conception of physical, material, atomism. For does not this conception necessarily imply a definite discreteness in the atoms? And is it not precisely this discreteness which Galileo has lost with his *atomi non quanti*? Much of Galileo's achievement in mechanics depended upon his employment of the infinitesimal calculus. This is a mathematical procedure, able to deal with diminishingly small extensional extents, which thus enabled Galileo to avoid the problem presented by discrete minimal

[4] cf. 'Discorsi e Dimostrazione Matematiche', *Opere di Galileo Galilei*, (Milano, 1811), pp. 50, 63.
[5] See above, pp. 165f.

extents. But if from this it be concluded that physical atoms are devoid of extent they are thereby also without discreteness, as was clear to Galileo.

Galileo's doctrine thus in the end involves the reduction of the physical to the mathematical. That is to say, the concept of physical matter is emptied of all content except the mathematical. A consequence of this reduction is that Galileo is then strictly left with nothing whereby to account, for example, for the mass of bodies. For since his atoms are without size they must also be without any bulk whatever, and how can constituents which are themselves without bulk constitute a body with bulk?

We here run into an issue, in which the problems of the continuum are indeed involved, but which goes much beyond them. This issue is that concerning the ontological status of body, an issue which became of increasing importance in the seventeenth century. We shall deal with it here only in so far as it affected Galileo's theory and one alternative to his position – that which came in the main to dominate.

The development of the atomistic theory in the first quarter of the seventeenth century, as we have seen, arose out of an identification of the new concept of matter with the ultimate constituents of bodies which are composites. These constituents, it was thought, must themselves therefore necessarily be bodily – they were not only small bodies, corpuscles, but the minimal bodies. It is entailed in this conception that a sensible body, as composite of these corporeal atoms, cannot be different in kind, and thus in ultimate character, from its constituents. The essential features of the composite, such as its extensiveness, are necessarily derivable from those of its constituents – the extensiveness of the composite body is constituted by the sum of the juxtaposed extents of the corpuscles. Accordingly, sensible bodies are to be distinguished from atoms, apart from the compositeness of the former as opposed to the latter, only by the greater size of the sensible bodies.

Galileo's theory, by its reduction of the physical to the mathematical, constituted a radical departure from this conception of corporeal atomism. For his atoms, as *non quanti*, are without the features, such as size, shape, etc., which bodies manifestly exhibit, and which were thought to constitute the 'primary qualities' of

bodies – as opposed to the 'secondary qualities', colour, etc., which
were by all proponents of the new thought of the seventeenth
century ascribed to perceiving minds as the subjective appearances of the bodies to minds. Thus Galileo's theory in this respect
entails an important difference between the atoms and the bodies
they constitute, for on his theory the discrete size and shape of
bodies cannot derive from the mere sum of juxtaposed units,
since his atoms are not discrete units with definite sizes and
shapes. We shall not now pursue the implications which this
entailed for the ontological status of body, implications which were
first clearly appreciated by Descartes and carried to their full
conclusion by Leibniz, as we shall see later.

Much aware of the difficulties attendant upon the identification of the physical and the mathematical, many thinkers who
maintained corporeal atomism, like Gassendi, thought that the
problems of the continuum could be successfully solved by a clear
and definite separation of the mathematical and the physical.
Gassendi's thought, characteristic of this line, has the merit of
bringing out with particular clarity some of the important consequences of the separation of the mathematical and the physical.
Gassendi's attempt was to maintain the theory of corporeal
atomism, from which Galileo had deviated, by explicitly rejecting
the conception that the atom in its essential character is mathematical, maintaining instead that the atom in its essential nature
is a solid bulk.

In his early period especially, Gassendi participated vigorously
in the contemporary anti-Aristotelian movement, but it was not,
as with others, in Neoplatonism that he sought an alternative;
he went for this to Epicurus. This means that for the grounding
and developing of his theory Gassendi returned to the atomism of
Democritus, and consequently came to take a different position
respecting the void from that of most of his contemporaries.
Gassendi was very clear about the difficulties which face the
theory of atomism in finding a principle in terms of which to
secure the distinctness and discreteness of the atoms. It was in
this respect that Galileo's theory was fatally deficient. The issue
is whether the nature of matter, qua matter, requires that it exist
in discrete indivisible units, that is, atoms. It was clear to Gassendi
that there cannot be a ground for atomicity in matter as such,
even if the mathematical be extruded entirely from the nature of

matter and it be conceived only as solid bulk. For if to be is to be solid bulk, there is no reason in solid bulkiness as such that it be divided into bodies of any particular size and shape, or indeed that it be divided at all. There is only one way to secure not only plurality but also atomicity, Gassendi maintained, and that is the way of the ancient atomists, namely to admit something which is completely contrary in nature to matter as the principle of discreteness and plurality, that is, as that whereby there can be discreteness and thus plurality at all. In other words, if we assume a plurality of discrete atoms, it is necessary to assume something of a completely contrary nature to introduce discreteness into solid bulk by separating the parts of matter from each other. Since it is essential to the nature of matter that it is solid full stuff, the contrary of solid fullness is the not-full, the not-solid, the not-stuff, in one word, the void. Hence, Gassendi insisted, the void is a metaphysical necessity if atomism is to be maintained.

In Gassendi's doctrine the ultimate principles in terms of which the universe is to be understood are therefore the absolute full and the absolute empty, or void. The absolute full means the absolutely solid, which thus excludes the contrary principle. Accordingly the atoms are absolute solids because they do not have any interstices of void. This means that they are atoms, that is, not further divided into parts, not because further divisibility is not possible – because of smallness or density – but because of the actual absence of void between their parts.

The absolutely solid atoms are bodily since they have extension and size (*magnitudo*), whence they can be called *corpuscula*, small bodies. Gassendi thus explicitly maintained the conception of corporeal atomism. Magnitude is sheer quantity of stuff, and this implies extension, that is, *partes extra partes*. It also implies shape (*figura*). There can be no reason in extensive solidity as such, however, for the atoms to be all of one size and shape, or even of a few specific sizes and shapes. There must therefore be an indefinite number of atoms of an indefinite variety of sizes and shapes – not an infinite number or an infinite variety, however, as the ancient atomists had maintained; a finite though very large number and variety suffices to account for the observed differences between sensible bodies.

Besides magnitude and shape, Gassendi held that the atoms

also possess weight. This is constituted by and reducible to the inner power or *impetus* whereby the atom moves. This power or *impetus* derives from God at the creation of each atom; and since it is the donation of God this *impetus* is constant and unchangeable, whatever the direction of motion. With this conception of *impetus* Gassendi retained what Aristotle had insisted was entailed in the concept of *physis*, the natural, the physical, namely that it has the principle, source, of its *kinēsis*, motion, in itself. But in Gassendi's doctrine, it is to be noted, this *impetus* does not involve any internal change in the atom, and secondly it itself is not subject to any change – changes in velocity arise from impact, but thereby the *impetus* or power to move is not affected. Thirdly, this power to move is not inherent in matter in the sense that it is entailed in the very nature of matter as solid bulk; on the contrary, since it is not so entailed, it is necessarily extrinsic to matter, coming as a donation of God.

When we consider this theory of corporeal atomism with reference to the problems of the continuum it is clear that it runs into serious difficulty. Gassendi's basic ground for rejecting the identification of the physical and the mathematical was that if the mathematical were intrinsic to the nature of matter there could be no escaping infinite divisibility and thus Galileo's *atomi non quanti*, thereby making corporeal atomism impossible. To maintain the conception of corporeal atomism Gassendi accordingly insisted on the full separation of the mathematical from the physical, and to do so he explicitly conceived geometry as a speculative science, having its truths in itself; geometry is thus not to be carried over into the physical material or sensible. Gassendi grounded his justification of this on Plato's distinction between the intellectual and the sensible.[6] Geometrically considered, therefore, the atoms are certainly divisible, and indeed *ad infinitum*. But physically they are not divided, and physically they are not further divisible. In taking this position Gassendi was, it is clear, departing from the conception of the relation of the physical and the mathematical derived from Cusanus,

6 cf. P. Gassendi, *Opera Omnia: Syntagmatis Philosophici*, Pt. II, Bk. III, Ch. 5; in ed. Lugduni, 1658 (repr. Frommann Verlag, 1964), Vol. I, p. 265: '*Responderi deinde potest Geometriam ex se scientiam esse speculativam, neque ideo usum curare, sed habere solum pro fine conclusionum suarum veritatem, voluptatemque ex eo perceptam, quod tam evidenter, ac certo, cum sint adeo mirabiles, consequantur: unde & visum est, quantum Plato refugerit, ut in materiam Physicam, seu sensibilem traducatur.*'

which was playing an increasingly important role in the new science of the seventeenth century.

But this separation of the mathematical from the physical involves Gassendi's position in difficulties no less great than those he had sought to escape by asserting this separation. In the first place, if geometry or mathematics belongs essentially to the intellect and not to physical matter, he is then faced with the problem of how there is any relation of mathematics to the physical at all. For the profound problem which is involved here and which became increasingly the concern of thinkers up to and including Kant was that of the basis of measurement. That the difficulties inherent in his conception of the status of the mathematical did not fully impinge on Gassendi was due to his in fact having maintained this conception in only a part of his thought. He was unable to maintain it consistently for the reason that he was precluded from doing so by his conception of matter as solidity. And with this we come to the second main difficulty in which Gassendi was involved in his attempted separation of the mathematical from the physical.

The need for this separation was in order to be able to maintain the concept of atomism. To do so Gassendi had conceived the essence of matter as solidity as opposed to Galileo's mathematical conception. But the solid atom is extended, and to be extended is to be *ipso facto* geometrical. It is an evasion to suppose that it is geometrical only in thought; if the atom is actually extended it is in a fundamental sense actually geometrical, and this implies that it is actually divisible, which means that the body in question cannot be a true atom. It is to be noted that Gassendi is not able, as is Aristotle, to conceive an extended body as 'potentially divisible', because the modern doctrine of corporeal matter, which Gassendi shared, excluded all potentiality from matter: each material atom is in itself completely what it is, fully actual.

This difficulty in which Gassendi's doctrine is involved is more far-reaching still. It is not that, in conceiving the atom as necessarily extended by virtue of its essential solidity, he has implicitly adopted the position of Bruno and Galileo of the identification of the mathematical and the physical. Gassendi identified the physical with solidity and not with the geometrical, but that this solidity must be admitted to be geometrically extensive does not imply that thereby Gassendi has identified the physical with the geometrical. For in Gassendi's doctrine it is not *only* solid matter, that is, the physical, which is geometrically extensive, but equally so is the void, that is, the non-physical. Thus for Gassendi the universe as a whole is geometrically extensive. Since the geometrical extensiveness is not identifiable with the solid physical, neither can it be with the non-physical void. What can then be the ontological status of the fundamental geometrical extensiveness? To this problem the philosophy of corporeal atomism can furnish no valid solution.

16

DESCARTES' THEORY OF
THE PHYSICAL: *RES EXTENSA*

Descartes was very much alive to the issues which were examined in the previous chapter, and saw very clearly the difficulties in which the theories of Galileo and Gassendi were involved. Fully recognizing the fundamental role of mathematics in the new science, Descartes appreciated more keenly than most the problem which this presented as to the ontological status of the mathematical. The complete separation of the mathematical from the physical, such as had been attempted by Gassendi, could not be consistently carried through. Descartes decided that the tradition deriving from Cusanus which identified the mathematical with the physical was fundamentally correct.

The reason why the position of Galileo was involved in fatal difficulties, as Descartes saw it, was not that of his identification of the mathematical and the physical, but stemmed from his identification of the physical, that is, matter, with the corporeal. Descartes accordingly took the bold step of distinguishing, of separating, the corporeal from matter.

This was a bold step because it constituted a radical divergence from the conception which was foundational to the modern concept of nature, namely that of corporeal matter as the fundamental physical existent. In the generation before Descartes, as we have seen, the slow process of change in the concept of matter had resulted in the conception of matter as an independent existent, that is, substance, which was identified with the corporeal elements as the ultimate physical existents. This conception, although for a time strongly challenged by Cartesianism, remained the dominant one and was finally secured by the achievements of Newton.

Bruno's doctrine, which had preceded the development of the modern doctrine of matter, had involved a distinction of matter as such from the corporeal existents. The position which Descartes developed is much different from that of Bruno, however. In Bruno's doctrine matter was conceived as the metaphysical source of the physical and not as itself the physical; the physical, for Bruno, was identified with the individual corporeal existents which were the contractions to plurality of the universal matter of the universe. In Descartes' new position, matter is the physical, that is, the physical existent is matter, but the physical or matter is not conceived by him as essentially corporeal; the physical is instead conceived as essentially mathematical.

This identification of the physical with the mathematical involves certain very definite implications, Descartes saw. Extensiveness is a fundamental feature of the physical, of matter, because of the mathematical constituting the very essence of the physical. Further, because matter in its fundamental nature is mathematical, the extensiveness of matter must be continuous, and of one kind, that is completely homogeneous. Hence the physical existent or matter must be one single continuous *res extensa*.

There can be no reason in sheer geometrical extendedness for it to have any termination or any bounds or limits whatever, and since this extendedness is the essence of the physical existent there can be no other extended existent whereby it could be limited. Hence this *res extensa* must be *interminatum*, boundless, or *indefinitum*, indefinite.[1] And equally this prohibition of bounds or limits applies within the interminate extended whole; that is to say, there is nothing in extendedness as such whereby parts can be bounded and separated from each other, which means that by its essential nature *res extensa* is single and homogeneous.[2]

But although in itself undivided, by its essential continuity it is divisible, and indeed *ad infinitum*. It is by this divisibility of *res extensa* that bodies come into existence, as we shall see presently. For the moment, however, it is the necessary implication of this divisibility we have to note, namely that it renders atomism impossible. For atomism entails non-divisible extents – in this respect Galileo's doctrine of *atomi non quanti* involved a con-

---

[1] Descartes, *Principles of Philosophy*, Pt II, 21. Like Cusanus, Descartes reserved the term *infinitum* as pertaining properly only to God; see *Reply to Objections I* (Haldane & Ross, Vol. II, p. 17), and *Princ.*, Pt I, 26, 27.
[2] cf. *Princ.*, Pt. II, 23.

tradiction – and by the essential continuity of physical extension, every physical extent, however small, is actually divisible.[3]

The rejection of atomism also disposes of any need, such as had been insisted on by Gassendi, for a distinction of a physical and a non-physical, the void. Descartes fully agreed with the Aristotelian argument that the concept of a void involves a contradiction : there can be no extended nothingness.[4] The existence of extension necessarily entails something extended, that is, an extended substance, and this means the physical substance, matter.[5] Matter is the sole extended.

Descartes' position thus completely avoids the kind of difficulty facing Gassendi and the theory of corporeal atomism in general, of explaining the relation of the mathematical to the extended physical. For Descartes the extendedness of the universe is the mathematical, actually existing. Descartes accordingly does not have to derive the mathematical nature of the physical, matter, from a principle more ultimate.

From this point of view it is evident that in Descartes' doctrine the universal matter of Bruno has become the actual physical existent, with all the fundamental mathematical nature which Bruno had ascribed to it. As Bruno had put it: 'that matter, through being actually all that which it can be, has all measurements, has all species of figures and dimensions, and because it has them all, it has none; because it is necessary that that which is so many different things be not any one of those particular things. It is fitting to that which is all to exclude every particular being.'[6] The doctrine of Descartes is in full accord with this. His physical existent, matter, the one *res extensa*, by virtue of its mathematical essence has dimensionality, but it has no particular dimensions since its parts are not, qua matter, distinguished into discrete sizes and shapes. Its mathematical dimensionality means that it is the source of the particular dimensions of the plurality of bodies deriving from it.

For in Descartes' theory, just as in Bruno's, bodies are ontologically derivative from matter, and thereby also their mathematical character is derived. Now while in both theories bodies are derivative, that is, they are not ontologically on the same level as the matter from which they are derived, the principle

3 ibid., Pt II, 20.   4 ibid., Pt II, 16.
5 ibid., Pt II, 16.   6 See above, pp. 133f.

of derivation is different in the two theories. Descartes' principle
of the derivation of bodies constitutes a most important and
distinctive feature of his system.

In Bruno's theory bodies are derived from universal matter
through being contractions of that matter to individual actuality.
Such a contraction to actuality is not possible for Descartes since
in his doctrine the actual is the physical which is matter.
Descartes required a different, but analogous, principle of the
derivation of bodies. It had to be different not only because of
the difference in ontological status of his matter from that of
Bruno – his being the actual physical existent while Bruno's was
the metaphysical source of the physical – but also because of a
most important difference in the ultimate ontological character
of matter in the two systems. In Bruno's doctrine universal matter
is God manifested. And since God is pure act, universal matter
has its inherent principle of agency, the *spiritus mundi*. Now
seventeenth-century thought had in general come to abandon
the conception of a world soul, so characteristic of the sixteenth
century, and Descartes in this respect as in others typified the
new conception, carrying through its implications. Descartes
retained from the Cusanus-Bruno doctrine the fundamental
mathematical extensiveness of matter, and regarded this as alone
comprising its essence. This rejection of the conception of ensouled
matter necessitated not only ascribing to soul an independent
ontological status – whence Descartes' doctrine of a plurality of
res cogitantes – but also that the mathematical matter be without
any inherent agency. In Bruno's system matter had its own
agency whereby the contraction to plural individuality could
occur. In the seventeenth-century conception of matter as without agency, there was no alternative but to accord the agency
whereby there was movement of matter to God alone. We have
already observed this in Gassendi, and Descartes fully accepted
this position too.

In the new conception of matter, as we have seen, the only
motion or change possible is locomotion or change of place. And
this locomotion, Descartes maintained,[7] is all that is required,
given his theory of matter as *res extensa*, as the principle of the
derivation of bodies. For if parts of the one *res extensa* – which
in itself in undivided though divisible – were to move differen-

[7] cf. *Princ.*, Pt II, 23.

tially, that would be all which is necessary for the parts to be distinguished and distinct from each other, and no more than such a distinction is required by the concept of body.

In Descartes' doctrine accordingly bodies come into being through the agency of God[8] effecting a differential motion in the parts of the one *res extensa*. But although Descartes' principle of the derivation of bodies in this way differs from that of Bruno, yet that derivation is analogous in accounting for the essential character of the derived bodies as mathematical. For Descartes, since a body consists in nothing but a part of *res extensa* moving differentially from other parts, the nature or essence of bodies is that of extension alone.[9]

The big and important difference of Descartes' system from those of his contemporaries is that in his the corporeal is not identified with the primary physical existent; in Descartes' doctrine body is ontologically of a derivative status. This has the enormous advantage that while he is able consistently to regard bodies as essentially mathematical, he is able to avoid the difficulties which beset the other systems, such as those of Galileo, Gassendi, Hobbes, etc., in respect of the problems of the continuum. For they are involved in the dilemma of either admitting infinite divisibility and thereby losing corporeality (for instance, Galileo), or retaining corporeality and then running into incoherence with mathematics (for instance, Gassendi). The advantages of Descartes' position are great indeed, and attempts were subsequently made to secure them while avoiding the disadvantages of Descartes' theory.

For Descartes' doctrine involves difficulties no less grave than those from which he has escaped. Gassendi had very clearly seen, as we have noted,[10] that a principle is required whereby bodies can be distinct and distinguished from each other – the absence of such a principle was a fatal weakness in the theory of Galileo. To obtain such a principle Gassendi had introduced the void, the non-physical, for the reason that there is nothing in the physical conceived as solid bulk necessitating a plurality of bodies. That is, with his conception of matter Gassendi had no alternative but to supply the required principle from outside matter. Besides

---

[8] cf. ibid., Pt II, 36.
[9] cf. ibid., Pt II, 4.
[10] See above, pp. 181f.

the objections to this theory previously discussed, there is the further and even more fundamental one that it involves a basic incoherence in the system. Gassendi's two ultimates, solid matter and the void, are, as far as the essential nature of each is concerned, entirely disconnected. That is to say, the essence of neither requires the existence of the other. Matter, qua solid stuff, does not require the void, the non-matter. The void is arbitrarily introduced in order to furnish a diversity and separateness in matter which matter by its essential nature excludes.

Descartes too, for analogous reasons, requires a principle whereby bodies can be distinct and distinguished from each other, for there is nothing in the physical conceived as mathematical extension necessitating a plurality of bodies. As was Gassendi, so was Descartes also driven to find the required principle outside matter. In Descartes' theory this required principle is motion, and this involves him in an incoherence analogous to that in Gassendi's doctrine. For the physical as mathematical extension neither entails motion, nor does it require motion. Motion is thus arbitrarily introduced to account for a diversity and separateness of the parts of matter which matter in its essential nature excludes. In the second place, as Leibniz particularly insisted, since motion is in no respect entailed in the physical for Descartes, he is compelled to introduce motion by a *deus ex machina*.

There is a further and different difficulty respecting motion in Descartes' doctrine, involving another set of issues, which came into increasing prominence in the seventeenth century and which were crucial to subsequent development. These come to the fore with the explicit consideration of the problem of the analysis of motion. The new seventeenth-century concept of matter as in itself fully actual and therefore excluding all internal change or becoming had, as we have seen, involved the rejection of the Aristotelian plurality of kind of *motus*, motion; the only motion possible, given the new conception of matter, is locomotion or change of place. Although Descartes had diverged from the modern doctrine in respect of corporeality, matter in his theory is in itself no less fully actual, having therefore the same implications for motion.

Since motion is change of place,[11] the precise analysis of motion necessitates the definition of the concept of place. Descartes'

11 cf. ibid., Pt II, 24, 25.

treatment of the problem is quite evidently the outcome of the century-long debate on the issue. There is, Descartes maintained, a *locus internus*, internal place, constituted by the *spatium*, space or extent, equivalent to the volume of the body and coincident with it.[12] It is, however, not to be identified with the dimensional extent of the body as such since, if the body is to move, that is, change to another place, that place from which the transition starts must be left behind. Thus we see that in addition to space or dimensional extent, the connotation of place must include *situs*, situation.[13]

This, however, does not suffice for the concept of place. The *locus internus*, internal place, is the dimensional extent 'in which' the body is situated. A different definition is required for the external place 'to which' a body moves. Descartes was obviously very much aware of the Aristotelian argument that place cannot be a dimensional extent existing apart from body, that is, the physical; the only actual dimensional extent is that of the physical. Hence the *locus internus* or *spatium* is not different from the dimensional extent of body except 'in our mode of conceiving it'.[14] But external place must likewise be related to body. Aristotle had been correct in relating it to a containing body;[15] accordingly, Descartes held, 'external place is rightly taken to be the superficies of the surrounding body'.[16] The attempt of some thinkers to identify place with void space was completely rejected by Descartes for the same reasons as this conception had been rejected by Aristotle.[17]

But although the outcome of Descartes' analysis of place is in the end so close to that of Aristotle, there is nevertheless a difference between them of the greatest consequence. This becomes clear when, considering motion as change of place, we seek to analyse that motion. For since there is no ontological difference between place and body, whereby place can be distinguished from body, by reference to what are the respective places determined? Clearly place can only be determined by reference to body – the place from which motion starts by reference to the body about to move, and the place to which it is to move by reference to another body connected with that

12 ibid., Pt II, 10. 13 ibid., Pt II, 14.
14 ibid., Pt II, 10, 12. 15 See above, p. 154.
16 ibid., Pt II, 15. 17 See above, pp. 153f.

place. But if the second body be simultaneously changing its place with reference to a third body, and that likewise to a fourth, and so on – as will indeed be the general case with all bodies as Descartes conceived them, for they are constituted by the shifting of parts of *res extensa* relatively to each other – it is accordingly manifest that there can be no such thing as an absolutely fixed, immovable place, that every place must of necessity be relative. Descartes is thus committed to a complete relativity of motion and place, as he acknowledged.[18]

Aristotle was able to avoid this universal relativity of motion and place because of his doctrine of a finite universe. Because there is in no sense anything whatever beyond the universe, the supposition of any 'place beyond' is completely invalid; and this means that there is nothing whatever whereby the universe as such can be said to move or not to move. The universe is that by reference to which in the final instance all place is determinable. Thus Aristotle is validly able to have the concept of an absolute place by reference to which motion of bodies is determinable, and he can thus have a valid concept of absolute as opposed to relative motion.

By contrast with this Descartes' *res extensa* is interminate, and Descartes was thereby logically committed to a thoroughgoing relativity – a consequence which Bruno had embraced, following Cusanus, as entailed in the conception of an infinite universe.

The result for Descartes of this complete relativity entailed by the conception of an infinite universe is a fatal imprecision in the concept of motion. This is of great and far-reaching consequence because of the quite fundamental role of motion, that is, locomotion, in the modern concept of nature. This imprecision comes out especially clearly in Descartes' doctrine. Motion is evidenced and constituted by a shifting of parts of *res extensa* relatively to each other. Thus motion depends upon a distinction of parts – if there be no distinction of parts there is no motion – but for there to be any distinction of parts at all requires motion. That is, motion cannot be understood except in terms of a distinction of parts, and a distinction of parts cannot be understood except in terms of motion. Descartes has no way out of this circularity by use of the concept of place, first, because for him the distinction of place is dependent upon the parts of *res extensa*, and secondly

[18] ibid., Pt II, 13.

G

because place in his doctrine shares the universal relativity. Thus the very concept of motion as change of place becomes vague.

This ontological imprecision in the concept of motion has the consequence not only that it is accordingly impossible to say of any particular body that it has in fact moved, in any absolute sense – such a sense is indeed quite inadmissible in Descartes' system – but also that a motion from any place A to another B is not precisely determinable.

As we shall see, it became clear to Newton that the concept of motion, so fundamental to the modern concept of nature, could be rescued from this imprecision only by a concept of place which is exempt from relativity. And furthermore, without the concept of absolute place, the foundation requisite for measurement too will be lacking – and not least of all the measurement of motion, which is quite fundamental in modern physics.

Before proceeding to the examination of the development of the Newtonian position, we must look at one other feature of the doctrine of Descartes which is highly important for the inquiry into the concept of nature and particularly for the issue of the relation of the physical and the mathematical.

We have seen that the seventeenth-century identification of nature, the physical, with an independently existent matter entailed the ontological separation – which Descartes was one of the earliest explicitly and systematically to carry through – of soul or mind as constituting a quite distinct substance. All of what Aristotle had designated as the qualitative, as distinct from the quantitative, attributes of the physical existent were, in the new doctrine, wholly extruded from the physical and were ascribed entirely to mind, as subjective appearances to mind of the exclusively quantitative physical.

Now the quantitative attributes of the physical were for Descartes the very essence of the physical, that is, the very nature of the physical as mathematical. In other words, the physical for Descartes is the extended mathematical actually existing as such. By contrast with this actual physical realization of the mathematical, in the mental substance there is the conceptual or intellectual realization of the mathematical. The two kinds of substance, *res extensa* and *res cogitans*, are accordingly for Descartes not wholly different in essence. They are both, in a fundamental respect, mathematical : one is the mathematical

existing in actual extension, and the other is the m.
existing in intellectual manifestation. The influen
Timaeus of Plato is clear: on the one hand the act
matical figures coming into the receptacle and com;
three-dimensional bodies, and on the other hand the ....ccts
grasp of these (mathematical) forms. There is also the influence
of the doctrine of Cusanus (which is also fundamentally
Platonic): the universe exists as mathematically extensive –in the
original sense of exist, 'to stand up or forth, to appear, be manifest' – which means that the mathematical extensiveness of the
universe is the manifestation of the infinity of God; but God
manifests himself not only in the mathematical extensiveness of
the universe, but equally so in the mathematical ideas which
are the intellectual grasp of the actual mathematical extensiveness.

Thus for Descartes the science of pure mathematics is the
knowledge of the essence of the physical,[19] knowledge as such
consisting in the intellectual possession of the forms constituting
the very essence or being of the physical. The mathematical ideas,
however, were not for Descartes, as they were for Aristotle,
derived by abstraction from the physical, but by direct donation
from God. This involves a great difference in the conception of
the nature of intellection or cogitation between these two positions
respectively. In Descartes' theory intellection can involve none of
the activity of abstraction which is so basic in the Aristotelian
theory; for Descartes the activity of thinking which constitutes
the very being or essence of a *res cogitans* consists in the explication, unfolding, of what is contained *complicans* in the fundamental innate ideas – Descartes clearly is, in this respect too,
definitely in the Neoplatonic tradition coming down through
Cusanus and Bruno. Such being the fundamental nature of thinking for Descartes, philosophy must also, if it is to attain truth
and avoid error, proceed by the method of mathematics, namely,
deductively from clear and distinct premises, consisting in innate
ideas received from God. This means indeed that philosophy, as
the science of first principles, must itself be the most general
mathematical science. In Descartes' doctrine it is not only the
physical which in its essential nature is mathematical; equally so
is the mental.

This being his position it is fully intelligible that Descartes was

19 *Meditation* V, last paragraph; cf. also *Princ.*, Pt II, 64.

not disturbed by the claims of critics that his ontological dualism had disastrous epistemological consequences. With his conception of the physical as mathematical, and knowledge also as mathematical, Descartes avoided the kind of insuperable epistemological difficulty involved in theories which identified the physical with the corporeal and grounded knowledge in the sensory.

The difficulties in which Descartes' doctrine was involved with regard to motion and bodies rather than epistemological ones arising from ontological dualism were, however, what impelled thinkers to develop other alternatives.

17

INFINITE PLACE AND
THE PRINCIPLE OF MOTION

The new seventeenth-century science of physics – that is, know-ledge of the physical or nature – was the science of bodies in motion. For in the new doctrine, as we have seen, the physical was identified with the corporeal. Descartes' theory, which iden-tified the primary physical existent not with bodies but with the mathematical *res extensa*, was thus in significant inconsistency with this modern conception of the science of physics. Strictly for Descartes the science of the physical was the science of *res extensa*, and this science was pure mathematics.[1] The science of bodies in motion was for Descartes accordingly the science of physics only in a derivative sense. Descartes however did not press this implication of his position, namely that the science of physics as it was being developed in his time was concerned with entities of a derivative and subordinate status. Rather he tended to blur this implication by his frequent ambiguity in regard to the status of bodies, often writing of them as if identical with *res extensa*.

The great achievement of the century was the science of the motion of bodies, and Descartes was not only fully in accord with his time in this respect but he and his school also played a considerable part in advancing that science. For Descartes, as for his contemporaries, the primary bodies with which this science was concerned were the particles or corpuscles constituting the elements, from which the perceptible bodies were to be regarded as made up. It was with the follower of Descartes, Christiaan Huygens, that was achieved the most extensive and consistent development of this science as an atomic kinetics, in which all phenomena were accounted for on the basis of atoms and their

---

[1] This is why Descartes maintained (*Princ.*, Pt II, 64) 'That I do not accept or desire any other principle in Physics than in Geometry or abstract mathematics . . .'

motion – including gravitation, which was explained in terms of the Cartesian theory of vortices.[2]

This pursuit of the science of motion of bodies gradually brought to the fore a discrepancy between it and Descartes' theory of the nature and derivation of bodies. For in this science bodies not only move but they also impact, and impaction clearly seemed to imply hardness and impenetrability as basic features of bodies. Huygens and many others accordingly abandoned the Cartesian conception of bodies, and accepted Gassendi's doctrine in this respect.

Faced with this issue – for example in his correspondence with Henry More[3] – Descartes maintained that hardness as such is a mere sensory property, the corresponding feature intrinsic to bodies being impenetrability which, he held, is nothing other than the extension of one body preventing the simultaneous occupation of a particular place by another body. On the basis of Descartes' doctrine of *res extensa*, however, extension as such cannot constitute impenetrability. Bodies are, on Descartes' theory, constituted and distinguished from each other not by their feature of extendedness, but by differential motion. Thus impenetrability is not explicable as the extension in one place prohibiting another portion of extension to be there, but by the resistance offered by the extension occupying that place being at rest relatively to the moving extension constituting the impinging body. Since there is no reason in extension as such for any particular portion of extension to involve resistance, and since there is also no ground for resistance to be found in motion as such, it means that Descartes has ascribed resistance as a peculiar property of rest. In maintaining this conception Descartes was adhering to the Aristotelian conception of rest as the contrary of motion, as opposed to the new conception of Galileo of rest as the zero of motion, or more precisely, the infinite slowness of motion, a conception which was coming into increasing acceptance – except by Cartesians – and which in the end completely dominated. Descartes' conception of rest as having such a unique status and property is, however, hardly reconcilable with the thoroughgoing relativity of his system. Further, this implies still another

---

[2] cf. 'Dissertatio de causa gravitatis' in *Christiani Hugenii Zuilichemii, dum viveret Zelhemii toparchae, opuscula posthuma* (Amstelodami, 1728).

[3] Descartes' letter of 16 April 1649 to More.

arbitrary introduction of a factor which is not required by his conception of the physical as having extension as its sole essence.

The science of physics steadily advanced in the seventeenth century as the science of bodies in motion, despite the philosophical difficulties in which it was involved, especially those arising from the problems of the composition of the continuum and the relation of the mathematical and the physical, problems which it had been a fundamental aim of Descartes' theory of *res extensa* to resolve. Although Descartes' theory had not succeeded in furnishing a satisfactory solution to the philosophical difficulties facing the new science of physics in the first half of the seventeenth century, it nevertheless constituted a vital contribution to the development, now to be examined, which resulted in a new theory whose singular merit was finally to have provided the solution for which thinkers had been searching. This theory was that of Isaac Newton, and with it the evolution of the modern concept of nature entered its final stage.

Newton's theory was the outcome of a direct line of development from Descartes via Henry More. More was strongly affected by Descartes' thought; in his earlier period he much admired the Cartesian system, becoming however increasingly hostile to it as his own theories matured. From the beginning however More insisted that Descartes' doctrine required modification in two chief and most important respects. First, he maintained, bodies could not be regarded, as they were by Descartes, as being constituted by extension alone. Along with the majority of thinkers More was of the conviction that bodies must be regarded as having hardness and solidity as their essential character. Basically the situation is that More found unacceptable Descartes' distinction and separation of matter from the corporeal, his identifying of matter with mathematical extension alone. More adhered firmly to the conception which we have seen to be basic to the modern concept of nature, namely that matter is the corporeal. Matter, for More, was hard, solid stuff.

Descartes, More maintained, was in error in an even more fundamental respect. This error was not merely in his having regarded extension as the sole essence of matter, but in having regarded extension as confined to matter. In other words, More

held that it is not only matter, the physical, which is extended.
More's theory of extension was the crucial factor in the development which we are investigating.

More attained his theory of extension by a very significant
reversion to the situation of sixteenth-century thought. It is not
the case, as is often supposed, of More's being a mere throw-
back; he was recovering a factor which seventeenth-century
thought had tended to lose sight of.

In the sixteenth century, as we have seen, the gradual change
in the concept of matter had resulted in conceiving it as an
independent existent or substance. But to be an actual existent,
it was held, meant being in act, and this implied having its own
inherent principle of activity. This principle, it was thought,
could only be form, hence the conception of ensouled matter.
Then in the first quarter of the seventeenth century there had
occurred the important development of the conception of matter
as in itself fully actual, devoid of any internal process of change
or becoming. Since soul was a principle of internal change or
becoming, in the new conception matter could not be regarded
as ensouled, and therefore soul was accorded the status of a
separate existent or substance.

This ontological dualism, which had so clearly and forcefully
been represented by Descartes' system, was entirely embraced by
Henry More – it indeed constituted his most important agreement
with Descartes. More maintained, however, that although matter
in the new doctrine could not have any principle of internal
change, of becoming, matter nevertheless still required a principle
of the change of place, that is, locomotion. Descartes, Gassendi,
and others had cast God in the role of the principle of locomotion.
But a transcendent God is in this situation inevitably a *deus ex
machina*. More presented an alternative theory as to the requisite
principle of motion.

The necessary principle of activity of matter or nature cannot
itself be material; hence it can only be immaterial or spiritual.
Also, it is necessary that the principle of activity function from
within matter and not externally – the conception of a transcendent God pushing matter around is quite unacceptable. More
reverted, for this required principle of activity, to the conception
which had been in strong favour in the sixteenth century, namely
that of a *spiritus mundi*. The principle of activity of matter, that

is, of the physical, of nature, More accordingly maintained, is a *spiritus naturae*, a spirit of nature.

In More's doctrine, however, this spirit of nature is not pluralized through contractions to individual souls in each material existent. On the contrary, it remains one and unitary, constituting 'an *All-comprehensive and Eternal Council* for the *ordering* and the *guiding* of the Motion of the *Matter* in the Universe to what is for the *best*'.[4] This *spiritus naturae* does not have the power of thought – intellect pertains to the individual souls, as in Descartes' system – but it is alive (*vitalis*), ordering matter according to certain general laws, constituting the manifestation of God's wisdom. This spirit, in his words, is 'a substance incorporeal, but without Sense and Animadversion, pervading the whole Matter of the Universe, and exercising a Plastical power therein according to the sundry predispositions and occasions in the parts it works upon, raising such *Phenomena* in the World, by directing the parts of the Matter and their Motion, as cannot be resolved into mere Mechanical powers'.[5]

Since this spirit of nature is one and unitary, and since it is the principle of activity within all matter, it follows not only that it must be extended everywhere but also that it must completely penetrate matter. That is, extension pertains not only to matter, as Descartes held, but equally to spirit, and particularly to the spirit of nature. Secondly, while the extension of material bodies involves their necessarily being mutually exclusive of each other – that is, by virtue of their hardness and solidity they cannot interpenetrate – the contrary is the case in respect of spirit. The *spiritus naturae*, in order to be operative within matter as its principle of activity, must necessarily penetrate matter; so that the extension of matter and the extension of spirit are not mutually exclusive.

More recognized that this conception of the extension of spirit led to some most important conclusions when its implications were developed. First, the extension of this *spiritus naturae* must be more general than the extension of corporeal matter. For, since it is one and unitary, the *spiritus naturae* must exist even where there are no bodies. This means, secondly, that in this

[4] Henry More, 'An Antidote against Atheism', Bk II, Ch. II, §7; in *A Collection of Several Philosophical Writings* (London, 1662), p. 43

[5] Henry More, 'The Immortality of the Soul', Bk III, Ch. XII, §1; in ibid., p. 193.

conception of a *spiritus naturae* extending everywhere is to be found a complete solution to the problem of the void, which had hitherto proved so troublesome to the theory of corporeal atomism and in general to the modern doctrine of matter as corporeal substance. This doctrine, More agreed, necessitated the conception of extents, spaces, without bodies in them. Descartes and Aristotle had been right, however, in maintaining that there could be no extents of mere nothingness, that extendedness necessarily implies something extended. It is the universal spirit of nature which extends and fills the spaces in between bodies, More contended.

Thirdly, the spirit of nature, as one and unitary, and extended everywhere, must be not only 'homogeneous and everywhere similar to itself',[6] but also infinite in extent.[7] Fourthly, it follows from its character as unitary, homogeneous, and infinite in extent that this *spiritus naturae* cannot itself move. Fifthly, since it is totally immobile, and everywhere, whatever motion occurs cannot occur to it, but must occur in it. This means that this spirit of nature must constitute the ultimate place, the *locus*, of motion. That is, it is this spirit, which is uniformly everywhere, that is the *spatium vel locus internus*, the space or internal place, the concept of which the century-long debate had shown to be required by the conception of the locomotion, change of place, of bodies.

In this conception of a *spiritus naturae*, therefore, Henry More had a solution not only to the problem of the principle of activity of matter, but also to the problems entailed by the concept of locomotion, problems which had involved Descartes in grave difficulty. For the concept of locomotion or change of place raises the problem of the nature and status of place, and Descartes, as we have seen, was not able on the basis of his theory of *res extensa* to provide a satisfactory solution to this problem. Descartes had agreed that one outcome of the debate over the previous several decades on this issue had been that place must be identified with the dimensional extent or space in which a body is. But Descartes' doctrine had landed him with a complete relativity of place, with the result of a fatal imprecision in the concept of motion. What is fundamentally required, More main-

---

[6] Henry More, *Enchiridium metaphysicum*, Ch. VIII, 9; in *Opera Omnia*, (London, 1679), Vol. II, Pt I, p. 167.
[7] ibid., pp. 167–8.

tained, is a concept of this *locus internus* as itself immovable, so that thereby we can have an absolute referent in terms of which motion as the change of place is to be understood, for only thus can the concept of motion have a precise meaning – by contrast with the imprecision of the concept in Descartes' theory. But to fulfil this requirement it is necessary that the concept of place be distinguished from that of matter in a way which was not possible for Descartes. For Descartes, place was distinguished from body only 'in our mode of conceiving it'.[8] whereas the distinction required needed to be a real one. It was this most important real distinction which More saw his theory of a *spiritus naturae* as able to furnish. For this infinitely extended spirit, because it is 'distinct from matter',[9] and because it is 'One, Simple, and Immovable',[10] necessarily constitutes the place, the *spatium vel locus internus*, in which matter or body is, as both absolute and distinct from body.

Thus Henry More was not only in full accord with the modern conception of the science of physics as the science of motion of bodies – the physical, nature, for him was the corporeal – but his theory furnished what the modern science of physics so much demanded and what had not been provided by other theories, namely a clear and definite concept of place, distinct from and not dependent upon matter, as the requisite basis for the concept of motion as change of place. It was this, as we shall see, which was so very important to Newton.

It has been usual to interpret More as having, in this theory of his, propounded the concept of 'space', albeit under an outmoded metaphysical and theological guise, which is dispensable as so much lumber surviving from an unenlightened age. The consequence of such an interpretation, however, is that the fundamental problem, which More and after him Newton saw to be at issue, is lost sight of.

More's explicit concern was the concept of 'place'[11] and the problem of the ontological status of place. We have seen that in

---

8 See above, p. 192.
9 ibid., Ch. VIII, 9; *Op. om.*, p. 167.
10 ibid.
11 More's text should be taken quite strictly as it stands. To read 'space' for More's 'place' – as has been usual during the last hundred years – is to fall prey to the error of projecting on to earlier thought, conceptions which belong to a later period.

the sixteenth century a number of thinkers had rejected the Aristotelian theory of place which had identified place with boundary surfaces, maintaining that it is to be identified instead with the whole interior volume. To emphasize the contrast with boundary surfaces they spoke of *locus internus*, the 'internal place', which is the dimensional extent, space (in the original sense) occupied by the body. The basic objection to the Aristotelian theory had been that in it place was completely tied to body – there could be no place at all without body – and this involved difficulties for the concept of the motion of bodies, their change from one place to another. Aristotle had correlated place with body because place could not be an independent existent, an *ousia* – the only independent existents or *ousiai* for Aristotle were the natural bodily existents. Descartes, faced with this problem of the ontological status of place, had identified place with *res extensa*. But since his *res extensa* was infinite, Descartes was committed to a thoroughgoing relativity of place, with fatal consequences for the concept of motion.

For More this but emphasized that Scaliger, Telesio, and others, had been correct in insisting on the necessity of place being distinct from body, from the physical. But the unresolved problem was how place could be conceived as thus distinct from body. What sort of existence or being could place have? Aristotle and Descartes were right that place as such could be no independent existent. More saw his theory as providing a complete answer to this problem. Place, as all previous analysis had shown, has the character of extensiveness. Since there could be no independent existent which is extensiveness as such, antecedent thought had identified the extensiveness of place with the extensiveness of the physical existent. The concept of motion, however, necessitated that place be ontologically distinct from the physical existent. The alternative is evident, More maintained: place must be identified with a non-physical, a non-corporeal, extended actual existent. Such an existent is precisely what his theory provided. This existent, because it is infinite and immobile, constitutes the infinite *locus internus* for the motion of all bodies.

The fundamental issue in this which was determinative for More was the problem of the ontological status of place. Place could not be a mere extendedness, distinct from corporeal matter.

Since the extendedness in question must be that of some actual extended existent, the only possibility is that it be the extendedness of a spiritual existent. And when we examine carefully all the characteristics required by such an existent as the ultimate and infinite place, *locus internus*, in which motion occurs, it becomes clear that these are precisely the characteristics which thinkers had found it necessary to ascribe to the Divine. As More himself put this :

'Enumeration of about twenty titles which the metaphysicians attribute to God and which fit the immobile extended [entity] or internal place (locus).

'When we shall have enumerated those names and titles appropriate to it, this infinite, immobile, extended [entity] will appear to be not only something real (as we have just pointed out) but even something Divine (which so certainly is found in nature); this will give us further assurance that it cannot be nothing since that to which so many and such magnificent attributes pertain cannot be nothing. Of this kind are the following, which metaphysicians attribute particularly to the First Being, such as : *One, Simple, Immobile, Eternal, Complete, Independent, Existing in itself, Subsisting by itself, Incorruptible, Necessary, Immense, Uncreated, Uncircumscribed, Incomprehensible, Omnipresent, Incorporeal, All-penetrating, All-embracing, Being by its essence, Actual Being, Pure Act.*

'There are not less than twenty titles by which the Divine Numen is wont to be designated, and which perfectly fit this infinite internal place (*locus*) the existence of which in nature we have demonstrated; omitting moreover that the very Divine Numen is called, by the Cabalists, MAKOM, that is, Place (*locus*). Indeed it would be astonishing and a kind of prodigy if the thing about which so much can be said proved to be a mere nothing.'[12]

What we have here is none other than More's version of Cusanus' doctrine of *explicatio Dei* which had pervaded so much sixteenth-century thought. More's *spiritus naturae* is God *explicans*; that is, it is God existing everywhere, in an actual manifestation of himself. More's position is in this respect quite obviously essentially similar to that of Bruno.

[12] ibid., Ch. VIII, 8. I have used Koyré's translation in his *From the Closed World to the Infinite Universe*, p. 148: cf. More's *Opera Omnia*, p. 167.

Further, through this theory of the *spiritus naturae* conceived as the *explicatio Dei*, More has provided the principle of activity of matter, the agency whereby there is movement, change of place, of bodies. This agency is that of God, but not God as a transcendent being; by his conception of the spirit of nature as *explicatio Dei* More has escaped the objection, which is rightly to be directed against Descartes, Gassendi, and others, of a *deus ex machina*.

This conception of an infinitely extended spirit acting everywhere – its acting constituting the principle of motion of matter, and 'where' it acts constituting the absolute place in which matter is – this conception was fundamental to the final stage in the development of the modern concept of nature with Newton.

18

NEWTON:
THE PHYSICAL EXISTENT AND
THE MATHEMATICAL EXISTENT

That Newton was profoundly influenced by the doctrine of Henry More has been sufficiently amply demonstrated[1] and does not require to be belaboured here. We need only emphasize certain points in this which are of special importance to our inquiry. The grounds for Newton's acceptance of More's doctrine were not primarily religious ones, as has too often been supposed; his basic reasons were philosophical, arising from a keen appreciation of the fundamental problems involved in the conception of the motion of bodies.

The philosophical debates of the century had resulted in a clarification of the issues. The difficulties in which the Cartesian doctrine was involved in respect of place and motion had become more evident. To Newton, More's theory by contrast provided what was requisite for the science of physics as the science of bodies in motion, namely a concept of place in terms of which the concept of motion as the change of place was fully and unambiguously intelligible. Further, and beyond what More had appreciated, Newton saw that this was the basis which was requisite for the science of physics as it had increasingly become, namely the mathematical analysis of the motion of bodies. This mathematical analysis of the motion of bodies is what he explicitly undertook in his *Philosophiae Naturalis Principia Mathematica*, achieving thereby an epoch-making advance in the science of physics. But this was upon a particular new philosophical basis.

Newton's explicit concern in his work was with the 'mathematical principles'; he made no attempt to undertake a 'principles of philosophy' in the manner of Descartes. Indeed on the whole

---

[1] cf. A. Koyré, op. cit., p. 159 and *passim*; E. A. Burtt, *Metaphysical Foundations of Modern Science*, (New York, 1925; 2nd ed. London, 1932); K. Lasswitz, *Geschichte der Atomistik*, Vol. II, p. 536.

he tended rather to fight shy of expressing himself on philosophical principles at all. Yet it is evident to any careful scrutiny of the few statements of a general philosophical kind which he permitted himself that he had deeply pondered philosophical problems – the careful cautious precision of these statements would not have been possible had he not done so. With this realization it should not be entirely a surprise that Newton did in fact make an important philosophical advance on the position of More.

Indirect evidence of this is provided by Joseph Raphson, a Cambridge mathematician and younger contemporary of Newton, who was an enthusiastic proponent of the Newtonian system. Fifteen years after the appearance of Newton's *Principia* Raphson published, in a second edition of his *Analysis Aequationum Universalis*,[2] an appendix entitled 'De Spatio Reali seu Ente Infinito conamen Mathematico Metaphysicum', which is an explication of the philosophical basis of Newton's work. It consists in an exposition of More's doctrine with the Newtonian development of it.

This development consisted basically in adding to the characteristics which More had ascribed to his *spiritus naturae* the mathematical ones, which Descartes and Bruno before him had seen to be all-important, but the significance of which More himself had largely failed to appreciate. The implications of this addition were considerable, indeed effecting a vital change in More's conception of extension.

More had conceived the extension of his *spiritus naturae* as in contrast with the extension of matter; for him there was the extension of spirit and there was the ontologically distinct extension of matter. More did not, however, face the problem of the relation of the mathematical to the physical. He implicitly assumed from Descartes the correlation of the mathematical with the extension of matter, but did not see the difficulty this presented when matter was identified with body, the difficulty which Descartes had avoided by rejecting that identification. More maintained that matter is divisible, but not infinitely so; division terminates in certain indivisible units or atoms of matter, called by him *monades physicae*.[3] But, as we have seen, if body be

---

[2] Second ed., London, 1702.
[3] cf. *Enchiridium metaphysicum*, Ch. 9; *Op. Om.*, Vol. II, Pt 1, p. 174.

intrinsically mathematical it must be infinitely divisible, which means that atoms are impossible.

In More's doctrine the mathematical had not been included among the 'twenty titles' attributed to the spirit of nature. But Raphson the mathematician, like Descartes, was more deeply affected by the logic of the doctrine of Nicolaus Cusanus. Accordingly for him, as for Descartes, extensiveness connoted the mathematical. Since More's spirit of nature was extensive, this implied that it was essentially mathematical. Further, this spirit was not only extended; it was infinitely extended. And here the Cusanian inheritance came fully to the fore in Raphson. Infinity, he pointed out, is the attribute of Divinity. Moreover, infinity connotes perfection, absolute perfection, which can only pertain to God. Raphson's conclusion was that if anything be infinitely extended it could only be divine. This meant that Descartes' doctrine was untenable; the logical outcome of regarding matter as infinitely extended was the pantheism of Spinoza. If this is to be avoided, then infinite extension must be regarded as pertaining to spirit alone.

The position at which Raphson had arrived is significantly similar to that of Bruno, in a number of respects. One of these is that in Raphson's doctrine as in that of Bruno the definite distinction which Cusanus had made between God and the primary extended entity tends to disappear – as indeed it did for More too in his later thought, and also, as we shall see, for Newton. This point is of considerable importance in the further development of Raphson's position, which in this respect is also Newton's.

Because infinity connotes perfection, and extension is infinite, extension is perfect, Raphson argued. This perfection of extension can only be that of the infinite spirit. The doctrine that extension is of the essence of matter must be rejected as implying either pantheism or atheism. Now it is from the infinite as creator that all the finite derives, and whatever limited perfection the finite possesses it does so by virtue of this derivation from the infinite. Thus whatever degree of perfection is attained by our finite discursive thought is by virtue of its derivation from, and indeed imitation of, the infinite divine thought. And likewise whatever perfection there be in material things is by virtue of their derived extension. As Raphson expressed this :

'The infinite amplitude of extension expresses the immense diffusion of being in the First Cause, or its infinite and truly interminate essence. This [amplitude] is that originary *extensive* perfection, which we have found, so imperfectly counterfeited, in matter.

'The infinite (whatever it be) and most perfect energy, everywhere indivisibly the same, which produces and perpetually conserves everything (and which this never-sufficiently-to-be-admired series of *Divine Ratiocination*, that is, the whole fabric of nature, more than sufficiently demonstrates to us *a posteriori*), is this *intensive* perfection, which though [distant from it] by an infinite interval in kind as well as in degree, we, miserable examples of the infinite Archetype, flatter ourselves to imitate.'[4]

The point in this of particular relevance to our inquiry is that extension, and thus the mathematical, does not belong to matter as its essence. The essence of matter is hard solidity.

This ontological distinction and separation of the mathematical from matter or the physical – in contrast to the doctrine of Descartes which had identified them – is the fundamental position of Newton, and it was achieved on the basis displayed by Raphson. Thus Newton, like Bruno and Descartes, held that there is an infinitely extended existent which is one, simple, homogeneous, and mathematical. For Bruno this had been a *meta*-physical existent from which the physical is derived. For Descartes this existent was identical with the physical or matter. For Newton this existent was spiritual, and distinct from the physical or matter.

Let us turn now to display this in Newton's own writing. Newton's interest was primarily scientific. In his great work[5] he restricted himself to the 'mathematical principles' of natural philosophy, without elaborating the natural philosophy itself. He not only avoided as much as he could making philosophical pronouncements, but in this book, as well as in the others, his *System of the World* and his *Opticks*, he abstracted as much as possible from the philosophical in respect of the fundamental

[4] J. Raphson, op. cit., p. 85. I have used Koyré's translation, in his book *From the Closed World to the Infinite Universe*, p. 200.

[5] *Philosophiae Naturalis Principia Mathematica*, 1686. Quotations will be from the revision by Florian Cajori of the Andrew Motte translation and published by the University of California Press, 1962.

concepts he employed, even though, as we shall see, he had a very definite philosophical position regarding them. This abstraction from the philosophical is very evident in the case of the basic concepts which occur in the initial Definitions in the *Principia*, concepts such as 'matter', 'quantity of matter', 'motion', 'quantity of motion', 'force'. This abstraction is equally true of his treatment of the concepts of 'time' and 'space' in the Scholium following the Definitions, though that this is the case has usually been overlooked. Such abstractions were indeed all that were necessary for the purposes of the mathematical principles. When the Definitions, and especially the Scholium, are read in the light of his full philosophy, the fact of the abstraction of the basic concepts becomes very evident. Further, reading the Scholium and Definitions from this standpoint rescues them from the appearance of dogmatic assumptions which in the absence of their philosophical basis they certainly have.

It proved not entirely possible for Newton to avoid some expression of his philosophy; he was driven as a result of controversy surrounding his work to the addition of some philosophical statements in later editions of both the *Principia*[6] and the *Opticks*.[7] In subsequent centuries a dislike of the theological ingredient in Newton's philosophical pronouncements resulted in their being dismissed as irrelevant to his physics. This dismissal is symptomatic of the loss of comprehension of the full extent and depth of the philosophical problems and issues involved in the modern scientific developments, a loss which became widespread in the eighteenth and nineteenth centuries. Newton was very much conversant with the philosophical problems, and the theological component was integral to his solution of them.

One of the philosophical problems which was becoming acute in the latter half of the seventeenth century was that of the principles of motion. The problem was constituted by the fact that since the physical existent was conceived as matter which is fully actual and in itself changeless, it could not, as had the physical existent of Aristotle, have the principle, source, of its motion in itself. Most thinkers, as we have seen, had recourse for the principle of motion of matter to God as a *deus ex machina*. The problem had become acute because of the recognition of the

---

[6] Especially the General Scholium at the end of the *Principia*.
[7] The thirty-one Queries at the end of the *Opticks*.

philosophical unsatisfactoriness of this conception. For Newton the way to an alternative had been pointed out by Henry More.

Newton adhered firmly to the conception of material atomism. As he expressed his view in Query 31 of his *Opticks*:

'All these things being consider'd, it seems probable to me, that God in the Beginning form'd Matter in solid, massy, hard, impenetrable, movable Particles, of such Sizes and Figures, and with such other Properties, and in such Proportion to Space, as most conduced to the End for which he form'd them; and that these primitive Particles being Solids, are incomparably harder than any porous Bodies compounded of them; even so very hard, as never to wear or break in pieces; no ordinary Power being able to divide what God himself made one in the first Creation.'[8]

These particles, as Newton says, are in themselves 'movable', that is, capable of being moved. They themselves do not contain any power or force whereby they could move themselves. The only power or force inherent in them is a *vis inertiae*, a 'power of inactivity'. Now, as Newton observed:

'The *Vis inertiae* is a passive Principle by which Bodies persist in their Motion or Rest, receive Motion in proportion to the Force impressing it, and resist as much as they are resisted. *By this Principle alone there never could have been any Motion in the World. Some other Principle was necessary for putting Bodies into Motion; and now they are in Motion, some other Principle is necessary for conserving the Motion.*'[9]

Considerable evidence was adduced by Newton for the existence of such a principle of motion. It manifested itself in the attractive forces which were to be found everywhere, the forces whereby the planets were maintained in their orbits and the 'Particles of Bodies stick together',[10] in the repulsive forces which together with attractive forces must be operative in the 'Reflexions and Inflexions of the Rays of Light',[11] in fermentation, electricity,

[8] Isaac Newton, *Optiks*, 1704. The edition here used is the fourth, of 1730, in the reprint by Dover Publications, Inc., 1952, p. 400.

[9] ibid., p. 397 (italics added).

[10] ibid., p. 394.

[11] ibid., p. 395.

chemical change, etc. Moreover there is another factor demonstrating the insufficiency of a *vis inertiae* alone, that which subsequently became generalized as the second law of thermodynamics. As Newton stated his argument:

'Seeing therefore the variety of Motion which we find in the World is always decreasing, there is a necessity of conserving and recruiting it by active Principles, such as are the cause of Gravity, by which Planets and Comets keep their Motions in their Orbs, and Bodies acquire great Motion in falling; and the cause of Fermentation, by which the Heart and Blood of Animals are kept in perpetual Motion and Heat; the inward Parts of the Earth are constantly warm'd, and in some places grow very hot; Bodies burn and shine, Mountains take fire, the Caverns of the Earth are blown up, and the Sun continues violently hot and lucid, and warms all things by his Light. For we meet with very little Motion in the World, besides what is owing to these active Principles.[12]

It is clear, therefore:

'that these Particles have not only a *Vis inertiae*, accompanied with such passive Laws of Motion as naturally result from that Force, but also that they are moved by certain active Principles, such as is that of Gravity, and that which causes Fermentation, and the Cohesion of Bodies.'[13]

It is to be noted that Newton says that the bodies 'are moved' by these principles, for these sources of motion are not inherent in the particles or bodies themselves. Newton emphasized the point that the force of gravity could not be inherent in bodies themselves.[14]

[12] ibid., p. 399.   [13] ibid., p. 401.
[14] cf. e.g. his letters to Bentley, in *Works of Richard Bentley*, Vol. 3 (London, 1838), pp. 210, 211–12: 'You sometimes speak of gravity as essential and inherent to matter. Pray, do not ascribe that notion to me. . . .' 'It is inconceivable that inanimate brute matter should, without the mediation of something else, which is not material, operate upon and affect other matter without mutual contact, as it must be, if gravitation, in the sense of Epicurus, be essential and inherent in it. And this is one reason why I desired you would not ascribe innate gravity to me. That gravity should be innate, inherent, and essential to matter, so that one body may act upon another at a distance through a *vacuum*, without the mediation of anything else, by and through which their action and force may be conveyed from one to another, is

Further, it is necessary to appreciate that the various 'active principles' mentioned above were not by Newton conceived as ultimate; for him they were so many manifestations of the truly ultimate principle of motion. For scientific purposes these various manifestations are distinguished and referred to as if they were distinct, it being not strictly necessary for scientific purposes to discuss the question of their foundation :

'But to derive two or three general Principles of Motion from Phaenomena, and afterwards to tell us how the Properties and Actions of all corporeal Things follow from those manifest Principles, would be a very great step in Philosophy, though the Causes of those Principles were not yet discover'd : And therefore I scruple not to propose the Principles of Motion above-mention'd, they being of very general Extent, and leave their Causes to be found out.'[15]

In later editions of his works Newton was driven to add some statement of his conviction respecting these ultimate causes, instead of simply leaving this to 'the consideration of my readers', in the General Scholium at the end of the *Principia* and in Query 31 in the *Opticks*. In the former he stated it as follows :

'Hitherto we have explained the phenomena of the heavens and of our sea by the power of gravity, but have not yet assigned the cause of this power. This is certain, that it must proceed from a cause that penetrates to the very centres of the sun and planets, without suffering the least diminution of its force; that operates not according to the quantity of the surfaces of the particles upon which it acts (as mechanical causes used to do), but according to the quantity of the solid matter which they contain, and propagates its virtue on all sides to immense distances, decreasing always as the inverse square of the distances.'[16]

Newton's theory of the cause of this power is based upon his acceptance of Henry More's doctrine of extension pertaining

to me so great an absurdity, that I believe no man, who has in philosophical matters a competent faculty of thinking, can ever fall into it. Gravity must be caused by an agent acting constantly according to certain laws; but whether this agent be material or immaterial, I have left to the consideration of my readers.'

[15] *Opticks*, pp. 401–2.   [16] op. cit., 546.

fundamentally to spirit, and that this extension is constituted by the activity of spirit pervading everywhere.

'And now we might add something concerning a certain most subtle spirit which pervades and lies hid in all gross bodies; by the force and action of which spirit the particles of bodies attract one another at near distances, and cohere, if contiguous; and electric bodies operate to greater distances, as well repelling as attracting the neighbouring corpuscles; and light is emitted, reflected, refracted, inflected, and heats bodies; and all sensation is excited, and the members of animal bodies move at the command of the will, namely, by the vibrations of this spirit, mutually propagated along the solid filaments of the nerves, from the outward organs of sense to the brain, and from the brain into the muscles.'[17]

The ultimate principle, source, of all motion is thus by Newton explicitly maintained to be spirit, an all-pervading, acting spirit. Henry More, in his doctrine as we have seen, had reverted to the sixteenth-century conception of a *spiritus mundi*. Newton, however, rejected this view. If God is spirit, and if spirit is extended, then the all-pervading spirit which is the principle of motion must be God. Newton expressed it thus in the *Opticks* :[18]

'Also the first Contrivance of these very artificial Parts of Animals, the Eyes, Ears, Brain, Muscles, Heart, Lungs, Midriff, Glands, Larynx, Hands, Wings, swimming Bladders, natural Spectacles, and other Organs of Sense and Motion; and the Instinct of Brutes and Insects, can be the effect of nothing else than the Wisdom and Skill of a powerful ever-living Agent, who being in all Places, is more able by his Will to move the Bodies within his boundless uniform Sensorium, and thereby to form and reform the Parts of the Universe, than we are by our Will to move the Parts of our own Bodies.'

God is necessary as the agent moving the parts of animals since animal bodies are matter, and thus themselves without a source of motion. To continue :

'And yet we are not to consider the World as the Body of God, or the several Parts thereof, as the Parts of God. He is an uniform

[17] ibid., p. 547.   [18] op. cit., pp. 403-4.

Being, void of Organs, Members or Parts, and they are his Creatures subordinate to him, and subservient to his Will; and he is no more the Soul of them, than the Soul of Man is the Soul of the Species of Things carried through the Organs of Sense into the place of its Sensation, where it perceives them by means of its immediate Presence, without the Intervention of any third thing. The Organs of Sense are not for enabling the Soul to perceive the Species of Things in its Sensorium, but only for conveying them thither; and God has no need of such Organs, he being every where present to the Things themselves. And since Space is divisible *in infinitum*, and Matter is not necessarily in all places, it may be also allow'd that God is able to create Particles of Matter of several Sizes and Figures, and in several Proportions to Space, and perhaps of different Densities and Forces, and thereby to vary the Laws of Nature, and make Worlds of several sorts in several Parts of the Universe.'

Thus while his predecessors and contemporaries continued to maintain the medieval conception of God as wholly transcendent, Newton held that since matter is without any principle of motion in itself, God must be conceived as immanent in the universe as its principle of activity. Newton's God is thus not *ex machina*, but integral to the world machine. He has stated his philosophy even more fully in the General Scholium of the *Principia*. His formulation is careful, precise, and compact, and reveals the extent, subtlety, and penetration of his philosophical understanding. The relevant passage is important not only for his conception of God, but also for his conception of space, there being a very close relation between the two conceptions:

'This Being governs all things, not as the soul of the world, but as Lord over all; and on account of his dominion he is wont to be called *Lord God* παντοκράτωρ, or *Universal Ruler*; for *God* is a relative word, and has a respect to servants; and Deity is the dominion of God not over his own body, as those imagine who fancy God to be the soul of the world, but over servants. The Supreme God is a Being eternal, infinite, absolutely perfect; but a being, however perfect, without dominion, cannot be said to be Lord God; for we say, my God, your God, the God of *Israel*, the God of Gods, and Lord of Lords; but we do not say, my

Eternal, your Eternal, the Eternal of *Israel*, the Eternal of Gods; we do not say, my Infinite, or my Perfect: these are titles which have no respect to servants. The word God usually signifies Lord; but every lord is not a God. It is the dominion of a spiritual being which constitutes a God: a true, supreme, or imaginary dominion makes a true, supreme, or imaginary God. And from his true dominion it follows that the true God is a living, intelligent, and powerful Being; and, from his other perfections, that he is supreme, or most perfect. He is eternal and infinite, omnipotent and omniscient; that is, his duration reaches from eternity to eternity; his presence from infinity to infinity; he governs all things, and knows all things that are or can be done.'[19]

In this statement that God's presence reaches 'from infinity to infinity' we see Newton's agreement with the doctrine of Henry More of the all-pervading extension of the divine spirit. It recalls Newton's phrase occurring in the first Scholium of the *Principia*:[20]

'Now no other places are immovable but those that, from infinity to infinity, do all retain the same given position one to another; and upon this account must ever remain unmoved; and do thereby constitute, what I call, immovable space.'

That both the absolute places and the presence of God reach 'from infinity to infinity' is because of the very close connection between them, as Newton makes clear in the immediately succeeding sentence of the General Scholium:

'He is not eternity and infinity, but eternal and infinite; he is not duration or space, but he endures and is present. He endures forever, and is everywhere present; and, by existing always and everywhere, he constitutes duration and space. Since every particle of space is *always*, and every indivisible moment of duration is *everywhere*, certainly the Maker and Lord of all things cannot be *never* and *nowhere*.'

---

[19] op. cit., pp. 544–5.
[20] op. cit., p. 9. In this edition the phrase, 'what I call', which occurs in the edition of 1729, has been omitted. The original reads: '. . . *spatiumque constituunt quod immobile appello.*'

n Newton's doctrine time and space are ontologically from the presence of God: 'by existing always and re, he constitutes duration and space'. Further, when we quate account of the fundamental role of God in Newton's metaphysical scheme, it becomes clear that time and space are not as ontologically distinct and separate from each other as they became to subsequent thinkers who accepted Newton's physics but repudiated his philosophy.

The next point relevant in this is that for Newton, as for More, 'place' is a basic concept. This is clear from the antecedent passage from the first Scholium: it is *places* which 'ever remain unmoved; and do thereby constitute, what I call, immovable space'. In this passage we have an explicit statement by Newton of the meaning of the word 'space' which had become current in his time. We have seen the earlier seventeenth-century meaning of the term as *locus internus*, internal place. For Newton and his contemporaries, such as Leibniz,[21] as well as later thinkers into the eighteenth century,[22] the word 'space' continued to have this connotation, but there was added the further meaning of 'totality of places', that is, the internal extent constituted by the totality of places. In the later eighteenth century this meaning of 'space' became lost when space came to be conceived as itself some kind of existent. It is a serious error, in the last couple of centuries almost universally pervasive, to read this latter conception into Newton.

In the first Scholium Newton was concerned with time and place as the concepts fundamental to motion, in the new seventeenth-century conception of motion as transition from one place to another. Newton saw with great clarity the need for precision respecting the concept of motion. On the basis of the Cartesian and other doctrines which were committed to a relativism, it was impossible unambiguously and finally to say, for example, of a body A that *it* had moved when there was the apparent occurrence of motion. Moreover in these doctrines with place relative, it was impossible precisely to conceive the motion of body A from place x to place y. The only way that precision

---

[21] That this was the conception held by Leibniz will be shown later.

[22] I have shown this to have been Kant's conception in a paper, 'The meaning of "Space" in Kant', in *Proceedings of the Third International Kant Congress* (Dordrecht/Holland, 1972).

could be attainable, Newton maintained, was with a conception of place as absolute, that is, in itself immovable. The totality of places constitutes space, and consequently places, as Newton mentions repeatedly in the first Scholium, are parts of space. The places constitute an immutable order of situation; that is, the places are where they are and cannot themselves move – to talk of places moving is a contradiction :

'As the order of the parts of time is immutable, so also is the order of the parts of space. Suppose those parts to be moved out of their places, and they will be moved (if the expression may be allowed) out of themselves. For times and spaces[23] are, as it were, the places as well of themselves as of all other things. All things are placed in time as to order of succession; and in space as to order of situation. It is from their essence or nature that they are places; and that the primary places of things should be movable, is absurd. These are therefore the absolute places; and translations out of those places, are the only absolute motions.'[24]

This analysis in the first Scholium, as has been pointed out above, is abstract. When we raise the question of the ontological status of place, that is, the question. What *is* place?, then Newton's answer is : place is 'where' God is active. And space is the totality of places because, as Newton said in the preceding passage quoted from the General Scholium, God is *everywhere*. Space or the totality of places is constituted by *where* God is active. Newton therefore, unlike More, does not identify place with the divine spirit : place is 'where' God is active, as time is 'when' God is active. Newton brings out this ontological distinction in the succeeding portion of the General Scholium :

'Every soul that has perception is, though in different times and in different organs of sense and motion, still the same indivisible person. There are given successive parts in duration, coexistent parts in space, but neither the one nor the other in the person of a man, or his thinking principle; and much less can they be found in the thinking substance of God.'[25]

[23] The plural 'spaces' here makes it clear that the word is being used in the sense of *locus internus*, internal *place*.
[24] op. cit., p. 8.   [25] ibid., p. 545.

The 'where' and 'when' of God's activity are not *parts* of God; God is not a being who can have 'parts'. God is act, and every acting, Newton maintains, following More, has a locus. But the loci of the activity are not to be identified with the activity; they merely manifest the extensive structure of the activity. In the case of God that activity is always and everywhere, and so space and time manifest the infinite structure of God's activity in distinction from God as such :

'God is the same God, always and everywhere. He is omnipresent not *virtually* only, but also *substantially*; for virtue cannot subsist without substance. In him are all things contained and moved; yet neither affects the other : God suffers nothing from the motion of bodies; bodies find no resistance from the omnipresence of God. It is allowed by all that the Supreme God exists necessarily; and by the same necessity he exists *always* and *everywhere*.'[26]

This last conclusion only holds with the premise that the activity of God is extensive, a premise which Leibniz, in his controversy with Clarke, refused to admit.

There are two important points to be noted about this ontological distinction Newton made between God and space. The first is that this distinction does not imply that space or place is some kind of separate existent – which it became for subsequent thinkers who accepted Newton's physics but rejected the basis upon which he had constructed it. Repudiating Newton's theology in particular, these thinkers, without providing the requisite philosophical justification, assumed space as some kind of actual, but of course non-material, existent. It was this latter conception which so quickly became mistaken for Newton's doctrine and which Leibniz and Kant rejected as philosophically untenable.[27] This philosophical criticism failed to stem the increasingly rapid acceptance of this supposedly Newtonian conception of space, secured by the overwhelming success of Newton's physics and a concomitant decline of interest in the philosophical issues involved in physics.

[26] ibid.
[27] cf. e.g. Leibniz's correspondence with Clarke, and Kant's Inaugural Dissertation, *De mundi sensibilis*, in which he referred to this conception as an 'empty figment of reason' (§ 15, D).

The second point to be noted about Newton's conception – and again it is different from what later became accepted as the 'Newtonian' conception of space – is that according to his theory it is not space which is extended but it is God who is extended. As is clear from the last quotation from Newton, he saw clearly that attributes cannot exist without substances, and extension is an attribute. Since for him space is not a substantial existent, extension could not be an attribute of space. The only relevant substantial existent here is God, and extension is thus to be ascribed to God. In Newton's doctrine, God's presence reaches from infinity to infinity, that is, he is everywhere present, because everywhere active. Place is 'where' God is active, and space or the totality of places constitutes the abstract structure of the where of God's activity.

Newton's doctrine and its implications can now most conveniently be further elaborated by a contrast with the positions of Bruno and Descartes. Both these thinkers held that there is an infinitely extended existent which is one, simple, homogeneous, and mathematical. For Bruno it was a metaphysical existent, the universe, from which the physical, matter, is derived by contraction. Descartes identified the infinitely extended existent with the physical or matter. Newton maintained that the infinitely extended existent is God.

All three thinkers were agreed that this infinite extension, qua extension, is mathematical. Further, they were all three agreed that it is entailed in the conception of an infinite continuous mathematical extendedness that, as Bruno put it, it 'has all the species of figures and dimensions, and because it has them all, it has none', in other words, that it is dimensional but in itself without any specific dimensions, that it is from this general mathematical dimensionality that all specific dimensions derive.

Newton's position, however, differs significantly from those of the other two thinkers in respect of the manner of this derivation. For Bruno the dimensional features of bodies, that is, the physical, derive by virtue of bodies being contractions to individuality of the infinite mathematical entity. Thereby the physical is itself intrinsically mathematical. But this involves a fatal difficulty, as we have seen : if bodies be essentially mathematical they must be infinitely divisible, and this contradicts the conception of bodies maintained by Bruno as ultimately atomic. Descartes had sought to avoid this whole difficulty respecting the divisibility of bodies by providing for the derivation of the mathematical features of bodies in a different way. In his doctrine this derivation is the function of motion. This conception, however, had landed Descartes' system in insuperable incoherence and also imprecision in regard to the concept of motion.

Now Newton maintained, with the majority of thinkers and against Descartes, that matter or the physical is corporeal. But he saw that the extensiveness and thereby mathematical character of bodies cannot belong to them intrinsically and essentially as matter, that is, as hard, solid, massy, impenetrable stuff. For if it were the case that bodies were intrinsically mathematical they would of necessity be divisible *in infinitum*, which would imply that material bodies would be impossible. Newton, therefore, like Descartes, has the mathematical character of bodies not intrinsic to them but derivative, and for the same reason as Descartes does, namely in order to meet the implications of the continuity of extensiveness. But Newton, following Henry More, saw a new way of providing for this derivation, a way which was exempt from the difficulties besetting his predecessors.

The particular appeal of More's system to Newton, as we have indicated earlier, is that it provided a concept of place in terms of which the concept of motion as the change of place was fully and unambiguously intelligible. Newton's view, as we have seen, is accordingly that the activity of the infinitely extended mathematical entity, God, constitutes the places in which bodies are. It is Newton's conception that it is by virtue of their occupation of places that bodies derive their actual dimensions. In other words, God's activity as continuously everywhere is the essence of the mathematical. Space or the totality of places as 'where' this activity is, constitutes the manifestation of the extensive structure of this activity. The particular dimensions of bodies are derived by their occupation of particular places. It is in this way, derivatively, that bodies have an extensive, mathematical character. And because this mathematical character of bodies is derivative and not belonging to their essence as solid matter, they are not infinitely divisible. This is accordingly why there can be atoms.

This conception of an independent mathematical existent from which dimensions derive to bodies, to the physical, Newton further saw, gives the foundation for measurement which is requisite for mathematical physics, that is, for the mathematical analysis of the motion of bodies. Bodies are measurable because of the mathematical character they derive by their occupation of places in the infinite mathematical extension; and motion is measurable because the places, as immobile, are absolute referents in terms of which it can be determined that there is movement from one absolute place to another, which accordingly enables this movement to be exactly measured. And ultimately measurement is possible at all because the places constitute an absolute order of situation which is the mathematical.

In Newton's doctrine, therefore, there are not two extensivenesses as in More's, the extensiveness of spirit and the quite separate extensiveness of matter; for Newton there is one fundamental infinite mathematical extensiveness, from which the particular, finite, mathematical extensive features derive to bodies, that is, to matter, the physical. The similarity of Newton's position to that of Descartes in this respect is indeed close. They both have an ultimate infinitely extended mathematical entity from which the particular finite mathematical features of bodies are derived. The basic difference between them is that whereas Descartes had identified the ultimate extended entity with the physical, with matter, Newton separated it from matter, the physical, identifying matter with body, and regarding the infinitely extended existent as spiritual.

It has been usual to view Newton's following Henry More as being philosophically gratuitous, an aberration due to a mystical and theosophical temperament. The injustice thereby done to Newton's capacity as a philosophical thinker is of slight consequence compared with the loss of appreciation of Newton's solutions to a number of philosophical issues and of the significance of those solutions. Another problem which is in this way lost sight of, one which is of great importance in the whole modern development, is that of the infinite.

By regarding the infinitely extended entity as spiritual Newton, in common with More, was able to resolve a difficulty which troubled Descartes. The problem at issue here was that of whether an actual infinite is possible. Descartes had ascribed the fundamental character of extension to matter, and was thereby up against this problem, which he sought to meet by regarding the extended existent as 'indefinite' or 'interminate' rather than 'infinite'. Since for Newton the ultimate extended entity is God, the attribution of 'infinity' was to be regarded as entirely appropriate. Moreover, thereby the ambiguity in which Descartes had been landed is avoided : for when Descartes was dealing with his extended entity as a 'being', that is, considering it in respect of its ontological status, he regarded it as 'indefinite', but when he was considering it in respect of its essential character as mathematical, he had perforce to regard it as 'infinite'. Newton's extended entity is infinite both as divine and as mathematical.

The significance of Newton's position is much more than only the achievement of greater consistency. It is that Newton is able on its basis to meet the important Aristotelian argument that an infinitely extended actual existent is impossible, an argument which Descartes had attempted to evade by regarding res extensa as only 'indefinite', not 'infinite', and which most thinkers after Kepler[28] had tended largely to ignore. The answer of Newton's position to the Aristotelian argument is that an infinitely extended actual existent is possible if this existent be spiritual, not physical. It is to be noted that Newton's followers, who conceived space as an infinitely extended actual existent, do not have Newton's counter to the Aristotelian argument; for in that later view space is neither spiritual nor divine.

It is to be noted that Newton's position is a new one, and that it is the culmination of the long slow development of the concept of infinity which we investigated in Part I. Aristotle had shown conclusively that the infinite or infinity could not pertain to physical actuality, arguing on the contrary that it could pertain only to potentiality, to the mathematical. The outcome of the medieval development had been the doctrine that the infinite pertains to God, that infinity is that which is unique to divinity, to the creator, to the source and origin of physical actuality. Then came the crucial contribution of Cusanus with his doctrine of the world as explicatio Dei, that God had particularly chosen to manifest his absolute infinity in mathematical extensiveness. By this doctrine was brought together, what in the medieval tradition had been kept completely apart, namely infinity as pertaining to God and infinity as pertaining to mathematics. Now the Cusanian doctrine of explicatio Dei, which had pervaded so

28 See above, pp. 91–3.

much of the seminal thought of the sixteenth and seventeenth centuries, found its final outcome in Newton. Cusanus still retained something of the antecedent gap between the divine infinity and the mathematical infinity, for the mathematical extended is but a manifestation of the unextended divine infinity. Newton's position identifies the divine and the mathematical infinite, as Raphson made clear.

19

THE MODERN CONCEPTION OF
NATURE

The modern conception of nature, of the physical universe, that which has dominated down to our own time, was not Newton's but a post-Newtonian development, emerging in the course of the eighteenth century. It was not the creation of any one particular thinker; it was rather the product of a conflation of the great systems of the seventeenth century, chiefly the Cartesian, the Newtonian, and the Leibnizian, through the elimination of their incompatible features and those, such as Newton's theology and Leibniz's doctrine of pre-established harmony, which were found especially hard to accept.

A very considerable contribution to this conflation, indeed without which it would not have been possible, was the rapid loss in the eighteenth century of an adequate grasp of the fundamental issues of the philosophy of nature. Kant was the last great thinker to possess such an understanding, but after him, and in some measure the product of his critical philosophy, that understanding tended increasingly to dwindle.

Without doubt the major factor in this philosophical decline was the increasing success of the Newtonian physics. Consequently, as Whitehead has observed: 'Having regard to this triumph, can we wonder that scientists placed their ultimate principles upon a materialistic basis, and thereafter ceased to worry about philosophy?'[1] And philosophers, capitulating to this belief that the fundamental problems of natural philosophy had been finally resolved, and that the elaboration of detailed knowledge in this field could safely be left to specialists (who came to be known as 'scientists', from 'science', 'knowledge'), turned all their attention to the mental or spiritual which, as a consequence of the

---

[1] A. N. Whitehead, *Science and the Modern World* (Cambridge, 1926), p. 61; (New York, 1925), p. 71. Henceforth the pagination of the New York edition will be in square brackets.

earlier seventeenth-century identification of the physical with matter conceived as substance, had come to have the status of an independent substantial existent. Hume set out explicitly to do for human nature what Newton had done for material nature.[2] The two domains, natural philosophy and mental philosophy were thus disastrously separated – disastrously for both. From the standpoint of our present interest the immediate consequence was the gradual emergence, increasingly freed from philosophical criticism, of a new conception of nature. It will not be necessary for our purposes to trace in any detail the process of emergence of this new conception; it will suffice to concentrate on its general features.

Towards the end of the seventeenth century the dominant Cartesian natural philosophy began giving way to the Newtonian. Preparing the ground for this there had been, prior to the advent of Newton's work, a considerable divergence from Descartes among his followers on certain basic doctrines. Among the most important was the abandonment, by thinkers such as Huygens, Cordemoy, Jakob and Johann Bernoulli, Hartsoeker, of Descartes' one *res extensa* and his conception of bodies as derivative, going over instead to Gassendi's conception of solid atomic bodies as matter, as the physical. This brought these Cartesians in this respect into accord with Newton. Thus was facilitated too the abandonment of the Cartesian theory of vortices, as for example by Huygens, upon reading Newton's *Principia*.

This conception of the physical existent as matter, conceived in the Gassendist way as impenetrable, solid atomic bodies, came increasingly into general acceptance, despite the Leibnizian criticism – which we shall have occasion to consider later, when we examine in some detail the philosophical implications of this conception of the physical.

The most significant development, which was particularly the outcome of a conflation of Cartesian and Newtonian conceptions, was that of a new concept of space, a concept which was basic to the new conception of nature and which more than any other specially characterizes it. Newton's conception of space was widely

---

[2] David Hume, *Treatise of Human Nature* (London, 1739), I, I, 4. cf. Charles W. Hendel's introduction, 'The Philosophy of Hume', p. xii of his edition of *Hume Selections* (New York, 1927, 1955), and p. 159 of C. W. Hendel's *Studies in the Philosophy of David Hume* (New York, 1963).

misunderstood even in his lifetime, as is amply evidenced by the contemporary controversies, one of the most enlightening of which was that between Newton's friend Samuel Clarke[3] and Leibniz. The fundamental reason for the failure to grasp Newton's concept of space was Newton's doctrine, derived from More, of God as extended. To most thinkers this seemed so erroneous a doctrine that they did not credit it or take it seriously; in respect of this Newton seemed to them philosophically naïve. Thus they had an obstacle to the entertainment of the concept of space as derivative, the place of God's activity, without this place being any kind of existent in itself. To his critics it seemed that the only possible interpretations of Newton's doctrine were either that space is an attribute of God, or that space is itself a self-subsistent existent, a creature of God. Leibniz attacked both these alternatives, and demonstrated conclusively their untenability. That he did not convince Clarke was because neither of the conceptions which he attacked were the doctrine of Newton. As Clarke said in his Fifth Reply to Leibniz:

'God does not exist In Space, and In Time; but His Existence causes Space and Time. And when, according to the Analogy of vulgar Speech we say that he exists in All Space and in All Time; the Words mean only that he is Omnipresent and Eternal, that is, that Boundless Space and Time are necessary Consequences of his Existence; and not, that Space and Time are Beings distinct from him, and IN which he exists'.[4]

It is desirable to elaborate here on the connotation of the word 'space' as understood by both protagonists in this debate, which was also the general understanding of the term at that time; this is desirable in order adequately to grasp the difference in the concept which came into existence in the eighteenth century. It is important to appreciate that the seventeenth-century connotation of the word 'space' is complex, the outcome of the century-long development which we investigated earlier in this Part.[5] The

---

[3] It seems to me that Koyré is correct in maintaining that Newton saw and approved Clarke's replies to Leibniz; cf. Koyré, op. cit., note 3 to Ch. XI, pp. 300–1.

[4] In G. W. Leibniz, *Die philosophischen Schriften*, Ed. C. J. Gerhardt (Berlin, 1875–90, Hildesheim, 1965), Vol. VII, p. 427. All succeeding references to this edition will be abbreviated to 'G'.

[5] See above, Ch. 13 especially pp. 160–63.

primary and original meaning of the word is 'extent, stretch, interval', and this continued to be a basic ingredient in the connotation. In the latter sixteenth century there developed the additional connotation of the extent in which body is or might be as the *locus internus*, the internal place of body. This addition of 'place' (in the new conception of place as opposed to the Aristotelian) to the original meaning of 'extent' was that which constituted the seventeenth-century connotation of the term 'space', with an increasing tendency to use the term in the sense of extended place in general or in totality. When seventeenth-century texts are read with care it is seen that the term is used with this connotation, but also in more restricted senses, involving only part of the whole connotation; for example, sometimes with only the original sense of 'extent', sometimes as 'internal place' and sometimes as simply 'place' alone.

Newton's writing certainly exemplifies all these senses, and in the previous chapter we have seen that in the first Scholium of the *Principia* he explicitly brought out the meaning of space as the totality of places.[6] Leibniz also felt himself compelled to explicate this meaning, in his Fifth Letter to Clarke:

'to give a kind of definition, *place* is that which we say is the same to *A* and to *B*, when the relation of the coexistence of *B*, with *C, E, F, G*, etc., agrees perfectly with the relation of the coexistence which *A* had with the same *C, E, F, G*, etc., supposing there has been no cause of change in *C, E, F, G*, etc. It might be said also, without entering into any further particularity, that place is that which is the same in different moments to different existent things when their relations of coexistence with certain other existents which are supposed to continue fixed from one of those moments to the other agree entirely together. And *fixed existents* are those in which there has been no cause of any change of the order of their coexistence with others, or (which is the same thing) in which there has been no motion. Lastly, *space* is that which results from places taken together.[7]

Leibniz's failure to understand Newton's conception of space is in a certain respect curious since their conceptions were not

6 cf. above, pp. 218ff.
7 §47; Loemker 703, G. VII., 400.

so much different from each other as they were from the conceptions which Leibniz criticized. Also Clarke failed to see this, and it was their different conception of God which was responsible for their failure. Completely rejecting the conception of space as itself some kind of actual existent, Leibniz maintained that 'space is nothing but the order of existence of things possible at the same time',[8] in other words, that 'Space is the order of coexisting things'.[9] Now this order is not an attribute of things, but it exists, and can only exist, *with reference to* things. As Leibniz put it in his Third Letter to Clarke: 'space is nothing else but that order or relation, and is nothing at all without bodies but the possibility of placing them'.[10] In Leibniz's view space, or place, 'is nothing at all without bodies', and in Newton's doctrine analogously space, or place, is nothing at all without God, that is, without the presence of God. In other words, for Newton space is neither a self-existent thing nor an attribute of God; it exists *with reference to* the presence of God; as I had put it earlier, it is the 'where' of God's activity.

If Leibniz missed this conception, despite Clarke's efforts, it is not surprising that Newton's conception failed to be understood by all but a very few. Newton's conception of God not being accepted by many, the conception of space as an attribute of God was rejected, and the other alternative, that of space as a self-subsistent existent was gradually and increasingly accepted, despite the criticism of this conception by Leibniz and his followers, and also by Kant.

Strongly contributing to the acceptance of this conception of space as a self-subsistent existent was the influence of Descartes' conception of *res extensa*. The divergence from Descartes by his followers in respect of this doctrine, which we noted above, consisted in their identifying atomic bodies as material substance, as the physical. But the virtues of Descartes' conception of a one, infinite, mathematical extended, were not lightly to be given up. These could all be retained if the conception of this infinite mathematical extended conceived as (supposedly Newtonian) space be accepted. Most important in this conflation of Newton and Des-

---

[8] Leibniz's letter to De Volder, June 30, 1704; Loemker, p. 536, G. II, 269.
[9] Leibniz, *Mathematische Schriften*, Ed. C. J. Gerhardt (Berlin & Halle, 1849–55), hereafter cited as 'GM', Vol. VII, p. 17; Loemker, p. 666.
[10] §5; Loemker, p. 682, G. VII, 364.

cartes, was the ultimate mathematical character thereby involved in this new conception of space. In this new conception, as in Newton's doctrine, but not as in Descartes', the mathematical is separate from the physical. Accordingly the concept of material atoms is rescued from the problem constituted by the infinite divisibility of continuous magnitudes; it is space which is an infinitely extended continuum, and which is infinitely divisible. Matter derives dimensionality and measureability by its occupation of space, and thus matter is exempted from infinite divisibility. In this respect the advantage of Newton's doctrine was preserved.

Moreover, this new conception of space was interpretable as in full accord with Newton's first Scholium. This self-subsistent existent space is immutable and changeless, constituting the absolute places of things. With this was therefore retained all that Newton had secured in regard to the intelligibility of the concept of motion.

It is to be noted that this new conception inverts the relative status of space and place which they had in Newton's doctrine. Newton had maintained that place is derivative from God's activity, from God's presence, as the 'where' of God's activity, and space is the totality of places since God's presence is 'everywhere'. That is, in Newton's doctrine place is the fundamental concept and space is derivative. In the new eighteenth-century doctrine space supplants God – Laplace's statement that God is an unnecessary hypothesis is an epitomization of this new position – and place becomes the derivative. It is not only in Newton's doctrine that place is a fundamental concept in the philosophy of nature; we have seen that it was so all the way back to Aristotle. The new doctrine is thus an inversion of all antecendent thought. As a consequence the concept of place fell into the background; indeed in the new doctrine it virtually disappeared, the concept of a geometrical point functioning in its stead. Its elimination as a fundamental concept is manifested too in the scholarship of the last century and a half failing almost entirely to recognize the significance of the status of place in the antecedent philosophy of nature, with the result that 'place' is read as meaning 'space',[11] and indeed even in commentaries on and

11 cf. e.g., Max Jammer, *Concepts of Space: the History of the Theories of Space in Physics* (Harvard, 1954), Chs 1–3; Werner Gent, *Die Philosophie des Raumes und der*

translations of Aristotle *topos*, 'place', is rendered as 'space'.[12] Nevertheless, despite this deposition of the concept of place, it has not become wholly lost; it persists, for the most part unrecognized, as a subordinate ingredient in the connotation of the term 'space', evidenced by the fact that in many occasions of the contemporary use of the term it is with the meaning of 'place'.

An important implication of the new concept of space, which became explicitly accepted in the eighteenth century, was that geometry is to be regarded as the science of space – and not, as the etymology of the word implies, and as had been the explicit Aristotelian view, the science of the extensive features of bodies. In this new conception of geometry the Cartesian inheritance is evident; in Descartes' doctrine, as we noted earlier,[13] pure geometry was the knowledge of the essence of *res extensa*. This new conception of geometry was profoundly affected by the development of non-Euclidean geometries in the nineteenth century.

Another advantage of this new concept of space as an infinitely extended, but non-material existent, is that it could be substituted for Gassendi's void, and the earlier objections to Gassendi's void, thereby could be overcome namely that an extended nothing is a contradiction; while retaining all which Gassendi sought to have by his concept of a void, as a requisite for the occurrence of motion, and as the principle of discreteness and plurality.

There was one further fundamental development from seventeenth-century thought to complete the modern conception of nature. It had been very clear to the seventeenth-century thinkers, as we have seen, that matter, conceived as substance, fully actual and in itself changeless, necessarily was without an inherent principle of motion. The recognition of this had led almost all thinkers to recourse to God as the principle, source, of motion of matter. This doctrine had also been a fundamental feature of Newton's philosophy of nature.

Leibniz rejected this doctrine as maintained by all his contem-

---

Zeit: *Historische, Kritische und Analytische Untersuchengen* (Hildesheim, 1962), esp. pp. 76–83; Jonas Cohn, *Geschichte des Unendlichkeitsproblems im Abendländischen Denken bis Kant* (Darmstadt, 1960), pp. 114ff.; Markus Fierz, 'Uber den Ursprung und die Beudeutung der Lehre Isaac Newtons vom absoluten Raum' in *Gesnerus*, Vol. XI, facs. 3/4, 1954, sec. 2, pp. 75–85.

[12] cf. e.g., G. S. Kirk and J. E. Raven, op. cit., pp. 297, 407–8; K. Lasswitz, op. cit., Vol. I, p. 106; E. Zeller, op. cit., II, II, p. 398; W. Gent, op. cit., pp. 9ff.

[13] See above, p. 195.

poraries and predecessors as involving the fallacy of a *deus ex machina*.[14] He insisted that it was essential to find the principle of motion within matter, and this led him to a different conception of matter. We shall examine Leibniz's alternative conception subsequently; it will not be necessary to discuss it in detail now. What is immediately relevant is the consequence of Leibniz's thought for the eighteenth-century development which we are investigating. Leibniz's impact was less directly philosophical than scientific.

Modern physics had been firmly established by Galileo as the science of the motion of bodies. In this the concept of motion was fundamental, and it was a new concept of motion radically different from the Aristotelian. In the seventeenth-century concept of material substance, matter is fully actual, without any kind of internal change or becoming. That is, it involved no potentiality. The new concept eliminated the concept of potentiality entirely from the physical.

Consequently motion could not be conceived, as by Aristotle, as a process of transition from potentiality to actuality.[15] Motion was conceived as nothing but the transition of a body from one place to another. The problem then arose as to the fundamental nature of this motion, of its ultimate analysis, and two alternatives were adopted in the seventeenth century. Their reconciliation was achieved in the eighteenth century in a new theory of matter.

The problem was that with matter as a fully actual substance, conceived essentially as simply extended with Descartes, or as solid stuff with Gassendi and most other thinkers including Newton, it was impossible that matter could have the source of motion within it; in itself, as Newton said, matter is merely 'movable'.

One alternative, of which the chief proponents were Galileo and Huygens, was to accord motion a quasi-independent, absolute or ultimate status. Bodies just are in motion. There are

14 Typical of the many attacks of Leibniz on this doctrine is the following statement in a letter to De Volder (G., II, 195; Loemker, p. 523): '. . . the mind is surely gradually freed from the false notions of matter, motion, and corporeal substance which are held popularly and by the Cartesians, when it comes to understand that the rules of force and action cannot be derived from these notions and that we must either take refuge in a *deus ex machina* or hold that there is something higher in bodies themselves.'
15 See above, pp. 108–11.

changes in motion, but the totality of motion remains constant. With this as a presupposition a complete mathematical analysis of motion was possible, and achieved. With Huygens the high point was reached of physics as a pure kinetics.

Other thinkers, however, were more alive to the question of the philosophical tenability of this conception. Motion is not itself a kind of existent; motion is the motion of something, as Aristotle had insisted. In the prevailing conception of the seventeenth century, it was the motion of bodies. This entailed that motion is essentially related to or essentially pertains to bodies. But since it can pertain to material bodies only as movable, that is, as capable of motion and not as moving themselves, the question has to be raised as to their actual motion, that is to say, how they come to be in motion, what is the cause of their motion, the source of the motion.

This is an issue not only on the general philosophical plane; it became acute too at the physical level in respect of the question of the interaction of bodies in motion. The crucial case is that of two bodies of equivalent mass and equivalent velocity moving straight towards each other on a plane even with their centres of gravity. What would happen upon their impact? Newton was quite clear that they would both stop dead, that is, lose their motion entirely:

'For Bodies which are either absolutely hard, or so soft as to be void of Elasticity, will not rebound from one another. Impenetrability makes them only stop. If two equal Bodies meet directly *in vacuo*, they will by the Laws of Motion stop where they meet, and lose all their Motion, and remain in rest. . . .'[16]

The plain empirical fact, however, acknowledged by all three, Newton, Huygens, and Leibniz, is that the bodies will rebound upon impact. These three thinkers drew very different conclusions from this fact. Huygens maintained that this proved his conception of motion – expressed in physics as the law of the constancy of energy; motion is not dependent upon the nature of bodies, so that their being absolutely hard and inelastic will not prohibit their rebound. Newton, with greater philosophical perspicacity, saw this to be untenable. He concluded that the

16 *Opticks*, p. 398.

only possible explanation of the rebound is that there must be 'active Principles',[17] and this means ultimately God's activity. Leibniz regarded both these positions as untenable. Both views accepted the conception of matter as absolute solidity. The above-mentioned empirical fact, to Leibniz, demonstrated that this conception of matter was in error, and that a different conception was requisite, for with that conception of matter there could be no other result than Newton had stated, namely the complete loss of motion.

Leibniz was fully in agreement with Newton in his insistence on some 'active principle' as the source of motion. To look for this active principle wholly outside body or matter, however, Leibniz argued, is to commit the fallacy of a *deus ex machina*. The active principle must be found within matter. But this is possible only with a different conception of matter or body from that which was then current, in either the Cartesian or the atomistic schools.

To distinguish his physics, based on his new theory of matter, from the kinetic physics of Huygens and Newton and the phoronomic physics of Descartes, Leibniz called his a 'dynamics'. By this term he intended to signify that the *dynamis*, 'power', or 'force', is in bodies. This conception was taken over in the eighteenth century, but with a significant difference, as we shall see.

The new conception of matter and body which Leibniz introduced involved a divergence from antecedent theories in a number of fundamental respects. The atomistic theory, from Basso and Gassendi up to Huygens and Newton, had identified the physical substance with matter conceived as bodily; physical substance is matter is body. Descartes on the other hand had identified the physical substance with matter, but he conceived matter as pure extension, and body as derivative by motion. That is, Descartes did not identify matter and body, as was done in the atomistic theory. A different alternative was introduced by the Cartesian, Cordemoy.[18] Rejecting Descartes' one *res extensa*, and accepting atomism as fundamental, he conceived the atoms as the physical substances and as being extended, solid bodies. But matter for him was derivative, constituted by an aggregation of atoms. Leibniz was influenced by Cordemoy's conception, but he

17 ibid., p. 399.
18 cf. Lasswitz, op. cit., Vol. II, pp. 415–21.

saw that it retained all the difficulties of material atomism. Leibniz went along with the anti-Cartesian trend in accepting atoms as the fundamental physical existents, as substances, but he introduced a radically different conception of atoms. His atoms – which he came to call 'monads' – are non-extensive, non-bodily, and non-material; he identified them rather with the *res cogitantes* of Descartes. In Leibniz's new doctrine extension, body, and matter are conceived as derivative from the atomic substances, in the way in which matter was derivative for Cordemoy, that is by being constituted by aggregations of atoms.[19] Thus in Leibniz's conception matter is identified with extended body, but body and matter are not substance.

The radical novelty of the Leibnizian doctrine made it difficult to accept and, further, the increasing success of the Newtonian science, based upon the conception of material bodily atoms, militated strongly against it. Also Leibniz's doctrine of pre-established harmony was felt to strain credibility too greatly.

One aspect of Leibniz's doctrine did, however, prove acceptable and influential. This was his conception of atomic substances as active, as agents, and thus as the sources of motion. Within a couple of generations there occurred a conflation of the Leibnizian conception of active substantial atoms with the older theory of material bodily atoms. The essential characteristics of material atoms as solid extended bodies were retained in the new eighteenth-century conception of physical substance, and to these were added the characteristic of activity, of agency. But it was not a spiritual activity, as with Leibniz. A new conception of activity was the product of the influence of Newton's insistence on active principles combined with Newton's theory of gravitation. Both Leibniz and Newton had spoken of the active principles as 'forces', and unheeding of Newton's insistence that it is inadmissible to ascribe gravitational forces to bodies as inherent properties of bodies, it is precisely this ascription which was made, even in Newton's lifetime. It was erroneously supposed that Newton was swayed by theological considerations in refusing to make this ascription; the sound philosophical reasons, grounded in the conception of material substance, which in fact determined

---

[19] 'A body is an aggregate of substances; it is not, properly speaking, one substance' (Loemker, p. 360). 'But since only simple things are true things . . . the rest are beings by aggregation' (Loemker, p. 531).

Newton's view, were ignored. Thus by this arbitrary combination of Leibnizian and Newtonian conceptions there arose the eighteenth-century theory of 'dynamic' matter – a conception which was, however, not accepted by the pre-critical Kant in his 'physical monadology'.[20] This theory of matter had the additional advantage of being able to accommodate the physical concept of 'energy', and thus to be in consonance with the Galileo-Huygens conception of the ultimacy of motion.

There was one final ultimate ingredient in the modern conception of nature, the concept of absolute time which, like space, was conceived as some kind of independent existent, independent that is from the other ultimates, matter, motion, and space. It is worth noting that in respect of this concept of time too there is a significant difference from the Newtonian conception. Newton accorded only matter an independent status, as the physical existent, as substance. For him neither space nor time were independent existents; the concepts were abstract derivatives as the 'where' and 'when' of God's activity. And since God is one, space and time are not separate from each other; for as Newton said in the General Scholium, since God necessarily 'exists *always* and *everywhere*', therefore 'every particle of space is *always*, and every indivisible moment of duration is *everywhere*'.

There is one important respect in which the eighteenth-century scheme is unclear in comparison with the Newtonian. For Newton the physical is matter; that is to say, the only physical existents were the material atoms. Thus for Newton the physical world is unambiguously constituted by the plurality of material atoms. But the eighteenth-century scheme admits space and time as independent existents. What kind of existents are they? Are they also to be regarded as 'physical'? – for they were not regarded as mental or spiritual. This is one reason why the term 'nature' ceased after the later eighteenth century to have any particular philosophical significance, and 'physical' came to be accepted as the adjective from 'physics', understood as the science of motion of bodies, while the older sense, in which I have been using the word, went almost completely out of currency.

In regard to space and time twentieth-century thought, with Minkowski and Einstein, has brought together again what in the

20 We shall see in Ch. 22 below that Kant's physical monads were not conceived as 'material'.

eighteenth century had been put asunder. This recent thought has also brought matter and motion into closer relation with space and time than that which had been accorded them in the scheme which dominated in the two previous centuries. But what precisely is the relation between them is by no means yet clear. In some interpretations of twentieth-century developments space-time seems to be regarded as fundamental, and matter, now shorn of its characteristic as solid stuff, and combined with the conception of an energy field, seems to be accorded a somewhat subordinate or derivative status – Einstein has noted that his position has certain important analogies to that of Descartes.

Philosophically, however, such interpretations remain obscure. What precisely is here being identified as the physical existent, and how is it being conceived? It is essential to pursue the problem in terms of the ultimate philosophical issues involved. To this we shall turn in the next Part.

PART IV

Prolegomena to a new concept of nature

We are in our time in the process of the development of a new concept of nature, of physical existence. This concept is still far from having been achieved, and what is being done here does not pretend to be more than a contribution to the prolegomena to such a concept. All work at this stage can perhaps appropriately be regarded as in a broad sense in the nature of prolegomena.

The development of this concept is inevitably the joint product of the labours of many thinkers, extending over the last few centuries. The present book is not a history, and in this Part no attempt will be made to bring into review the many significant contributory strands to this development. Rather it will concentrate on one of these only.

In the seventeenth century there was commenced a highly important process of the critical evaluation of the concept of nature then emerging. Subsequently this line of inquiry became greatly slowed down, practically brought to a stop, by the growing positivistic temper of the eighteenth and nineteenth centuries. The result has been a great loss of appreciation of the fundamental problems and issues pertaining to the philosophy of nature.

A return to the critical inquiry of that time is perhaps the most effective means of recovering that understanding of the fundamental issues which is so urgently requisite today. In successive chapters we shall examine the issues which were seen to be basic. As we proceed we shall bring these into focus on the present-day situation.

20

MATTER, BODY, AND EXTENSION

The twentieth-century developments in physical science have involved very considerable divergences from the scheme of ideas, discussed in the previous chapter, which constituted the basis of physics in the preceding two centuries – now usually referred to as 'classical' physics in distinction from the recent physics of the relativity and quantum theories. This divergence has evoked quite a bit of attention to philosophical considerations, in varying degrees of penetration, by a number of leading physicists and a few philosophers.

The approach of almost all the philosophical thought on the recent scientific developments has been to seek to discern the philosophical implications of these developments, what they entail respecting philosophical questions, the epistemology involved, for example, but also what is implied for wider metaphysical problems. Especially valuable for its systematic range and its penetration of the issues is the recent book by Milič Čapek, *The Philosophical Impact of Contemporary Physics.*[1] Starting with a systematic examination of the concepts of space, time, matter, and motion, it has then displayed their untenability for contemporary physics and the modifications and transformations they have undergone in the recent physical theories. Whitehead's earlier philosophical work up to and including *Science and the Modern World* has also conformed to this general approach.

However, legitimate and valuable as is this approach, it requires to be complemented by another, which considers the philosophical issues directly and in some disengagement from the contemporary scientific developments. Such was, for example, Whitehead's procedure in *Process and Reality*. It is the latter general approach which is adopted in the present inquiry, though in a more historical way than has been usual with Whitehead.

In this final Part we shall revert to the seventeenth century

[1] Princeton, 1961.

241

to take advantage of and build upon the very considerable elucidation which had at that time been achieved of the fundamental philosophical issues relevant to science. This insight was largely lost during the eighteenth century, with the consequence that contemporary thought has been deeply disadvantaged. This is evidenced, for example, in the comparative lack of appreciation displayed in contemporary thought of the basic relevance of the issue of ontological status in respect of concepts such as space-time, motion, the various 'particles', energy, and so on. Likewise in contemporary thought the term 'matter' continues to be used; the contemporary concept, however, is considerably different from that which antecedently prevailed, but there is a singular lack of clarity as to what precisely the contemporary concept of matter is.

We shall commence our inquiry with the concept of matter. We have seen that it was the new early seventeeth-century conception, which accorded to matter an independent status as itself substance, as the physical existent, which had initiated the development of the modern concept of nature. Moreover, it was this conception of matter as a fully actual existent, without any internal change or becoming, which was the one ingredient in the modern conception which has remained constant throughout the entire three centuries.

By the late seventeeth century what is entailed in this conception had become considerably clarified. The most thoroughgoing and penetrating analysis to which the conception was subjected was that of Leibniz in his later period. The outcome was too radical for his time and its significance was lost; with the twentieth-century scientific developments its import ought to be more readily appreciated.

There were two main varieties of the seventeenth-century conception of matter as substance. One was the doctrine of Descartes, and the other was that which was common to Basso, Gassendi, Hobbes, and Newton. That which was general to both varieties, besides the fundamental character of matter as fully actual and devoid of any change in itself, was its character as extensive. Extension, that is, was conceived as a general and ultimate feature of matter, as Descartes said, constituting its essence as matter. The other thinkers diverged from Descartes only in maintaining that extension is not the sole feature of the essence of matter, holding that solidity or impenetrability had to be added; for them matter was to be regarded not only as extensive, but as the extensive full. Leibniz turned his attention to both these characters. Here we shall concentrate on his analysis of extension as a general and ultimate feature of matter.

In both varieties matter is conceived as fundamentally extensive; that is, it is not only basically extended, spread out, but this extendedness is, as such, an ultimate and irreducible character. As Leibniz put it to De Volder : 'The Cartesians think that some substance can be constituted by extension alone because they conceive of extension as something primitive.'[2] This conception of extension as ultimate and not further analysable is not that of the Cartesians alone; it is shared by all proponents of the theory of material substance.

Now Leibniz challenged this assumption of the ultimacy and unanalysability of extension, of 'extension as something absolute, irresolvable, ineffable, or primitive'.[3] On the contrary, Leibniz maintained : 'I do not think that substance is constituted by extension alone, since the concept of extension is incomplete. Nor do I think that extension can be conceived in itself, but I consider it an analysable and relative concept, for it can be resolved into plurality, continuity, and coexistence or the existence of parts at one and the same time.'[4] The concept of extension is incomplete in the sense that it is not itself some kind of existent, but it is the 'extension of' some existent. Further, extension implies parts, and what is more, *partes extra partes*, which is to say it entails plurality. And, this division into parts is infinite; that is, there is no division in which the parts will not themselves be extensive, and this is what is meant by continuity.[5] Clearly, too, those parts are coexistent. The feature of continuity involved in extension rules out the conception of material *atoms*, for every extension is divisible *ad infinitum*.[6] This infinite divisibilty of extension is equally fatal to Descartes' theory, for by reason of it extension

[2] Loemker, p. 527; G.II, 240–1.

[3] Loemker, pp. 536–7; G.II, 269.

[4] Loemker, p. 516; G.II, 169.

[5] cf. Kant, *Critique of Pure Reason*, B 211 : 'The property of magnitudes by which no part of them is the smallest possible, that is, by which no part is simple, is called their continuity.' (tr. Kemp Smith).

[6] cf. Leibniz's paper 'First Truths', Loemker, pp. 269–70. cf. also Loemker, p. 456.

cannot constitute a one single substance; there can be a unity only in an abstract sense : 'I think that the extended has a unity only in an abstract sense, namely, when we leave out of consideration the internal motion of the parts, for each part of matter is itself subdivided further into actually different parts'.[7]

What this comes to then, Leibniz concluded, is that extension is not a character which can pertain to any one single existent. Rather it is a character of a plurality. This is what he meant in speaking, in the passage quoted above, of extension as a 'relative concept' : there is extension only *in relation to* a plurality, that is, the concept of extension can strictly pertain only to a plurality of entities and not to a single entity. 'Extension is itself, for me, an attribute resulting from many substances existing continuously at the same time.'[8] 'To make extension possible, moreover, there must clearly be something which is repeated continuously, or a plurality of things which coexist continuously.'[9]

Since extension cannot validly be identified with substance as it was by Descartes, but is the extension of something, it is evident that extension is an abstraction. In his words : 'extension is an abstraction from the extended and can no more be considered substance than can number or a multitude, for it expresses nothing but a certain non-successive (i.e., unlike duration) but simultaneous diffusion or repetition of some particular nature, or what amounts to the same thing, a multitude of things of this same nature which exist together with some order between them; and it is this nature, I say, which is said to be extended or diffused.'[10]

The fundamental conclusion to be drawn from these considerations and arguments, Leibniz maintained, is that what is truly to be taken as a substantial existent cannot be extensive.

If matter therefore cannot be substance, what follows for the concept of matter? Is the concept to be dismissed as simply an error, as a mere confusion of thought? Leibniz did not thus reject the validity of the concept. He accepted it, maintaining that the error lay in identifying matter as substance.

Leibniz fully accepted the doctrine, which had originated in the first quarter of the century with Basso and others, that a body is a composite entity and not itself a single unitary substance. 'A body is an aggregate of substances; it is not, properly speaking,

[7] Loemker, p. 516; G.II, 170.   [8] Loemker, p. 520; G.II, 184.
[9] Loemker, p. 525; G.II, 227.   [10] Loemker, p. 536; G.II, 269.

one substance.'[11] Moreover, it is properly speaking such an aggregate of substances which constitutes matter with its mass – Leibniz
explicitly agreed with Gassendi, Newton and others against Descartes, that mass has to be added to extension as an attribute of
matter. Thus Leibniz identified body and matter, but distinguished these from substance. Leibniz therefore accorded body
or matter a definitely different ontological status from that of
substances or monads; body or matter had the status of a derivative from substance.

This is a very important point, the full significance of which is
usually overlooked. This point can be most readily appreciated
by contrast with the doctrine of material atomism. In this, as
in Leibniz's theory, bodies are regarded as composite entities,
their constituents being the material atoms. But in this doctrine
the atoms are themselves regarded as corporeal, as corpuscles, as
little bodies. The acceptance by Newton of this position is singularly explicitly stated in the Third of the Rules of Reasoning
which are given at the beginning of Book III of his *Principia*:[12]

'We no other way know the extension of bodies than by our
senses, nor do these reach it in all bodies; but because we perceive
extension in all that are sensible, therefore we ascribe it universally to all others also. That abundance of bodies are hard, we
learn by experience; and because the hardness of the whole arises
from the hardness of the parts, we therefore justly infer the hardness of the undivided particles not only of the bodies we feel
but of all others. That all bodies are impenetrable, we gather
not from reason, but from sensation. The bodies which we handle
we find impenetrable, and thence conclude impenetrability to be
an universal property of all bodies whatsoever. That all bodies
are movable, and endowed with certain powers (which we call
the inertia) of persevering in their motion, or in their rest, we
only infer from the like properties observed in the bodies
which we have seen. The extension, hardness, impenetrability,
mobility, and inertia of the whole, result from the extension, hardness, impenetrability, mobility, and inertia of the parts; and
hence we conclude the least particles of all bodies to be also
all extended, and hard and impenetrable, and movable, and en-

[11] Loemker, p. 360; G.II, 135.
[12] op. cit., p. 399.

dowed with their proper inertia. And this is the foundation of all philosophy.'

This is the general argument, whether explicitly stated or not, which is adhered to by all proponents of material atomism.

Now in this theory the material atoms are the true substantial existents; a composite body, constituted by an aggregate of atoms, is not properly a substance, but is to be accorded the status of a derivative, ontologically considered. In this respect Leibniz and Newton are in agreement.

But for Newton and the theory of material atomism in general, there is no difference in ontological nature between the atoms and the composite body. The latter is to be regarded as merely an arithmetical sum of the former; that is, ontologically considered, body is a mere collective term, and does not signify any difference in ontological nature from the material atoms. In this respect there is a fundamental divergence between this theory and that of Leibniz. For Leibniz, bodies do not share the ontological nature of the substances. Leibniz agreed in general with Newton in his characterization of the fundamental features of body, namely, extensiveness, impenetrability, mobility, and inertia – he agreed with Locke in rejecting hardness as a true character of body.[13] But he rejected the argument that these must also be the characters of the constituent substances.

The core of Newton's argument, clearly stated in the foregoing passage, on the basis of which he ascribed the observed characters of bodies to the constituent substances, is that the character of the whole must 'arise' or 'result' from the characters of the parts or constituents. Now Leibniz is fully in agreement with the general position that the character of the whole must arise or result or derive from the character of the constituents; there is no other way by which the character of the whole can be derived. But Leibniz maintains that Newton's inference from this premise is invalid. It does not follow from this that the constituents must necessarily have the character of the whole. It follows only that the constituents must have such a nature that the character of the whole can be derivable from the constituents. The constituents and the whole can have ultimately different characters, but the character of the whole can neverthless be derivable from that of

13 cf. Locke, *Essay*, II, IV, 4; Leibniz, *Nouveaux Essais*, Bk II, Ch. IV.

the constituents. This is a point of the utmost importance for the contemporary situation in respect of the philosophical analysis of scientific concepts.

Leibniz is accordingly faced with the necessity of showing how the character of extension, which he and the atomists agree is a primary feature of a composite body, can be derived from constituent substances which are conceived by him as essentially non-extensive. It was this necessity which impelled him to the analysis of extension examined above. The outcome of this analysis, as we have seen, was that extension cannot pertain to a single entity but must pertain only to a plurality. That is, extension cannot be an attribute of a single substance; there is extension only in relation to a plurality. In other words, extension is not a mode of substance, a manner in which substance exists (that is, as extensive); extension is a relation, a relation between substances. Thus Leibniz's doctrine is that substances, which in themselves are non-extensive, can be in extensive relations with each other. Accordingly, if the very nature of extension is that it is a relation and not an attribute, it is clear how the character of a plurality is derivable from the nature of the constituents. Of course, the nature of the constituent substances must be such that they are intrinsically capable of relatedness, but that is a further point, to the consideration of which we shall turn subsequently. For the moment our concern is only the question of the derivability of the character of extension from substances which in their nature are non-extensive. In respect of this Leibniz's position is fully satisfactory.

Further, Leibniz's position enables him to have a clear conception of the ontological status of body, concerning which the theory of material atomism is definitely ambiguous : for in this theory body is not substance but an aggregate, yet body does not differ in its fundamental nature from the constituent material substances; the latter indeed are also bodies. This ambiguity has had serious consequences in twentieth-century thought.

A statement by Leibniz in his correspondence with De Volder further clarifies his conception of the status of extension and of matter : 'Accurately speaking, moreover, extension is merely something modal like number and time, and not a thing, since it is an abstract designation of the continuous possible plurality of coexisting things, while matter is in fact this very plurality of things itself and hence an aggregate of the things which contain entelechies.'[14] That is, extension is not to be identified with matter as by Descartes and the atomists. When we consider extension as such we are dealing with an abstract structure of possible relatedness, 'an abstract designation of the continuous possible plurality of coexisting things'. Leibniz is very insistent that extension is not any kind of actual existent, but is the order of possible existence. He makes the point repeatedly; thus to De Volder: 'I had said that extension is the order of possible coexistents and that time is the order of possible inconsistents.'[15] In his doctrine therefore, as in that of Descartes, the concepts of duration and space are not different from time and extension, 'except in our mode of considering them', that is, except for the context of their use. Accordingly Leibniz defines space equivalently with extension: 'For *space* is nothing but the order of existence of things possible at the same time, while *time* is the order of existence of things possible successively', he writes to De Volder.[16] This formulation is repeated many times in his writings.

The implications of this position are of enormous consequence, so it is very important to be clear about Leibniz's doctrine. His doctrine rejects the position that extension is, as such, a character of actual existents. This latter position runs foul of all the problems of the continuum, not only of infinite divisibility, but also that of the composition of the continuum; as Leibniz wrote to Nicolas Remond: 'The source of our difficulties with the composition of the continuum comes from the fact that we think of matter and space as substances'.[17] Leibniz was more keenly alive to the problems of the continuum and their significance for the whole issue of physical existence than were any of his contemporaries. These considerations were determinative in his analysis of the concepts of matter and substance. It was by reason of these considerations that he saw the necessity to distinguish extension ontologically from the actual existents, and to deny extension the status of an attribute.

We have seen that Leibniz's alternative position is that extension is a relation, that there is extension only in relation to a plurality. The latter formulation is preferable to the former, which might be misunderstood as maintaining the identification of

[14] Loemker, p. 523; G.II, 195.
[15] Loemker, p. 531; G.II, 253.
[16] Loemker, p. 536; G.II, 269.
[17] Loemker, p. 656; G.III, 612.

extension with relation. This would not be acceptable, for if relations are actual, then extension would still be an attribute of actuality, and thus again be enmeshed in the problems of the continuum.

Leibniz's doctrine is that the alternative to according extension the status of actuality is to accord it the status of possibility. In this doctrine Leibniz was reintroducing the Aristotelian distinction which, as we have seen, the modern conception of matter had eliminated from natural philosophy as otiose and indeed completely false. But if this conception of matter as substance be rejected, then the ground for the elimination of the category of possibility vanishes. Leibniz saw, with Aristotle, that its introduction was the only way to resolve the problems of the continuum. In respect of this doctrine, too, Leibniz won scant recognition, with serious consequences for thought in this century.

This distinction was stated by Leibniz to De Volder as follows:[18] 'in actual bodies there is only a discrete quantity, that is, a multitude of monads or of simple substances. . . . But a continuous quantity is something ideal which pertains to possibles and to actualities only in so far as they are possible. A continuum, that is, involves indeterminate parts, while on the other hand, there is nothing indefinite in actual things, in which every division is made that can be made. Actual things are compounded as is a number out of unities, ideal things as is a number out of fractions; the parts are actually in the real whole but not in the ideal whole. But we confuse ideal [entities][19] with real substances when we seek for actual parts in the order of possibilities, and indeterminate parts in the aggregate of actual things, and so entangle ouselves in the labyrinth of the continuum and in contradictions that cannot be explained.'

One of the few thinkers of this century to recognize this distinction and its relevance for the contemporary situation in scientific thought is Whitehead – I think he arrived at this position independently from Leibniz, and from Aristotle. In *Process and Reality* he wrote: 'It cannot be too clearly understood that some chief notions of European thought were framed under the influence of a misapprehension, only partially corrected by the scientific progress of the last century. This mistake consists in the confusion of mere potentiality with actuality. Continuity concerns what is potential; whereas actuality is incurably atomic.'[20] We shall be pursuing the implications of this position as we proceed.

In doing so, it is helpful to understand Leibniz's doctrine more fully in regard to the status respectively of extension and body. First, we must be quite clear that when we are dealing with extension or space we are concerned with possibilities, not with actualities. Bodies are actual, and it is in bodies therefore and not in extension that definite, determinate parts are to be found. As Leibniz put it to Nicolas Remond: *'space is exactly the same as the order of coexistence.* . . . In so far as they are not designated in extension by factual phenomena, parts consist only in possibility; there are no parts in a line except as there are fractions in unity. But if we assume that all possible points actually exist in the whole – as we should have to say if this whole were a substantial thing composed of all its parts – we should be lost in an inextricable labyrinth.'[21]

The next point is that the order of possibilities which constitute extension, or space, and time, is ontologically distinct from the actual bodies; and it constitutes the ultimate framework of possibility for these bodies actually existing there and then. Leibniz stated this as follows, in his reply to a criticism of his system made by Bayle in his *Dictionary*:

'I acknowledge that time, extension, motion, and the continuum in general, as we understand them in mathematics, are only ideal things – that is, they express possibilities, just as do numbers. Even Hobbes has defined space as a phantasm of the existent. But to speak more accurately, *extension* is the order of possible coexistence, just as *time* is the order of possibilities that are inconsistent but nevertheless have a connection. Thus the former considers simultaneous things or those which exist together, the latter those which are incompatible but which we nevertheless conceive as all existing; it is this which makes them successive. But space and time taken together constitute the order of possibilities

---

[20] op. cit., (Cambridge, 1929), p. 84; (New York, 1929), p. 95. Henceforth this work will be cited as 'PR', and the pagination of the New York edition will be in square brackets.

[21] Loemker, p. 656; G.III, 612.

of the one entire universe, so that these orders – space and time, that is – relate not only to what actually is but also to anything that could be put in its place, just as numbers are indifferent to the things which can be enumerated. This inclusion of the possible with the existent makes a continuity which is uniform and in- different to every division.'[22]

The last two sentences make very explicit Leibniz's doctrine of the ontological distinction of space and time from actuality, that they are not actual but constitute the order of possibilities for actual existence. The necessity that space and time 'relate not only to what actually is but also to anything that could be put in its place' is fundamental. In this Leibniz has taken very seriously and carried through the implications of the sixteenth-century analyses, examined earlier,[23] which had resulted in the insistence on the necessity of a distinction between the concepts of place and body. These considerations were strong with Newton too, and the result was that on this point Newton and Leibniz were in full accord, and were opposed to the doctrine of Descartes which did not make this ontological distinction.[24]

The import of the foregoing considerations became lost in the course of the eighteenth century, with the consequence of a lack of appreciation in contemporary thought of these issues, resulting in an unawareness of the fundamental difficulties involved in those theories, now dominant, which accord space-time the status of actuality, in many indeed the ultimate physical actuality, from which matter is derivative.

Whitehead is one twentieth-century thinker fully alive to these issues. Like Leibniz he saw the necessity both of making an onto-logical distinction between space and time on the one hand and physical actuality on the other, and also of refusing to accord space and time, or space-time, the status of actuality. Whitehead conceived of an 'extensive continuum' as constituting 'the most general scheme of real potentiality, providing the background for all other organic relations'.[25] His doctrine is 'that the real

---

[22] Loemker, p. 583; G.IV, 568.   [23] Chs 12 and 13.

[24] When Whitehead says (PR 105 [118]): that 'Descartes, with Newton, assumes that the extensive continuum is actual in the full sense of being an actual entity', he is following the eighteenth-century interpretation of Newton which, as we have seen, differs from the position Newton in fact held.

[25] PR 93 [105].

potentialities relative to all standpoints are co-ordinated as diverse determinations of one extensive continuum. This extensive continuum is one relational complex in which all potential objectifications find their niche. It underlies the whole world, past, present, and future.'[26] 'This extensive continuum expresses the solidarity of all possible standpoints throughout the whole process of the world. It is not a fact prior to the world; it is the first determination of order – that is, of real potentiality – arising out of the general character of the world.'[27]

Like Leibniz, Whitehead insists on the fundamental importance of the category of potentiality or possibility in contrast with that of actuality, and makes the same basic criticism of past and contemporary thought for its neglect of potentiality. Thus Whitehead writes: 'The most general notions underlying the words "space" and "time" are those which this discussion has aimed at expressing in their true connection with the actual world. The alternative doctrine, which is the Newtonian cosmology, emphasized the "receptacle" theory of space-time, and minimized the factor of potentiality. Thus bits of space and time were conceived as being as actual as anything else, and as being "occupied" by other actualities which were the bits of matter. This is the Newtonian "absolute" theory of space-time, which philosophers have never accepted, though at times some have acquiesced.'[28]

Also, like Leibniz, Whitehead maintains that continuity, which is the fundamental character of extension, pertains to potentiality and not to actuality. 'The notion of a "continuum" involves both the property of indefinite divisibility and the property of unbounded extension.'[29] By contrast, actuality is discrete, and in Whitehead's doctrine this discreteness is the direct result of the act of the ultimate existents: 'Actual entities atomize the extensive continuum. This continuum is in itself merely the potentiality for division; an actual entity effects this division.'[30] In this respect there is an important divergence between Whitehead and Leibniz; in Leibniz's doctrine extensive discreteness is not to be ascribed to the act of the ultimate existents, but is derivative, pertaining to the relatedness of a plurality of these existents constituting a body.

We shall have to probe this divergence much further later.

26 PR 91 [103].   27 PR 92 [103].   28 PR 97 [108–9].
29 PR 91 [103].   30 PR 92 [104].

However, this divergence in no way affects the fundamental position which Whitehead and Leibniz, and indeed also Newton (in his true view and not the later misinterpretation of him) hold in common, namely that extension must be regarded as onto-logically distinct from physical existence, by contrast with the position of Descartes and some interpretations of the recent theory of relativity which identify them. In regard to the problem of the ultimate ontological status of extension, Whitehead, Leibniz, and Newton hold views which are not quite as far apart as is sometimes supposed; but this, too, is a topic for later examination.

Our main concern in this chapter has been to bring out that careful philosophical examination of the fundamental concept of the modern theory of nature, namely that of matter as sub-stance and as in its essential nature extensive, shows that it is untenable. This analysis was achieved already in the seventeenth century, by Leibniz. In this century Whitehead undertook a renewed inquiry into the concept, with the same outcome. Čapek and some other thinkers have demonstrated that, in fact, the twentieth-century developments in physics involve the abandon-ment of the earlier conception of material substance. Čapek has also shown the extent to which contemporary thought has never-theless continued to be bedevilled by the carrying-over as an implicit presupposition of this earlier conception, for example in the use of the term 'particle', and in the continued supposition of 'matter' as the physical existent. The question must be raised whether matter can at all be considered tenable as the physical existent, that is, whether the physical existent is to be conceived as 'material' at all. To this we shall turn in the following chapter.

MATTER, MOTION, AND SUBSTANCE

We have previously[1] discussed at some length Newton's arguments that matter in no way entails an 'active principle' and that motion cannot be accounted for from matter alone, indeed that without some active principle the motion of matter must inevitably cease. Newton was by no means alone in seeing this; it was recognized by most of the leading thinkers of the seventeenth century, such as Descartes, Gassendi, and the Occasionalists. Newton's arguments are of special importance because of his insistence that the 'active principle' must be operative within the scheme of nature and not *ex machina* as in the case of Descartes, Gassendi, and the Occasionalists. In regard to this last point, we have seen[2] that Leibniz concurred with Newton on the necessity of the active principle being within nature but maintained that Newton's doctrine also involved the *deus ex machina* fallacy. Leibniz's arguments respecting how the active principle is to be conceived as within nature are of singular significance and must be considered in some detail.

In his *Specimen Dynamicum* Leibniz made the general criticism that 'The fact that the nature of body, and indeed of substance in general, is not well enough understood has resulted, as we have already suggested, in outstanding philosophers of our time locating the notion of body in extension alone and being driven therefore to take refuge in God to explain the union between soul and body and even the communication between bodies themselves',[3] and also to explain the motion of bodies. But even in physics itself the conception of a merely extensive mass moving does not suffice for the laws of motion; for example, it does not explain how there can be rebound upon impact. Leibniz came to the same conclusion as Newton : 'after trying to explore the principles of mechanics itself in order to account for the laws

---

[1] Ch. 18.   [2] Ch. 19, pp. 235f.
[3] Loemker, p. 444; GM.VI, 246.

of nature which we learn from experience, I perceived that the
sole consideration of *extended mass* was not enough but that it
is necessary, in addition, to use the concept of *force*'.[4] That is to
say, 'the principles of mechanism, of which the laws of motion
are the result, cannot be derived from what is purely passive,
geometrical, or material, or proved by the axioms of mathematics alone'.[5] Leibniz stated his conclusion somewhat more fully
to De Volder:[6] 'it is impossible for matter as it is commonly
thought of as formed solely out of the modifications of extension,
or if you prefer, out of passive mass, to suffice for filling the
universe, but that it is obviously necessary to assume something
else in matter from which we may get a principle of change and
one by which to distinguish among phenomena; and hence we
need some alteration, and therefore some heterogeneity,[7] in matter
in addition to increase, diminution, and motion.'

We have to be very clear about the issue confronting us. First,
there is one fundamental point : 'If nothing is active by its own
nature, there will be nothing active at all.'[8] Now the question is
whether matter can be conceived as active in its own nature,
that is, whether matter can have in itself, qua matter, a source
of change. Leibniz examined this question repeatedly in various
writings and came to the conclusion that the analysis of the concept of matter makes it impossible that activity or a source of
motion or change can validly be attributed to matter *per se*. In
his essay, 'On Nature Itself, or on the Inherent Force and Actions
of Created Things', he wrote : 'it must be admitted that extension,
or the geometric nature of a body, taken alone contains nothing
from which action and motion can arise. Indeed, matter rather
resists being moved by its own *natural inertia*, as Kepler has
fittingly named it'.[9] Nor does it help to add the character of
impenetrability – what Leibniz usually referred to as 'antitypy' :
'For not only extension but also the antitypy attributed to bodies
are purely passive things, and as a result the origin of action

---

[4] Loemker, p. 454; G.IV, 478.   [5] Loemker, p. 624; G.VI, 588.
[6] Loemker, p. 529; G.II, 250.
[7] cf. Loemker, p. 525 (G.II, 226–7) : 'So if we say, as is usually done, that a body
contains nothing but extension, and then conceive extension as a kind of simple and
primitive attribute, we can in no way explain how any variation can arise in bodies
or how a plurality of bodies can exist... ; that if matter were not heterogeneous... ,
there could arise no variety of phenomena.'
[8] Loemker, p. 534; G.II, 263.   [9] Loemker, p. 503; G.IV, 510.

cannot be a modification of matter. Hence movement as well as thought must come from another source.'[10]

Leibniz's conclusion is that since the source of motion cannot be ascribed to matter *per se*, it must be ascribed to something else. As he made the point to De Volder : 'We cannot dispense with this active principle or ground of activity, for accidental or changing active forces and their motions are themselves certain modifications of some substantial thing, but forces and actions cannot be modifications of a merely passive thing such as matter. It follows, therefore, that there is a primary active or substantial being which is modified by an added disposition of matter or of passivity.'[11]

But what exactly does this come to? It does not assert an ontological dualism, in which an active substance moves a passive substance, matter. The controversies on this point to which Descartes' doctrine had given rise had sufficiently demonstrated the untenability of that position. What we have here, on the contrary, is the explicit rejection of the position that matter is to be accorded the ontological status of substance; Leibniz is ascribing to matter an ontologically derivative status.

Leibniz's fundamental ontological position, implicit in the foregoing passage as a primary premise, is that activity pertains to substance, that is, substance is an acting entity above all else, and only substance is in this sense active. With this as his premise, Leibniz's argument in that passage is that, since there must be a source of the motion of matter, some principle of activity, and since this source or principle cannot belong to matter *per se*, in its nature as matter, we have to conclude, first, that matter cannot be substance, secondly, that matter must be derivative from that which is truly substance, and thirdly, that motion comes to matter by virtue of and through this derivative status, that is, that it is the activity of substance which manifests itself as the motion of matter.

Before we proceed to explicate Leibniz's theory, it will be well to appreciate in general the position which he put forward as an alternative to the prevailing doctrines of matter. The seventeenth-century conception of matter identified matter as substance. All doctrines of material substance, excepting that of Descartes – but including the interpretation of Descartes by a

[10] Loemker, p. 623; G.VI, 587.   [11] Loemker, p. 517; G.II, 171.

good many of his followers – conceived material substance as corporeal; that is, matter and body were identified in this conception. In face of the issue of the principle or source of the motion of matter, seventeenth-century thinkers in general, including Newton, had recourse to God as this source or principle. It is well to be reminded in this context, since Leibniz's analysis is equally relevant to the eighteenth-century conception of matter which has since prevailed, that in the eighteenth century the philosophical problem of the principle of the motion of matter was simply ignored, and force or activity was ascribed to matter as substance – in the light of the philosophical analyses of the preceding century, a clearly arbitrary procedure.

Leibniz maintained the position that the only valid alternative to the prevalent theories was to deny matter the status of substance. In the previous chapter we saw that he had also arrived at this conclusion regarding matter from an analysis of the concept of extension, a conclusion which is now fully confirmed by the consideration of the requirement of a principle of activity.

We have observed that basically involved in his argument is the conception of substance as fundamentally active. This doctrine of course goes back in the philosophical tradition to the Greeks, and in this context of the philosophy of nature Leibniz was well aware that in maintaining this position he was returning to the doctrine of Aristotle, according to which the physical existent is that which has the principle, source, of its *kinēsis* in itself, the doctrine whose rejection had been fundamental in the seventeenth century theory of matter as substance. Leibniz saw very clearly that the inevitable price for the rejection of this doctrine of Aristotle's, was incoherence in the philosophy of nature. The recognition of this incoherence in the modern philosophy of nature has been fundamental, too, in the thought of Whitehead in this century, bringing Whitehead also back to the Aristotelian position.

It would be a mistake to suppose that the eighteenth-century conception of matter as dynamic also tacitly involved a return to the position of Aristotle. For the Aristotelian doctrine is that the physical existent, by virtue of its inherent activity, is necessarily involved in internal change, while, as was pointed out in the previous chapter,[12] the denial of internal change in matter is the

[12] p. 242.

I

one feature of the modern conception of matter which has persisted until this century. In the persistence of a lack of internal change in the conception of matter as dynamic we have another manifestation of the incoherence of the conception of dynamic matter.

In respect of the necessity of internal change implied in its inherent activity, Leibniz's conception of substance accorded with the Aristotelian, and even more explicitly so does that of Whitehead, in which it is maintained of substance or actual entity that 'Its "being" is constituted by its "becoming" '.[13]

We must now resume the inquiry into how exactly Leibniz conceived the connection between substance and matter and how from the activity of substance there derives the motion of matter. To De Volder, Leibniz wrote: 'Primitive concepts lie concealed in derivative ones but are hard to distinguish in them. I doubt that a body can be conceived apart from motion; I admit that motion cannot be conceived apart from body. But in the concept of motion there are included not only body and change but a reason and a determinant of change as well, which cannot be found in a body if its nature is considered to be purely passive, that is, to consist in extension alone or even in extension and impenetrability. In extension I think of many things together – on the one hand, continuity, which it has in common with time and motion, and on the other, coexistence. So it is not necessary to think of extension either as a whole or as nothing at all. To make extension possible, moreover, there must clearly be something which is repeated continuously, or a plurality of things which coexist continuously.'[14] What is particularly relevant here is the connection not only between motion and body, but also between motion and plurality. The many coexistent things constitute an extensive body, and it is body which moves.

The many coexistent things are the substances – which Leibniz calls monads – and qua substances they act. Now this acting is a process of internal change:[15] it is an actualizing of potentiality.

13 PR 31 [34–5].

14 cf. Loemker, p. 525; G.II, 227.

15 cf. Loemker, p. 534; G.II, 263: 'But since every action contains change, we must have in it precisely what you would seem to deny it, namely, a tendency toward internal change and a temporal succession following from the nature of the thing' – this to De Volder, a Cartesian.

Fundamental in this process from potentiality to actuality is that there must be a potency, power, by reason of which the actualization is attained. That is, potentiality is not merely a capacity for actualization, a capacity which requires some agency to effect it; potentiality *per se* entails the spring or source of activity. Leibniz insists on the fundamental sense of 'potency', 'power', that which is basic too in the Greek word *dynamis*. Because through the Neoplatonic influence down the ages this sense of 'potency' or 'power' had become weakened, potency being understood rather as a capacity to act than an acting itself, Leibniz preferred to use the word 'force'. His statment of this in his short paper 'On the Correction of Metaphysics and the Concept of Substance' is as follows :

'the concept of *forces* or *powers*, which the Germans call *Kraft* and the French *la force*, and for whose explanation I have set up a distinct science of *dynamics*, brings the strongest light to bear upon our understanding of the true concept of *substance*. Active force differs from the mere power familiar to the Schools, for the active power or faculty of the Scholastics is nothing but a close [*propinqua*] possibility of acting, which needs an external excitation or a stimulus, as it were, to be transferred into action. Active force, in contrast, contains a certain act or entelechy and is thus midway between the faculty of acting and the act itself and involves a conatus. It is thus carried into action by itself and needs no help but only the removal of an impediment.'[16]

Leibniz saw, and made much of, the connection between this and the conception of 'substantial form'. As he put it in his paper on 'A New System of Nature' : 'It was thus necessary to restore and as it were, to rehabilitate the *substantial forms* which are in such disrepute today, but in a way which makes them intelligible and separates their proper use from their previous abuse. I found then that their nature consists of force. . . . Aristotle calls them *first entelechies*. I call them, more intelligibly perhaps, *primitive forces*, which contain not only the *actuality* or the *completion* of possibility but an original *activity* as well.'[17]

Now a body is constituted by a plurality of acting monads or

16 Loemker, p. 433; G.IV, 469.
17 Loemker, p. 454; G.IV, 478–9.

substances. That is, body as such is a derivative entity. What Leibniz calls active or primitive force is the force of acting of each individual monad. Body, which is derivative, manifests this force derivatively, and Leibniz distinguishes this force as pertaining to body from the primary forces of the monads by referring to the force pertaining to body as secondary.[18] The essential point is that the force which we must recognize in bodies – a conception necessitated, as we have seen earlier in this chapter, by an adequate science of physics – cannot be a primary active force since bodies are not substances, and must therefore be a derivative force, derivative from the true primary force, that of the constituent monads.

With these concepts clear we are in a position to understand the concept of motion. Motion, Leibniz maintains, pertains to body and not to the individual monads. Motion, however, is not to be identified with derivative force; it is a consequence of derivative force. Leibniz emphasized this to De Volder:[19] 'I, however, do not consider motion to be a derivative force but think rather that motion, being change, follows from such force.' The individual monads act, and when this acting is considered, not in itself, that is, with respect to the individual subjects of acting, but with reference to the plurality of monads, those constituting the body in question and those constituting other bodies, one outcome of this acting will be a change of situation of the monads, and consequently of bodies, relatively to each other. It is this resultant change of situation relatively to each other which is motion.

It is clear that for Leibniz the concept of motion, like that of extension, is not ultimate, simple, and unanalysable, but is, as he said of the latter, 'an analysable and relative concept'. The concept of motion pertains to a plurality, being analysable into the change of situation of a number of individuals with reference to each other; there can be no change of situation in respect of itself. Thus motion is a relative concept; it can only pertain to a number of entities relatively to each other.

We might note at this point that Whitehead, quite independently of Leibniz, has arrived at an essentially similar analysis of motion. Motion in the modern sense is 'locomotion', change

---

[18] cf. *Specimen Dynamicum*, Part I, Loemker, pp. 435–7; GM.VI, 234–7.
[19] Loemker, p. 533; G.II, 262.

of locus (place or situation), or 'local change'. Whitehead writes:

'a molecule in the sense of a moving body, with a history of local change, is not an actual occasion [substance]; it must therefore be some kind of nexus of actual occasions. In this sense it is an event, but not an actual occasion. The fundamental meaning of the notion of [local] "change" is "the difference between actual occasions comprised in some determinate event".'[20]

It is clear that for Whitehead, too, the concept of motion is relative to a plurality and does not pertain to an individual substance.

In a statement to De Volder, Leibniz has given an important elucidation of his doctrine:

'every change, spiritual as well as material, has its own place [sedes], so to speak, in the order of time, as well as its own location in the order of coexistents, or in space. For although monads are not extended, they nevertheless have a certain kind of situation [situs] in extension, that is, they have a certain ordered relation of coexistence with others, namely, through the machine which they control [i.e. body]. I do not think that any finite substances exist apart from a body and that they therefore lack a position or an order in relation to the other things coexisting in the universe. Extended things involve a plurality of things endowed with position, but things which are simple, though they do not have extension, must yet have a position in extension, though it is impossible to designate these positions precisely as in the case of [bodies].'[21]

His statement should be noted that finite substances do not 'exist apart from a body' – only the infinite substance, God, does;[22] this means that finite monads are always associated in collectives. It is these collectives which constitute bodies, and it is the 'ordered relation of coexistence' between them which constitutes the extension of the body. Thus each constituent monad must have a situation in the extension of that body – it could not be outside

20 PR 101 [114].   21 Loemker, p. 531; G.II, 253.
22 cf. Loemker, p. 552; G.VI, 506–7.

it, for example. But when we so consider its situation this can be done only relatively to the others.

At one period Leibniz had indeed been of the opinion that the position of individual monads could be exactly designated, for he thought that the position of the monads could be identified with geometrical points.[23] He came to see however that, with a more careful consideration of the nature of substance as active, such a view is erroneous.[24] Some of the relevant points respecting the nature of substance we shall discuss later; here we shall content ourselves with only one. This is that since the concept of extension is derivative, equally so must be that of a point in extension, and therefore his earlier view locating monads in points 'contains a certain confusion of classes, so to speak'.[25]

So far we have concentrated on the one feature which all adherents to the doctrine of material substance are agreed is fundamental to matter, namely extension. We need to take account, however, that, as Leibniz observed:[26] 'Philosophers who are not Cartesians will not agree that extension is enough to form a body; they will demand something more which the ancients called antitypy, that, namely, which makes one body impenetrable to another.' Newton maintained the characters of hardness and solidity in addition. Locke, with good reason, rejected hardness as a feature of matter, and identified solidity with impenetrability. Leibniz agreed with this, and put the emphasis on the concept of impenetrability as fundamental. Leibniz is therefore faced with the need to show that this feature of impenetrability is also a derivative one, and not an ultimate feature of substance, and further, to explain how impenetrability is derivative from activity.

We have seen Leibniz's reasons for holding that there must be a primary active force, and that this must be conceived as 'a force which does not consist merely in a simple faculty such as that with which the Scholastics seem to have contented themselves but which is provided besides with a striving or effort [*conatus seu nisus*] which has its full effect unless impeded by a contrary

[23] cf. 'A New System of the Nature and Communication of Substances', especially Loemker, p. 456; G.IV, 482–3.

[24] cf. especially the P.S. to his letter of April 30, 1709 to Des Bosses, in Loemker, p. 599; G.II, 372.

[25] ibid.

[26] Loemker, p. 619; G.VI, 580.

striving'.[27] The last clause is of special relevance in the present context. How is this 'contrary striving' to be analysed? Since *conatus* or striving must primarily be that of acting substances, the contrary striving must equally be ascribable to the monads or substances themselves. Leibniz maintains that the 'contrary striving' is the obverse, as it were, of striving; it is constituted by the resistance necessarily offered by any instance of striving to another striving. That is to say, every 'activity' necessarily has an aspect of 'passivity'. Thus besides a primitive active force, we must recognize also a 'primitive force of suffering or of resisting'.[28] And just as a body, which is constituted by a plurality of acting monads, manifests that acting as a derivative force, so correspondingly a body manifests too the primitive passive force as antitypy or impenetrability. It is by virtue of this 'that one body is not penetrated by another but opposes an obstacle to it and is at the same time possessed of a kind of laziness, so to speak, or a repugnance to motion, and so does not allow itself to be set in motion without somewhat breaking the force of the body acting upon it'.[29] In this way therefore Leibniz accounts for the character of antitypy or impenetrability, which he agrees is correctly to be regarded as an essential feature of matter or body, as derivative and pertaining to a plurality. This at the same time explains the other feature of matter or body, which Newton, Descartes, Kepler and others were agreed must be ascribed to it, namely, a *vis inertiae*. And further, it also explains the feature of 'mass' which contemporary thought had regarded as also attributable to matter or body as a fundamental character – Newton in his *Opticks* had characterized matter as 'solid, massy, hard, impenetrable', and in his *Principia* had defined mass as quantity of matter.[30] The concept of mass, like the others, Leibniz insists, is complex: it involves extension, antitypy and inertia; extension in that it pertains to a body or plurality, and antitypy and inertia in that mass is the quantitative measure of inertia which is constituted by antitypy.

In summary, therefore, we see that Leibniz has shown that matter or body cannot validly be taken as substance, but that it

[27] Loemker, p. 435; GM.VI, 235.
[28] Loemker, p. 437; GM.VI, 236.
[29] Loemker, 437; GM.VI, 237.
[30] cf. op. cit., Definition I.

is a derivative entity constituted by a plurality, and further that all the characters which thinkers had correctly ascribed to matter as its essential features, namely, extension, impenetrability, inertia, are all upon analysis to be seen as features pertaining to a plurality and not to a single individual substance. Finally, motion too must be seen as pertaining to a plurality, and not to a single substance.

Whitehead in this century has come to the same conclusion as Leibniz on all these points, and he has done so independently of Leibniz, proceeding from a consideration of the philosophical implications of the twentieth-century developments in physical science.[31]

Central to the recent theory of relativity is that motion is relative, but not many contemporary thinkers have seen the full implications of this, and especially that the conception of motion as relative means that motion is not a concept pertaining to an ultimate actuality or substance, but that it pertains to pluralities, as a feature of pluralities. In contemporary thought, however, there persists as a tacit presupposition that motion is fundamentally ascribable to individual ultimate existents, and most thinking in physical science still proceeds upon this basis.

The concept of something as relative means that it must be conceived *in relation to* something else. Leibniz has argued that extension, impenetrability, and inertia are relative concepts, and that matter and body are relative concepts, and also that motion is a relative concept. It is evident that the concept of 'relation' is in need of the most careful scrutiny. This will be the topic of the next chapter.

[31] With regard to the concept of mass, cf. the following in *Science and the Modern World*, pp. 127–8 [149]: 'The notion of *mass* was losing its unique pre-eminence as being the one final permanent quantity. Later on, we find the relations of mass and energy inverted; so that mass now becomes the name for a quantity of energy considered in relation to some of its dynamical effects. This train of thought leads to the notion of energy being fundamental, thus displacing matter from that position. But energy is merely the name for the quantitative aspect of a structure of happenings; in short, it depends on the notion of the functioning of an organism.'

22

RELATION, ACTION, AND
SUBSTANCE

The concept of relation is anything but a simple and straight-forward one, and there are a number of relations of different kinds, to instance but a few relevant in the philosophy of nature, spatial, temporal, and causal relations. For the philosophical understanding of the nature and status of relations, what is of primary importance is that relations must be grounded in substances, that is, in ultimate existents.

In a theory of substance as matter, in itself fully actual, all relations between substances must be completely external to the substances. Since the substances are fully actual, relations of distance from each other, for example, can make no difference whatever to the substances in question. The same is true of temporal relations. Any individual substance remains exactly what it is, in no way affected by other substances, and it would indeed remain unaffected even if all other substances were annihilated. All relations which are quantitatively specifiable are of this kind; in this theory they must necessarily be entirely external to the material substances.

But if they are external to the material substances and they are nevertheless relations, to be such they must be grounded in some substance. In Newton's doctrine (as we have expounded it and not as it was understood in the eighteenth century) the spatial and temporal relations between the material substances were grounded in the spiritual substance, God. Since God's activity is everywhere and everywhen, it is this which constitutes the ultimate places of the material substances, and thereby also the mathematical framework in terms of which the spatial and temporal relations between the material substances can be specified. These relations are primarily specified by God in his activity, and secondarily so by finite minds through their comprehension of mathematics. Basic in this philosophy is the Platonic doctrine of Ideas or Forms, in its Christian Neoplatonic understanding which had become so influential in the Renaissance, and which continued to play a profound role in the thought of the seventeenth century, as we shall see. The finite comprehension of mathematics was constituted by the possession by finite minds of mathematical Ideas or Forms, the archetypes of which are in the mind of God and are those according to which he acts in respect of matter.

Descartes' theory differed from this in that for him *res extensa* was the actual mathematical *explicatio* of God's thought, so that the quantitative relations of bodies are derivative from the mathematical structure of *res extensa* as matter. Thus in Descartes' doctrine the quantitative relations of bodies (which are not themselves substances) are grounded in *res extensa*, the material substance. Thinking, as the essence of *res cogitans*, is ultimately mathematical, and consists in the explication of the mathematical Ideas innate in finite minds by God's creation, and accordingly the comprehension of pure mathematics is the comprehension of the essence of matter, and thereby derivatively, in applied mathematics, the quantitative relations between bodies are specifiable.

For both these theories it is clear that the explanation of how mathematical thinking is applicable to and true of physical existence is in terms of this Platonic doctrine of Ideas. This was the view most widely current at the time, rather than the Aristotelian doctrine of mathematics as a conceptual abstraction from the physical.

Leibniz, having rejected entirely the conception of matter as substance, had accordingly to provide a different theory of relations from that currently accepted. Substances for him are essentially acting, and thus relations must be grounded in the acting of the non-material substances. Crucial here will clearly be his conception of the *character* of that acting.

But before we come to the examination of Leibniz's conception of the character of the acting of substances, there is one fundamental implication of his conception which needs to be brought out. We have this in the following statement by Leibniz in his 'Principles of Nature and of Grace':[1] 'Everywhere there are simple substances actually separated from each other by their own actions, which continually change their relations.' The relevant

---

[1] Loemker, p. 636–7; G.VI, 598.

point is that by virtue of their acting the substances are separate and distinct from each other. The actings constitute their principle of individuation. Actings are mutually exclusive, and thus necessitate the respective monads being elsewhere in relation to each other. So it is impossible, for example, for two monads to coincide in the same point. Since all monads are necessarily, by virtue of their acting, elsewhere in relation to each other, it follows that there must necessarily be an order of this relatedness of the monads to each other. The question now is, what is the status of that order? Since it is an order of *relations*, it must be grounded in the substances. This brings us to the question of the nature of the acting of the substances, for the order of relations must be grounded in the actings of the substances.

Now in regard to this question, what is determinative for Leibniz in his acceptance, too, of the Neoplatonic doctrine of Ideas. It comes out very clearly in the following passage:

'Thus the idea of things in us is nothing but the fact that God, the author alike of things and of mind, has impressed the power of thinking upon the mind, so that it can by its own operations produce what corresponds perfectly to events which follow from things.'[2]

Mental activity or 'operation' consists in explicating the Ideas implanted in the mind by God. There is a correspondence between the Ideas in the mind and things because, in terms of the Platonic doctrine, the Ideas also inform things. Because through God's creative activity the same Ideas inform respectively things and minds, the correspondence between the two will be perfect. This is Leibniz's theory of pre-established harmony.

In this doctrine mental activity consists basically in the explication of ideas. The paradigm of this is mathematics, especially geometry, which consists in the explication of what is implicit or *complicans* (to use Cusanus' term) in certain primary ideas as axioms. In this conception any kind of direct contact between mind and things is entirely redundant. Strictly, accordingly, the object of the mind in thinking is its own Ideas, and not external

---

[2] G.VII, 264: '*Ideam itaque rerum in nobis esse, nihil aliud est, quam DEUM, autorem pariter et rerum et mentis, eam menti facultatem cogitandi impressisse, ut ex suis operationibus ea ducere possit, quae perfecte respondeant his quae sequuntur ex rebus.*' cf. Loemker, p. 208.

things. This conception also entered British empiricism through Locke, though Locke, and still less so his followers, did not very clearly appreciate the foundation of their position and thus what this position logically committed them to. Leibniz, on the contrary, was very clear about what is entailed in this position, and developed his theory of mental activity accordingly.

For Leibniz is was this mental activity which is the fundamental acting of substance. That is, since matter must be denied the status of substance, the only alternative, Leibniz concluded, is that substance must be what Descartes termed a *res cogitans.* Leibniz himself expressed it thus in his paper on 'A New System of the Nature and Communication of Substances':[3] 'I found then that their nature consists of force and that there follows from this something analogous to sense and appetite, so that we must think of them in terms similar to the concept which we have of *souls.*'

Now, what follows for the problem of relations from this conception of substance and the nature of its acting? We have seen that according to this doctrine, to quote Leibniz's formulation, 'speaking with metaphysical rigour, there is no real influence of one created substance upon another and that all things, with all their reality, are continually produced by the power of God'.[4] And as he emphasized to De Volder:[5] 'I do not admit any action of substances upon each other in the proper sense, since no reason can be found for one monad influencing another.' This is a strict consequence of the adoption of the Platonic doctrine of Ideas in the Christian Neoplatonic interpretation, and both Leibniz and Descartes were completely consistent in their adherence to it. Leibniz saw especially clearly that it followed that relations between substances could not be other than ideas in the individual substances severally. In other words, a relation cannot be an *ens reale*; it can only be an *ens mentale*. This means that a relation is a 'phenomenon', an appearance, and not any kind of thing in itself.

We have seen Leibniz's analysis of extension, that it is the order of a coexistent plurality. We have also seen earlier in this chapter that since, by virtue of their acting, all monads are necessarily elsewhere in relation to each other, there must accordingly be an order of this relation of the monads to each other.

---

[3] Loemker, p. 454; G.IV, 479.   [4] Loemker, p. 457; G.IV, 483.
[5] Loemker, p. 530; G.II, 251.

It is evident that this order is none other than that which constitutes extension. This brings out again what we have seen before[6] to be Leibniz's doctrine, that extension is an order of *relatedness* of coexistents. The present considerations respecting the ontological status of relations brings out that this order of relatedness of coexistents must be phenomenal. This makes clearer too Leibniz's argument that, since extension or space cannot be any kind of actual existent, it is the order of *possible* relatedness between coexistents.

In each of the monads severally this order of possible relatedness is an idea. This is the ground for Leibniz's insistence, which we have seen earlier,[7] that continuity – which is a necessary feature of extension – is 'ideal', as opposed to actual. Further, the archetype of the ideas of extensive relatedness in the individual substances is the idea of that relatedness in the mind of God in his creating of the substances each elsewhere in relation to each other. From this perspective, therefore, we can see that Leibniz's conception of space, and time, is not as much different from that of Newton as is usually supposed.[8] There is the further point of tremendous importance, namely that the archetypal idea of the order of relatedness of monads is essentially mathematical, and hence there is the mathematical character of the idea of extension in the finite substances.

The previous two chapters have brought out that in Leibniz's analysis all the characters which have been, and correctly so, ascribed as the attributes or features of body, extension and impenetrability and mass being the chief, must be seen as relative to a plurality and not as attributes which can pertain to a single substance; that is, these features are characters displayed by relations, and not by substances. Now in this chapter it has emerged that, as a consequence of Leibniz's doctrine of the nature of the acting of substance, *all* relations must be phenomenal. Since therefore the features of body (extension, mass impenetrability) are phenomenal, body *per se* must be accorded the status of a phenomenon. Leibniz states this doctrine repeatedly. For example : 'But since only simple things are true things . . . the rest are things by aggregation and therefore phenomena . . .';[9] 'a body is not a true unity; it is only an aggregate . . . a collection

6 cf. Ch. 20, pp. 248–9.   7 cf. Ch. 20, pp. 249–51.
8 cf. Ch. 19, pp. 229–30.   9 Loemker, p. 531; G.II, 252.

like a herd. Its unity comes from our perception. It is a being of *reason* or rather, of *imagination,* a *phenomenon.*[10] The term 'imagination' does not connote 'illusory'; the word comes from 'image', a likeness or copy – in the Platonic doctrine the ideas in the mind are images of the Ideas in themselves.

We have also seen that the concept of motion cannot validly pertain to an individual substance, according to Leibniz's analysis, but is relative to a plurality. The motion of body too, therefore, Leibniz maintains, must be phenomenal : 'motion apart from force (or in so far as it involves only a consideration of the geometric concepts of magnitude, ·figure, and their variations) is in fact nothing but change of situation; and thus . . . *motion in so far as it is phenomenal consists in a mere relationship'.*[11]

When the theory of material substance was introduced in the first quarter of the seventeenth century by Basso, Galileo and others, the implication was clearly seen, by these two thinkers in particular, that features of bodies such as colour, heat, sound, etc., cannot be accepted as in fact belonging to bodies, that they are appearances in the mind of what in bodies is far different from them. Galileo had proclaimed very firmly that what we perceive as heat in bodies is in the bodies themselves nothing but the motion of particles. This doctrine very soon came into widespread acceptance and, following Locke, became terminologically fixed as the distinction between primary and secondary qualities. Bodies in themselves had only the primary qualities of extension, shape, impenetrability, mass; colours, heat, sound, etc., belonged entirely to observing minds as the appearances in the mind of the primary qualities external to them in bodies.

Leibniz fully accepted the apparent or phenomenal status of colours, sounds, heat, and so forth. But according to his analysis the primary qualities are equally apparent, phenomenal. For him therefore bodies, with all their observed qualities or features, are phenomenal : 'It can even be demonstrated that the concepts of size, figure, and motion are not so distinct as has been imagined and that they include something imaginary and relative to our perceptions, as do also (though to a greater extent) colour, heat, and other similar qualities which one may doubt truly are found

10 Loemker, p. 623; G.VI, 586.
11 Loemker, p. 445; GM.VI, 247.

in the nature of things outside of ourselves', he writes in his 'Discourse on Metaphysics'.[12]

But although for Leibniz all the features of body are phenomenal, yet there is a difference between colours, heat, etc., on the one hand, and size, figure, extension, etc., on the other. While all are ideas in the mind, the difference is that the former ideas do not have anything in bodies exactly corresponding to them; that is, they are not images of features in bodies. But the latter group of ideas do constitute true images. Thus Leibniz spoke of them as *phaenomena bene fundata*, well-grounded phenomena.

For Leibniz the latter group of ideas are true images, not as with Locke by virtue of the direct action of the bodies on the mind, but through the pre-established harmony. Accordingly he is not faced with Locke's insuperable problem – that of material atomism – of explaining how the action of bodies, which Locke is very clear can only consist in impact,[13] can produce an effect on mind which by definition is unextended and not of such a kind as to be able to be impacted on.

Nevertheless it was Leibniz's theory of body as phenomenal and his doctrine of pre-established harmony which most of his contemporaries and successors felt to be the more unacceptable. Basically what they could not accept was the conception of substance as in itself without direct effect on others. In this respect Locke and his followers, despite their acceptance of the Christian Neoplatonic doctrine of Ideas, inconsistently adhered to the Aristotelian doctrine of causal efficacy. The continued adherence to these two inconsistent positions has continued to bedevil much philosophical thought down to the present day, especially that of the empiricist tradition.

In this century Whitehead sought to resolve the endemic difficulty of empiricism by cutting the Gordian knot. He secured causal efficacy by insisting on relations as real and not apparent or phenomenal. Relations must be grounded in substances, and moreover in the acting of substances. Whitehead proclaimed the doctrine that the acting of substances is a grasping, a prehending (in the original etymological sense) of other substances. By its act of prehending, a substance or actual entity effects a contact with

---

[12] Loemker, p. 309; G.IV, 436.
[13] cf. John Locke, *Essay Concerning Human Understanding*, Bk II, Ch. 8, 11.

another, thereby including the character and efficacy of that other in itself. It is important to note that in this doctrine the relation is effected by the prehending entity, by its act of prehending. There is not a mutual act of prehending; in this relation the prehended entity is not itself active. Its activity has ceased; it is in the 'past' of the prehending entity. Whitehead maintains that contemporary actual entities are causally independent of each other, that is, that there is no relation of prehension between them – contemporaries do not prehend each other. There can be prehension only of an entity in the past of the prehender, that is, of one whose process of acting has terminated.

Now the question can be raised respecting this doctrine whether Whitehead had as effectively cut the Gordian knot as he had supposed. For in the act of prehension as Whitehead conceives it, there remains a very significant feature of the Neoplatonic doctrine of Ideas as inherited from traditional, especially British, empiricism. In the empiricist tradition the ideas are in the mind, and moreover it is these ideas which are the objects of the mental activity[14] – whether they be termed 'ideas' with Locke, or 'impressions' with Hume, or 'sense data' by contemporary thinkers. Whitehead certainly rejects this theory; for him the objects are other, past, actual entities. Nevertheless he conceives the act of prehending as essentially a 'perceiving'. As he has made clear in *Science and the Modern World*,[15] 'perception' for him is '*taking account of* the essential character of the thing perceived'. Moreover, this *perception* (which is more than the *act* of perceiv*ing*) is located in the perceiver. As he says : 'Accordingly, there is a prehension, *here* in this place, of things which have a reference to *other* places.'[16] The point I wish to make is that in the empiricist tradition mental activity is conceived as essentially 'perception', and Whitehead accepted this conception of it. This too is Leibniz's doctrine; we have seen that he conceived the action of monads as 'perception and appetition'. What is fundamental in a monad is 'actions, and these can only be its *perceptions* – that is to say, the representations of the compound, or of that which is without, in the simple – and its *appetitions* – that is to say, its tendencies from one perception to

[14] cf. Locke, *Essay*, Bk I, Ch. I, 8, and Bk II, Ch. I, 1; Ch. 8, 7.
[15] op. cit., p. 86 [101].
[16] ibid.

another – which are the principles of change'.[17] Determinative in all these theories is the Neoplatonic doctrine of Ideas: 'perception' is having ideas in the mind as images of what is without. With regard to Whitehead, I wish to raise the question whether the acting of substance as 'prehension' or 'grasping' is adequately construed as 'perception'. I have come to the conclusion that it is not, and only the implicit continuation of the Neoplatonic doctrine has obscured from Whitehead, and his followers, that it is not.

In the search for a more adequate conception of the nature of the acting of a substance it is worth noting a certain significant inconsistency in Leibniz's thought. As we have seen in the previous chapter, when Leibniz was considering the fundamental nature of substance, more particularly as required from the point of view of physics, he concluded that it must consist in 'force' or 'power':

'the concept of *forces* or *powers*, which the Germans call *Kraft* and the French *la force*, and for whose explanation I have set up a distinct science of *dynamics*, brings the strongest light to bear upon our understanding of the true concept of *substance*.'[18]

But when his acceptance of the Neoplatonic doctrine of Ideas asserts itself he characterizes the fundamental nature of substance as 'perception'. He brings the two concepts of 'force' and 'perception' together in a passage already quoted:[19] 'I found then that their nature consists of force and that there follows from this something analogous to sense and appetite'.

The question must be raised whether indeed 'sense and appetite' *follow from* 'force'. It seemed to Leibniz that there is this implication because he had the Neoplatonic doctrine as a premise. But if that premise be not accepted, then 'force' does not imply 'perception and appetite'. Moreover, without that tacit premise, 'force' and 'power' construed as 'perception' is both without foundation and also a pretty implausible theory.

It seems to me that in the attempt to gain an understanding

[17] Loemker, p. 636; G.VI, 598.
[18] cf. p. 259 above; Loemker, p. 433; G.IV, 469.
[19] See above, p. 268; Loemker, p. 454.

of the nature of the activity of substance it will be worth exploring Leibniz's suggestion of 'force' or 'power'. The concept of 'force' was basic in Leibniz's physics, and in that of Newton. With regard to the concept in Newton, Whitehead has observed:

'The force acting on a body, whether by touch or by action at a distance, was [in effect] defined as being equal to the mass of the body multiplied by the rate of change of the body's velocity, so far as this rate of change is produced by that force. In this way the force is discerned by its effect on the motion of the body.'[20]

Leibniz is in agreement: as regards force and power, he writes in the paper 'On the Elements of Natural Science',[21] 'it must be recognized that it is to be estimated from the quantity of its effect'. This effect is motion. 'As concerns physics, we must understand the nature of force; that it is entirely different from motion, which is something more relative. This force must be measured by the quantity of the effect.'[22] But this is not to say that 'force' *means* 'quantity of motion'. On the contrary, it is important to observe carefully the distinction between 'force' and 'motion', both in physics and in philosophy:

'For considering only what it means narrowly and formally, that is, a change of place, motion is not something entirely real; when a number of bodies change their position with respect to each other, it is impossible, merely from a consideration of these changes, to determine to which bodies motion ought to be ascribed and which should be regarded as at rest. . . . But the force or the immediate cause of these changes is something more real, and there is a sufficient basis for ascribing it to one body rather than to another. This, therefore, is also the way to learn to which body the motion preferably belongs. Now this force is something different from size, figure, and motion, and from this we can conclude that not everything which is conceived in a body consists solely in extension and its modifications, as our moderns have persuaded themselves. Thus we are compelled to restore also certain beings or forms which they have banished.'[23]

[20] *Science and the Modern World*, p. 57 [66–7].   [21] Loemker, p. 279.
[22] Loemker, p. 360; G.II, 137.   [23] Loemker, p. 315; G.IV, 444.

And in a reply to Bayle, Leibniz stresses that:

'As for *motion*, that which is real in it is *force* or power, namely, something in the present state which carries with it a change for the future. The rest is only phenomena and relations.'[24]

We have seen in sufficient detail that the concept of motion is relative, and therefore in Leibniz's theory must be phenomenal. The force which enters into physics (as the science of bodies in motion) is what previously we have seen to be 'derivative force'. The 'primitive force' from which this is derivative is the acting of the individual monads.

Now force or power as 'something in the present state which carries with it a change for the future' means that it must essentially involve a *conatus seu nisus*, a striving or effort. This striving or effort must be ascribed to the individual monads as an intrinsic feature of their acting. When Leibniz turns explicitly to the analysis of the acting of the monads he does so, as we have shown, with the implicit presupposition of the Neoplatonic doctrine of Ideas. In terms of this the acting is analysed as perception and appetition, and it is in the latter that must be found the 'striving or effort', for appetition is the principle of change in the monad: 'The action of the internal principle which brings about change or the passage from one perception to another can be called *appetition*.'[25] But can this change or passage from one perception to another, even with the acknowledgement that the monad is itself the source of that change, be accepted as adequate to constitute the 'striving or effort' required for force as the 'motive power' of bodies? According to this analysis, the acting of the monads, when the plurality of them constituting a body is considered, manifests itself as the change of position relatively to each other which is motion. In this way certainly the monads are validly to be considered as the principle or source of the motion of the bodies, but hardly as the 'motive power' whereby there is motion. That is to say, in this analysis the factor of 'power' has been lost.

The same outcome follows for Whitehead's doctrine, as a consequence of his conception of the acting of substance or actual

24 Loemker, p. 496; G.IV, 523.
25 Loemker, p. 644; G.VI, 609.

entity. Indeed the concept of 'force' does not figure in his philosophy at all, and the factor of 'power' has disappeared from 'potentiality', reducing the latter concept to 'possibility' – and the two terms are thus used synonymously by Whitehead. There is no 'motive force' in Whitehead's doctrine; there is a 'motive' for motion (though Whitehead does not use the term), analysable as the teleological aspect involved in the anticipation each actual entity has of the future. But an actual entity cannot be efficacious on its successor or any other actual entity by its own direct agency. Thus for Whitehead the word 'efficacy', too, has a weakened sense in his conception of 'causal efficacy'. In Whitehead's analysis of transeunt causality the antecedent in this relationship, which is the 'cause', is efficacious only by constituting the datum for the prehensive activity of the consequent. In the generally accepted conception of transeunt causality it is the antecedent which is efficacious by its activity, 'acting on' the consequent, thereby 'causing' the effect; in Whitehead's doctrine the agency whereby there is transeunt causality is the exact reverse of the generally accepted understanding.

There is much to be gained in respect of the implications of the concept of force for substance, it seems to me, by a perusal of Kant's pre-critical thought. Kant, both as mathematical physicist and as philosopher, was early influenced by Leibniz's doctrine of force. His first published work was the dissertation entitled *Gedanken von der wahren Schätzung der lebendigen Kräfte and Beurteilung der Beweise, derer sich Herr von Leibniz und andere Mechaniker in dieser Streitsache bedienet haben, nebst einigen vorhergehenden Betrachtungen, welche die Kraft der Körper überhaupt betreffen.*[26] The philosophical position involved in this work was elaborated ten years later in the important dissertation known by the shortened title of *Monadologia physica.*[27]

Kant accepted from Leibniz that we must recognize in body an essential force inhering in it indeed prior to extension.[28] Body is a composite entity, and this composition is a relation.[29] The ultimate constituents of body must be simple entities, that is, ones

[26] This will be cited under the shortened title of *Living Forces.*

[27] *Metaphysicae cum geometria iunctae usus in philosophia naturali, cuius specimen I, continet monadologiam physicam,* 1756.

[28] cf. *Living Forces,* § 1.

[29] cf. *Monadologia physica,* Prop. 2.

themselves without parts; they must be monads.[30] The force inherent in body must accordingly be identified as the action of the monads. Motion is the external appearance of this force, and the effort to maintain motion thus has its basis in the activity of the monads.[31]

Now Kant completely rejected Leibniz's conception of the acting of the physical monad as 'perceiving' – in fact Kant retained the generally accepted modern doctrine of a dualism of ultimate existents, physical and spiritual or mental. For Kant the acting of a physical monad is a *wirkende Kraft*, an active power or force. The verb *wirken*, literally 'to work', is the German equivalent of 'to act'; it retains strongly, what has been considerably lost in the English word, the connotation of 'efficacy', and especially an efficacy *on*, which is there too in the Latin *actus*, in its derivation from *ago*, 'to drive, lead, impel'; *actus* is 'the moving or driving of an object'.[32] In the preface to the *Monadologia physica* Kant states explicitly his conception of the motive force or power of bodies which is the acting of the monads : for him the principle of all inner action or inherent force of the elements is necessarily motive, and thus externally directed, for that which is present [and acted on] is external, and it is thus not possible otherwise to conceive a force moving that which is present.[33]

That is, Kant holds that, to constitute a motive force, the acting of a monad or substance must be more than only a process of internal change; it must be outward directed, an acting *on* another. He had stated this very clearly too in his first book :[34] 'There is nothing easier than to derive the origin of that which we call motion from the general concepts we have of active force. Substance A, whose force (power) is determined by its acting

---

[30] ibid., also Prop. 1.

[31] cf. *Living Forces*, § 117.

[32] cf. Lewis and Short, *A Latin Dictionary*.

[33] op. cit.: '*cum principium omnium internarum actionum s. vim elementorum insitam motricem esse necesse sit, et extrinsecus quidem applicatam, quoniam illa praesens est externis, nec aliam ad movenda compraesentia vim concipere possimus, nisi quae illa vel repellere vel trahere conatur . . .*'

[34] *Living Forces*, § 4: '*Es ist aber nichts leichter, als den Ursprung dessen, was wir Bewegung nennen, aus den allgemeinen Begriffen der würkenden Kraft herzuleiten. Die Substanz A, deren Kraft dahin bestimmt wird, ausser sich zu würken (das ist den innern Zustand anderer Substanzen zu ändern), findet entweder in dem ersten Augenblick eihrer Bemühung sogleich einen Gegenstand, der ihre ganze Kraft erduldet, oder er findet einen solchen nicht.*'

beyond itself (that is changing the inner condition of other substances), in the first instants of its effort either directly finds an
object which suffers its entire force, or it does not find such an
object.' It is to be noted that, for Kant, the concept of active
force entails not only outward direction, an efficacy on, but that
this efficacy is constituted by an inner change in the substances
affected.

Indeed Kant goes even further than this and insists that 'it is
only possible for a change to occur in substances in so far as they
are connected with others, this mutual dependence determining
the changed condition.'[35] He points out that 'consequently a
simple substance free from all external connection, and thus left
alone to itself, is completely unchanging'.[36] Thus Kant entirely
rejects Leibniz's doctrine of monads as existing without any direct
effect from (and upon) each other.

For Kant, therefore, monads must necessarily be in relation
with each other; that is, the acting which is fundamental to the
being of a monad is essentially an activity of relating itself to
others. This brings the concept of relation right into the fore-
ground in Kant's philosophy. Relation is no mere accident of
substance; relation is essential to substance, as an intrinsic feature
of its acting.

Now Kant agreed with Leibniz that extension and thus space
must be relative, that is that they are constituted by relations
between substances. For Kant the extensive relation is accordingly a fundamental one, existing by virtue of the very acting
of the substances. As Kant said in his first work:[37] 'It is
easy to show that there would be no space and no extension if
substances did not have the power to act beyond themselves. For
without this power there is no connection or relation, without
this no order, and without this finally no space.' Not only space
but the concepts of place and situation have no meaning apart
from the acting of substance effecting relations with others: 'with-

---

[35] *Principiorum primorum cognitionis metaphysicae nova dilucidatio*, 1755, Section III,
Prop. 12: '*Nulla substantiis accidere potest mutatio, nisi quatenus cum aliis connexae sunt,
quarum dependentia reciproca mutuam status mutationem determinat.*'

[36] ibid.: '*Hinc substantia simplex omni nexu externo exempta, sibique adeo solitario relicta,
per se plane est immutabilis.*'

[37] *Living Forces*, § 9: '*Es ist leicht zu erweisen, dass kein Raum und keine Ausdehnung
sein würden, wenn die Substanzen keine Kraft hätten, ausser sich zu würken. Denn ohne diese
Kraft ist keine Verbindung, ohne diese keine Ordnung, und ohne diese endlich kein Raum.*'

out external connections, situations and relations there is no place'.[38] For Kant therefore space is in no respect a container pre-existing the physical substances or presupposed by their existence; the contrary is the case, for space is brought into being by the acting of the substances. This acting is a getting into relation with others, and only in so far as that relation is effected is there space. Now because relations for Kant are real and by no means merely apparent or phenomenal, space for him, by contrast with Leibniz, is not phenomenal.

After some further more detailed consideration of the philosophical implications, Kant came to see that substances acting on each other implies their being in existence elsewhere in relation to each other. This means that in a certain basic respect the situation of substances is presupposed by the acting of the substances and cannot be derivative from it. In other words, their being elsewhere in relation to each other is presupposed by their acting, and this relation is thus not brought into being by the acting. But what then is the ontological status of situation? It cannot itself be an actual existent, a substance; it must thus be either an attribute of substance or relative to substance. It is not a relation grounded in the physical substance, as we have seen; is it thus to be regarded as an attribute of a physical substance? This cannot be, for the concept of situation has no sense in regard to the monad simply in itself; the concept implies a plurality – the word means 'place in relation to other things' – and is thus a relative concept.

At that time – that is when Kant wrote the dissertation *Principiorum primorum cognitionis metaphysicae nova dilucidatio*, 1755, the year before the *Monadologia physica* – he saw no alternative to regarding the situation of the physical monads as grounded in the mind of God: 'Finite substances, solely by their existence, do not stand in relation with each other, and clearly comprise no community, except to the extent that they are sustained conformally in mutual dependence by the common source of their existence, namely the mind of God.'[39] It is evident that the outcome of this conclusion is to put Kant in a position

---

[38] ibid., § 7: '*Weil nun ohne aüsserliche Verknüpfungen, Lagen und Relationen kein Ort statt findet.*'

[39] op. cit., Section III, Prop. 13: '*Substantiae finitae per solam ipsarum exsistentiam nullis se relationibus respiciunt, nulloque plane commercio continentur, nisi quatenus a communi exsistentiae suae principio, divino nempe intellectu, mutuis respectibus conformatae sustinentur.*'

analogous to that of Leibniz, and of Newton; for both these thinkers, too, as we saw at the beginning of this chapter, grounded the situation of finite substances in the activity of God.

Thirteen years later, when Kant wrote the short paper which proved to be the turning-point in his thought, the outcome of which was his 'Copernican revolution', namely the paper entitled 'Von dem ersten Grunde des Unterschiedes der Gegenden im Raume', he had apparently come to be dissatisfied with the position of the earlier dissertation – dissatisfied in particular, one can conjecture, with the role which it assigns to God in the physical order; generally in the eighteenth century the disinclination to ascribing this kind of role to God was growing ever stronger. The crucial argument of this paper was that with a conception of space as relative to substances it is impossible to account for the fact of incongruent counterparts. This fact implies that there must be a certain absoluteness of direction in space, and this is entirely missing if space be derivative from the actings of the physical monads on each other. In the following year, 1769, according to Kant's correspondence, a 'great light' dawned on him; he had found the solution to this problem. It was explicated in his Inaugural Dissertation *De mundi sensibilis atque intelligibilis forma et principiis*, 1770, in terms of the new position of the critical philosophy. In this, space, and time, while still conceived as relational, are grounded, not in the activity of the physical monads, but in perceiving substances as the *a priori* form of their perceiving. The implications of this new conception are indeed far-reaching, and its consequences for the philosophy of nature have reached into this century; it has, for example, had a profound influence on Einstein's thought in his theory of relativity. A feasible alternative to the way of the critical philosophy in respect of the problem presented by incongruent counterparts was, however, open to Kant in terms of the position of his dissertation of 1755; basically that position was not as untenable as Kant thought in 1768, as we shall have occasion to see.

To further this line of thought it is necessary to pursue Kant's analysis of the acting of physical monads or substances in somewhat more detail. It follows from this conception 'that space, which is entirely without substantiality and an appearance of the external relations of unitary monads' is consequently 'not at all exhausted by a continuous division in infinitum'.[40] A body, since it is composite, is divided into constituent monads, but there cannot be an infinite number of them,[41] contrary to Leibniz. But since extension or space is ontologically different from the actual existents or monads, the infinite divisibility of extension does not entail the infinite division of body. On the other hand it can validly be said that a monad 'fills an assignable space'.[42]

To say that a monad 'fills a space', Kant is clear, does not entail that extension is an attribute of a monad, the monad thus filling the space by reason of its extension. Kant, with Leibniz, rejects the conception of extension as an attribute of substance. He states his alternative as follows: 'The monad determines the little space of its present not through a plurality of its substantial parts, but through a sphere of activity by which it keeps at a distance those external and present on both sides of itself and from a closer approach.'[43] Thus a particular extensive quantity can be assigned to a monad, that constituted by the periphery of its activity;[44] but this does not entail that the activity as such is extensively divisible.[45]

In Kant's doctrine, therefore, the acting of a physical monad is an outward directed power, effecting a change in other monads. The monads affected or acted on, however, are themselves also active; that is, their acting is also a power directed outward. Thus any monad, in coming into contact with another, encounters the active power of that other, and encounters it as a repulsive force. But in so far as the other is being acted on or affected, it is in that relationship passive, in the strict sense of 'acted on or receiving'. Thus passivity is an aspect of activity; that is, every activity is also a passivity; every activity at once affects and is affected.

---

[40] *Monadologia physica*, Section I, Scholium to Prop. IV: '*spatium, quod est substantialitatis plane expers et relationis externae unitarum monadum phaenomenon, vel in infinitum continuata divisione plane non exhauriri . . .*'

[41] ibid., Corollary.

[42] '. . . *spatium assignabile implebit. . .*'. Cf. ibid., Prop. V, and Scholium.

[43] ibid., Prop. VI: '*Monas spatiolum praesentiae suae definit non pluralitate partium suarum substantialium, sed sphaera activitatis, qua externas utrinque sibi praesentes arcet ab ulteriori ad se invicem appropinquatione.*'

[44] ibid., Prop. VII: '*Monas itaque, quae est elementum corporis primitivum, quatenus spatium implet, utique quidem quandam habet quantitatem extensivam, nempe ambitum ctivitatis, in quo vero non reperies plura, quorum unum ab alio separatum, h.e. absque alio sibi olitarium propriam habeat perdurabilitatem.*'

[45] ibid.

We have seen in the previous chapter[46] that this was Leibniz's doctrine too. Further, it was in terms of this that Leibniz accounted for the feature of antitypy or impenetrability. Kant likewise explains impenetrability by the power of resistance offered by the activity of a monad to another monad's activity attaining a closer approach.[47] Thus Kant, in the same way as does Leibniz, explains all the characters of body, extension, impenetrability, inertia,[48] elasticity,[49] and motion, as derivative from the acting of the monads.[50]

Kant consistently conceives the acting of a physical monad as a power or force outward directed and effecting a change in other monads. Thus in Kant's pre-critical doctrine relations are not, as in Leibniz's *entia mentalia*. Kant is thus, by contrast with both Leibniz and Whitehead, able to retain the full connotation of 'power' as a force acting on. In this doctrine accordingly the acting of a physical monad is a 'motive force', and Kant can retain the full concept of transeunt causality.

To confuse Kant's physical monadology with the eighteenth-century doctrine of dynamic matter would be a serious error. This doctrine, as we have seen, accepted the fundamental seventeenth-century conception of matter as in itself changeless, whereas Kant's monads effect an internal change in each other. For Kant quite explicitly the physical monads are not 'material'; that is, Kant does not identify the physical existent with matter. For him, on the contrary, matter is identified with body,[51] and body, and thus matter, is a derivative entity constituted by a plurality of monads. Kant's doctrine is not involved in the ontological confusion which we have seen to be the case in Newton's view and the doctrine of material atomism in general,[52] in which the atoms and body are regarded as ontologically of the same character and kind. For Kant body, and matter, is constituted

---

[46] See pp. 262–3.
[47] *Monadologia physica*, Section I, Prop. VIII.
[48] ibid., Section II, Prop. XI.
[49] ibid., Section II, Prop. XIII.
[50] With regard to extension and impenetrability, cf. also Kant's paper of 1764, 'Untersuchung über die Deutlichkeit der Grundsätze der natürlichen Theologie und der Moral', the Section entitled 'Der einzig sichern Methode der Metaphysik, an der Erkenntnis der Natur der Körper'.
[51] cf. on this also Pt I, Ch. 1 of 'Träume eines Geistersehers, erläutert durch Träume der Metaphysik', 1766.
[52] See above, pp. 245–7.

by the relations between monads, and an entity constituted by relations must be ontologically different from the entities which are the subjects of the relations, those in which the relations are grounded.

Since relations for Kant, by contrast with Leibniz, are not *entia mentalia*, Kant's pre-critical doctrine can be regarded as rescuing body from the phenomenal status to which Leibniz's doctrine consigns it. But this conception of the acting of the substances effecting real relations has to be subjected to much further analysis for its acceptability to be assessed. This can only be pursued in the context of a wider inquiry respecting the nature of the physical existent.

23

THE PHYSICAL EXISTENT AND BODY

With the introduction of the doctrine of material atomism towards the end of the first quarter of the seventeenth century, there entered modern thought a fundamental metaphysical position which soon came to receive widespread adherence and by the end of the century was dominant. Descartes was the one outstanding thinker of the new movement of thought who did not accept it, but it was common to Basso and the early atomists as well as the later atomists, Gassendi, Hobbes, Boyle, Newton, Locke, and it was accepted also by Leibniz and his school who repudiated material atomism, and, following him, by Kant in his physical monadology. By the end of the eighteenth century this metaphysical position had acquired the status of a tacit presupposition of thought in physical science and in the philosophy concerned with physics, and has continued so down into this century. It seemed that Whitehead might have abandoned it in *Science and the Modern World*, but the presupposition of this position exerted itself fully when he came to elaborate his metaphysics in *Process and Reality*.

This metaphysical position is that the ultimate physical existent or substance in the strict sense of the term is to be identified with the final constituents of compounds, and that consequently no compound entity can be a substance.

The long dominance of this position has given it a seeming obviousness, and any alternative to it appears hardly conceivable or so implausible as to be completely discounted. One of the fundamental tasks of philosophy, however, is to inquire into presuppositions, and as Whitehead has remarked, it is precisely those assumptions which 'appear so obvious that people do not know what they are assuming because no other way of putting things has ever occurred to them'[1] that most deserve examination.

[1] *Science and the Modern World*, p. 61 [71].

The metaphysical assumption with which we are here concerned was very explicit at the time of its original adoption, it having been introduced in opposition to the Aristotelian doctrine of body. In the Aristotelian view, taking organic body as the paradigm instance, a body is one single unitary whole, the principle of its unity being its form. As thus formed there exists a single *ousia* or substance. Such a unitary organic entity is to be contrasted with the kind of whole constituted by an aggregate collection, a mere heap. A stone is an example, for if a stone be pounded and broken up it is found to be constituted of smaller stones; that is, division of a stone does not destroy its character as stone. But if the body of an ox, say, be subjected to division the ox as such would cease to exist; the divided parts would not be oxen but butcher's meat, and thus quite different substantially. For what had constituted the ox one unitary being was its substantial form, and the division of the ox's body involved the destruction of that form, so that thereby the original substance ceased to exist. The early seventeenth-century thinkers, as we have seen,[2] especially the medical men, rejected this doctrine, maintaining that the organic body is a compound, an aggregation, and not a single substantial whole, and that the true substances are its ultimate constituents, the material atoms.

It was clear to the early protagonists of this doctrine such as Basso, Galileo, and Gassendi, that an immediate implication is that the unity which Aristotle had proclaimed is merely apparent. That is, the body only appears to be one single whole, whereas it is in fact an aggregate of discrete entities; it only appears to be continuously extensive, whereas in fact its extension is discontinuous, being divided into ultimate atomic parts. Indeed all the sensible features of a compound body, such as colour, heat, etc., must be recognized as apparent, and what is more, such appearances must be wholly subjective to the observer, and not at all inhering in the atomic constituents. There was general agreement about the subjectivity of the qualities of body presented to us in sensory perception. Most thinkers, explicitly or implicitly following the argument which was stated by Newton,[3] ascribed the quantitative features to the atoms as their 'primary qualities'.

The validity of this argument, as we have seen,[4] was challenged

---

[2] See above, Ch. 11.   [3] See above, pp. 245f.
[4] See above, pp. 247ff.

by Leibniz, who came to the conclusion that the reputed 'primary qualities' are no less apparent than are the sensible ones, and that accordingly, since all the features of body are apparent, body as such must be phenomenal. But Leibniz agreed with the fundamental metaphysical position of the material atomists, namely that body is not substance but a compound and thus an ontologically derivative entity. For Leibniz the true substances are not material atoms but non-material or spiritual atoms.

Kant, too, accepted the same metaphysical position. For him also, a body is a compound entity and not a true substance; the substances are the physical monads, which are the ultimate constituents of all compounds.

Through into this century the sciences of physics and chemistry adhered to this metaphysical position as a tacit presupposition. In the nineteenth century, chemical theory was put firmly on an atomic basis, all chemical 'substances' being displayed as constituted as compounds, each of a definite number of atoms, these being all alike in their nature. In this century, when these atoms were found to be not atomic after all but themselves compounds, the search has continued for the ultimate constituents as the final physical existents.

This procedure was carried to the limit by Whitehead in *Process and Reality* in his conception of the final existents or actual entities as being not only atomic extensively but also durationally so; they are of a certain minimal extension and endure very briefly. The simplest compound entity is one constituted by one single actual entity superseding another in a single chain. Whitehead has conjectured that electrons, for example, might be such chains or routes of single actual entities – that is, unless it be found that electrons are themselves compound in the way the 'atoms' were found to be. More complex compounds, those constituting the 'atoms', molecules, and on to macroscopic bodies, consist of bundles or groups of such routes of supersession. Fundamental in this doctrine is that it is the ultimate constituents into which all compounds are analysable that are the true physical existents, the substances. All compounds, and bodies in particular, are derivative entities, of a different ontological status from that of actual entities. In Whitehead's theory all these derivative entities are 'societies', constituted by particular ordered relationships between the constituent actual entities.

Now it is certainly the case that one of the most significant results of modern research in physics is to have displayed bodies as compounds, not only of an enormous degree of complexity but also of constituents of extremely minute magnitudes. Any philosophical theory to count as tenable at all has to take the fullest account of this scientific result. But the question has to be examined whether these constituents are to be identified as the true physical existents, the substances, and that only they can be regarded as being such. It is also necessary to inquire to what extent the philosophical theories are able satisfactorily to account for the compounds and the features they are found to exhibit.

Let us start with the theory of material atomism. Since material atoms are by their nature devoid of any internal change, it follows ineluctably that groups or collections of them can have no character other than that which is the sum of the characters of the constituent atoms. Groups of atoms can be no more than bare aggregate collections, and can have no feature qua group which is other than the arithmetical sum of the features of the individual atoms. Newton saw this very clearly in the passage referred to above.[5] Moreover, these aggregate collections can be no more than purely fortuitous, there being nothing in the nature of matter – extension, solidity, mass, inertia – necessitating atoms to collect in groups. Yet right at the beginning of the modern theory of material atomism it was found necessary to distinguish specific groups of atoms, staying together and behaving as groups, and indeed exhibiting a particular group structure and character. That is, the mere conception of atoms and their bare aggregation was not found sufficient for scientific purposes, indeed not even by the very originators of the modern theory of material atomism; Basso earliest, then others, introduced the conception of groups of atoms in a particular structure, Gassendi giving them the name 'molecules' (little masses) which was thence-forward adopted. The molecular theory has continued to be of great importance in scientific theory down to the present day.

From the philosophical point of view, the problem is that we have the conception of a group which has a particular character as that group, with a group structure and behaviour which is something over and above and not reducible to the individual

5 See above, pp. 245–6.

characters of the constituents. For there is nothing in the concept of material atoms whereby a togetherness of atoms in a group in a particular pattern or structure should result in a particular character of the group – for example, that one particular patterned structure should have the character of water, another of salt, another of sulphur, and so on. In recent theory there is more than only the number of constituents involved; there is also a particular mathematical pattern, a geometrical structure, for example. But the conception of a geometrical pattern or structure goes beyond what is entailed in the conception of the constituents individually, for the geometrical structure of the group is not reducible to or derivable from the individual extendedness of the atoms. All this in addition to the question, which exercised the ingenuity of a good many thinkers in the seventeenth century, of how the atoms come to adhere in groups at all. Newton explained this adherence by an attractive force, and this came to be the generally accepted explanation. Newton saw clearly, however, that it is impossible to ascribe this force to matter, given the nature of matter, and he grounded it in the action of God. But in the eighteenth century the philosophical problem was ignored; attractive force was ascribed to matter without any consideration of the question whether such an ascription can consistently be made. The theory worked for scientific purposes, and positivistically that was regarded as sufficient. Likewise the geometrical structure of the group was also positivistically accepted, without regard to the question of the philosophical consistency of the conception.

In respect of these philosophical issues, therefore, it is manifest that the theory of material atomism is extremely inadequate. The basic reason for this inadequacy is that in this theory, given the nature of matter, it is impossible for the atoms to have relations to each other.[6] For there to be groups of atoms which are more than mere aggregates, however, implies that there must be relations between the members of the group.

Leibniz saw the necessity of this very clearly, and his philosophy does furnish relations. Indeed as we have seen, in his doctrine all the features of body – extension, impenetrability or solidity, mass, inertia – are relational, and the very concept of body is a relational concept. So he is able in principle to account

6 See above, Ch. 22, pp. 265f.

for all the features of a group and group behaviour for which the theory of material atomism can have no explanation at all.

Now in Leibniz's theory all relations are phenomenal. That is, they have the status of ideas in the monads. Thus for him, body, too, is an idea in the monads. Apart from that idea there is a mere aggregate; it is the idea which provides the unity whereby there is one thing, a body, and not a mere plurality. This means, however, that in Leibniz's theory while body is not a substance but a plurality, the plurality in itself as that plurality does not have a unity whereby it is a body; the unity of that plurality for Leibniz is no more than an experiential feature within the constituents of the plurality severally. That is, what exists in actuality is a mere aggregate, and the members of the group act in a certain harmony, which gives to it an appearance of a group character, by virtue of a co-ordination pre-established by God of the actions of the constituent monads which are in themselves separate from each other. This theory would be acceptable only if no alternative were indeed possible, as Leibniz maintained.

One possible alternative is the doctrine of Whitehead, which is in many respects close to that of Leibniz, but differs from the latter in this crucial respect of relations. Whitehead has sought to develop a theory of relations which would provide a real, as opposed to Leibniz's merely phenomenal, connection between the substances. Thereby a body as a 'society' of actual entities could truly be something more than an aggregate collection as it is for Leibniz in the end. To assess Whitehead's alternative it is necessary to examine his theory of 'society'.

A 'society' is a derivative entity constituted by a plurality of actual entities which are in a genetic interrelatedness by virtue of their prehensive activities. What constitutes the group of actual entities in this society as opposed to some other is the particular form or character exhibited by the individual prehensive actings, that form or character being common to all members of the group. This common form or character Whitehead terms the 'defining characteristic' of the particular society in question.[7] That is to say, it is by reason of this shared or common character that a body is distinguished as having this geometrical shape and size, these features whereby we designate it wood as opposed to metal, and so on. The 'defining characteristic' of a society is thus very similar

[7] PR, Pt I, Ch. 3, Section 2.

K

to the 'substantial form' of the Aristotelian theory. But whereas Aristotle conceived this as the form of one single substance, Whitehead conceives it as the form which is common to a plurality of individual substances, that is, each of them individually manifesting that form in their prehensive actings. And since each of the prehensive acts is an act of relating the subjects of the acts to other actual entities, the common form will be the form of the individual relations. Thus it can be said that Whitehead does have what Leibniz is unable to have, namely a plurality which is something more than a mere aggregate. As Whitehead has said, 'a society is more than a set of entities to which the same class-name applies'.[8] A set of entities to which the same class-name applies would be a mere aggregate, but in a society the constituent entities are related to each other by their prehensive acts and the common form is the form of the acts severally.

There is, however, a difficulty with this theory. This difficulty is rooted in Whitehead's conception, which we examined in the previous chapter,[9] of the prehensive acts as acts of 'perception'. According to this conception there is a perception by an actual entity 'here' of the others as 'there' and 'there' and 'there'. Each 'there' and 'there' and 'there' from 'here' specifies a different geometrical relationship from the standpoint 'here', and the totality of these relationships is co-ordinated in a specific geometrical pattern. Each actual entity has its particular perspective of the total geometrical pattern. That is, each perceives the others as in that particular geometrical perspective to itself. That perception of the geometrical perspective is 'in' the perceiving actual entity; there is nothing as it were 'reaching out beyond' the perceiver. This is confirmed by a consideration of Whitehead's analysis of a 'physical prehension' as 'the feeling of another actuality'.[10] 'Thus a simple physical feeling is one feeling which feels another feeling',[11] he explains, and this means that 'the subjective form of a physical feeling is re-enaction of the subjective form of the feeling felt'.[12] It is clear, therefore, that for Whitehead the prehensive relation of one actual entity to another is a feeling in the prehender, that is, it is an item within the prehending actual entity. It turns out therefore that relations in Whitehead's doc-

[8] PR 124 [137].   [9] See Ch. 22, pp. 272–3.
[10] PR 317 [343].   [11] ibid., p. 335 [362].
[12] ibid.

trine are not so different from what they are in Leibniz's; in both relations exist strictly as a feature within each of the monads or actual entities constituting a body or society. In Whitehead's theory the constituent actual entities have feelings conformally with each other, and in Leibniz's theory the constituent monads have ideas conformally with each other. In Whitehead's theory the act of feeling of the felt actual entity is strictly over when it becomes the object of the feeling of the prehending actual entity. Thus that the feelings are conformal does not suffice to render the constituent actual entities any less existentially separate than are Leibniz's monads with their conformal ideas. That in Whitehead's case the conformity of the feelings is by derivation from each other, whereas in Leibniz's the conformity of the ideas derives from God, does not affect the point about the existential separateness of the constituents. That is to say, in Whitehead's theory, too, in the end the constituents of a body constitute an aggregate.

Let us now examine Kant's doctrine to see whether with his conception of relations there is any different an outcome. Relations in Kant's theory are constituted by the actings of the monads being outward directed and affecting a change in other monads. His monads are fully in interaction; existentially they are not in isolation as are material atoms, the monads of Leibniz, and the actual entities of Whitehead. Thus Kant's theory supplies part at least of what is required for an adequate conception of body. But there is the other equally indispensable requirement, namely that the constituents must be not only in interrelation but that this interrelation must constitute the group of related entities a 'unity', that unity being manifested as the particular character or form of the body in question.

Kant's conception of the acting of the monads, as we have seen, satisfactorily furnishes a motive force – which is lacking in the other theories – but does this acting at the same time provide a *unity* among the monads acting on and reacting to each other? Kant maintained that it did by his providing the reason for the monads cohering in groups – a reason which is completely lacking in the materialistic doctrine. In the previous chapter we investigated Kant's theory that a monad fills or occupies a specific volume or space by virtue of its activity, and that its 'sphere of activity' is determined by the repulsive force of the monads acted on. Now Kant argues further that 'through the power of impenetrability alone a body would not enjoy a definite volume, if there were not in addition an inherent equal attraction, both together defining the limits of extension'.[13] Kant maintains[14] that the force which is operative in the direction contrary to that of the repulsion must be an attractive force. Now that force which is contrary to the repulsive force is clearly the active force, the force of 'acting on'. This therefore is identified by Kant as the 'attractive force' – the force which Newton's work had brought into prominence as required to account for the factor of gravitation. Kant maintains that his two forces, attractive and repulsive, manifest the inverse square law in their operation, thus satisfying the requirements of Newton's physics.[15] The question is however whether a force 'acting on' can consistently be regarded as being an 'attractive' force. The most that could be said, it seems to me, is that the force 'acting on' could be regarded as *analogous to* an 'attractive' force, and that for the purposes of physics this would entirely suffice. That might well be granted, but philosophically considered this does not constitute a *unity* between the entities in question, that is if there be only an 'acting on' and an equivalent 'repulsion'. For that would leave the entities existentially separate and thus not truly in relation. But even an 'attractive' force could not effect a true unity, since such a force could not effect a relation, a relation implying, as Kant was clear,[16] effecting a change in the inner condition of the other entity.

It is only with relations conceived as effecting an inner change in the entity acted on that a unity is possible between entities, and moreover a unity which is manifested as the particular form or character of the group of entities so related. In his pre-critical writings Kant does not work out such a theory of unity, and it may be that the difficulties facing him in being able to do so were part of the reason for his 'Copernican revolution'. For in the critical writings, starting with the *De mundi sensibilis*, Kant turned immediately to the problem of unity. In this dissertation Kant dealt with the 'form' which is requisite for unity in so far

---

[13] *Monadologia physica*, Section II, Prop. X: '*Corpora per vim solam impenetrabilitatis non gauderent definito volumine, nisi adforet alia pariter insita attractionis, cum illa coniunctim limitem definiens extensionis.*'

[14] ibid.: '*Qui cum repulsioni exadversum agat, est attractio.*'

[15] cf. ibid., Prop. X, Scholium.

[16] See above, pp. 277f.

as the sensible is concerned, and he carried this endeavour through in the *Critik der reinen Vernunft*, providing there the intellectual forms which are also requisite. It will not be necessary to elaborate his doctrine in detail since it is sufficiently known. For our purposes it is necessary only to note that in this later doctrine the requisite forms are grounded in the experiencing mind as the *a priori* conditions of experience. The significant point is that these forms are the essential forms of relatedness. Thus the outcome of Kant's new doctrine for the problem of relations is to bring him to a position very close to that of Leibniz. Relations for Kant, spatial, temporal, and causal, are all grounded in the mind. Accordingly the concept of body, too, is mind-dependent, phenomenal — though it is, to use Leibniz's phrase, a *phaenomenon bene fundatum*. For two centuries a vast proportion of the labour of philosophers has consisted in a struggle with the insuperable problems bequeathed by this position. I agree with Whitehead that the time is more than ripe to admit that the position is untenable and to search for another. This is a main part of the effort of this book.

At this point it becomes important to examine more closely the reasons for the inadequacy of Kant's pre-critical position on relations. Kant had recognized that if an acting entity is to be veridically related to another by its acting, then the other must be internally changed by that acting. Why was Kant not able to give effect to this recognition? The reason, it seems to me, was that Kant, although he had rejected the doctrine of material atomism and did not conceive his physical monads as 'material', was nevertheless implicitly deeply influenced by the modern doctrine of material atomism which, by his time, was completely dominant in physics. This influence is manifest in his adherence to an ontological dualism of physical and mental substances. Indeed it is in this dualism that lies the root of his difficulty. For by it he had deprived himself of the means of being able to conceive his monads as involving internal change. He had thereby also deprived himself of in fact being able to have relations which effect such an internal change. It is not without significance that in his new doctrine he turned to the other side of the ontological dichotomy for a grounding of relations.

These considerations seem to me fully to confirm Whitehead's contention that the ontological dualism introduced in the seventeenth century with its doctrine of matter as substance has been a disaster and must be rejected entirely. The clear need is for a different ontological conception of the physical existent from that which has dominated thought for nearly four centuries.

Whitehead's has been the major effort of our time to develop an alternative conception of the physical existent. We have seen however that his system involves difficulties in respect of this crucial issue of relations. His difficulty is the contrary to that of the Kant of the pre-critical writings, for in this respect White- head is completely unaffected by the materialistic doctrine. Nor does it consist in the fact of his conceiving the acting of sub- stances as acts of prehending – indeed as such there is an impor- tant analogy between Whitehead's conception and that of the pre-critical Kant. The difficulty for Whitehead's doctrine is rooted in his having been too strongly influenced by the Neoplatonic inheritance in the British empiricist tradition and consequently conceiving prehension as perception. But not perception as such, but perception understood as the having of 'ideas' by the per- ceiver – whether they be 'images', or 'representations', or 'feelings conformal with' the perceived, is irrelevant to the issue.

There is an alternative doctrine of perception to be found in Plato's *Theaetetus*[17] divergent from that of the Neoplatonic Plato. In this, perception is not the having, the subjective entertaining of ideas; perception in this theory is something which is the out- come of the 'motion' (*kinēsis*) of both the perceiver and the per- ceived. This *kinēsis* is an acting on the part both of the perceiver and the perceived, and in both the 'action' also has its aspect of 'passion'.[18] That the 'active' must have the reciprocal aspect of the 'passive', we have seen was recognized too by both Leibniz and Kant.[19]

If Whitehead had recognized this he would have had a rather different conception of prehension, even if thought of as 'per- ception'. It would have brought him closer to Kant's conception of acting as an 'acting on', and thus of acting as a *relating*. It is true that Whitehead does seek to have prehension a relation; that is indeed a main strength of his theory. But he is frustrated

---

[17] cf. Plato, *Theaetetus*, 156–7. I do not intend to maintain that this is Plato's own doctrine; but this does not affect my argument.
[18] ibid.
[19] cf. above, pp. 262f. and 281f.

in this by his Neoplatonic presuppositions, the outcome of which is that the relations turn out to be 'feelings of conformity'. We have seen the insufficiency of this conception; what is needed is Kant's conception of relations as effecting a change in the other. I am aware that Whitehead would raise the objection that such a conception would raise difficulties for epistemology; we shall deal with that issue later.

Let us attempt to see what such a conception of acting as relating would come to. If an entity acts on another and thereby effects an internal change in the other, this implies that in their transaction the entity acted on must be in one respect passive, as the recipient of that effect; but in another respect, in order to 'receive', it must be 'active' – that is, 'receiving' is an 'acting'. Every passivity has its corresponding aspect of activity, and every activity has its corresponding aspect of passivity. This implies that the entity 'acting on' is itself affected by the activity of the other entity. It is this mutual acting and being affected which constitues the *relating*. And further, the 'character' of the relation will be constituted by the particular mode of the effect. For what the effect is will depend upon the initially acting entity, that is, its character and the character of its acting, and upon the character of the recipient. This means that the character of the relation will be the outcome of the mutual actings. The relation is clearly not something apart from the entities in relation, a *tertium quid*. But it does constitute the unity effected by the relation as something more than the entities conceived as not in that relation. Moreover, the character of the relation will be the character of the unity. It is obvious that there is no need for this relationship to be confined to two entities; there can be a unity constituted by a mutual relatedness between a considerable plurality of entities.

The character of the relatedness and therefore of the unity must, we have seen, inevitably depend upon the character of the actings of the entities involved. There is clearly no need to assume a like character in every entity, nor that, taking a particular entity for consideration, the character of its acting in respect of different entities must in each case be the same or alike. The contrary is rather the necessity, since the character of the acting will be determined by the character of the entity affected. Thus there must be a vast variety of kinds of relationship, and thus of unity. Also it is clear that there can be no necessity for the acting of an entity to affect another in every case to an equal degree and extent; that is, a vast variety, extent, and degree of change is possible in various affected entities, the change in some instances being slight in comparison with that in other instances. Accordingly, the unity in some instances will be trivial compared with that effected in other instances of relatedness.

In some instances the change will be so partial and of so particular a character as to leave the entities in question for the most part unaffected in their character. An instance of this kind of relationship would be that which results in motion, that is, locomotion or change of place.

At the other end of the spectrum, the unity constituted by the interacting, and thus interrelated, entities could be of such a kind as to exhibit the interrelated group of entities in question as distinct in character from other groups. There will in this way be a group character, qua that group, which will be derivable from the individual characters of the constituents, but not reducible to them as their sum, since the group character will be the character of the *relation between* the constituents, and not the collection or arithmetical sum of the individual characters. In terms of this theory, therefore, we are able to have a conception of body which is not an aggregate.

This theory can be pushed still further. We need to bring into consideration at this point the issue raised at the beginning of this chapter, namely whether only the constituents of compounds are to be identified as substances, as the true existents, all compounds being derivative existents and thus having an ontological status different from that of the constituents. I wish to argue that it is possible validly to conceive a plurality of entities in a particular interactive unity such as to constitute the whole a substantive existent. I shall develop this in the next chapter.

24

THE PHYSICAL EXISTENT,
SIMPLE AND COMPOUND

At the beginning of his *Monadology* Leibniz formulated tersely
what had quite early been fundamental in his philosophy : 'There
must be simple substances, since there are compounds, for the
compounded is but a collection or an *aggregate* of simples.'[1] These
simple substances he termed 'monads', from '*Monas* . . . a Greek
word signifying unity or that which is one'.[2] Until his correspondence with Des Bosses, which occurred during the last ten years
of his life, he had maintained the position that only these simples
were to be regarded as substances; then he came to waver in this
and admitted also 'compound' or 'composite' substances, instances
of which are 'animals or other organic beings'.[3] In his *Principles
of Nature and of Grace* (1714) he also specified 'compound substance' which 'is a collection of simple substances, or *monads*'.[4]
There were significant moves toward this position in his correspondence with De Volder, which had occurred earlier (1699–
1706). This change in his position is important because it arose
as a result of grappling with some basic issues in the concept of
substance.

Quite early Leibniz had gaind a clear appreciation that crucial
in the concept of substance is *unity*. This was an insight going
back to Plato and Aristotle, and which had been prominent also
in medieval thought. Throughout most of his career Leibniz had
maintained that unity can be ascribed only to the simple constituents of compounds, since 'the compounded is but a collection
or an *aggregate* of simples'. This to him had been the ultimate
justification for the metaphysical position which we saw, in the

---

[1] op. cit., § 2; Loemker, p. 643, G.VI, 607.
[2] *The Principles of Nature and of Grace*, § 1; Loemker p. 636, G.VI, 598.
[3] Loemker, p. 617; G.II, 506.
[4] op. cit., § 1; Loemker, p. 636, G.VI, 598.

previous chapter, that Leibniz shared with most of his contemporaries.

In his later years, however, there began impinging on him that there is a significant difference between organic and non-organic compounds, and that the former are not satisfactorily to be regarded as mere aggregates, for on this basis there is no means of making any such distinction as that between organic and non-organic.

Now as long as he retained as a fundamental metaphysical position that only the simples are to be regarded as true substances, he was committed to having to ground the difference between the organic and non-organic in the constituent monads individually. Pressed on this fundamental issue by Des Bosses, Leibniz for a time sought a way of resolving the problem by resuscitating the late scholastic conception of a *vinculum substantiale* (substantial chain), but in the end he had to confess that on his basis he could not consistently admit such an entity : 'Therefore I should prefer to say that there are no substances over and above monads, but only appearances.'[5]

In the De Volder correspondence Leibniz sought to work out a conception of organic body consistently in terms of his fundamental metaphysical position. He wrote :

'If you think of mass as an aggregate containing many substances, you can still conceive of a single pre-eminent substance or primary entelechy in it. For the rest, I arrange in the monad or the simple substance, complete with an entelechy, only one primitive passive force which is related to the whole mass of the organic body. The other subordinate monads placed in the organs do not make up a part of it, though they are immediately required by it, and they combine with the primary monad to make the organic corporeal substance, or the animal or plant. I therefore distinguish : (1) the primitive entelechy or soul; (2) primary matter or primitive passive power; (3) the complete monad formed by these two; (4) mass or secondary matter, or the organic machine in which innumerable subordinate monads concur; and (5) the animal or corporeal substance which the dominating monad makes into one machine.'[6]

5 Loemker, p. 614; G.II, 504.
6 Loemker, pp. 530–1; G.II, 252.

We see here that Leibniz recognizes in an organic body a singular kind of unity, which induces him even to speak twice in this passage of the 'organic corporeal *substance*', and that on his basis this unity cannot be a feature or attribute of the whole, of the aggregate *per se*, but that it can be found only in either the plurality of constituent monads severally or in one of them as 'dominant'. He chooses the latter alternative since in organisms, especially animal ones, there seems to be a control of the whole by a particular centre. That is, the unity of the organic whole is furnished by one dominant monad. The other point relevant here is that, for reasons we examined in an earlier chapter,[7] this unity must be an 'idea' in the dominant monad.

But there is another aspect of Leibniz's doctrine which is important to our inquiry, though it is not readily brought into consistency with the foregoing conception of unity. Consider the following statement to De Volder :

'When I say that even if it is corporeal, a substance contains an infinity of machines, I think it must be added at the same time that it forms one machine composed of these machines and that it is actuated, besides, by one entelechy, without which it would contain no principle of true unity.'[8]

There are two points in this to which I wish to draw attention. The first is the conception of a 'machine'. Leibniz uses the term in the strict sense of a whole of parts, these moving in a specific manner, through each being adapted for a specific function, designed to produce a specific effect. This is to be contrasted with the conception of 'organism', which is a whole in which the parts are 'organs', in the original sense of 'instruments', each *functioning with reference to the whole*. On his basis Leibniz cannot admit an organism in this strict sense, for the parts, the constituent monads, do not function with reference to the whole as its 'instruments', since they are existentially separate from each other; their acting, that is, perceptions, are predetermined by God to be in conformity with each other. So Leibniz is left with a mechanism, as comes out clearly in the following passage in *The Principles*

[7] See above, pp. 269ff; also pp. 288f.
[8] Loemker, p. 529; G.II, 250.

of Nature and of Grace,[9] which I wish here also to take into consideration together with the previously quoted one :

'And each outstanding simple substance or monad which forms the centre of a compound substance (such as an animal, for example), and is the principle of its uniqueness, is surrounded by a mass composed of an infinity of other monads which constitute the body belonging to this central monad, corresponding to the affections by which it represents, as in a kind of centre, the things which are outside of it. This body is *organic* when it forms a kind of automaton or natural machine, which is a machine not only as a whole but also in its smallest observable parts.'

That is, an organic body is in the end only *apparently* 'organic'.

But, and this is the second point, both passages, and more especially so the former, bring out Leibniz's contention that a mechanism nevertheless requires to be 'actuated, besides, by one entelechy, without which it would contain no principle of true unity'. It is to be noted that this contention is, first, that there is a need for a 'principle of activity' whereby the machine is 'actuated'; this is what we had previously discussed as the necessary 'active force'. Secondly, this principle of activity is also to be a 'principle of unity'; that is, it is to be the source of the unity of the bodily whole, that which unifies it into a one which is not merely an aggregate.

The question which arises is how, on his basis, this is possible at all. Our analysis in the preceding chapters has shown that in terms of his fundamental metaphysical position Leibniz is not able to have a principle of activity which can constitute a 'motive force' capable of 'actuating' a body, since the acting of a monad is, as he finally conceives it, not a force 'acting on' but is an activity of perception confined to the subjectivity of the monad. For the same reason Leibniz cannot have his principle of activity an 'activity of unifying'; the unity is a perceptual one, phenomenal only.

Yet it is significant that Leibniz saw clearly the need for a principle of activity which is a principle of unity. And further, it is this recognition which drove him in his later years to admit

9 Loemker, p. 637; G.VI, 598–9.

a 'compound substance'. In doing so he was being impelled toward a very important change in his conception of substance, and indeed even of his conception of a monad. There is evidence of his moving toward this, prior to his correspondence with Des Basses or at least independently of the considerations there raised, in his paper 'On Nature Itself' (1698):[10]

'it can be concluded that there must be found in corporeal substance a *primary entelechy* or first recipient [πρῶτον δεκτιηὸν] of activity, that is, a primitive motive force which, superadded to extension, or what is merely geometrical, and mass, or what is merely material, always acts indeed and yet is modified in various ways by the concourse of bodies, through a conatus or impetus. It is this substantial principle itself which is called the *soul* in living beings and *substantial form* in other beings, and inasmuch as it truly constitutes one substance with matter, or a unit in itself, it makes up what I call a monad.'

A minor point in this passage is the statement that the dominant monad 'always acts indeed and yet is *modified* in various ways by the concourse of bodies'. Strictly in his doctrine monads cannot be modified by each other; at most it is '*as if* they were modified'. It is not without significance, however, that Leibniz said what he did; it accords with what follows.

The next point, which is of considerable importance, is Leibniz's statement that the acting or 'primitive force' of the dominant monad is the 'substantial principle' of the 'corporeal substance'. That is, it is this acting which is the 'principle' of that whole being a 'substance'. In maintaining this, Leibniz has moved away from the position of conceiving the dominant monad as only one substance among other substances in an aggregate collection. That there has occurred a shift in his position is confirmed in the next point.

This is that the 'substantial principle' is not conceived simply as an act or 'force' but as a 'formed act', and it is this 'formed act' which is the 'substantial form' of the 'corporeal substance' – in living substances this substantial form is the 'soul' of the substance. Again here the dominant monad is conceived as something more than just one monad among others, as in his earlier posi-

[10] Loemker, pp. 503–4; G.IV, 511.

tion. The earlier position, it could be said, was Platonic: the soul is one substance in the body, that is, one among others. But the position adopted in the passage under consideration is the quite different, the Aristotelian one, of the soul conceived as the 'substantial form' of the body.

It seems to me that Leibniz's thought was definitely at that stage in a transition from a Platonic to an Aristotelian position, but that Leibniz did not fully appreciate this and accordingly did not consistently push it through. In this respect the concluding portion of the sentence we have under consideration is especially interesting. It states: 'and inasmuch as it truly constitutes one substance with matter, or a unit in itself, it makes up what I call a monad.' What, in this statement, is meant by 'matter'? It could be said (and Leibniz, pressed on it, might have said), in accordance with the passage in a letter to De Volder quoted above,[11] that 'matter' means the 'primitive passive power' of the dominant monad, that which is the 'passivity' correspondent to the 'activity' of the monad. With this interpretation Leibniz would retain his Platonic position. But on that basis the activity of the dominant monad could not constitute the 'substantial form' of the whole. This Aristotelian position could be maintained, however, with a different interpretation of 'matter' in this statement, namely with 'matter' conceived as the aspect of passivity, not of only one monad among others, but the aspect of passivity of the activities of all the monads making up that particular whole of which the dominant act is the substantial form.

The question is whether such a conception is at all consistently possible. The one condition requisite for its possibility is the abandonement of Leibniz's earlier position, the Neoplatonic one, of the acting of substance as perception, conceived as the purely subjective having of 'ideas' – this position is completely inconsistent with the Aristotelian conception of 'substantial form'. What is needed is a conception of the acting of substance as an 'acting on' – the position of the Kant of the pre-critical writings.

With such a conception of acting, there would be a whole constituted by the plurality of monads reciprocally acting on each other and being affected by each other. The being affected would be the passivity relatively to the activity causing the effect. If there were a dominant monad, by its activity affecting all the

11 Page 298.

rest, their being affected by it would constitute a passivity in relation to the activity of the dominant monad, and in this respect these monads would constitute the 'matter' which is 'formed' by the activity of the dominant monad. The term 'matter' here clearly has the Aristotelian sense of 'that which receives form' or 'that which is formed'; and the 'form' will be the character of the acting of the dominant monad. In this way it is possible to have – and Leibniz could have had – a valid conception of the dominant monad as the 'substantial form' of the 'corporeal sub-stance'. What is more, this dominant acting, with its 'matter', would constitute a 'unit in itself', and would thus fully accord with what Leibniz termed a 'monad', for what is fundamental in the conception of a monad is precisely the 'unity'.

In the position thus developed, there would be a true unity constituted by the acting of the dominant monad, for the acting in this conception is a true 'relating'. The acting of the dominant monad relates it to every other, and thereby relates all with itself into a true unit – very different from a phenomenal one.

It is important to be clear about the implications of the position thus developed. The fundamental point to be noted is that there is a most important difference between the dominant monad and the other constituents of the 'corporeal substance'. The dominant monad will not be simply one monad among the others, differing from them only in having a greater internal complexity – having consciousness, for example; the dominant monad will in a certain respect be inclusive of the others. This it would have to be to constitute the substantial form and the unity of the whole. Thus there is involved here a definite departure from the metaphysical presupposition which has ruled modern thought, namely that only the constituents of compounds can be substances. For what has emerged in this new position is the conception of a monad or substance which is not a constituent of a compound but itself a compound.

Leibniz's statement in the *Monadology* that 'there must be simple substances, since there are compounds', can be accepted as valid and true; but the rest of his statement, which reads, 'for the compounded is but a collection or an *aggregate* of simples', does not hold without qualification. The conception of a 'com-pound substance' is not a logical self-contradiction, nor is there sufficient reason for regarding it as metaphysically impossible. Leibniz thought earlier that there is such a metaphysical impossibility, but this was because he assumed that only a 'simple' can be a 'unit' or 'unitary'. This is, however, an unwarrantable assumption. 'Unity' implies, as Leibniz was well aware, the 'unity' or 'unifying' of *many*; and logically the 'many' could be 'many simples'.

In a certain respect Leibniz could be said to have Aristotle on his side in respect of this issue, for Aristotle had often said that 'no substance is composed of substances'.[12] However, if Aristotle's doctrine be examined carefully it will be seen that Aristotle does not hold that statement without qualification. More fully his statement of his position is: 'A substance cannot consist of substances present in it in complete reality; for things that are thus in complete reality two are never in complete reality one, though if they are *potentially* two, they can be one'.[13]

A most important exemplification of Aristotle's doctrine in this respect is to be found in his theory of chemical combination, which we expounded earlier.[14] We saw that Aristotle distinguished a genuine *mixis* or chemical combination from, on the one hand, a *genesis* or coming-into-being of a substance which has involved the complete *phthora*, passing-away or destruction, of one or more substances, and from, on the other hand, a mere aggregate juxtaposition, *synthesis*, in which the constituents remain fully existent in the compound. There would be no *mixis*, Aristotle held, if the constituents of the compound either entirely ceased to exist in coming into the combination or remained fully existent in the compound. His answer to the question of how the constituents of a *mixis* can exist in it without their being 'fully existent' in it, was that their existence must be 'potential' and not 'actual'. Accordingly, to return to the passage quoted above, if substances are 'potentially' two, they can be 'actually' one.

This Aristotelian analysis is very relevant to the problem with which we are concerned, namely, how a compound substance can be regarded as constituted of simple substances. If the simple substances remain in every respect fully actual, then a compound

---

[12] *Met.*, 1041a4–5: οὔτ' ἐστὶν οὐσία οὐδεμία ἐξ οὐσιῶν. (Ross tr.).

[13] *Met.*, 1039a3–6 (Ross tr.): ἀδύνατον γὰρ οὐσίαν ἐξ οὐσιῶν εἶναι ἐνυπαρχουσῶν ὡς ἐντελεχείᾳ· τὰ γὰρ δύο οὕτως ἐντελεχείᾳ οὐδέποτε ἓν ἐντελεχείᾳ, ἀλλ' ἐὰν δυνάμει δύο ᾖ, ἔσται ἕν.

[14] See above, pp. 141f.

substance with them as constituents is impossible. This had been very clear to the early seventeenth-century protagonists of material atomism – who knew their Aristotle – and was the basic ground upon which they rejected the Aristotelian doctrine of a whole bodily being as one substance. For in the new theory, the material atoms are substances, and they are each fully actual; so that a compound of them cannot constitute a substance.

The Platonism which was so strongly influential in this doctrine – contributing the conception of substance as fully actual and in itself changeless – also affected Leibniz; he accordingly conceived his simple monads as in themselves fully actual.[15] He did not sufficiently appreciate, however, that this is inconsistent with the conception of monads as involving internal change by virtue of their acting. This is therefore a further aspect of the Platonism in Leibniz's conception of substance which must be rejected, the more especially so if we adopt the conception of the acting of substances as an acting on each other and effecting changes in each other. Now, with the repudiation of the conception of substance as fully actual and changeless, the factor of 'potentiality' involved in substance must be explicitly and fully recognized.

With this let us return to the analysis of the conception of a compound substance constituted by a number of simple substances. In so far as the compound is a 'substance' it is 'actual', that is, an actually achieved unity. What is unified will be the plurality of constituents. Now the actual unity of necessity transcends the constituents individually, and since it is the *unity* which is actual, *in relation to it* the constituents must necessarily be potential; this is necessarily entailed in the relationship. In themselves, however (that is, not in reference to the actual unity) they are actual substances, and must be such in order to be able to be constituents. Furthermore, they must be in themselves actual in order to be able to act; the actualized unity is not due solely to the acting of the dominant or unifying monad, for the latter acting, to be an 'acting on' requires a responsive acting in the others. Thus the constituents must necessarily, by their acting, contribute to the achieved unity. So there is required, for a unity to be possible at all, the actings of the constituents unified, *and* the transcendent acting unifying the constituents. To say that

<hr>

15 cf. *Monadology*, §§ 4–9.

there is a unity is to say that the unity is actual; and with reference to that actual unity, the constituents are potential. Thus there is a compound which is a substance by virtue of its acting achieving unity, and as such it is actual; and it will be constituted of substances, which are actual substances by virtue of their acting, but which, in reference to the actual unity of the compound, are potential.

The previous chapter has shown the necessity for the conception of compounds which are more than mere aggregates. It has been argued that neither the doctrine of material atomism nor the spiritual atomism of Leibniz or the Whiteheadian theory of actual entities is able to have such a conception of a compound. The reason is that none of these theories is able to have a compound with a unity qua compound. Such a unity, we have shown in this chapter, must be a substantial unity, the unity of a substance, and further such a unity must be the achievement of an act of unifying. An act of unifying must be an 'acting on' those entities which are unified, effecting changes in them, and this implies a reciprocal acting on their part, so that the entities acted on must be substances acting. The compound of these constituents will be a true substance, by its act of unifying and the resultant unity. The unity will thus be the form or character of the unifying act, and this form or character will accordingly be the 'substantial form' or the 'defining character' of the compound whole.

This conception of substantial form obviously requires justification. 'Form' is usually thought of as a quality of a thing, typified by the colour spread over the surface of the thing. We have previously[16] discussed Leibniz's highly important arguments demonstrating that the conception, common to the material atomists and Descartes, of extension and other characters as *qualities* of individual substances is erroneous, and that these characters must be conceived instead as the characters of *relations*. I am here following Leibniz in this argument, and generalizing it; *all* characters, qualitative as well as quantitative, are characters of relations. In other words, the usual conception of form as a quality of an individual substance on the analogy of a colour spread over a surface, is being entirely rejected. Form or character pertains to relations, and to substances only in respect of their relation to others. I am going further than Leibniz by

 all qualities are characters of relations

16 See above, Ch. 20, pp. 243ff.

maintaining that the so-called 'secondary qualities', colours, sounds and so forth, are also all relational. We shall see the significance of this later.

It needs further to be pointed out that in maintaining this conception of form, and thus substantial form, as relational, I am rejecting Leibniz's conception of the acting of substance as a process of explicating what is implicit or *complicans*, that is, of his conception of acting as thinking, epitomized by mathematical thinking. In other words, I am repudiating the conception of substance as *res cogitans*, the conception of being as thinking, the conception which has played so prominent a role in philosophy from the time of the Greeks. The view I am proposing maintains thought as resulting from, but not as the very essence, of the acting of substance.[17] The basic point is that the acting of substance must be a relating, and a relating must be an 'acting on' – and this thinking cannot do. The *character* of the relating which is the acting of a substance will be the 'substantial form' of that substance.

This view of substantial form is, I think, not so very different from that of Aristotle – but it is importantly different from the Neoplatonic understanding of Aristotle. For in the latter form tends strongly to be *identified* with act; whereas the view I am putting forward conceives form as the *form of* act, the character of act. Thus character is to act as form is to matter.

The conception of acting maintained here, as was shown in the previous chapter, has the full connotation of 'potency', 'power'. It is a power of affecting others. In relation to the effect as actual, the power is potential; the effect is the form of the act. This is fully in accord with Aristotle when he made a certain identification of *dynamis*, potency, and *hylē*, matter.[18] For our immediate purposes, however, this need not be stressed. What is important is that the acting is potential in relation to the effect,

---

[17] In this is contained the answer to the objection mentioned earlier (on p. 294) as one which might be raised against the theory here being developed, namely that it will involve a difficulty in respect of perception. In the position I am maintaining, the fundamental acting of a physical existent is not conceived as 'perceiving' – as by Leibniz and Whitehead. I agree with Descartes in holding that perception is a species of *cogitatio*, thinking. Thus perception will be derivative from the relational acting of physical existents, and accordingly the epistemological difficulty anticipated above is circumvented. It is beyond the scope of the present volume to enter into this in further detail.

[18] See above, Ch. 11.

both the effect which is the outcome of the acting, and the effect of its being acted on. The effect is the achieved actuality.

It would be a very serious misunderstanding of this conception to take the 'actuality' to be the substance in a final, achieved, and thus static 'state'. The actuality is the *substance in relation*, so that the actualized form is the actualized relation. And there can be no relation actualized apart from the act*ing*, the relat*ing*. So the substance, and hence the relation, actualized must necessarily be the substance *en-ergeia*, in-act.

It should now not be difficult to appreciate that substance so conceived necessarily involves a process of coming to be, a process of transition from potentiality to full achievement (*entelecheia*). Substance cannot be understood apart from this process (*kinēsis*), but must be conceived as in the process.

Although there is an important similarity between this conception of substance and the doctrine of Whitehead, yet there is also an important difference. In Whitehead's doctrine the grasping, prehending, of others constitutes but the first phase of the process toward achieved actuality. This phase is that of the appropriation of data; thereupon the remainder of the process is internal to the substance in becoming, and the 'actuality' will be itself as fully become. In my theory there can be no such separation of substances from each other. The acting of substances is a mutual acting on, whereby they are in relation, and the relation is intrinsic to their actualization. This does not entail that the form of the relation must be in every respect identical for the different substances in that relation; the form will necessarily vary in accordance with the act of the different substances – for these cannot be all alike or there could be no variety in the universe, as Leibniz correctly pointed out.[19] Further detail in respect of this theory necessitates the consideration of another range of problems which will be the topic of the next chapter.

I shall conclude this chapter with one further point relevant to the issue of simple and compound substances. In our previous discussion, starting from Leibniz, we have analysed a 'corporeal substance' as being constituted by a plurality of simple substances and one compound substance. However, from early on in the seventeenth century, as we saw in the previous chapter, it was found necessary to admit groups of simples in varying degrees

[19] cf. e.g., Loemker, p. 525; G.II, 226–7.

of complexity, ranging (if we put this in terms of present-day scientific theory) from the compound 'atoms', through molecules in an ascending order of complexity of compounds, to cells, each analysable as constituted by various molecules in increasing orders of complexity, and on to macroscopic organic beings, animals, etc., constituted by a vast complexity of cells, themselves being grouped in ordered structures constituting the muscles, bones, organs, etc., of the animals.

The compound 'atoms', molecules, and cells very clearly are not mere aggregates; they are each unitary compounds, of a very definite order and structure, exhibiting a specific character and behaviour. That is, in each of these the constituents have a very definite ordered and structured relationship to each other, and the whole constitutes a very definite unity.

Now our analysis has made clear that there can be a relationship between entities only through a reciprocal acting of the entities on each other. The crucial issue is that of the 'unity' of the whole. We have examined above the unity of a substance, substantial unity. Now clearly not every unity is a substantial unity. The question is whether the unities of compound 'atoms', molecules, and cells, are to be regarded as substantial unities. An aggregate can constitute a kind of unity, but such a unity is no more than the sum of its parts; that is, the character of this unity is not anything more than the characters of the constitutents collectively. The unity of molecules, etc., we have seen, must be something more than that of aggregates.

The weakness of the theories of Leibniz and Whitehead with respect to this problem, we have seen, is that in the end for them the 'unity' of the whole is an item within each constituent individually. This is because in both doctrines the acting of the constituent substances is an act of perception, essentially subjective to the substances.

But what is the outcome for this issue with the acting conceived as an 'acting on' and thus as a 'relating'? The entities in relation act on each other reciprocally, and are thus each modified, in some respect, by the relationship, that is, by their acting. This reciprocal acting constitutes a tie or bond between them, this bond being the relation – which exists only in the acting, and not as some *tertium quid*. The word 'relation' – in this respect like the word 'perception' – connotes both the act, the relat*ing*, and *what* the act achieves. The 'whatness' is the form or character of the relation. This means that by virtue of the mutual activity of relating, there exists a form or character common to the entities acting. This form or character is not one inhering in each entity separately and individually – in which case the character would be a mere class name – but is a character of a relation.

With this, it is clear, there is a unity between the entities so related, and what is more, a unity which is more than that of an aggregate. Now the problem is, what precisely is the ontological status of this unity? The problem we have here is an enormously difficult and subtle one, the adequate analysis of which is quite beyond the scope of the present volume. There is a weighty consensus, from Plato and Aristotle down the ages to Leibniz and Whitehead, that unity must be grounded in substance. This means that in the ultimate and primary sense unity is the unity of substance *per se*. The unity of an aggregate is not ascribable to the aggregate as a feature of the aggregate *per se* – for an aggregate is by definition not a 'one' but a plurality – so there can be a unity of an aggregate only with reference to some or other 'observer'; that is, the 'unity' of an aggregate is grounded in some substance as an *ens rationis*.

The question now is whether any *via media* is possible. That is, is it possible for there to be a unity which is not either the unity of a substance, or the unity of an aggregate which is an *ens rationis*? In regard to substances in relation, does their being in relation constitute them 'one' in a respect which is not the 'oneness' of a substance? The alternatives seem to be that either the relating unifies the acting substances into a one which is a substance transcending but constituted by them, or there is a unity by virtue of the relation, leaving the substances themselves basically diverse. The latter alternative, however, is unsatisfactory. For either the entities in relation remain a plurality and not a unity, or the relation unifies them. But if the relation does unify them, bringing them into one, why is this not to be regarded as a substantial unity? It seems to me that this is essentially a substantial unity. For the relation has a form or character which is the character of that whole, of the unity.

Now form must be grounded in substance; there cannot be form or character without substance. Is this form to be regarded as grounded in the plurality of substances constituting the whole, each individually? But it is the form of the whole, one unitary form; so how can it be grounded in many substances? Besides, it is the form or character of a relational unity; thus it cannot be grounded in the many substances individually, but in them in relation. As thus relational, the form is the form of *one* whole, not of a plurality. I conclude therefore that this one form must be the form of one substance, that this form must be a substantial form.

How precisely are we to conceive this substance? It is certainly not one among the others, as in Leibniz's earlier theory. It can only be one constituted by the many. The problem is how precisely are many substances to be conceived as constituting one substance. The theory being here advanced conceives the acting of substances as an acting on each other. Now when the acting of the substances on each other is fully reciprocal, I wish to suggest, these actings combine into one single total act, with one single form, the relational form we discussed above. An aspect of this fully reciprocal acting of a plurality combining to constitute one single acting is probably what is manifested in the compound 'atom' as a balance or neutralization of positive and negative electrical charges. It is by reason of this combined acting constituting a one acting, that the compound entity acts as a whole, that is, as one, with reference to, and on, other wholes. The action of one compound 'atom' on another is not, by the scientific evidence, an aggregate acting of the electrons and protons individually on each other, but of each 'atom' as a whole on others – it is precisely this which necessitated early in the seventeenth century the introduction of groups of simples, or molecules, etc. Now the acting of the compound as a whole, that is, as one, implies one acting of that whole; and this one acting of the compound is the many fully reciprocal actings combined into one.

As so combined into one, this one must transcend the many constituents – for we have a 'one' here which is not that of an aggregate. Further, this one is an actual one, that is, an actualized unity; and with reference to this actual one, the many constituents are potential, although in themselves they are each actual substances. In the same way there could be compounds with the previous compounds as their constituents, and so on in increasing orders of complexity, each compound, on this basis, being a unitary substance, that is, having a single unitary act and a single unitary form of that act, the 'substantial form' of that compound.

There is another aspect of the status of 'potentiality' of the constituents which is important. The constituent substances are potential in reference to the actuality of the whole they constitute. That is, as constituents of that whole they are potential. But their potentiality in that relationship also implies that although they are in that relationship, they might cease being so. If they ceased being in that relationship it would entail the resumption of their status as independent actual substances. Thus electrons, 'atoms', molecules, cells, etc., are capable of and do exist as independent substances in separation from compound wholes of which they had previously been constituents. And as such independent actual substances, they have the potentiality of entering into relationships with others, including becoming again constituents of other compound substances.

I have spoken of the actings of the constituents of compound substances as 'fully' reciprocal because, since all actings of substances will be actings on each other and thereby reciprocal, it does not follow that all reciprocal actings will constitute compound substantial wholes. If the acting of a particular substance in response to the acting on it of another be more strongly a passive response or reception than itself an acting on, that is, if the feature of acting on in this relationship be recessive by contrast with the aspect of reception, the relation will not be a unity of a substantial kind, but one in which the recipient substance will be in some way changed, but will remain substantially quite distinct. In this way substances by their actings will affect each other, the substances so affected remaining substantially distinct, though they will be, by their acting on each other, in relationships of various kinds, including that which constitutes them aggregates – the 'adhering' in aggregates necessarily must be a relationship. It is only the actings on each other which are fully reciprocal that will constitute a compound substance.

The instances of substances by their relational acting constituting aggregates will be those which we know as 'inorganic' wholes. Compound substances are all 'organic', for in them the constituents act with reference to the whole – this is the essence of the relationship of the constituents to the substantial whole which we discussed above. Thus compound 'atoms' and molecules as well as cells will be organisms. Organisms in ever greater degrees of complexity are constituted by compound substances constituted of compounds which are compounds of compounds. This is fully in accord with the following statement by Whitehead in *Science and the Modern World* : [20]

'The concrete enduring entities are organisms, so that the plan of the *whole* influences the very characters of the various subordinate organisms which enter into it. In the case of an animal, the mental states enter into the plan of the total organism and thus modify the plans of the successive subordinate organisms until the ultimate smallest organisms, such as electrons, are reached. Thus an electron within a living body is different from an electron outside it, by reason of the plan of the body. The electron blindly runs either within or without the body; but it runs within the body in accordance with its character within the body; that is to say, in accordance with the general plan of the body, and this plan includes the mental state. But the principle of modification is perfectly general throughout nature, and represents no property peculiar to living bodies.'

It will be noted that for Whitehead 'organic' is not synonymous with 'living'; that is, not all organisms will be 'living'. This is entirely consistent with the theory I have been developing. Living organisms will be ones in which the dominant substance of the organism has achieved a degree of complexity, arising from its constituents, enabling it to dominate and control, by its acting, the acting of the constituents to some appreciable extent. Obviously the character of livingness will be a question of degree and not of kind. The highest organisms will be those living ones in which the dominant substance is capable of a high degree of consciousness and thought. This brings us to the consideration of another range of issues, to which we shall turn in the next chapter.

[20] op. cit., pp. 98–9 [115–16].

25

PHYSICAL EXISTENCE, CONTINUITY, AND DISCRETENESS

The modern concept of nature, of the physical, was determined by the introduction, early in the seventeenth century, of the concept of matter as substance. This entailed an ontological dualism which has ruled thought down to the present day. In this doctrine physical existence was conceived as material, implying the exclusion from the physical existent of anything of the kind of perception, thought, feeling, emotion, etc., all of which were relegated to an ontologically separate existent or substance. Even when the doctrine of material substance was rejected, as by Leibniz, the influence of the ontological dualism was determinative; for Leibniz and other opponents of materialism conceived substance by contrast with that doctrine as 'spiritual' or 'mental'. This is true not only of the seventeenth century but of thought down into this century, a good instance of this being the 'pan-psychism' of Peirce, Whitehead, and other thinkers. In the early part of the present century the theory of 'neutral monism' gained some prominence, but it too was determined by the dualism inherited from the seventeenth century, for in this theory substance was conceived as neither material nor mental, but neutral to both, from which they arise.

One clear outcome of the present inquiry is the complete untenability of the conception of 'material substance'. This conception must be rejected entirely, and with it all the implications consequent upon it, including, most importantly, also the conception of 'spiritual or mental substance'.

The vital need of our time is a conception of physical existence untrammelled by erroneous presuppositions inherited from the scheme of thought which has dominated the modern era. With a clear realization of the implications of the modern ontological dualism we can avoid these.

First and most urgently the connotation of 'material' which

has in the modern period become attached to the concept of the 'physical' has to be utterly rejected. It is certainly not easy to eliminate a conception such as that of matter as substance which has been fundamental to the thought of centuries, but it is definitely necessary to do so. Recent physics has departed from this concept, but this concept has over the centuries so moulded the modes of thinking that it continues nevertheless prominently to exert itself in the thinking of physicists. In physics as well as in philosophy it is vital to purge the term 'physical' of this erroneous connotation. With this connotation the word 'physical' means, of or pertaining to matter, in contrast to mind or the spiritual – in accordance with the modern ontological dualism. In rejecting this we need to emphasize the other currently main meaning of 'physical', namely of or relating to physics, and to bring back into prominence the basic and original meaning of the physical, of the natural, which the word still retains, though somewhat subordinately. This is what has been attempted in this book.

With the elimination of the connotation of 'material' from the concept of the physical we are able to proceed to the development of the implications of the conception at which we had arrived in the last chapter of the physical existent as organic, by contrast with the mechanistic conception of the modern period.

The physical existent, we have seen, must be an acting entity, and the acting must essentially be a relating, a relating both between existents and within the existents or substances. This accords with the Greek conception of *physis*, of the physical, in a number of respects. Clearly in the conception of the physical at which we have arrived, the physical existent is that which has the principle, the source, of its *kinēsis* in itself. Its *kinēsis* is its process of acting; for we have seen that a substance must be in a process of change, and not, as in the conception of substance as matter, in itself changeless and fully actual. The acting of the substance is the substance becoming actual. This clearly implies a transition from potentiality to actuality, on which Aristotle had also insisted in respect of the physical existent.

We have dealt in the previous chapter with some aspects of the concept of potentiality and the contrast of potentiality and actuality. We must now examine some other aspects of the concept. A substance, antecedently to its actualization, must have been potential, both in the sense of possible to be actual, and in the sense of a power or potency to effect that actualization. Now this means that the acting, which is potency, must be *directed to* the achievement of an actualization which in a particular respect transcends the process toward it. This implies that the actualization is an end toward which the acting is directed. As such an end it is a possibility of achievement, not yet actualized.

The question now arises as to what is implied in the conception of an end as a possibility. What is entailed in saying, there is an end as a possibility? In what sense can the possible end *be*? Is it merely an *ens rationis* in the mind of an analysing thinker? That is, does it mean that possibility exists only in intellectual analysis, so that we are making a mere distinction of thought in saying that, considered from the standpoint of the achieved actualization, antecedently to that actualization, it must have been possible?

But in the process of actualization of the substance itself, the end as a possibility must be in some respect efficacious in it in order that the acting be directed toward that end.[1] And for a possibility to be *efficacious* in a substance implies that in some respect the possibility must *be in* the substance. But in what respect can the possibility *be* in the substance? To say that it 'is' implies its being in some respect 'actual'.[2] But it cannot be actual in the sense of the 'end actualized', that is, in full achievement (Aristotle's *entelecheia*), for then it would not be 'possible'. In what respect then can the possible 'be', and 'be actual' as efficacious?

One respect of this existence of the possible we have seen in the previous chapter in the case of a constituent substance in a compound existing actually and contributing its acting as a

[1] Unless this be so we are not talking and thinking about the physical existent, but about subjective contents of the mind. This latter is a widely current position, based ultimately upon the tacit acceptance of the Neoplatonic doctrine of mind which we discussed in Ch. 22, pp. 267ff., a doctrine which we saw good reason to reject.

[2] It does not suffice to say as Aristotle did that 'is' has many senses, and that we must distinguish between 'is-actual' and 'is-potential'. To leave it at that, as he did in his analysis of how the constituents exist in a *mixis* (see above Ch. 11, pp. 141–2, and Ch. 24, pp. 304f.), is to give only part of the answer which is requisite. It still leaves the problem of how this 'potential being' is to be conceived and analysed, the problem which occupied thinkers for centuries, in the Middle Ages and on into the seventeenth century, as we saw in Ch. 11, the problem to which we are attempting to give a solution, in the previous chapter and this one.

potentiality to the achievement of an actuality transcending itself. But what we are concerned with here is a somewhat different aspect of possibility, which is indeed entailed in the former. What we are trying to distinguish here is not the potency of the acting whereby the end is achieved, but the possibility of that end antecedently to its achievement, as that in terms of which the acting is *directed*. This is the Aristotelian telic cause, 'that for the sake of which' (*to hou heneka*). Once we admit substance as in a process of becoming, in a process of transition from potentiality to actuality, we are committed to admitting possibility as efficacious in the process as an 'end-cause'. This possibility, in other words, is entailed in potentiality; the potency must be directed in accordance with a possibility of the end. To refuse to admit this, for example on the ground that it involves anthropomorphism, is simply to display a continued adherence to the ontological dualism which has to be rejected.

We are now in a position to give an answer to the question raised above as to the respect in which the possible can 'be' and 'be actual' as efficacious in a substance. The possible is efficacious by being the end actually entertained as the goal of the acting. This actual entertainment of the end as possible obviously stands in contrast with the end as achieved, the *entelecheia*, and must also be distinguished from the process of acting by which that full achievement is attained. This kind of entertainment[3] of possibility is that which we know in ourselves as 'conceptual'[4] or 'mental'. We must accordingly, with Aristotle and Whitehead, admit it as intrinsic to the physical as the only way in which possibility can be accorded a status in physical existence.

In formulating this we are in something of a difficulty with regard to terminology, for words like 'conceptual' and 'mental' not only tend heavily to have the connotation of consciousness – which of course has to be excluded as not being general to all substance – but in their modern understanding these terms are also shot through with the ontological dualism which we reject. Thus even Whitehead, who accepts the position I am advancing, *contrasts* the term 'conceptual' with the 'physical' in his doctrine

---

[3] 'Entertain' is used in the strict etymological sense (from *inter* and *tenere*): to hold, to possess; to preserve, guard; to maintain, support.

[4] Again the basic etymological sense is important; from *concipio*, to take or lay hold of, to take to one's self, to take in.

of each actual entity having a 'physical' and a 'conceptual' or 'mental' pole. This survival in Whitehead of the influence of the ontological dualism which he rejects has had the effect of his use of the term 'physical' being somewhat narrower than that in which I have used the term. His usage of 'physical' is nevertheless not contrary to mine; basically it is in accord with the classical meaning of the term from the Greeks till into the eighteenth century. The explicit retention of this full sense will, I suggest, assist in avoiding confusions of thought, especially those deriving from the modern ontological dualism.

This mode of existence of the possible, namely as an entertainment in the physical existent of the end to be attained by its acting, is fundamentally important, for, as we shall see, in terms of this doctrine a solution can be found for a range of difficult problems which are not coherently soluble on other bases. Many of these problems arise in connection with relations, relations between substances and within compound substances.

In the theory we have been advancing, substances act on each other, thereby effecting relations. It is implied in this conception of substances acting on each other that each is elsewhere in reference to others, as we have seen.[5] Each such acting substance, as Kant insisted, must have a *sphaera activitatis*, bounded by the resistance constituted by the spheres of activity of its neighbours.[6] By its acting therefore each substance occupies a certain volume.[7] That is, a substance is not in itself extensive, in the sense that extension is an attribute of the substance; in this we are accepting the arguments of Leibniz,[8] Kant,[9] and Whitehead[10] against the conception of extension as an attribute of substance, holding with them that extension pertains rather to relations.

But to say that extension pertains to relations and not to substances as attributes nevertheless entails, as we have seen,[11] that extension must be grounded in substances. On the basis of his conception of substance Leibniz had concluded that extensive

---

5 See above, pp. 278f; cf. also pp. 266f.
6 See above, pp. 281f.   7 See above, p. 281.
8 See above, pp. 243f.   9 See above, pp. 278f.
10 cf. PR 135 [148]: 'The inclusion of *extensive quantity* among fundamental categoreal notions is a complete mistake.' Also, PR 408 [441]: 'For Descartes the primary *attribute* of physical bodies is *extension*; for the philosophy of organism the primary *relationship* of physical occasions is *extensive connection.*'
11 See above, pp. 266ff.

relations can only be grounded in substances as phenomena, that is, they must be ideas in the monads, and ultimately ideas in the divine creating monad. This phenomenal status for extensive relations was rejected by Kant in his pre-critical thought; he maintained that they must be real. In Kant's doctrine of acting monads, extensive relations are brought into being by the acting of the monads on each other.[12]

Kant however saw that there is a difficult problem involved in this. For monads to act on each other implies that they must each have, antecedently to the acting, a situation in reference to each other which is presupposed in their acting, since as acting they must each be elsewhere with respect to each other.[13] In other words, there is a relation of situation with reference to each other which is presupposed by the acting and not brought into being by the acting. In what substance is this relation of situation grounded? Since it is presupposed by the acting of the physical monads it cannot be grounded in them. Kant concluded, like Leibniz, and Newton, that it must be grounded in God.[14]

But there is a difficulty in this for Kant. In his theory the relation of situation is distinguished and separated from the relation of extension; the former is grounded in God, and the latter in the acting of the physical monads. But does not a relation of situation entail extensiveness? Thus it cannot be the case that the acting of the monads originates extensiveness as such, as was maintained by Kant in holding that without the acting of the monads 'there is no connection or relation, without this no order, and without this finally no space'.[15] Kant was caught by an equivocation. The acting of the monads brings an extensive relation into being. This must be accepted on the basis of his conception of acting. This means that the acting brings a *relation* into existence; but it is not entailed in this, that the very *extensiveness* of the relation is brought into existence, for the extensiveness is presupposed by the acting, since the acting is an acting on others elsewhere.

What, then, is the ontological status of the presupposed extendedness and relation of situation? It is not that of itself an actuality; this is what is denied in rejecting the theory that

---

[12] See above, pp. 278f.   [13] See above, p. 279.
[14] ibid.   [15] See above, p. 278.

extendedness is originated by the acting, for this theory implies that there actually is extendedness only as the achievement of the acting. On the other hand, to say that extendedness is presupposed by the acting is to say that it is not an actuality but a possibility for actuality. Now we have seen that it was Leibniz's doctrine that extendedness is a possibility. But did this doctrine entail that possibility is a *possibility for actuality*? By according possibility a purely phenomenal status, Leibniz deprived himself of being able to have possibility a 'possibility for actuality'. That is, he cannot in this way have it a possibility which is a potential for actualization. His possibility is condemned to remain phenomenal; it can never achieve actualization, for its being phenomenal means that it is an appearance in an 'observer', and not in any respect 'actual' as a possibility in a physical existent itself. It is precisely what Leibniz's doctrine cannot allow which is requisite for a valid theory of extendedness as presupposed by acting as a relating. This being 'presupposed' means that it must in some respect be actual as a possibility in the acting of the physical existent, 'directing' that acting.

Earlier in this chapter we saw how possibility can be actual and efficacious qua possibility in a physical existent; namely by the possibility being 'entertained' by the physical existent. It is in this way that extendedness is 'presupposed' by acting which is a relating to others. Thus also the acting can actualize an extended relatedness, that is, bring a relation as extended into being. In so doing, as Whitehead has insisted, 'extensiveness becomes, but "becoming" is not itself extensive'.[16]

That relational acting necessarily presupposes extendedness was most clearly seen by Whitehead. Accordingly, he maintained:[17] 'Extension is the most general scheme of real potentiality, providing the background for all other organic relations.' That is:[18] 'This extensiveness is the pervading generic form to which the morphological structures of the organisms of the world conform.' Whitehead's doctrine, which we have already had occasion to discuss in an earlier chapter,[19] is that it is necessary to admit an 'extensive continuum' which is a structure of all possible situations or standpoints relatively to each other; we must admit, in

---

16 PR 48 [53].   17 PR 93 [105].
18 PR 406 [439]. cf. also, p. 408 [441].
19 See above, pp. 251f.

his words,[20] 'that the real potentialities relative to all standpoints are co-ordinated as diverse determinations of one extensive continuum'. This is a structure of 'possible' standpoints, which are actualized by substances in acting; whence Whitehead speaks of them as 'real potentialities'. The actualization is necessarily discrete – expressed in terms of our theory, each substance has a sphere of activity which is definitely bounded by the spheres of activity of its neighbours; but this scheme or structure of relatedness, as possible, is continuous. A 'continuum' entails 'possibility of division'; the division is actualized by the acting.

In one of his statements quoted above, in explication of this conception of extensiveness, Whitehead speaks of it as a 'pervading generic form'. Extensiveness is the form which is actualized in the relating activity; it is the form of the acting whereby that acting actualizes an extensive relation, that is, whereby the relation actualized by the acting is extensive.

Antecedent to the actualization, the extensiveness is a possibility 'entertained' by the substance in its process of acting. With the achievement of the relation, the relation is extensive. Earlier we examined the contrast between a possibility as 'entertained' and as actualized. But there is a further issue to be discussed that is entailed in the conception of a possibility as entertained by a physical existent, which is of special relevance for the conception of extensiveness. In our previous discussion we had been particularly concerned with the case of an end entertained as a possibility. Now an end is fairly specific, whereas extendedness as a possibility is a form of relatedness, and what is more, a 'pervading generic form', a structure of all possible standpoints or situations in their relatedness to each other. We have to raise the question, as Kant did,[21] regarding the grounding of this general structure of relatedness. Since it is presupposed by the acting of any and every individual physical existent, it cannot be regarded as grounded in the physical existents. Whitehead, too, explicitly faced the question of the grounding of this general form of relatedness, the extensive continuum, and came to the same conclusion as had Kant, Leibniz, and Newton, namely that it must be grounded in God, holding that : 'Here "God" is that actuality in the world, in virtue of which there is physical

[20] PR 91 [103].
[21] See above, pp. 319 and 279f.

L

"law".[22] And indeed it is difficult to see how there could be an alternative to this position. Adequately to justify the concept of 'God' as necessitated by the order of physical existence will take us well beyond the scope of our present considerations and must be postponed. Here we might just mention it as highly significant that these four who among modern thinkers had most penetratingly and comprehensively faced this issue have come to the same conclusion.

Further, we might also point out that the position of Kant in his critical philosophy is definitely unsatisfactory as a solution to this issue. For him this general form of relatedness is grounded in the perceiving mind as the form of perception. This view however suffers from the same defect as does the phenomenalism of Leibniz; Kant's position precludes him from being able to have the form of extensive relatedness as a possibility effective *in physical existents themselves* as a possibility for actualization. It is true that in his doctrine this form of possible relatedness (space and time) transcends the individual perceivers – that it is transcendental. But his adherence to the ontological dualism prevents his being able to ascribe this form to physical existents – indeed the fundamental move of the critical philosophy had been precisely to deny it to the physical and to locate it in the perceiving mind, that is, in the other kind of fundamental existent, mental or spiritual substance. In regard to this issue, in the critical philosophy the transcendental ego takes the place of God in his pre-critical doctrine, but this leaves the problem with which we are here concerned basically insoluble, whereas this is not true of the position of the pre-critical philosophy.

In the alternative theory being advanced here – which is in this respect close to that of Whitehead – each physical existent 'entertains' the generic form of extended relatedness in having a 'situation' relatively to others from which it is able to act. Exactly how it acquires this entertainment we must leave to later examination. Here I wish to point out that it is by virtue of this that a physical existent has a 'place'. The extensive continuum is the structure of every possible 'where' and 'when' – in this respect, it is worth noting, there is a close agreement between Whitehead and Newton (not the later misconception of Newton) – so that the extensive continuum is the absolute structure of the

22 PR 402 [434].

'places' of things. Because the term 'place' has had so strongly a connotation of the spatial alone, Whitehead has preferred to use the term 'standpoint'. But Newton did not so restrictedly use the term 'place' in his General Scholium :[23]

'As the order of the parts of time is immutable, so also is the order of the parts of space. Suppose those parts to be moved out of their places, and they will be moved (if the expression may be allowed) out of themselves. For times and spaces are, as it were, the places as well of themselves as of all other things. All things are placed in time as to order of succession; and in space as to order of situation. It is from their essence or nature that they are places; and that the primary places of things should be movable, is absurd. These are therefore the absolute places; and translations out of those places, are the only absolute motions.'

Bearing in mind that, as we have seen,[24] this absolute structure of 'places' is not for Newton itself any actual existent, we can see that his doctrine is close to Whitehead's conception of an 'extensive continuum' as the absolute structure of the 'places' of things. This theory fully accords with what the analyses of the sixteenth and seventeenth centuries had brought out as necessary, namely that 'place' must be ontologically distinct from the physical, and yet be that in terms of which physical activity is determined, and the motion and measurability of the physical existents is derivable.[25]

Before we are able to proceed to the analysis of motion in terms of the theory here being advanced, there are some prior issues to be examined.

In the previous chapter we have argued for a conception of substance or the physical existent as compound. To be compound means to be composed of constituents. These constituents, as has been shown, can themselves be compound, and need to be so if we are to have a conception of the physical existent as a unitary substance which is able adequately to provide a philosophical

[23] op. cit., p. 8.
[24] Ch. 18, *passim* and Ch. 19, pp. 227ff.
[25] This problem of measurability is a highly complex one and will not be further investigated in this book – it requires a volume to itself. Whitehead devoted Part IV of *Process and Reality* to the topic in a very compressed treatment.

account of the evidence furnished in scientific theory. Now if these constituents be compound, they must be constituted by other entities as constituents, but there cannot be an infinite regress of compound constituents. Ultimately there must be simples as constituents. These simples must be the ultimate elements of all compounds. That is, the conception of compound substance implies the conception of elements,[26] and these elements must be certain minima.

The question now is whether the elements are themselves to be considered to be substances. It will be valuable for the analysis of this problem to revert to some important distinctions which were made by Aristotle.[27] Aristotle pointed out that the fact of change implies some substratum underlying change. There would not be 'change' if there occurred the existence of one thing which then, in an absolute and unqualified sense, ceased to exist and another thing came into existence in its stead, again in an absolute and unqualified sense. When Whitehead states that, 'The fundamental meaning of the notion of "change" is "the difference between actual occasions comprised in some determinate event" ',[28] some substratum is implied : it is that whereby there is an 'event' – we shall come to that presently. For there to be change there must in some respect be something undergoing change, some substratum continuing through the process of change.

Further, Aristotle pointed out,[29] in the theory of Democritean atomism, the atoms, which are the elements, also constitute the substratum of change; in this theory change is accordingly analysable as a difference of situation with reference to each other of the atoms in a compound, so that change pertains to the compound, the atoms being the continuing substratum, they being in themselves changeless. This is clearly also the position in modern materialistic atomism. Aristotle showed[30] that with this conception of the substratum as elements in themselves changeless, it is impossible to give a valid account of the change occurring in compounds. We have demonstrated this at length in regard to the modern theory of material atoms, in themselves changeless. Aristotle concluded that for there to be change in compounds the elements could not be changeless, but had themselves to be subject

---

[26] Element means ultimate constituent. cf. above, pp. 135f.
[27] See above, pp. 136ff.   [28] PR 101 [114].
[29] See above, p. 136f.   [30] ibid.

to change; indeed, that the elements had to be subject to generation and destruction.[31] This implied that there had to be something different from the elements to constitute the substratum
of change.

Our earlier analyses had also led us to the conception of substance as necessarily involving change in itself.[32] This implies that
the elements themselves must undergo change, and accordingly
the elements cannot constitute the substratum of change. What
then are we to identify as the substratum of change? Aristotle
had maintained that the substratum must be sought in the *archai*,
the principles or sources of change. These principles for Aristotle
are *hylē* and *eidos*.[33] The substratum of change he identified
as *hylē*, that which receives or takes form and remains throughout
the changes of form. We have seen[34] that there is a certain ambiguity in Aristotle's writings as to exactly what is to be identified
as the principle of change or *kinēsis*, the 'that from which as a
source' (*hothen hē archē*); sometimes he identified this as *eidos*,
form, but as against this he insisted on a close connection between
the concepts of *hylē* and *dynamis*, potentiality, and *dynamis*
connotes potency, power.[35]

Taking a lead from this latter position, we shall identify the
substratum of change as the factor of 'acting' which we have found
to be fundamental in substance. This acting is to be regarded
as an *archē*, principle or source. Moreover, thus regarded it can
be identified with Aristotle's *hylē* as that which is formed.[36] This
is Whitehead's doctrine too in his conception of a 'category of the
ultimate' which he terms 'creativity',[37] that is creative activity,
and which he has himself noted corresponds to the Aristotelian
prime matter.[38] The acting is the principle, source, of change;
and this acting is the substratum of change, taking different forms.

We are now in a position to deal with the question whether,
in the theory here being advanced, the elements of a compound
substance are to be regarded as being themselves substances. The
elements must involve change in themselves; they do so by virtue
of acting. Now since the elements are not the substratum, the
substratum being the fundamental underlying activity, the actings

---

[31] ibid.   [32] See above, especially p. 305.
[33] See above, pp. 136f.   [34] See above, Ch. 8, *passim*.
[35] ibid.   [36] See above, pp. 307 and 309f.
[37] PR 28–9 [31–2].   [38] PR 42–3 [46–7].

of the elements must be the individualizations of this substrate acting, and this means that they are individual units of acting. But to be units of acting implies that they must be unitary substances. This accords with Aristotle, who also maintained that the elements must be *ousiai*, substances.[39] This also accords with Whitehead, for whom the elements of all compounds are the actual entities, that is, substances – indeed for him the only substances.

Now the theory which I am developing brings into prominence a particular problem connected with the relation of constituent substances in a compound. This problem exists also for Aristotle and Whitehead, for their theories also involve the relatedness of substances in compounds. But this problem comes more fully to the fore with the explicit conception of acting as a relating.

The acting of a substance, we have seen, presupposes a place or situation in reference to others, and by its acting a substance occupies a particular volume or region – I shall here adopt Whitehead's term 'region' rather than 'volume' which so strongly has a purely spacial connotation; a region is a 'where' and 'when', that is, it includes a temporal aspect. The extension of the region is not an attribute of the acting; the extensiveness of the acting is derived from the extensive continuum, as an actualization of the possibility constituted by the extensive continuum.

Since the substance is a unit, it must be an undivided whole. The region which it occupies, on the other hand, is indefinitely divisible, because it is a portion of the continuum, and a continuum implies infinite divisibility.[40] Now since by its acting a substance occupies a region, the acting of the substance must, as Whitehead has insisted,[41] share in the divisibility of the region. This means that the acting, which is an extensive relating to others, is divisible into sub-acts corresponding to sub-regions of the whole region. Whitehead has pointed out that each sub-act might itself be a substance, but for its sharing the one 'subjective form' (which is indeed the 'substantial form') of the whole actual entity or substance. Whitehead has also pointed out that if we ignore this factor of 'subjective form', analogously to the co-ordinate division of an actual entity or substance into many parts

[39] See above, pp. 135ff.
[40] See above, pp. 321 and 243f.
[41] cf. PR Pt IV, Ch. I, §§ I and II.

which could be taken to be themselves substances, we can also treat a plurality of substances as if it constituted one single substance : [42]

'just as, for some purposes, one atomic actuality can be treated as though it were many co-ordinate actualities, in the same way, for other purposes, a nexus of many actualities can be treated as though it were one actuality. This is what we habitually do in the case of the span of life of a molecule, or of a piece of rock, or of a human body.'

Now since the divisibility of the region implies the divisibility of the extensiveness of the acting into sub-actings, is it to be concluded that this divisibility of the acting can proceed *ad infinitum*? The answer seems to me to be clear, that while the extensiveness is infinitely divisible, acting cannot be. Acting involves, as we have seen, a process of transition from potentiality to actuality, and this implies a certain minimum, without which there could be no 'transition'. We can consistently maintain an atomicity of acting because we have insisted that extensiveness is not grounded in physical substance.[43]

The position we arrive at, therefore, is that if we take any substance and 'divide' its acting, we must necessarily arrive at certain minima, minimal acts. To be minimal acts means that they must be minimal units of acting, and this implies that the minima must be substances. These minima will accordingly be the true elements.

As substances the minima must be discrete; that is, their acting constitutes a definite actualized unit. This discreteness is manifested both in the acting, which is a unit of acting, and in the form of the acting, the substantial form, which must accordingly also be unitary.

But when the elements are constituents of a compound, they will be in interaction with each other to constitute the compound substance. There will be one unitary acting, the acting of the

42 PR 406 [439].

43 cf. above, pp. 321–3 and p. 252. Kant, in Prop. VII of Section I of his *Monadologia physica* maintained the atomicity of the monads in this same way of distinguishing extendedness ontologically from the physical. This, however, is not quite consistent with his doctrine elsewhere, in which he regarded extensiveness as originated by the acting of the monads (see above, pp. 319f).

compound substance as an actual whole. With reference to this unitary acting of the compound substance, the actings of the constituents will be sub-acts, which, but for the unitary substantial form that they share (by virtue of having contributed to it), would themselves be separate individual substances – in exact parallel with Whitehead's doctrine. As constituents of a compound they are not actually separate, but only potentially so, as we have seen. In the same way, compound substances by their reciprocal interacting combine to constitute other more complex compound substances or physical existents, their actings thus having the status of sub-actings of the unitary acting of the substance they constitute.

A compound substance is one single physical existent, having a single unitary acting and a single unitary form of that acting, which is its 'substantial form' – corresponding to the 'defining characteristic' of Whitehead's 'societies'. Thus there is one substantial form for a physical existent which is a molecule, or a cell, or an animal, or a human being. The destruction of that particular form entails the destruction of that particular unitary physical existent. In such a destruction the constituents, which antecedently to that destruction were only potentially separate, attain an actual separation – this process of actual separation continuing downward according to the particular new unitary substances constituted consequent upon that destruction.

The acting of a single compound existent, since it is constituted by the actings of the constituents, must necessarily occupy a region which is a totality of the regions of the constituents. The acting of the compound existent, and consequently its extension, will be single, undivided, and continuous; its acting, that is, will be divisible but undivided. But there is a sub-acting corresponding to each 'division' of the region. Since these sub-actings are contributary 'parts' of a unitary whole, they will not themselves be 'divided' and separate actually, but only potentially so. But each constituent, as itself a substance, has its own unitary acting and form; this does not simply disappear on becoming a constituent, for then it could not be a constituent. The 'division' must terminate, as we have seen, with atomic units, the elementary constituents, as the minima.

This distinction made here between compounds as actual and their constituents as potential should be of the greatest importance in science in gaining an accurate understanding of the nature and status of the entities with which it is concerned. Current thinking in science continues to proceed upon the tacit presupposition of all compounds as aggregates, and supposes that there is no difference at all between an entity as constituent of a compound and not a constituent. Thus characteristics which are found in entities separately are assumed to remain unchanged in a compound. Thus for example if a 'free' electron is found to exhibit the characteristics of a moving 'particle', it is assumed that it continues to do so in a compound 'atom'. But if the conception of compounds as aggregates is false, as we have shown it to be, then this kind of assumption regarding the constituents can effectively hinder or block scientific understanding – and I would say is doing so today.

Further, in contrast with this modern doctrine of aggregates and unchanging elements, we have seen the necessity to conceive substances and thus also the elements as involving change in themselves. Fundamentally this change is the *kinēsis* involved in the process of becoming. Now the elements must be atomic minima; this means that their acting, their *kinēsis*, must be 'epochal' (to use Whitehead's term), a unitary whole of acting, as Whitehead too maintained. Aristotle had argued that the elements as *ousiai* must not only involve change in themselves, but that as natural *ousiai* they must also be subject to *genesis*, coming-into-being, and *phthora*, perishing.[44] The theory we are maintaining – which is in this respect close to that of Whitehead – fully accords with Aristotle on this; for this Aristotelian doctrine is exactly applicable to the elements as here conceived : they come into being and they perish.

Aristotle also maintained that the generation of the elements must be from something; it could not otherwise be 'generation'. He concluded, after considering the alternatives, that the only way this could be is that the elements must be generated by changing into each other.[45] Again this holds for the theory here advanced, though not exactly as Aristotle conceived it, for he did not conceive of the elements as 'epochal'. But on this theory an element must come into being from another, out of another; it cannot come into being simply and strictly 'out of nothing'. Thus

44 See above, pp. 137f.
45 See above, p. 138.

the 'perishing' of an element is its 'changing into another' through that other coming into being. This is fairly close to Whitehead's doctrine, though he tended more to emphasize the separateness between these unit elements and to minimize the continuity. But perishing and coming into being are closely interrelated, as Aristotle brought out, and as indeed Whitehead fully saw in his doctrine of 'process', namely that there is a process of transition internal to each actual entity and a process of transition from one actual entity to another.[46]

There is another, related, feature of Aristotle's theory of the elements which is very pertinent here. This is his emphasis on the necessity of contrariety in respect of the elements, without which it is impossible to explain the diversity we find in compounds.[47] Today we can readily reject Aristotle's two pairs of qualitative contraries, hot and cold, wet and dry, as archaic and no longer apposite to modern scientific research, but Aristotle's insistence on some basic contraries will be ignored at our peril. That there must be contraries seems to me to be a necessity. That certain particular contraries should be ultimate and necessary is not clear. Perhaps they differ in different cosmic epochs. Some such basic contraries in the present cosmic epoch are probably what are manifested, put in terms of current physical science, as positive and negative electrical charges. That characterization, however, is highly abstract; it will be one of the tasks of future philosophy to give it adequate characterization. However, that elements should be contrary in their total character, as the above example might be taken to suggest, is not necessary, nor indeed is it probable. A variety of combinations of contraries is more likely; perhaps this is what is being manifested in the variety of 'elementary particles' which current research has discovered. This may also account for the 'short-lived' character of many of them; for they require combination with other contrary ones as a condition of the perpetuation of their form – for contraries 'require' each other, as Plato was well aware.[48]

The theory being advanced here of the elements changing into one another by a process of generation and perishing differs from

[46] cf. PR Pt. II, Ch. 10.
[47] See above, pp. 138f.
[48] For example, such contraries, necessary to each other, play a fundamental role in his *Timaeus* in his theory of the coming into being of the world.

Whitehead's conception in an important respect. In his doctrine the generation of an entity initiates with the prehension of an entity which has perished. The acting is wholly confined to the entity in becoming. With this the separateness of the entities which he emphasizes consistently follows. In this respect my view is closer to that of Aristotle, who maintains the necessity of a continuous process of *kinēsis*.[49] In my view too the *kinēsis*, the process of acting, is continuous, but it is 'epochalized' into a plurality of actings – this is but another aspect of the position maintained above in making a distinction in respect of acting between the actual and the potential.

This conception of the process of acting, as I am maintaining it, has a special relevance for the theory of 'motion'. Acting, I have been holding, is a process of *kinēsis*. I am using this term in the full Aristotelian sense of the fundamental process of actualization.[50] In this process, every achieved actualization is a potentiality for a further actualization. At the level of the elements, as we have seen, the process of acting, and thus *kinēsis*, is necessarily 'epochal',[51] but this does not involve or imply that the process of acting is 'broken off', and then resumed anew; rather one phase of the *kinēsis* ends with the initiation of another phase. In this, one atomic element 'changes into' another. The fundamental process of *kinēsis* is a process of actualizing one element, the achieved actualization then being the potentiality in the continuing process of actualizing another. The achievement of actualization involves a whole complex process of change, and it is this which is *kinēsis*, motion (in the original sense of the term).[52]

Now consider such a process of continuous actualization of elements. Involved in this *kinēsis*, this process of actualization, as one aspect of it, could be a change of place of later actualizations relatively to antecedent ones. Thus would 'locomotion' be effected. Locomotion, that is, change of place, is one aspect of the total *kinēsis*, *motus*, and not something distinct, in a category

---

[49] We shall be examining this in the next chapter.
[50] See above, Ch. 7.
[51] I use the word, as does Whitehead, in the strict etymological sense of a check, cessation. cf. Whitehead, *Science and the Modern World*, p. 157: 'A duration, as the field of the pattern realized in the actualization of one of its contained events, is an epoch, i.e. an arrest.'
[52] See above, pp. 109ff.

of its own. That is, locomotion, where it occurs, is integrally involved in the total process of becoming, of actualization, of physical existents.

This means that in this theory locomotion is not, as it is in the theories of Leibniz and Whitehead, accorded a derivative status.[53] In these theories locomotion does not occur to the monads and actual entities; the concept of locomotion does not pertain to them but only to pluralities considered in relation to each other. In the theory here advanced, as in that of Aristotle, locomotion is one aspect of the total *kinēsis*, of the total process of actualization of physical existents, and thus properly pertains to them.

Thus both the elements and compound physical existents involve locomotion as an aspect of their acting. Since the process of acting or *kinēsis* of the elements is a continuous process of perpetual actualization, locomotion, where it occurs, will be continuous – as opposed to Whitehead's theory in which it is discontinuous. But it is important to be careful about the understanding of 'continuity' here. Since the acting of the individual elements is atomic and unitary, 'epochal', each such epoch of acting has a discreteness. But since this does not imply that the acting is cut off or broken off, but rather that the end of one phase is the beginning of another, the total process of acting will accordingly be continuous.

This is fully in accord with Aristotle's analysis of continuity.[54] He pointed out that there is a very close connection between 'continuity' and 'contiguity' – which is indeed the position we have stated above. He says: 'A thing that is in succession and touches is "contiguous" '.[55] A thing is 'in succession' when it is after the beginning 'and when further there is nothing of the *same* kind as itself between it and that to which it is in succession';[56] this latter provision constitutes the thing 'touching', and thus 'contiguous'. Aristotle then points out that accordingly:

'The "continuous" is a subdivision of the contiguous: things are called continuous when the touching limits of each become one and the same and are, as the word implies, contained in each other: continuity is impossible if these extremities are two. This

[53] See above, pp. 260–61; cf. also pp. 263f., 270, 274ff.
[54] *Physics*, Book V, Ch. 3.
[55] *Physics*, 227a6 (Hardie & Gaye tr.): ἐχόμενον δὲ ὃ ἂν ἐφεξῆς ὂν ἅπτηται.
[56] 226b31–227a1.(tr. Hardie and Gaye).

definition makes it plain that continuity belongs to things that naturally in virtue of their mutual contact form a unity.'[57]

The crucial point is that there is continuity only when 'the touching limits of each become one and the same and are, as the word implies, contained in each other'. It is in this precise sense that I am maintaining that there is a continuity in the process of *kinēsis* whereby one epochal element succeeds another; there is no 'break', but any two succeeding elements are contiguous in this sense of continuous, for the end of one is the beginning of another, the 'touching limits' thereby being one and the same.

This continuity of the process of acting, of the *kinēsis*, motion, pertains to a compound substance or physical existent in respect of its constituents; the actings of the constituents in constituting the one unitary compound existent, will be continuous when seen from the standpoint of the compound. But seen from its own standpoint, each constituent acting will be discrete, itself a unit.

We have seen earlier that continuity pertains to possibility, whereas actuality is discrete. This is exemplified in the analysis which we have just made. The acting and thus *kinēsis*, motion, of the actual compound existent is unitary and thus discrete. As such it is continuous, which means that it is divisible, but not divided. That is, the divisions are potential, from the standpoint of the actual whole. Considered purely in themselves the sub-actings of the constituents, since they are units, will be actual and discrete; but from each such standpoint, since the acting of each constituent contributes with others to the larger whole, its own acting will be continuous with that of the others.

Thus continuity for its adequate understanding, as also discreteness, requires to be considered in conjunction with the distinction between actuality and potentiality. Included in the latter concept, as we have seen, is that of possibility, and with this arises the issue of the status of the possible in physical existence which we discussed toward the beginning of the chapter. As was pointed out there, that issue requires the treatment of some further considerations which were left for the next chapter.

[57] 227a10–15 (tr. Hardie and Gaye): τὸ δὲ συνεχὲς ἔστι μὲν ὅπερ ἐχόμενόν τι, λέγω δ' εἶναι συνεχὲς· ὅταν ταὐτὸ γένηται καὶ ἓν τὸ ἑκατέρου πέρας οἷς ἅπτονται, καὶ ὥσπερ σημαίνει τοὔνομα, συνέχηται. τοῦτο δ' οὐχ οἷόν τε δυοῖν ὄντοιν εἶναι τοῖν ἐσχάτοιν. τούτου δὲ διωρισμένου φανερὸν ὅτι ἐν τούτοις ἐστὶ τὸ συνεχές, ἐξ ὧν ἕν τι πέφυκε γίγνεσθαι κατὰ τὴν σύναψιν.

26

NATURE, THE INFINITE, AND
THE FINITE

In the understanding of nature, of the physical, one of the fundamental issues we have encountered throughout this inquiry is
that of continuity, and the basic question which has always arisen
is that of the ontological status of continuity. This issue had been
brought into prominence by Aristotle, and it remained a fundamental issue in the seventeenth century. One most important
aspect of it was the problem of the relation of the physical and
the mathematical, and closely bound up with this was the problem of the infinite.

Decartes had brought all these together in his ultimate physical
existent, *res extensa*. In his doctrine *res extensa* was the physical
actuality, and it was conceived as basically mathematical. As such
it was both infinitely extended and essentially continuous. Thus
for Descartes continuity pertained to actuality, to physical actuality.

This conception of the physical as essentially continuous rendered material atomism impossible. But material atomism had
become accepted as the philosophical basis of modern science,
and accordingly a different status was requisite for continuity
and the mathematical. Finally in the eighteenth century this was
found in the conception of space as an existent independent of
the physical, matter; for to space was accorded the features of
infinite extension, continuity, and the mathematical – it was space
which was regarded as the object of the science of mathematics.
Thus in this doctrine continuity did not pertain to physical actuality, matter, but to a quasi-physical actuality, space – and also
to another quasi-physical actuality, time.

Leibniz's analysis, we have seen, brought out the untenability of
both these positions. One of his fundamental insights emerging
from his analysis – but almost completely ignored – was that continuity cannot pertain to actuality. Continuity, he held, pertains
to possibility, and this meant, he concluded, that its ontological

status is that of ideality. Thus he grounded continuity and the mathematical (infinity being included in this) in the mind of God.

But with this conception of extensive continuity as essentially thought, Leibniz is committed to an untenable position in regard to relations. Thus the theory of relations becomes crucial; and an adequate theory of relations, we have found, depends upon an adequate theory of acting.

Our inquiry into the theory of acting has brought us to the conception of the individual actings of the individual physical existents as the individualizations of an ultimate substrate acting,[1] what Whitehead referred to as the 'category of the ultimate' and explicated as follows:

'In all philosophic theory there is an ultimate which is actual in virtue of its accidents. It is only then capable of characterization through its accidental embodiments, and apart from these accidents is devoid of actuality. In the philosophy of organism this ultimate is termed "creativity".'[2]

This conception of an ultimate substrate acting entails that this acting is continuous. This substrate acting is individualized in the actings of physical existents, and these must, at the elementary level at least, be epochal;[3] but this does not imply 'breaks' between them, but rather that they must be continuous, as we have seen. In this theory, therefore, continuity pertains to the ultimate acting, and it is from this that derives the feature of continuity of acting which we have found necessary to recognize between constituent existents and within compound existents.[4]

In the theory we have been developing, however, continuity does not pertain only to the ultimate acting; continuity pertains equally fundamentally to the ultimate form of extensiveness, that which Whitehead has termed the 'extensive continuum'.[5] The connection between these two kinds of continuity is in obvious need of elucidation.

It is important to note that in this theory – which in this respect is close to that of Whitehead – neither the ultimate substrate acting nor the generic extensive form is an actual existent. Hence in

[1] See, above pp. 325ff.   [2] PR 9 [10].
[3] Lee, above p. 332.   [4] See above, pp. 330ff.
[5] See, above pp. 320f.

this theory continuity does not pertain to actuality. This makes acute the issue as to what exactly then is the status of these two, the ultimate acting and the generic form of extensiveness.

The ultimate substrate acting is not itself a substance, an actual existent; it is that from which all physical actual existents arise. This is to say that it is the source of actual existence. Implied in this is a distinction which was made by Plato in his *Timaeus* and systematically applied by Aristotle, namely a distinction between actual physical existents on the one hand, and *archai*, principles, sources, on the other.

This distinction is indeed fundamental to cosmological theory. Aristotle had maintained that the ultimate *archai*, sources, from which *ousiai* or actual existents come into being are *hylē*, matter, and *eidos*, form. For Plato in the *Timaeus* the *archai* were the forms and the receptacle, the recipient of form – which Aristotle accordingly identified as *hylē* in Plato's system. In the seventeenth century, however, the two Aristotelian *archai* were conceived as themselves actual existents; they became material substance and spiritual substance. But this development did not render the conception of an *archē* redundant or unnecessary; on the contrary, it is because it remained fundamentally necessary that in the seventeenth century God was brought in as an *archē*. This necessity of an *archē* – and not because of any mere survival of religious piety – is the basic reason why seventeenth-century thought had recourse to God as the principle, source, of motion and change. Leibniz protested the fallacy of a *deus ex machina* involved in this, but did not himself in the end, as we have seen, manage entirely to avoid that fallacy. The reason is that Leibniz, with his contemporaries, continued to adhere to the medieval conception of a transcendent God, the ultimate source and origin of all finite existence. From the eighteenth century onward God largely ceased to figure in cosmological thought, but with this went a neglect of the necessity of an *archē*. Contemporary thought is paying a heavy price for the continued neglect of this necessity of an *archē*.

Whitehead is the one recent thinker who has not ignored this issue. In respect of it he has returned to the position of Greek thought, having been strongly influenced in this by the *Timaeus*. For Whitehead the ultimate *archai*, sources, are creativity and eternal objects (his term for forms). By virtue of this position in respect of the *archai*, Whitehead is able to have a very different conception of the relation of God to nature, to physical existence, from that of antecedent modern thinkers. We shall see the significance of this in due course.

The theory which I am advancing is in full accord with Whitehead in respect of the *archai*; the sources of physical existence are the ultimate acting and form – the form or character of the acting. In this view the ultimate substrate acting is not itself actual; it is not an *ousia*, substance, physical existent, but the source, *archē*.

Now since it is an *archē*, source, of actual existence, it cannot itself come into being. That is, *genesis*, coming-into-being, does not pertain to this ultimate acting. On the contrary, coming-into-being pertains to the *ousiai*, the physical existents. It is they which come into being, with this ultimate acting as one of the *archai*, sources, from which they come into being. To say that this ultimate acting does not come into being is to say that it is eternal – 'eternal' means, without beginning or end, which is only another way of saying, not subject to generation or coming-into-being and perishing. This is one important implication of the conception of the ultimate acting as not itself actual, but as the source of actual physical existence.

Another consequence of the conception of the ultimate acting as not itself actual, is that it must accordingly be potential. It is the potentiality for actuality. For actualization is the individualization of this substrate acting in individual actings, and this substrate acting is thus the ultimate potential for actualization.

But to say that this ultimate substrate acting is 'potential' implies, in the first place, that it is the 'potency' whereby, and in virtue of which, there is actuality. Considered as such, this ultimate substrate acting is pure potency.

However, 'potentiality' connotes more than 'potency'; for included in it is the concept of 'possibility'. For it is evident that in saying that the ultimate acting is the potentiality for actuality is meant that it is capable of individualization in definite individual actings. But there can be no definite, individual acting unless it be in a particular 'where' and at a particular 'when'. Now this factor of particular 'where' and 'when' is not entailed in potency as such. It can only come from another source, and this must be the other *archē*, the generic form of extensiveness, which is the scheme of all possible standpoints.[6] Considered just in itself, this ultimate form of extensiveness is a pure possibility. It can become a potentiality only by integration with the other *archē*, pure potency. Thus it is the two *archai* together or conjointly which constitute the potentiality for actuality.

In this we have the answer to the question raised above as to the connection between the continuity which we found pertaining to the two *archai*. As *archai* these two are not existentially separate; on the contrary, they are co-ordinate and require each other. Thus continuity in its full ultimate sense pertains to these two conjointly, as the potentiality for actuality. When we consider these two, pure potency and pure extensiveness, separately in respect of continuity, we have an abstract consideration of continuity.

We can now see that it is not in this abstract sense of continuity that it was maintained above that the ultimate acting entails that this acting is continuous. When we consider continuity as it underlies and is manifested in actuality, both *archai* are involved; when we consider continuity abstractedly we will be dealing with it as manifested, for example, in mathematics.

Thus it is primarily continuity in the former sense which is involved when we say, as Whitehead does, that there is a continuity of becoming.[7] Now to say that the process of becoming, the process of actualization, *kinēsis*, is continuous implies that while there is a coming-into-being of actual existents, the process of becoming, the *kinēsis*, as such, does not come into being; it must be eternal. This is what Aristotle, too, maintained:

'But it is impossible that *kinēsis* should either have come into being or cease to be (for it must always have existed), or that time should. For there could not be a before and an after if time did not exist. *Kinēsis* also is continuous, then, in the sense in which time is; for time is either the same thing as *kinēsis* or an attribute of *kinēsis*.[8]

This identification of time and *kinēsis* is highly important. What is implied in it is that time is not some kind of separate

---

[6] See above, pp. 320f.   [7] cf. PR 48 [53] and above, p. 320.

[8] *Met.*, 1071b7–10; Ross translation, with the substitution of the Greek word *kinesis* for the English 'movement'.

existent as it is in the post-Newtonian doctrine, or in the recent variation of that position in which time is linked with space. Time is an aspect of *kinēsis*, of the fundamental process of actualization of physical existents; that is, what we know as time is one aspect of the fundamental process of *kinēsis*, and thus derivative from it. Time, in other words, is grounded in the ultimate acting; and it is by reason of this that time is continuous. This is why the continuity of time is something so different from abstract mathematical continuity. Time is one aspect of the acting of physical existence. The acting of a physical existent 'occupies' a durational stretch as it 'occupies' an extensive volume.[9]

In this century there has come into prominence what Whitehead has called an 'epochal theory of time',[10] sometimes referred to as a 'quantum' theory or 'chronon' theory of time, sometimes also as a 'pulsational' theory. This conception, used with proper care, is not inconsistent with what I am maintaining. On the contrary, since the ultimate acting, as we have seen, is necessarily epochalized in actualization, this epochalization will be reflected in a temporal as also in an extensive aspect. But just as when we are thinking about 'acting', we must be clear about precisely what acting we are referring to – that of individual existents or the ultimate substrate acting – so also in respect of time, and of extension, we must be clear about the exact referent of the term, or we are likely to run into confusion and error. I prefer Whitehead's term 'epoch' in respect of time to 'quantum' or 'chronon', for these two terms tend to over-emphasize the discreteness, as Čapek too has pointed out,[11] and thus lose sight of the necessary continuity. In respect of time, as of extension, and of acting, the proper understanding of the concept of continuity and what it entails is of the utmost importance.

We must now turn to a further implication of the conception of the ultimate substrate acting and of form as the *archai* of actual physical existence. We have said that these ultimates are not themselves actual, but are the potentiality for actuality. Now the concept of potentiality implies potentiality *for* actuality. But the concept of potentiality does not entail *necessary actualization*.

---

[9] See above, p. 318.
[10] cf. *Process and Reality*, pp. 94, 401 [105, 434], and *Science in the Modern World*, pp. 157ff. [183ff].
[11] cf. Čapek, op. cit., pp. 231–41.

This is clear with both components of potentiality, namely potency and possibility. With regard to potency, as Aristotle pointed out, 'that which has a potency need not exercise it'.[12] That is, the concept of potency entails a capacity for exercise, but not a necessity of exercise. This means, as Aristotle has frequently pointed out, that potency (*dynamis*) entails a capacity both of being and not being;[13] that is to say, 'that which is potentially may possibly not be'.[14]

It follows therefore that the two *archai*, the ultimate acting and form, that is, pure potency and pure possibility, are not alone sufficient for physical actualization. These two sources provide only the potentiality for actualization, but with only this, actuality might not be. Another factor is required to provide the necessity of actualization. In other words, there has to be an additional principle as the reason that there is actually a continuity of becoming, of *kinēsis*, that is, that the process of actualization proceeds and proceeds continuously. For while as *archai* the ultimate substrate acting and form are eternal, that is, not subject to coming-into-being, this does not entail that there will actually *be* a process of coming-into-being.

We have seen that the two *archai*, the ultimate acting and form, are co-ordinate and require each other. What is necessary is another *archē*, co-ordinate with these two, and required by them. The former two *archai* constitute the ultimate potentiality. Now potentiality is 'potentiality *for*', as we have seen. But potentiality as such does not furnish the 'for'. In other words, potentiality implies a telic factor, but this *telos*, end, is not contained in potentiality as such. That is, potentiality implies some or other end, but itself does not entail any specific end; potentiality in itself is purely general. Specificity can therefore come only from another source.

In the tradition of the last two millennia this source is assumed to be necessarily transcendent. A great many of the gravest difficulties with which Western thought has wrestled during this long period are the consequence of this conception of a completely transcendent *archē*. We have been arguing that the two *archai* which conjointly constitute the ultimate potentiality require a

---

[12] *Met.*, 1071b13. (Ross tr.)
[13] cf. e.g. ibid., 1039b29, 1050b11.
[14] ibid., 1071b19: ἐνδέχεται γὰρ τὸ δυνάμει ὂν μὴ εἶναι. (Ross tr.)

co-ordinate principle to complete them with specific ends. A transcendent principle cannot be co-ordinate; the supposition involves a contradiction. The requisite principle must be conceived as within the whole and not transcending it. This implies a return to the position of Greek thought, and a rejection of the fundamental position of medieval thought.

The problem is how to conceive this third *archē*. It must of necessity be other than the other two, or it would be a duplication of them. Now those two constitute potentiality; therefore the third principle must be the contrary of potentiality. This, as Aristotle pointed out,[15] can only be pure actuality. To say that it is 'pure' actuality is to say that it is actuality devoid of potentiality. This principle must exclude potentiality, for potentiality entails that it might not be, and it is precisely to ensure necessary actualization that this third principle is required, as Aristotle too had insisted.[16]

This third principle provides the necessity of actualization, we have seen, by being the source of ends. There cannot be individual actualization without specific ends, and actualization is the making of the end actual – as opposed to potential – by enacting the end.

Now is this third principle to be conceived analogously to the ultimate potentiality, which is individuated in individual existents? That is, is this third principle to be conceived analogously to the substrate acting which is individualized in particular actings, so that each existent is to be conceived as an individual actualization of a general end? That, however, would entail that the third principle is a potential actualization, a potentiality which is actualized. That would mean, as Aristotle put it,[17] that its essence is potentiality. But we have seen that it must necessarily exclude potentiality. Since the third principle cannot be simply ends in general, the only alternative open is that it must be itself an individual actualization, that is, en-action, of *all* ends, and this must mean that the third principle is all ends *complicans*, and it is as such that it is the *archē*, source, of ends. It is pure actuality because, without any potentiality and thus process of becoming, it is the pure enacting of ends.

15 cf. *Met.*, 1071b20–3.
16 cf. ibid., 1071b18–20.
17 ibid., 1071b18–19.

This, too, is Aristotle's doctrine in conceiving this *archē* or principle as *energeia*, without any *dynamis* or *kinēsis*;[18] it is pure *energeia*, en-action. For him too it was an individual enaction, and hence he referred to it as *ousia*. Thus, he said, it is something eternal which is both *ousia* and actuality, *energeia*.[19]

There is a certain divergence of this position, that is, that of Aristotle and the one I am developing, from that of Whitehead. For Whitehead insisted that God, like all actualities, is to be conceived as in becoming, arguing that it is one of the glaring incoherences in traditional doctrines to make God an exception to the general categories applying to all other actuality.[20] In maintaining this, however, Whitehead was losing sight of that most important distinction which we discussed above, and to which he to a considerable extent adhered, namely the distinction between physical existents on the one hand and *archai*, principles, sources, on the other. God is not a physical existent, but one of the *archai*, sources, of physical existence, and is therefore not to be conceived as co-ordinate with physical existents. It is fundamental to the nature of physical existence that it involves a process of becoming, *kinēsis*, and to conceive God as involved in becoming is to include God in the physical. Whitehead went to this extent, in part of his doctrine, in his endeavour to escape from the medieval conception of a wholly transcendent God – a conception which we have seen to entail insuperable difficulty for a philosophy of nature, of physical existence. Whitehead was certainly correct in his insistence on God as in intrinsic connection with the physical. But in this part of his doctrine Whitehead went too far; God is not to be 'included' in the physical by conceiving God as an actuality co-ordinate with physical actuality. The necessity is the route we have followed – which was also Whitehead's in some aspects of his doctrine as we have seen – namely that of conceiving God as an *archē* of the physical.

We have in the foregoing of course entered but a short way into an immense topic, much further exploration of which is, however, beyond the scope of this inquiry. It is necessary nevertheless to consider one further point in it which is most relevant to our investigation of physical existence. This is the problem

---

[18] cf. *Met.*, 1071b3–1072a18.
[19] ibid., 1072a25: ἀΐδιον καὶ οὐσία καὶ ἐνέργεια οὖσα.
[20] cf. PR 486 [521].

of how the individual aims necessary in the process of *kinēsis* or becoming come to inhere in the individual physical existents.

In his handling of this problem Aristotle had unfortunately expressed his answer to this in terms of the astronomical science of his day, with the result that his fundamental point has tended to be missed, especially in the modern period. His fundamental doctrine is not dependent upon that science, however, as has been too frequently supposed. His point is, first, that physical existents must derive their aim from the actuality which is the ultimate source of all aim; and secondly, that that aim is not simply individually received directly by each physical existent, but rather in mediation through the entire structure of all physical existents in relation to each other. That is to say, what is involved is not any simple two-termed relation between each individual physical existent and the source of its aim; the relation is a highly complex one, including all other existents in its scope, each according to its perspective from the existent in question. This implies the conjoint operation of all three *archai*, and none separately. In this entire relatedness of all physical existents there is manifested some very general features, such as the general order of extensive relatedness, which increasingly and progressively become more specific through actualization, for example, in the particular place (that is, 'where' and 'when') of each physical existent in reference to others. Put conversely, the process of becoming of each physical existent, in all its specificity, is determined by its place in reference to others, in an ever-widening order of generality of relatedness. Every aspect of its specific definiteness, that is, its individual form or character, is necessarily involved in a continuous progression to ever greater generality of relatedness. Each specific aim, therefore, is entailed in the general relatedness as a 'limit'.[21] It is as such a 'limit' in the general structured relatedness that the individual aim derives to the physical existent from the ultimate source of aim.

This too is Whitehead's doctrine, and it is this position which was presupposed in his statement, quoted above,[22] that ' "God" is that actuality in the world, in virtue of which there is physical "law" '.[23] By putting the term 'law' in quotation marks White-

---

[21] In the strict etymological sense of 'entail'.
[22] See above, pp. 321f.
[23] PR 402 [434].

head was making clear his rejection of any tacit implication of the fiat of a law-giver. What is known in science as 'physical law' is the structure of order manifested in and determining the relation of the physical existents. In contemporary physics this law is still conceived as pertaining primarily to the motion (locomotion) of the physical existents, and it is expressed and investigated mathematically. Clearly fundamental in this is extensiveness, for this motion is the extensive transition from one place to another. And extensiveness, we have seen, is a basic form of relatedness. Thus the scientific investigation concerns one aspect of the fundamental relatedness of physical existents.

In a more complete philosophical view each physical existent must be seen as in its relational acting manifesting a perspective of the structured order determining the relations of all physical existents. Now the aim determining the relational acting of each physical existent is in a primary aspect constituted by its 'entertainment' of that ordered structure in its perspective. Thereby is derived its place, its 'where' and 'when', and thus its *situs* with reference to others, which is presupposed in its acting. Thus the full character or form of a physical existent in its relational acting will necessarily be implicated in the generic form of extensive relatedness; its character will be separable from this only in abstraction.

This form of extensiveness is one aspect of structured order in general. The general structured order, in abstraction from actualization in physical existents, is form, and as such is pure possibility, and thus to be identified as one of the *archai*. This, in conjunction with the other *archē*, potency, constitutes potentiality. And in conjunction with the third *archē*, that is, as 'entertained' in pure actuality, form constitutes the aim of physical existence. Thus physical existence presupposes all three *archai* conjointly.

With the distinction we have been maintaining between physical actuality on the one hand and *archai*, principles, sources, on the other, we are able to have an understanding of the ontological status of continuity, and of the relation of the mathematical to the physical, which avoids the difficulties besetting the philosophies of the modern period.

In the theory here developed continuity pertains primarily to potentiality, and not to actuality. Actuality, on the other hand, is primarily discrete. It has to be discrete because each physical existent is necessarily finite, a particular definite actualization which, as definite, excludes alternative possibilities.

But in this theory the discrete and the continuous are not separated as they are in the ruling modern philosophy – that which still dominates thought in science – into two kinds of existents. Such a conception involves completely insuperable difficulties, as we have seen. The distinction needs to be, not between two or more kinds of physical actuality (or quasi-physical actuality), but between physical actuality on the one hand, and *archai*, sources, of that actuality, on the other. Thereby potentiality is not separated from actuality, but potentiality is involved in actuality as that which is actualized. Thus what is continuous becomes discrete in actualization.

In abstraction from actualization, and from the potency whereby there is actualization, we have only pure possibility. This is form, and it is to form that continuity essentially pertains. When we consider form as pure possibility we can refer to forms, in the plural – as we have been doing. But it is necessary to appreciate that forms as pure possibilities do not have the discreteness of actualized forms; on the contrary, there is an essential continuity of form in pure possibility. There is an essential interrelatedness of forms in pure possibility; and the 'form of interrelatedness' is itself one of the forms.

One form of interrelatedness is extensive interrelatedness. This form of extensive relatedness is what is the object of inquiry in some branches of mathematics. What is being maintained here is that the mathematical is primarily form, as Plato insisted. Thus the generic form of extensive relatedness, Whitehead's extensive continuum, is essentially mathematical. Therefore the mathematical is included in the character of physical existents by the actualization of extensive relatedness.

This conception of the physical as the actualization of the mathematical is very different from the conception of Descartes – which identifies the physical and the mathematical – and from the conception of Newton – in which mathematical features, such as measurability, are derived by the physical through its existing in a place as a 'container' – and also from the conception of Leibniz and of Kant – in which the physical is mathematical only 'ideally', that is, by virtue of thought; a doctrine which in one guise or another has become increasingly widespread during this century. The position I am maintaining is in essential agreement with Whitehead, the thinker who in this century has been most fully alive to the complexity of the issue.

The foregoing analysis also leads to the conclusion that Aristotle was correct in maintaining that the infinite pertains to potentiality and not to physical actuality. In particular he saw the concept of infinity as pertaining to mathematics, not only to geometrical extensiveness but also to the sequence of numbers. Actual physical existence is necessarily definite and thus finite. Thus there can be no one physical whole which is infinite.

Infinity cannot be restricted to the mathematical, however. It pertains to all form. That is, form in general is divisible into forms, *in infinitum*; this is entailed in the continuity of form. In regard to form, continuity is not constituted by contiguity, as in actuality;[24] in form there is pure continuity. It would be more precise, therefore, to say that continuity, and thus infinity, pertain primarily to possibility rather than to potentiality.

Now we have seen that the third *archē*, pure actuality, is the eternal enaction of all possibility, that this is eternal 'entertainment' of all possibility *complicans*. In virtue of this eternal enaction pure actuality is infinite.

But as soon as this is said, it is necessary to recall the other part of Aristotle's acute analysis of the concept of the infinite, namely that the concept of infinity cannot pertain to actuality as an attribute.[25] Can it be maintained that this does not hold for pure actuality as an *archē*? The fundamental point of Aristotle's argument is that an actual is, qua actual, necessarily a whole, complete, that is, something from which nothing is absent or wanting, and this is the very contrary to the concept of the infinite, which implies the not-whole, that which it is always possible to go beyond in some respect. But pure actuality must necessarily be a whole, or it would in some respect entail potentiality. Thus infinity cannot pertain to pure actuality as an attribute. Nor is the infinite possibility which is enacted by pure actuality to be regarded as an attribute of that actuality; this pure possibility is another *archē*.

The important conclusion of Aristotle's analysis is that infinity does not pertain to actuality as such at all, but that infinity must

24 See above, pp. 332f.
25 See above, Chapter 3, *passim*.

be seen as pertaining to *process*, to 'that which can be gone through'.[26]

Now the eternal *energeia*, enaction, of pure actuality is precisely such a 'process', an eternal process of en-acting. Thus infinity can be said to pertain to the *process* of enaction – which is quite different from conceiving infinity as an attribute of pure actuality. The *process* of enacting is never a whole, never complete – this is entailed in its being eternal.

The becoming, the *kinēsis*, of physical existence is also a process. This *kinēsis*, becoming, we have seen, is a process of actualization, and the source, *archē*, of this *kinēsis* is pure potency, the ultimate substrate acting. This acting, by reason of its necessary conjunction with the other two *archai*, is eternal, and from this follows the eternity of the process of becoming of actual existence. Thus the process of *kinēsis* is infinite; that is to say, it is a process, that is, that which essentially is gone through, but there is no end to it. In respect of its process of *kinēsis* or becoming, therefore, and only in respect of its *process*, physical existence too can be spoken of as infinite.

To regard the physical universe as infinitely extended is inadmissible and an error, for it entails conceiving extension as an attribute, a conception which we have seen has to be rejected; extension is a relation, not an attribute. A relation cannot be infinite since it entails terms.

This throws into strong relief the insufficiency of the modern conception of nature, that which is epitomized in the title of Alexandre Koyré's book, *From the Closed World to the Infinite Universe*. That conception can be viewed as having been consonant with a stage in the development of science. Scientific thought in the twentieth century has entered a new stage, in which the old conception of nature has become most seriously restrictive.

The present inquiry has brought out that every theory of nature, of physical existence, is necessarily faced with the fundamental issues of continuity and discreteness, of the infinite and the finite, of the relation of the mathematical to the physical, and also that of *archai*, sources, issues which are all closely interconnected.

In the light of these issues the modern conception of the physical as matter has been shown to entail a separation of

[26] See above, pp. 56–8.

continuity from the discrete, of the finite from the infinite, of the mathematical from the physical, separations which are bridgeable only by appeal to a transcendent *arche*. To the extent to which this conception of physical existence is retained, explicitly or tacitly, these implications will continue to have their effect on thought. The consequences in contemporary science are considerable.

What is needed is a conception of nature as essentially in becoming (and not as changeless actuality), that is as involving a process of *kinesis* (and not merely moving from place to place), and as having the *arche*, source of its *kinesis* in itself (and not transcendent) – an *arche* which must be understood in a threefold aspect.

THE PHILOSOPHY OF NATURE

In the course of the inquiry in the last three chapters there has gradually emerged a theory of my own concerning the nature of the physical existent. This is, however, incidental rather than intentional; for my intention in this book has been the elucidation and investigation of the fundamental issues and problems of the philosophy of nature. But fundamental issues and problems cannot be formulated *a priori* and investigated antecedently to the examination of theories; on the contrary, the elucidation of problems and the formulation of theories are two aspects of the same enterprise. Thus the elucidation of the problems and issues must occur in the context of the examination of theories, and the theories will necessarily be in a certain context of thought.

The classic exemplification of this is Aristotle's inquiry into the fundamental issues and problems of the philosophy of nature which constitutes his book known as the *Physics*. In it every problem and issue involves Aristotle's going back to antecedent theories, and the elucidation of the problems occurs in the examination of those theories, his own position then both emerging from that elucidation and also contributory to it. What is exemplified in Aristotle, therefore, is a dialectical process of the contrast of theories, the basic problems and issues being brought out and clarified in the process of that dialectic.

Subsequent thought – and in particular that of the sixteenth, seventeenth, and eighteenth centuries – is to be seen as also exemplifying a dialectical process in which the basic problems at issue were elucidated by the dialectical contrast of theories, the later theories both being a response to a better understanding of the problems consequent upon the contrast of earlier theories, and themselves contributing to that better understanding.

In this Part I have exemplified in dialectical contrast chiefly the earlier seventeenth-century theory of material atomism, the theories of Descartes, Newton, Leibniz, the pre-critical Kant,

Aristotle, and Whitehead. My aim has been by this contrast to bring out the fundamental issues and problems of the philosophy of nature as they face us today. In this context my own theory is also presented as contributory to that elucidation.

The reason why only Whitehead among recent thinkers has been included is that he so far outstrips others in an understanding of the issues in their depth and interconnected complexity.

This brings to the fore a question of great moment. Almost all contemporary discussions of issues of the kind with which we have been dealing here have been placed almost exclusively in the context of recent scientific theory.[1] Whitehead is exceptional in having seen clearly the inadequacy of this. The inadequacy consists not in the concern with recent scientific theory – indeed that must remain of the first importance – but in the failure to appreciate the full range and depth of the issues at stake, and that these require going much beyond the context of contemporary science. Thus, for example, an adequate philosophical analysis of the concept of 'space' in contemporary scientific theory must involve a consideration not only of the range of the problems of the continuum – infinity and finitude, continuity and discontinuity, divisibility and indivisibility – but also the problem of the ontological status of 'space', which must involve the problems of the relation of the mathematical and the physical, which in turn bring up the consideration of the quite basic problem of the nature of the physical existent.

These and a number of others are the problems, it has been a main aim of the present book to show, which are those finally at issue in the present-day context of thought. Further, it is with reference to these, as Whitehead has seen, that scientific theories require to be examined. It is this which is in the end requisite for the adequate assessment of scientific theories.

Put in another perspective, what I am maintaining is that the urgent need of our time is to heal the breach between philosophy and science which has existed since the eighteenth century. Such a step will necessarily involve the revaluation of both enterprises.

---

[1] It is not without significance that these discussions are generally conceived as 'philosophy of science' – a term which at the present time for the main part, and with justification, connotes the methodology and epistemology of science – rather than 'philosophy of nature'.

Since the eighteenth century they have been conceived as each separate and distinct from the other. Also science has come to be accepted, explicitly or implicitly, as the primary and basic enterprise, that by virtue of which positive knowledge is attained – whence this enterprise has been called 'science', that is, 'knowledge' – and philosophy, in so far as it has retained any relevance to science, is a second-order enterprise, reflecting upon science.

But in the light of an inquiry such as I have undertaken in this book, it becomes clear that such a valuation of what is termed the scientific enterprise is the product of the assumption that all the fundamental questions, those which previously had constituted the subject-matter of *philosophia naturalis*, the philosophy of nature, were finally resolved. In our century it ought however to be explicitly recognized that this assumption is definitely erroneous. The development of scientific thought itself has had the consequence of throwing open that entire arena of inquiry. Once again, as in the seventeenth century, the 'philosophy of nature' must not only be brought into the forefront, but the recognition of its intrinsic relevance to and need by the scientific enterprise must be restored. Then it will be seen that there are not two independent enterprises, science and philosophy, but one, the inquiry into nature, having two complementary and mutually dependent aspects.

INDEX

Descartes, René—*cont.*
physics as phoronomy, 235
Principles of Philosophy, 73, 81n
recognition that matter has no
principle of motion, 254
rejection of material atomism, 284
relations, and Neoplatonic doctrine of Ideas, conception of,
268
relation of the mathematical to
the physical, 96
relation of the physical and the
mathematical, problem of, 36
res cogitans, doctrine of, 189
res extensa, his conception of rejected by followers, 230
spatium, conception of, 163
universe, conception of, 96
universe as *interminatum,* conception of, 81
vis inertiae, conception of, 263
Discreteness, problem for Pythagoreans, 47–49
Divine, absolutely transcendent,
59–60
Dualism, ontological, criticism by
Whitehead, 293–94
ontological, implications of, 317,
318
ontological, implied in physical
existent as material, 314
ontological, in Kant, 277, 293
ontological, in Seventeenth Century, need of *archē,* 336
ontological, rejected by Leibniz,
256
Duns Scotus, conception of being,
central to, 71
theory of combination, 143
on knowledge of God, 76
positive conception of God's infinity, 67–69
doctrine of matter, 127
Dynamis, in analysis of *kinēsis,*
114–15
connected with *hylē* by Aristotle,
325
connection with *hylē,* problem of,
120–21
God without, for Aristotle, 62
involved in *kinēsis,* 109–10

Eidos, conception of by Aristotle,
contrasted with Neoplatonic
conception, 125–26
Einstein, concept of space and time,
237–38
influence on, of Kant's critical doctrine, 280

Electrons, Whitehead's analysis of,
286
Elements, Aristotelian, conceived as
ousiai, 326
Aristotelian, necessarily involve
change in themselves, 324–25
Aristotelian theory of, 135–38
bodily, 51
changeless in atomism, 324
conception of, 324
of compounds, as substances,
325–28
Empiricism, acceptance of Aristotelian conception of causal
efficacy, 271
British, influence on Whitehead,
294
British, inheritance of Neoplatonic
theory of Ideas, 267–68, 272
Empedocles, Sixteenth-Century revival of, 84
Energia, God as, for Aristotle, 61–62
in analysis of *kinēsis,* 109, 111,
115
Energy and matter in Eighteenth
Century, concept of, 237
problem of ontological status of,
242
Entelecheia, in analysis of *kinēsis,*
109, 115
Aristotle's concept of, 316, 317
Entertainment, concept analysed,
317, 320–22
Entities, compound, Whitehead's
analysis of, 286
Epicurus, resuscitation of, by Gas-
sendi, 181
Epistemology, difficulties involving
relations, 295, 314n
Epochal acting, Whitehead's theory,
335
Epochal theory of becoming, in
Whitehead, 329–32
Eternal objects, as *archai* of
actuality for Whitehead, 337
Euclid, Sixteenth-Century revival of,
84
Event, theory of, in Whitehead, 324
Existents, primary, atomic, for
Whitehead, 286
Explicatio, doctrine of, 75
Explicatio Dei, doctrine of, 75–81
doctrine of, in More's philosophy,
205
doctrine of world as, accepted in
Fifteenth and Sixteenth Cen-
turies, 130
Extension, as attribute for Descartes,
rejection of, by Whitehead, 318n

Whitehead, A. N.—*cont.*
God in relation to physical existence, 337
God as source of physical law, 343–44
influence on, of Aristotelian conception of active substance, 257
influence on, of Neoplatonic doctrine of Ideas, 272, 273, 294, 295
influence on, of Plato's *Timaeus*, 336
isolation of actual entities, 291
Kant's critical doctrine, untenability of, 293
locomotion as derivative, 331–32
locomotion as discontinuous, 332
mass, on concept of, 264n
the mathematical as form for, 345
measurability, analysis of, 323n
motive power, lacks concept of, 275–76
motion, concept of, similarity to Leibniz, 260–61
on influence of Newtonian physics on decline of philosophy of nature, 226
on Newton's concept of force, 274
organism, theory of, 313
pan-psychism of, influence of materialism, 314
philosophy of nature, analysis of problems of the, 350
physical, term used in classical sense, 317–18
place, conception of, 322–23

possibility intrinsic to physical existent, 317
prehending, theory of, 308
prehension as perception, 272–73, 290–91, 294–95
prehension as relation, 294–95
on presuppositions, 284
Process and Reality, 241, 284, 286
relations by acts of prehending, 290–91
relations, conception of, contrasted with Kant, 282
relations, conception of, close to that of Leibniz, 290–91
relations real, not phenomenal, 271
Science and the Modern World, 226n, 241, 264n, 272, 284, 313
society, theory of, 286, 289–90
societies, defining characteristic of, 328
subjective form, 327
theory of substrate acting, creativity, 335
substratum, conception of, 325–26
time, epochal theory of, 339
unity grounded in substance, 310
unity subjective to experiencer, 309
Woodbridge, F. J. E., 101n
World, dependence of on God, 123
conceived as *explicatio Dei*, see Universe

Zeller, E., *Die Philosophie der Griechen*, 46n, 63n
Outlines of the History of Philosophy, 46n